Computers@Libraries

COMPUTERS@LIBRARIES

V K J Jeevan

Ess Ess Publications

4837/24, Ansari Road, Darya Ganj,
New Delhi-110002
✆ : 23260807, 51563444
Fax : 011-51563334
E-mail: info@essessreference.com
url:http://www.essessreference.com

First Published 2005

ISBN : 81-7000-445-4

Price : Rs. 1675/-

Published by :

Ess Ess Publications

4837/24, Ansari Road, Darya Ganj,
New Delhi - 110 002
✆ : 23260807, 51563444
Fax : 011-51563334
E-mail: info@essessreference.com
url:http://www.essessreference.com

Laser Typesetting:

Mukesh Graphics

T-1264, Mangolpuri, New Delhi
Ph. : 27922304
E-mail:mukeshgraphics29@yahoo.com

Printed at :

Print Line

to

my young son Dipu

my student Minoo

Leena's parents

&

the memory of "raja" of my teachers

CONTENTS

Preface

Libraries, Library Science and librarians are currently invaded and surrounded from all quarters. The emerging information world attaches too much importance to media, information and knowledge all combined and intertwined and libraries are key players in this symbiosis. Thus in many institutions, non-library professionals are heading the libraries due to obviously known reasons. There are also cases where the professionals fail to take up the leadership role at the institutional and national levels. There are also problems of understaffing in libraries, underemployment to library professionals and merit and ability the last criteria in selections and promotions. Electronic information and digital resources in the market place dictates librarians to be more tech savvy and constant knowledge updating to conduct their professional activities in an efficient way. Being a librarian is the most dangerous role with such onslaught of technology and societal pressures. These papers are some of the reflections of justifying my own existence in this profession. I shall be happy and confirm that the purpose of this book will be served if this book finds some interest with all categories of professionals, computer comfy and traditional, young and old and teachers as well as librarians.

This book is organized in 6 parts and 25 chapters. The first part 'state of the art' deals with diverse aspects of the profession. The first chapter presents the relevance of Ranganathan in the digital era. The second chapter discusses the trends of job opportunities in the library profession which many ordinary students wish to pursue as a panacea to earn their livelihood. The third chapter describes the status of publication in journals from the Indian Institute of Technology Kharagpur which no doubt reflects the national status from premier academic and research institutions. The fourth chapter calls for quality auditing of our libraries on the lines of the nationwide procedure adopted in US. There is much hue and cry in the discipline about managing knowledge and we started with library management and then proceeded with information management that is still very relevant. The fifth chapter deals with the possibilities and dangers in managing knowledge. The technology is there to conduct e-learning library science but what is lacking is pragmatic application and a change in the mindset as discussed in chapter 6. Chapter 7 is a reflection of what needs to be done to preserve the intellectual output of developing countries with an illustration of superconductivity literature. The second part of the book covers two aspects of book acquisition. We have come a long way from just buying books to collection development and electronically enabling book collection and their access which is the theme of chapter 8. Chapter 9 discusses the futility of hanging to unilateral regimes like the present GOC which totally bypasses the diverse membership it accommodated once. Part 3 throws light on IT enabling public libraries (chapter 10), information support for rural development (chapter 11) and National Library (chapter 12). Libraries and librarians have to deal with electronic contents in wide variety and more quantity these days and that is the subject matter of part 4. Chapter 13 highlights the different resources available in a very potential and highly active area like Bioinformatics. Librarians through ages tried to provide client centred information services and the emerging computer and information technology provide effective tools and techniques to realize this and chapter 14 discusses some such technology and the portent area of personalization. Chapter 15 deals in lighter vein how education and learning could be made fun by combining media, web and information technology. Chapter 16 lists the different licensing models libraries have to bear with for accessing electronic contents and the need to counter the repacking trends adopted by publishers. Chapter 17 calls for more active strategies to lure back users to libraries because the electronic environment alienates many of them from the portals of the library. Part 5 encompasses different facets of computer applications in libraries. Chapter 18 is a tutorial on database management systems with some examples from the library domain. Chapter 19 is a similar effort on databanks. Chapter 20 details a dBase implementation for creating a system for managing inventory of consumables and other items in an information center or library. Web mails democratized email applications to a great extent and some discussion about this widely used tool is presented in chapter 21. Part 6 is about the 'big bang' in library science, digital libraries. Chapter 22 discusses how to build digital libraries in a pragmatic way.

Chapter 23 identifies the most important ingredient for digital libraries, content, which are aplenty in developing countries. Archiving digital contents is the next step in maintaining digital libraries which is the subject of chapter 24. Chapter 25 cautions about the difficulties libraries and librarians have to overcome before jumping into the bandwagon.

Subject matter in some of these chapters appeared in journals and proceedings of conferences and my thanks are due to the editors of those publications. I am thankful to many of the authors whose papers I have referred and they were like giants on whose shoulders I sat while presenting my ideas. Peers and teachers always cautioned me about 'how not to do' and 'why to do' whereas friends, professional colleagues and juniors inspired me 'how to do' and 'when to do'. My primary gratitude goes to my present employer, Indian Institute of Technology Kharagpur, the first, biggest, and the most diversified IIT. Before reaching here, I do not have a single publication and I used to treat authors as people from some other galaxy then. My eights years of stay in the Institute has been very rewarding due to the high academic ideals pursued in this Institute and the excellent infrastructure and the good company of educated community it offers. The successive heads of the Institute and the Central Library whole-heartedly supported my academic efforts and I would like to personally thank each one of them. My parents, brothers and their families, and in-laws deserve special mention for all they have done for me. This book has become a reality now due to the encouragement, support and togetherness of my wife Leena and two little sons. Minoo deserves special mention for collecting the references, endless discussions and proof reading the manuscript. I have great respect for the readers and the comments received from them while publishing earlier versions of these papers and my first book, only mustered enough courage to proceed with publishing this book. I request the readers to convey the feedback along with any suggestions and comments for further improvement of this book like many who did for my previous book. Mr. Sumit Sethi and his team at Ess Ess Publications deserve special acclamation for bringing out this publication in a pleasing appearance in such a short time.

Kharagpur **V K J Jeevan**

List of Appendix

List of Boxes

List of Figures

LIST OF TABLES

PART 1: STATE OF THE ART

1
Ranganathan's Ideas

1.0 INTRODUCTION

The greatest information scientist the world has seen in the twentieth century is no doubt, Dr. S R Ranganathan, regarded as the father of Library movement in India and recognised as the great conceptualist internationally. Many seminal contributions originated from the great master; and despite the origination of a lot of nascent ideas, due to the strong opposition to bring a money sieve between information and its users, he or his associates in India never practiced the commercialisation of these ideas. But these ideas reaped benefits in the west, who ever applied them for the betterment of information organisation and dissemination. In the recent years due to the myth that powerful computers can control the onslaught of information growth have lead to a deterioration in many of the areas where Ranganathan was active, like better classification systems for information organisation, intellectual and simple tools for information representation, bridging the gap between information rich and poor etc. The phenomenal growth of Internet and other digital information networks has demonstrated the need of strong classification and representation of information that will go into any database. The Indian software talent is globally recognised, and if some funds will come into, definitely a rejuvenation of Ranganathan's ideas for better information processing in the post internet information scenario could be tried out. Then only we can discourage the strong orthodoxism of functioning from some quarters, by a wrong interpretation of Ranganathan's theories.

1.1 Intellectual Neo Colonialism

There has been a recent report in newspapers about attributing the discovery of radio waves to Indian Scientist JC Bose. Every day news about patenting of traditional knowledge known to our ancestors and biological species by multinationals and the strong opposition to such activities by India and other developing countries is also coming out. It seems that the sophisticated weaponry had given way to hitech biotechnology and the new form of scientific colonialism is cultivated through pro-north ideas like terminator genes. The famous theorem associated to Pythagores has been known to our early artisans and formed the basis of many of our pristine architectural marvels. Due to the centuries of oppression by empirical rule and the first two generations of intellectuals breed in their institutions, some of us still feel ourselves inferior to westerners. If a C V Raman or Rabindranath Tagore can won Nobel Prizes under British Yoke, and a Khorana or Chandrasekhar or Sen can get the same out of their work in a foreign country, what's forbidding us from achieving laurels or making our inventions, ideas and research more visible internationally is a matter of introspection. We have to admit the fact that there is no monopoly of ideas to one country's citizens and we are not way behind any others in the development of nascent and path breaking ideas. Though international scientific databases admits only 2-3% as the contribution from India, it is difficult to assess the exact contribution by Indians as a considerable number of them work in many developed countries and their contribution is inadvertently attributed 'in toto' to such countries.

The greatest information scientist the world has seen in the twentieth century is no doubt, Dr. S R Ranganathan. Many of the seminal contributions originated from the great master include; Colon Classification - a classification scheme visualised for effective control of the Universe of knowledge, Classified Catalogue Code- a simplified code for designing catalogue and database entries, chain indexing- a semimechanical method to derive index entries from the title of the document; to name a few. The chain indexing found application in databases like the British National Bibliography, and prenatal processing of information sources got many takers in the developed world. The facet analysis and synthesis postulated by him in colon classification is finding increased adaptation in Dewey Decimal Classification (DDC) and Universal Decimal Classification (UDC). The page growth of DDC is not consonant now a days with the onset of new disciplines due to common 'add to' features and frequent application of tables, started earlier by UDC, both influenced by decades of consistent as well as high quality research done by Ranganathan and his Indian gharana of library classification research. The pragmatic ideas of Ranganathan that a catalogue is a pointer to represent the original source is finally receiving attention among the western mindset because of the intricacies of their practice of making such tools as a surrogate to the original source. If you keep on adding more and more inputs to make the substitute to stand for the original, finally you end up with 'information twins' and more information overload in the already exceeding flood of new information, which can be confirmed easily by a look at the quantity of each of the international databases. It is undoubted that identifying relevant and substantial inputs from Ranganathan's research on cataloguing will relieve some of the problems faced in designing workable search engines on huge databases.

1.2 Ranganathan and Information Science

The contributions of the great master along with other developments is highlighted in Table 1 to have an idea on the impact of Ranganathan's ideas to the development of library & information science.

Despite the origination of a host of nascent ideas, due to his wholesome democratic spirit and the strong opposition to bring a 'money sieve' between information and its users, he or

1852: C C Jewett, originated the idea of Centralised Cataloguing

1901: Library of Congress (LC) begins catalogue card distribution service and work on the National Union Catalogue. Centralised cataloguing resulted in a savings of ~ 79%

1932: LC's Co-operative cataloguing

1934: Colon Classification and Classified Catalogue Code by S R Ranganathan

1938: Canons of Cataloguing by S R Ranganathan

1945: Chain Indexing, a semi-mechanical method to arrive at Class Index Entries (Subject Headings) from Class Number (notational representation of a subject by the classification scheme), by S R Ranganathan

1950: British National Bibliography (BNB) started using Ranganathan's "Chain Indexing" technique to generate index entries from source titles, and continued till 1970. Abandoned for computerising the operation as the semi mechanical method needed intellectual inputs.

1951: S R Ranganathan, "Libraray service, bibliographic organisation and library classification recognise no national or political boundaries. They are international. The library profession is international. Bibiographers and documentalists are international." stressed the need for international co-operation

1952: S R Ranganathan advocated for prenatal cataloguing and classification, before the publication and release of information sources

1959: Cataloguing in Source (CIS), LC catalogued 1203 publications from 157 publishers using page proofs and 1082 publications printed it in the publication.

1965: LC, Mechanisation of cataloguing

1966: MARC I pilot project to generate and distribute catalogue entries through computer readable form (pilot project)

1967: Anglo American Cataloguing Rules I, as a result of the first International Conference on Cataloguing Principles

1968: MARC II, permanent program

1971: Pre-natal cataloguing and classification to avoid repetition of cataloguing process in each library introduced by LC. Cataloguing in Publication (CIP) using galley proofs and data returned within ten days to keep up with the publication schedule.

1978: Revised and consensus (between both sides of the Atlantic) edition of AACR I as AACR II

Box 1.1: Seminal Contributions of Ranganathan Vs. International Developments

his associates in India never practiced the commercialisation of these ideas. But these ideas reaped profits in the west, who ever applied them for the betterment of information organisation and dissemination. The chain indexing was successfully used by the British National Bibliography for about twenty years. Similarly the prenatal cataloguing and classification ideas of Dr. Ranganathan had been commercially exploited by Library of Congress (Cataloging in Source/ Publication programmes) and other firms selling catalogue cards. The so called developed world insists on getting proper recognition to their ideas and products by safe guarding their rights through all the concerned international forums, will never bother about the abuse of great ideas from pioneers like Ranganathan. It is a moral right on the part of all those concerned to channelise a part of their profits to invest in India for the research activities cherished by him. Perhaps India could have earned enormous amount of dear foreign exchange, had the new provisions of Intellectual Property Rights can be called to explain the previous violations.

1.3 RANGANATHAN AND DIGITAL AGE

In recent years, the myth that powerful computers can control the onslaught of information growth have lead to a deterioration of research in many of the areas where Ranganathan was active, like better classification systems for information organisation, intellectual and simple tools for information representation, bridging the gap between information rich and poor etc. The phenomenal growth of Internet and other digital information networks have demonstrated the need for strong classification and representation of information that will go into any database. The need for identification and application of very apt terms will increase with the quantity of information to be searched using that vocabulary. Most of the web search tools like Google, Yahoo, etc., flashes a long list of information to the screen against any search, and the relevance of many of them has to be researched and found out. Such a situation has crept in due to the total elimination of intellectual expertise vital for information organisation, in the development of such tools. In many information activites, a sensible and knowledgable librarian is a pre-requisite and be preferred to a high end sophisticated computer or other Information Technology gadget.

The pricing of information products and services also needs thorough restructuring in this context. Actually the important inputs inherent in all such products and services is information, which normally comes from a wide range of people and institutions (free of cost in a majority of the cases). It is justifiable that the producers spent quite a good deal of resources for organising the data and interfacing (value-addition in their terms) them with pointers to search, but that argument doesn't hold much when you are dealing with people who are unable to pay, even though they cherish to use such products, because they know well that any improvement to their present state of affairs can only result by effective use of information. It is not out of place to invoke conscience of database developers to design a more realistic pricing policy on their information products for the benefit of a whole lot of humanity who is toiling to meet both ends. The prices of databases to any country should be based on the GDP/GNP or other economic indicators which truly reflect the actual purchasing power of that country. The highly specialised Medline database is made available by its developer National Library of Medicine freely through its website (http://www.ncbi.nlm.nih.gov) is a positive step in this regard, which other developers may find difficult to digest.

The number of H-1B visas to USA is being increased by 77% over a three year period [1]. Despite a more staunch and vocal posture in the aftermath of Shakthi, the Americans demonstrated that they know their business well by offering 44% of H-1B visas issued in the first half of the current fiscal year to Indian citizens. There are many areas where the Indian software talent can be pooled and projected in the International information marketplace like retrospective conversion of databases, design and development of new information systems and services, as only a Sabeer Bhatia could think and implement a wonderful idea like hotmail. This talent is globally recognised, and if initiatives and funds will come into, definitely a rejuvenation of Ranganathan's ideas for better information processing in the post internet information scenario could be tried out. Then only we can discourage the strong orthodoxism of functioning by some library professionals, out of a wrong interpretation of Ranganathan's theories, who work just by reading his books and not by understanding, visualising or interpreting how he termed library as a growing organism.

1.4 CONCLUSION

India has laid strong foundations in classification, cataloguing, indexing due to the efforts of Ranganathan, and due to the special mentality of Institution building out of tax money, we have got well stocked libraries through out the length and breadth of the country. The recent years have witnessed a similar boom in software development. Perhaps a marriage of these two ideas could be tried out to put India to lead the world in quality info products and manpower. This may also go a long way to solve the unemployment rate persisting among library trained in this country.

The information professionals in India can be broadly classified into pro and anti Ranganathan, and even a large quantity of the former who respect and support him doesn't understand his writings and for what ideals he stood for. A philosophic prediction about libraries as an expanding entity, one of the first Indian in the discipline to accept computers as comfortable tools are not easy to be grasped by many fellow and succeeding professionals. Ranganathan has not become irrelevant, he was definitely a man walked ahead of his time.

REFERENCE

1. The Hindu Daily, Visakhapatnam Ed., 1998 July 26.

2
Library Jobs

2.0. INTRODUCTION

There has been a considerable rise in the number of Universities offering library science courses in the Bachelor and Master levels, some even in the self-financing as well as distance mode. These courses are cashing on the handful of library jobs advertised in the government and private sector. Since the designations followed in different institutions vary, it became absolutely impossible for a non-professional to judge them properly and students are deceived by inflated job prospects. With advances in computer and information technology enabled information services, the job of the librarian itself is getting redefined with demands for command over new technology attributes. It is always good to have realistic estimates about the total positions in different institutions as well as annual job openings at different levels in a profession not only to guide the professional aspirants and students but also to venture into effective continuing education programmes of working professionals. In-depth studies on both these aspects are scant largely due to the lack of proper data and statistical tools. A study on the advertised vacancies from April 1977 to March 1978 in the Employment News, the Hindustan Times, the Indian Express, the Times of India, and The Statesman revealed a total of 433 jobs broken up into 142 in Library, 58 in Documentation, and the remaining in translation, editorial, photography, extension, databank, and programming [7]. Another study on employment trends based on the Hindustan Times, the Times of India, and the Employment News, for the years 1981 and 1982 identified the sectors of employment, occupational titles, qualifications, pay scales, age and experience, and reservation of jobs [1]. Though an old study estimated the country needed 164,263 MLISc and BLISc holders, and 79,689 CLISc holders at the end of sixth five-year plan [6], however, no assessment is available on the annual outturn of jobs. This seems to be an overestimate made in 1970 about the anticipated total job prospects by 1985. The number of vacancies notified in 1997 was 160 (0.53% of the total) and 1995 was 69 (0.20% of the total) [3]. Since the latest statistics are absent, this author made some projections on the total jobs as on rolls of different libraries in 1997 as 54547 at an approximate annual 3% increase (1636) [4]. This projection has been made on the premise that the primary source of library jobs, the government sector is downsizing and most of the library posts advertised are due to resignations/retirements rather than creation of new openings. To have a feel of the trends in library related jobs, job notifications in the "Employment News" are scanned for 1998 and 1999 and the results of the study with analysis are presented in this paper.

2.1. Methodology

The publication 'Employment News' is not available in electronic form and the printed issues of the weekly over the years 1998 and 1999 are being used for the study [2]. Thus volume XXII, issue 39 to volume XXIII, issue 39 for the calendar year 1998 and volume XXIII, issue 40 to volume XXIV, issue 39 for the calendar year 1999 are included in this study. However due to non-receipt, the issue 40 of volume XXII and issues 10, 32, 42, 44, 47, 48, and 50 of volume XXIII are excluded from the purview of this study. Only job advertisements for library professionals in Institutions and non-professional vacancies in libraries are collected from the above mentioned issues of the Employment News. As the publication is largely regarded as an organ to disseminate jobs falling vacant under central government and its autonomous bodies, few jobs from state government and private sector find mention there. In data analysis, central government is used to designate not only its departments, but also autonomous institutions and other centrally funded bodies. The same terminology is applied to designate institutions affiliated to or supported by state governments. However, as a major carrier of job openings in a principal employer pool, the trends received from this publication largely reflect trends from other fields as well. These job notifications are sorted separately to assess:

* Type of Employer: Central/State Government Institutions or private sector.
* Type of Job: Permanent, deputation or temporary
* Reservation in professional jobs under SC, ST and OBC streams
* State in which the job is advertised
* Essential Qualifications such as VIII, X, XII, Graduate, Post-Graduate etc.,
* Professional Qualifications like Certificate, Diploma, Bachelor, Master or Ph. D in Library and Information Science
* Desirable Qualifications
* Experience in years
* Employers and category of jobs

Since the professional positions in different institutions follow different designations and different pay scales, such as the 'Librarian' in a School demands similar qualifications and pay scale of a 'Library Assistant' in an academic, research or special library, some groupings based on pay scales irrespective of designations, are attempted to draw patterns in tabulations and data analysis. Since the year 1998 and 1999 is the change over from IV Pay Commission (PC)/V PC in many institutions, merging of equivalent scales as per the reports of the PC implementation are made in data analysis.

2.2. Data Analysis

Information about pay scale, employer and nature of jobs in 1998 is shown in Table 2.1. The number of jobs in the central government, state government, and private institutions are respectively 319 (79.95%), 67 (16.79%) and 13 (3.26%) of the total 399. Out of 319 jobs in the central sector, 53 (16.61%) are in the pay scale 1640-2900/5500-9000, to be followed by 51 (15.99%) in 1400-2600/5000-8000 and 39 (12.23%) in the slots 2200-4000/8000-13500 and 950-1500/ 3050-4590. However, 26 (38.81%) out of 67 vacancies in the state sector are advertised in the supervisory cadre of 2200-4000/8000-13500. Only one job is marked as part-time and nine jobs show no pay scale. Of the 399 jobs, 346 (86.72%) are permanent and 23 (5.76%) are temporary, whereas 30 (7.52%) are to be filled by transfer on deputation. The significant slots for permanent posts are 58 (16.76%) in 2200-4000/8000-13500, 53 (15.32%) in 1640-2900/ 5500-9000, and 50 (14.45%) in 1400-2600/5000-8000. 17 (56.67%) out of 30 deputation posts fall in the supervisory cadre. All the temporary posts are either in short-term projects or as annual apprentices.

The reservation of jobs among various streams is presented in Table 2.2. 210 (65.83%) of the 319 jobs in central government are in the general quota, as against 31.58% in reserved streams; 36 (33.03%) for 'Scheduled Castes' (SC), 17 (15.59%) for 'Scheduled Tribes' (ST) and 56 (51.38%) for 'Other Backward Classes' (OBC). Of the 50 general posts in the state government, 17 (34%) are in the scale of 2200-4000/8000-13500 and 12 (70.59%) of the 17 reserved jobs are in the supervisory cadre. If data for both central and state governments are merged with private sector data, around 48 (17.58%) general posts are in the scale of 2200-4000/8000-13500, followed by 33 (12.09%) in 1400-2600/5000-8000 and 32 (11.72%) in 1640-2900/5500-9000. Most of the reserved positions are in the non-supervisory cadre, like 26 (20.63%) in 1640-2900/5500-9000, 24 (19.05%) in 950-1500/ 3050-4590 and 20 (15.87%) in 1400-2600/5000-8000.

As is the case with other government jobs, it was found

that there is more than one scale slot for library jobs in the attendant, assistant and supervisory grades and irrespective of pay scales; such a grouping is resorted in Table 2.3 for 1998 vacancies. Of the 319 jobs in central sector, 154 (48.28%) are as Assistants, 97 (30.41%) in the supervisory position, and 40 (12.54%) as Clerks. 26 (38.81%) of 67 jobs in the state sector fall in the scale of 2200-4000/8000-13500 with supervisory grades itself accounting for 45 (67.16%) positions. 162 (93%) of the Assistant posts and over 84% of the group A posts are permanent.

The reservation for different types of jobs in 1998 is provided in Table 2.4. 87 (41.43%) Assistant posts in the central sector got vacant in the general stream and 33 (58.93%) in the OBC stream. Of the 39 group A officers in 2200-4000/8000-13500, only 10 (25.64%) got earmarked for reserved categories, whereas one third of total posts in similar cadre for state sector were assigned to reserved categories.

The pay scale, employer and nature of jobs in 1999 are shown in Table 2.5. The number of jobs in the central government, state government, and private sector are respectively 149 (69.63%), 56 (26.17%) and 9 (4.21%) of the total 214. Out of 149 in the central sector, 25 (16.78%) are in the pay scale of 2200-4000/8000-13500, to be followed by 23 (15.44%) in 5000-8000 and 16 (10.74%) in the slot 1400-2300/4500-7000. However, 23 (41.07%) out of 56 in the state sector are advertised in the supervisory cadre of 2200-4000/8000-13500. Around 10 (17.86%) jobs in the state government are in 3700-5700/12000-18300. There are 8 (3.74%) jobs without any pay scale. Of the 214 jobs, 165 (77.10%) are permanent, 30 (14.02%) are temporary, and 19 (8.88%) are to be filled by transfer on deputation. The significant slots for permanent posts are 42 (25.45%) in 2200-4000/8000-13500, 19 (11.52%) in 3700-5700/12000-18300, and 17 (10.30%) in 1400-2300/4500-7000. 16 (84.21%) out of 19 deputation posts fall in the support cadre. 5 (16.67%) of the 30 temporary posts are in the scale of 2200-4000/8000-13500, and most of the remaining are in short-term projects or as annual apprentices.

Table 2.1: Pay Scale, Employer and Nature of LIS Jobs in 1998

Pay Scale 4PC/5PC	Employer			Nature of Job			Total
	Central Govt.	State Govt.	Private	Perma-nent	Depu-tation	Temp-orary	
800-1150	2			2			2
950-1500/ 3050-4590	39	1		39	1		40
975-1660		1		1			1
1000	5					5	5
1400	8					8	8
1350-2200		1		1			1
1640-2400			1	1			1
2550-3200	5			5			5
2650-4000	2			2			2
1200-2040/ 4000-6000	16	5	1	21	1		22
1400-2200			1	1			1
1400-2300/ 4500-7000	34	4		35	3		38
1400-2600/ 5000-8000	51	1	1	50	3		53
3750-8150	2			2			2
2558-5378	1			1			1
5000	2					2	2
5000-8500			2	2			2
1640-2900/ 5500-9000	53	5		53	5		58
5480-8925		1		1			1
5730	1					1	1
2000-3200, 2000-3500/ 6500-10500	17	3		12	8		20
2200-4000/ 8000-13500	39	26	2	58	4	5	67
3000-4500/ 10000-15200	8	1		6	3		9

Pay Scale 4PC/5PC	*Employer*			*Nature of Job*			*Total*
	Central Govt.	*State Govt.*	*Private*	*Perma-nent*	*Depu-tation*	*Temp-orary*	
3700-5000/ 12000-16500	6			4	2		6
3700-5700	15	9		24			24
12000-18300		1		1			1
14300-18300	3			3			3
4500-5700	2			1		1	2
4500-7300	6	4		10			10
16400-20000	1	1		2			2
No pay scale	1	3 (1PT)	5	8		1	9
Total	319	67	13	346	30	23	399

The reservation of jobs fallen vacant among various streams is presented in Table 2.6. 128 (85.91%) of the 149 jobs in central government are in the general quota, as against 8 (5.37%) for SC, 3 (2.01%) for ST and 10 (6.71%) for OBC. Around 20 (15.63%) general posts are in the scale of 5000-8000 and 16 (12.50%) each in the scales of 1400-2300/4500-7000 and 2200-4000/8000-13500. 10 (47.62%) out of 21 reserved positions are in the non-supervisory cadre. Of the 48 general posts in the state government, 18 (37.50%) are in the scale of 2200-4000/8000-13500, 10 (20.83%) each in the slots 3700-5700/12000-18300 and 4500-7300/16400-22400. 6 (66.67%) of the 9 reserved jobs are in the supervisory cadre. In the case of central, state and private sector together, 34 (18.38%) of 185 general posts carry the scale 2200-4000/8000-13500, 20 (10.81%) with 5000-8000 and 18 (9.73%) each for 1400-2300/4500-7000 and 3700-5700/12000-18300. 16 (55.17%) of the 29 reserved posts belonged to supervisory categories.

Table 2.2: General, SC, ST and OBC LIS Jobs in 1998

Pay Scale	Central Government				State Government				Private	General		SC/ST /OBC		Total
	General	SC	ST	OBC	General	SC	ST	OBC		#	%	#	%	
800-1150		1	1									2	0.50	2
950-1500/ 3050-4590	14	6	4	14	1					15	3.76	24	6.02	39
975-1660					1					1	0.25			1
1000	5									5	1.25			5
1400	8									8	2.01			8
1350-2200					1					1	0.25			1
1640-2400									1	1	0.25			1
2550-3200	5									5	1.25			5
2650-4000	2									2	0.50			2
3050-4950	1									1	0.25			1
1200-2040/ 4000-6000	11	1		4				5	1	12	3.01	10	2.51	22
1400-2200									1	1	0.25			1
1400-2300/ 4500-7000	18	6	2	8	4					22	5.51	16	4.01	38

Pay Scale	Central Government				State Government				Private	General		SC/ST /OBC		Total
	General	SC	ST	OBC	General	SC	ST	OBC		#	%	#	%	
1400-2600/ 5000-8000	31	8	2	10	1				1	33	8.27	20	5.01	53
3750-8150	2									2	0.50			2
2558-5378	1									1	0.25			1
5000	2									2	0.50			2
5000-8500									2	2	0.50			2
1640-2900/ 5500-9000	27	9	6	11	5					32	8.02	26	6.52	58
5480-8925					1					1	0.25			1
5730	1									1	0.25			1
2000-3200, 2000-3500/ 6500-10500	16			1	3					19	4.76	1	0.25	20
2200-4000/ 8000-13500	29	3	1	6	17	4	1	4	2	48	12.03	19	4.76	67
3000-4500/ 10000-15200	8						1			8	2.01	1	0.25	9
3700-5000/ 12000-16500	6									6	1.50			6

Pay Scale	Central Government				State Government				Private	General		SC/ST /OBC		Total
	General	SC	ST	OBC	General	SC	ST	OBC		#	%	#	%	
3700-5700	11	1	1	2	7	1	1			18	4.51	6	1.50	24
1200-18300					1					1	0.25			1
14300-18300	3									3	0.75			3
4500-5700	1	1								1	0.25	1	0.25	2
4500-7300	6				4					10	2.51			10
16400-20000	1				1					2	0.50			2
No pay scale	1				3				5	9	2.26			9
	210	36	17	56	50	5	3	9	13	273	68.42	126	31.58	399

Table 2.3: Types of LIS Jobs in 1998

Job Type	***Institution***						***Nature of Job***						***Total***
	Central Govt.		***State Govt.***		***Priv-ate***		***Perma-nent***		***Deput-ation***		***Temporary***		
	No	***%***	***No***	***%***	***No***	***%***	***No***	***%***	***No***	***%***	***No***	***%***	
Attendant	11	2.75	2	0.50	1	0.25	13	3.26	1	0.25			14
Trainee	13	3.26									13	3.26	13
Clerk	40	10.03	1	0.25	1	0.25	42	10.53					42
Assistant	154	38.59	16	4.01	4	1.00	162	40.60	12	3.01			174
Project Fellow	3	0.75									3	0.75	3
Gr. B Senior	17	4.26	3	0.75			12	3.01	8	2.01			20
Gr. A Entry	39	9.77	26	6.52	2	0.50	58	14.54	4	1.00	5	1.25	67
Gr. A Middle	29	7.27	11	2.76			35	8.77	5	1.25			40
Gr. A Senior	12	3.01	5	1.25			16	4.01			1	0.25	17
No pay scale	1	0.25	3	0.75	5	1.25	8	2.01			1	0.25	9
	319	79.95	67	16.79	13	3.26	346	86.72	30	7.52	23	5.76	399

Table 2.4: Reservation in different types of LIS Jobs in 1998

Job Type	Central Government				State Government				Private	General		SC/ST/OBC		Total
	General	SC	ST	OBC	General	SC	ST	OBC		#	%	#	%	
Attendant	9	1	1		2				1	12	3.01	2	0.50	14
Trainee	13									13	3.26			13
Clerk	16	6	4	14	1				1	18	4.51	24	6.02	42
Assistant	87	24	10	33	11			5	4	102	25.56	72	18.05	174
Project Fellow	3									3	0.75			3
Gr. B Senior	16			1	3					19	4.76	1	0.25	20
Gr. A Entry	29	3	1	6	17	4	1	4	2	48	12.03	19	4.76	67
Gr. A Middle	25	1	1	2	8	1	2			33	8.27	7	1.75	40
Gr. A Senior	11	1			5					16	4.01	1	0.25	17
No pay scale	1				3				5	9	2.26			9
	210	36	17	56	50	5	3	9	13	273	68.42	126	31.58	399

The classification of jobs in 1999 based on pay scales as job types is highlighted in Table 2.7. Of the 149 (69.63%) jobs in the central sector, 54 (36.24%) are as Assistants, 62 (41.61%) in the supervisory position, and 15 (10.07%) as Trainees. 23 (41.07%) of 56 jobs in the state sector fall in the scale of 2200-4000/8000-13500 with supervisory grades itself accounting for 44 (78.57%) positions. 33 (94.29%) of the group A middle level posts, 43 (87.76%) of group A entry positions and over 80% of the Assistant posts are permanent. 15 (78.95%) of 19 deputation positions and 23 (76.67%) out of 30 temporary posts are in the support cadre.

Table 2.5: Pay Scale, Employer and Nature of LIS Jobs in 1999

Pay Scale	Institution			Nature of Job			Total
	Central Govt.	State Govt.	Private	Permanent	Deputation	Temporary	
750-1350		1		1			1
950-1800		1		1			1
1400	2					2	2
2160-3540	1			1			1
2650-4000	4	1		3	2		5
3050-4590	4	1		4	1		5
3200-4900	1			1			1
4000-6000	1			1			1
1400-2300/ 4500-7000	16	1	1	17	1		18
3000	1					1	1
3500	6					6	6
4000	6					6	6
4690	1					1	1
5000	3					3	3
5000-8000	23			16	7		23
5000-8500			3	3			3
5500-9000	14	3		13	4		17
6000	1					1	1
6500	2					2	2

6000-10750			1	1			1
6500-10500	5			3	1	1	5
7000		1				1	1
2650-4200	1			1			1
2200-4000/ 8000-13500	25	23		42	1	5	48
10000-15200	9			7	2		9
3700-5000/ 12000-16500	4			4			4
3700-5700/ 12000-18300	9	10		19			19
14300-18300	2			2			2
4500-5700	1			1			1
4500-7300/ 16400-22400	5	11		16			16
22400-24500	1			1			1
No pay scale	1	3	4	7		1	8
Total	149	56	9	165	19	30	214

The reservation for different types of jobs in 1999 is provided in Table 2.8. 49 (85.19%) of 54 Assistants, 16 (61.54%) of 26 group A entry, and 24 (96%) of 25 group A middle posts in the central sector got vacant in the general stream. Of the 26 group A officers in 2200-4000/8000-13500, only 10 (38.46%) got assigned for reserved categories. Similarly, 18 (78.26%) of 23 group A entry, all 10 group A middle, and 10 (90.91%) of 11 group A senior posts in the state sector appeared in the general stream.

Till now, the data for the two years are analysed separately, and in Table 2.9, data for few common scales are presented. In the central government, four commonly occurring pay scales in both years are 5500-9000, 2200-4000/8000-13500, 5000-8000, and 1400-2300/4500-7000 whereas frequently advertised scales under the state government are 2200-4000/8000-13500, 3700-5700/12000-18300 and 4500-7300/16400-22400. Majority of jobs over the two-year period is permanent, and the number in each head for 1998 is higher than that for 1999, with the only exception of more temporary jobs in 1999.

Table 2.6: General, SC, ST and OBC LIS Jobs in 1999

Pay Scale	Central Government				State Government				Private	General		SC/ST/ OBC		Total
	General	SC	ST	OBC	General	SC	ST	OBC		#	%	#	%	
750-1350					1					1	0.47			1
950-1800					1					1	0.47			1
1400	2									2	0.94			2
2160-3540	1									1	0.47			1
2650-4000	4				1					5	2.34			5
3050-4590	3		1		1					4	1.87	1	0.47	5
3200-4900	1									1	0.47			1
4000-6000	1									1	0.47			1
1400-2300/ 4500-7000	16				1				1	18	8.41			18
3000	1									1	0.47			1
3500	3	1		2						3	1.40	3	1.40	6
4000	5			1						5	2.34	1	0.47	6
4690	1									1	0.47			1
5000	3									3	1.40			3
5000-8000	20	1		2						20	9.35	3	1.40	23

Pay Scale	*Central Government*				*State Government*				*Private*	*General*		*SC/ST/ OBC*		*Total*
	General	*SC*	*ST*	*OBC*	*General*	*SC*	*ST*	*OBC*		*#*	*%*	*#*	*%*	
5000-8500									3	3	1.40			3
5500-9000	12		1	1	1	1	1			13	6.07	4	1.87	17
6000	1									1	0.47			1
6500	2									2	0.94			2
6000-10750									1	1	0.47			1
6500-10500	5									5	2.34			5
7000					1					1	0.47			1
2650-4200			1							0		1	0.47	1
2200-4000/ 8000-13500	16	5		4	18	3	1	1		34	15.89	14	6.54	48
10000-15200	9									9	4.21			9
3700-5000/ 12000-16500	4									4	1.87			4
3700-5700/ 12000-18300	8	1			10					18	8.41	1	0.47	19
14300-18300	2									2	0.94			2
4500-5700	1									1	0.47			1

Pay Scale	Central Government				State Government				Private	General		SC/ST/OBC		Total
	General	SC	ST	OBC	General	SC	ST	OBC		#	%	#	%	
4500-7300/ 16400-22400	5				10			1		15	7.01	1	0.47	16
22400-24500	1									1	0.47			1
No pay scale	1				3				4	8	3.74			8
Total	128	8	3	10	48	4	2	2	9	185	86.45	29	13.55	214

Since some of the advertisements do not show the exact city/town in which the jobs are located, the number of jobs advertised for each state irrespective of central, state or private sector is tabulated in Table 2.10. May be due to the large concentration of central government and research installations, Delhi accounted for the highest tally, with 160 (40.10%) in 1998 and 64 (29.91%) in 1999. Uttar Pradesh with 69 (17.29%) and 29 (13.55%), West Bengal with 28 (7.02%) and 12 (5.61%), Karnataka with 12 (3.01%) and 23 (10.75%), Maharashtra with 17 (4.26%) and 10 (4.67%), and Madhya Pradesh with 14 (3.51%) and 10 (4.67%) are other states with more library jobs. The region wise tally of posts in 1998 and 1999 are respectively, north {222 (55.64%), 132 (61.68%)}, east {52 (13.03%), 21 (9.81%)}, south {34 (8.52%), 36 (16.82%)} and west {31 (7.77%), 25 (11.68%)}.

The essential qualifications sought from prospective employees are divided into pre-professional basic qualifications and professional qualifications in library science. The results of categorisation by basic qualifications are summarised in Table 2.11. Since many job advertisements are not very explicit about the qualifications, and merely mention the qualifications as per UGC norms, state government or institution rules, only 259 (64.91%) jobs from 1998 and 135 (63.07%) jobs from 1999 are included in this analysis. 159 (39.85%) jobs of 1998 and 57 (26.63%) of 1999 asked for a minimum qualification of graduation in any subject. Around 40 (10.03%) jobs in 1998 and 56 (26.17%) jobs in 1999 stipulated for post-graduate qualification. Three (0.75%) jobs in 1998 and 6 (2.80%) in 1999 demanded a BE/B.Tech degree. Only 57 (14.28%) jobs of 1998 and 13 (6.07%) jobs of 1999 are accessible to non-graduates, mainly as attendants/clerks.

Table 2.7: Types of LIS Jobs in 1999

Job Type	***Institution***						***Nature of Job***						***Total***
	Central Govt.		***State Govt.***		***Private***		***Permanent***		***Deputation***		***Temporary***		
	No	***%***	***No***	***%***	***No***	***%***	***No***	***%***	***No***	***%***	***No***	***%***	
Attendant	5	2.34	3	1.40			6	2.80	2	0.94			8
Trainee	15	7.01									15	7.01	15
Clerk	5	2.34	1	0.47			5	2.34	1	0.47			6
Assistant	54	25.23	4	1.87	4	1.87	50	23.36	12	5.61			62
Project Fellow	7	3.27	1	0.47							8	3.74	8
Gr. B Senior	5	2.34			1	0.47	4	1.87	1	0.47	1	0.47	6
Gr. A Entry	26	12.15	23	10.75			43	20.09	1	0.47	5	2.34	49
Gr. A Middle	25	11.68	10	4.67			33	15.42	2	0.94			35
Gr. A Senior	6	2.80	11	5.14			17	7.94					17
No pay scale	1	0.47	3	1.40	4	1.87	7	3.27			1	0.47	8
Total	149	69.63	56	26.17	9	4.21	165	77.10	19	8.88	30	14.01	214

Table 2.8: *Reservation in different types of LIS Jobs in 1999*

Job Type	**Central Government**				**State Government**				**Private**	**General**		**SC/ST/ OBC**		**Total**
	General	**SC**	**ST**	**OBC**	**General**	**SC**	**ST**	**OBC**		**#**	**%**	**#**	**%**	
Attendant	5				3					8	3.74			8
Trainee	11	1		3						11	5.14	4	1.87	15
Clerk	4		1		1					5	2.34	1	0.47	6
Assistant	49	1	1	3	2	1	1		4	55	25.70	7	3.27	62
Project Fellow	7				1					8	3.74			8
Gr. B Senior	5								1	6	2.80			6
Gr. A Entry	16	5	1	4	18	3	1	1		34	15.89	15	7.01	49
Gr. A Middle	24	1			10					34	15.89	1	0.47	35
Gr. A Senior	6				10			1		16	7.47	1	0.47	17
No pay scale	1				3				4	8	3.74			8
Total	128	8	3	10	48	4	2	2	9	185	86.45	29	13.55	214

Table 2.9: Comparison of LIS Jobs in 1998 Vs 1999

Pay Scale	Institution						Nature of Job						Total	
	Central Govt.		State Govt.		Private		Permanent		Deputation		Temporary			
	1998	1999	98	99	98	99	98	99	98	99	98	99	1998	1999
2650-4000	2	4		1			2	3		2			2	5
3050-4590		4		1				4		1			0	5
3200-4900		1						1					0	1
4000-6000	16	1	5		1		21	1	1				22	1
1400-2300/ 4500-7000	34	16	4	1		1	35	17	3	1			38	18
5000	2	3									2	3	2	3
5000-8000	51	23	1		1		50	16	3	7			53	23
5000-8500					2	3	2	3					2	3
5500-9000	53	14	5	3			53	13	5	4			58	17
6500-10500	17	5	3				12	3	8	1		1	20	5
2200-4000/ 8000-13500	39	25	26	23	2		58	42	4	1	5	5	67	48
10000-15200	8	9		1			6	7	2	3			8	10
3700-5000/ 12000-16500	6	4					4	4	2				6	4

Pay Scale	*Institution*						*Nature of Job*						*Total*	
	Central Govt.		*State Govt.*		*Private*		*Permanent*		*Deputation*		*Temporary*			
	1998	*1999*	*98*	*99*	*98*	*99*	*98*	*99*	*98*	*99*	*98*	*99*	*1998*	*1999*
3700-5700/ 12000-18300	15	9	10	10			25	19					25	19
14300-18300	3	2					3	2					3	2
4500-5700	2	1					1	1			1		2	1
4500-7300/ 16400-22400	6	5	4	11			10	16					10	16
No pay scale	1	1	3	3	5	4	8	7			1	1	9	8
Total	255	127	61	54	11	8	290	159	28	20	9	10	327	189

The professional qualifications required as essential by different jobs are classified in Table 2.12. Since the same job demands dual qualifications such as a Graduate with BLIS (used to designate Bachelor of Library and Information Science and all its equivalent degrees in this paper) or Post-graduate with MLIS (used to designate Master of Library and Information Science and all its equivalent degrees in this paper), each such job is posted for both BLIS and MLIS. Also, many of the advertisements though silent about basic qualifications but used to be specific for professional qualifications. Thus the total number of jobs counted in this table is slightly higher than the actual. The jobs which asked for a minimum professional qualification of BLIS for 1998 and 1999 respectively are 206 (51.63%) and 97 (45.33%). 57 (14.29%) jobs in 1998 and 63 (29.44%) jobs in 1999 sought a minimum of MLIS. Only 2 (0.50%) posts of 1998 and 4 (1.87%) posts of 1999 included the National Eligibility Test (NET) conducted by UGC as an essential qualification though there are 65 and 48 posts respectively in these two years advertised in the group A entry scale. One year training in IT is normally a qualification prescribed for Deputy Librarian and Librarian vacancies in academic libraries {10 (2.51%) vacancies in 1998 and 7 (3.27%) in 1999}, but the advertisements are silent about the details of this qualification; is it the PGDCA sort of courses or a specialized training at National Centre for Science Information (NCSI) or something else.

Table 2.10: LIS Jobs Vs State in 1998 and 1999

State	***1998***		***1999***	
	#	*%*	*#*	*%*
Andhra Pradesh	13	3.26	5	2.34
Arunachal Pradesh			1	0.47
Assam	3	0.75	5	2.34
Bihar	6	1.50	6	2.80
Chandigarh	11	2.76	2	0.94
Delhi	160	40.10	64	29.91

Goa	1	0.25	3	1.40
Gujarat	3	0.75	7	3.27
Haryana	8	2.01	5	2.34
Himachal Pradesh	11	2.76	1	0.47
Jammu & Kashmir			2	0.94
Karnataka	12	3.01	23	10.75
Kerala	5	1.25	3	1.40
Madhya Pradesh	14	3.51	10	4.67
Maharashtra	17	4.26	10	4.67
Manipur	3	0.75		
Meghalaya	16	4.01	1	0.47
Nagaland	2	0.50		
Orissa			2	0.94
Punjab	3	0.75	13	6.07
Rajasthan	10	2.51	5	2.34
Tamilnadu	4	1.00	5	2.34
Uttar Pradesh	69	17.29	29	13.55
West Bengal	28	7.02	12	5.61
Total	399	100.00	214	100.00

Table 2.11: Essential Qualifications for LIS Jobs in 1998 and 1999 - Basic

Qualifications	***1998***		***1999***	
	#	***% (399)***	***#***	***% (214)***
VIII	5	1.25	3	1.40
X	39	9.77	7	3.27
XII	13	3.26	3	1:40
Graduate	159	39.85	57	26.63
Post-Graduate	40	10.03	56	26.17
B.E./B.Tech.	3	0.75	6	2.80
PhD			3	1.40
Total	259	64.91	135	63.07

The desirable qualifications incorporated in some of the job advertisements (Table 2.13) make interesting reading. The employers are under the impression that a librarian should be proficient in a foreign language other than English and knowledge of one Indian language other than the mother tongue and Hindi. Though overemphasized in professional forums about the invasion of computer and information technology in the profession, only 51 (12.78%) jobs in 1998 and 30 (14.02%) jobs in 1999 underlined 'proficiency in computers' at least as a desirable qualification. A qualitative mention doing the rounds in essential qualifications is 'innovative library services', and it is sure that subjective assessment by the employers must definitely bias assessment of prospective job applicants by this criteria. It is painful to note that not only senior and supervisory job, but even jobs in the support cadre at lower scales also decorate advertisements with such ornamental desirable qualifications.

Table 2.12: Essential Qualifications for LIS Jobs in 1998 and 1999 - Professional

Qualifications	*1998*		*1999*	
	#	*% (399)*	*#*	*% (214)*
CLIS	48	12.03	8	3.74
DLIS	90	22.56	20	9.35
BLIS	206	51.63	97	45.33
MLIS	57	14.29	63	29.44
PhD	1	0.25	10	4.67
NET	2	0.50	4	1.87
PGDCA	3	0.75	3	1.40
1 Year IT	10	2.51	7	3.27
No Professional Qualifications mentioned	5	1.25	12	5.61
Total	422	105.76	224	104.67

Table 2.13: Desirable Qualifications for LIS Jobs in 1998 and 1999

Qualifications	***1998***		***1999***	
	#	*% (399)*	*#*	*% (214)*
CLIS	1	0.25		
DLIS	1	0.25	1	0.47
MLIS	16	4.01	10	4.67
MPhil/PhD	9	2.25	8	3.74
PhD	2	0.50	11	5.14
Knowledge of foreign language other than English	11	2.76	9	4.21
Proficiency in Computers	51	12.78	30	14.02
Typewriting	2	0.50	7	3.27
Innovative Library Services	7	1.75	6	2.80
Science Degree	23	5.76	12	5.61
Editing and Writing	1	0.25		
Film Library Experience	1	0.25	1	0.47
Practical knowledge of film techniques or Diploma in Cinema	1	0.25		
Certificate in Health Science	1	0.25		
Experience in Public Library	5	1.25		
Experience in Scientific Library	8	2.01		
Braille Certificate	3	0.75		
Training in Medical Librarianship	1	0.25		
LLB	1	0.25	1	0.47
DCA	3	0.75	6	2.80
NCSI Training	3	0.75		

MCA	5	1.25		
Experience in Manuscript Library			1	0.47
Teaching Ability			4	1.87
Knowledge of one Indian Language other than Hindi and Mother tongue			1	0.47
Knowledge of Urdu/ Persian/Arabic			3	1.40
Total	156	39.09	111	51.87

Table 2.14: Experience in Years for LIS Jobs in 1998 and 1999

Experience in years	***1998***		***1999***	
	#	***% (399)***	***#***	***% (214)***
1	13	3.26	4	1.87
2	38	9.52	24	11.21
3	25	6.27	20	9.35
4	6	1.50	5	2.34
5	22	5.51	27	12.62
6	2	0.50	2	0.94
7	5	1.25	6	2.80
8	14	3.51	7	3.27
9	2	0.50		
10	12	3.01	7	3.27
11	1	0.25		
12	5	1.25	1	0.47
13	2	0.50	4	1.87
14	1	0.25	1	0.47
15	4	1.00	5	2.34
18			1	0.47
Not mentioned	15	3.76	7	3.27
Total	167	41.85	121	56.54

Table 2.15: Employers & Category for LIS Jobs in 1998 and 1999

Employer	Category of Jobs																Total
	Attendant		Clerk		Assistant		Trainee/ Project		Group B Sr.		Group A entry		Group A middle		Group . A Sr		
	98	99	98	99	98	99	98	99	98	99	98	99	98	99	98	99	
Central Government	2	3	37		56	23			9	3	3	10	9	2	1	1	159
National Research/ Educational Institute	3		3		60	19	15	19	9	1	21	11	14	16	3	2	196
State Government					1		1										2
State Institute	2				12				2								16
Central University	3					12					14	4	10	5	1	4	53
State University	3	1			3	3		1			24	23	9	10	10	11	98
College		3			6	4					7	2					22
Polytechnic					1	1					2						4
School		1			49	11											61
Industry					1	1											2
Total	13	8	40		189	74	16	20	20	4	71	50	42	33	15	18	613

It is quite natural to seek some prior experience in a professional discipline, but there are inconsistencies such as seeking few years of experience for entry level positions in the support cadre and not seeking sufficient experience in the case of senior posts. The experience sought by individual advertisements is cumulated in Table 2.14. 38 (9.52%) jobs in 1998 and 24 (11.21%) in 1999 required minimum two years of experience. In 1998, 25 (6.27%), 22 (5.51%) and 14 (3.51%) jobs prescribed a minimum experience of 3, 5, and 8 years respectively. 27 (12.62%) and 20 (9.35%) jobs in 1999 stipulated respectively prior experience of 5 and 3 years.

An examination of employers and job types is conducted in Table 2.15. The major job givers in the library profession are national level research/educational institutes (196, 31.97%), central government departments (159, 25.94%), state universities (98, 15.98%), schools (61, 9.95%) and central universities (53, 8.65%).

2.3. SUGGESTIONS

2.3.1. Problems of job Characterisation

In the academic set up, all teachers are not called as Professors, as there are established categorizations for a particular job in the government. But one can see a multitude of problems in classifying library related jobs, as a library assistant and library attendant can be named as Librarian (manifested with some grade) in some institutions. Universities follow designations like library/professional assistants for the support cadre and at officer level, the Assistant Librarians (equivalent to Lecturers), Deputy Librarians (equivalent to Readers, but the term 'deputy' rhymes more with the bureaucracy, questioning the academic attributes of the profession, a term Associate Librarian would have been more better) and the Librarian (at Professor level, the head of the library). It is difficult to arrive at uniform designations for all library posts as the institutions fall under different departments which have their own job classifications. But the Institutions should be logical to some extent in arriving at meaningful designations for different cadres in the library. When browsing library related job notifications, a non-professional always would be confused and often gets the impression of overblown job potential because of this chaos in designating library related jobs, as different levels of jobs follow same or similar designations.

2.3.2. Why to tap more jobs?

There of course exist a rational question about what is the need to tap more jobs on the library front. The number of students acquiring library science degrees in a year either through regular or via distance mode is approximately 6000 [5]. The central government and its ancillary institutions advertise about their positions in 'Employment News', and the average annual output of such positions is roughly 300. How many other positions will come up in the state governments and other institutions is anybody's guess. There may be job notifications from these as well as other institutions and private sector in local dailies and now in web portals. The exact number of job openings in the LIS field is difficult to collect in the existing circumstance due to poor statistical information maintained for the same, and the employers fall in different sectors of government, autonomous, private and industry. If the employment exchanges disclose the number of library degree holders on their roster and our library schools keep live statistics of their students getting placed, then only the unemployment rate among library trained in the country could be assessed. The expected annual generation of library related jobs as per the present trend, assessed on a high end, is approximately around 1700 [5]. It is a known fact that a considerable number among the library trained are unable to get suitable placements in a reasonable time. The alternatives at their hand are rather limited since they have little or no mobility to jobs outside the country as is practiced for other professional streams, due to the obvious disadvantages of weak input, feeble infrastructure in library schools, prevalent curriculum and instruction methodology.

2.3.3. How to tap more jobs?

As library science is interdisciplinary in nature, chances exist for employment within and outside the profession like working as research assistants to scholars; with booksellers and publishers in locating books and information; preparing catalogues and bibliographies for wholesalers and publishers; preparing commercial indexing periodicals; and compilation of source books [8]. Schools affiliated to Central Education Boards have a full-fledged librarian, whereas most of the state government schools are managing (?) their libraries on a part time basis with the help of a teacher or clerical staff. At least the high schools can afford to have a librarian to opt for library oriented teaching followed in the technology intensive developed world. The life long teacher oriented 'spoon fed' instruction practiced is the great bane of this country, forcing many talents to drop out in between. Our achievements in the education front speak more in terms of quantity and failed relatively on the quality aspect. No need to search elsewhere reasons for the miserable state of economy and industry, even in the presence of the third largest scientific manpower.

The radio and television programmes are often disturbed by the trail of advertisements on a wide variety of products, since the industrial houses earmarked a certain percentage of their profit for product promotion. As far as in-house R & D is concerned, a 1000 of them have at least one [9], many of them doesn't have one and they are easily satisfied with the borrowed technology. The industrial confederations have realized that in the liberalized economy, the actual survival of internal industry can not be ensured by government control banning imported products, but by making our industry more competitive and better performing in the international market. How far they have considered the utility of information intermediaries on a wide variety of jobs for such an uphill task, if they really want to catch up with multinationals, could be verified only by studying new recruitment for library professionals in industries.

Most of the states and union territories have not so far enacted the library legislation to provide effective public library services to its people. Even in places where the Public Library Act was passed, the situation has not shown any visible improvement in the case of professional recruitment in public library system due to the lack of priority on the part of concerned administration ensemble. Most of the public libraries are now operated either through voluntary services of people or through untrained and inexperienced staff. The services of a professionally trained librarian for public library services could be explored and practiced in the right spirit in this country. If the authorities find it difficult to recruit librarians in all public libraries, they may try to recruit professionals at the Taluk/ Panchayat levels for the benefits of few libraries coming under its fold.

There may be new job areas for library professionals as digital resource managers, digital rights managers, content managers for website creation, internet enabled reference services, resource discovery managers to identify new products, processes or competitors, etc. Most of the library professionals have bachelors or masters degrees in another subject enabling them to look for avenues in interdisciplinary areas. Bioinformatics is getting increased attention in the country, with some technical institutions and universities offering courses in this area. If library professionals with bioscience background are able to acquire the skills required in this area, they may find new job prospects in this area.

2.3.4. Role of Library Associations

The professional associations work for the well being of the profession and they have the backing and support of a large number of professionals and institutions in this venture. The professional bodies have a cell to look in to the problems of job and unemployment. Since we are not very good in collecting and analysing statistics, it is not known whether any government department or the professional associations like ILA, IASLIC, SIS etc., have a live record about the library jobs generated in the country or the number of qualified but unemployed library professionals. It is high time to collect the relevant statistics from different organisations about their library positions, trends of annual recruitments with skill requirements, library degree holders on the rolls of Universities and employment exchanges etc. Only if such information is available, the requirements of library professionals and what sort of skills are in high demand etc. can be assessed. This exercise may also help in convincing the prospective employers about the need to recruit vacant positions or to create new ones. A database should be maintained by the professional associations with provision for updating when a person occupies/changes/retires from a job.

2.3.5. Role of Government

The objective of professional education is different from conventional university education and it has to be need-based. If there is no demand of professionals in a particular area and when they can not be accommodated for any related work, the best course of action on the part of Government is to prune such education activities or at least contain them to some extent. The reverse is happening on the library education front now. With out identifying any major jump in the demand for library graduates, more universities are starting library science courses, some are offering them on the distance mode too, a surprising thing is some have even identified it as a potential course to be offered on self financing basis along with management, computers, etc. Perhaps the UGC through its curriculum development exercises would be able to refine the library courses so that new professionals will be instilled vital skills to perform well in the highly demanding emerging information work place. What is needed is a NCTE/AICTE type of regulatory body to control the existing and emerging institutions offering library science courses, which should essentially look up the number of seats, required infrastructure, and other essential matters. Let us hope that the accreditation culture that is picking up late in this country may axe library courses with doubtful motives, and to put a brake on the new found interest to offer more library courses on the distance mode.

The government should also take initiative to immediately fill library posts vacated by retirement/ resignation, and to create and recruit suitable new positions as and when necessary. The motivation of the library staff in many organizations is victimized by the poor options available for career advancement. In some institutions, library professionals enter and retire in the same post even after serving long. Such anomalies should be axed, and equitary opportunities as for other professionals would be given for library personnel too.

2.3.6. Role of Students

Before venturing into any professional education, it is better to collect statistics about the job prospects and unemployment rate in the field. Most of the career guidance magazines publish such features nowadays. If one is really exemplary, s/he does not need professional education to get a job. Understanding one's weakness and strength is the right point to choose a profession. As such service to society is concerned, no profession is either superior or weak to another. It is one's tastes, resources, luck and destiny decides what profession would be selected ultimately. Fresh students must closely observe and assess their suitability and drive 'to compete with more persons for less jobs' before enrolling to any library science courses.

As far as the unemployed library degree holders or those now pursuing library courses are concerned, they can take up the lack of jobs in the profession at appropriate fora with the help of library associations and the peer group of faculty members. Such persuasion will help at least to speed up processes for recruitment of vacant positions.

2.3.7. Role of Library Schools

The curriculum needs constant updation to meet the challenges thrown by the emerging information set up where electronic processing is becoming more vital and relevant to effectively collect, process, organise and service the large chunk of information generated. It is imperative up on the part of learned faculty to modify the curriculum not only to accommodate computer related topics in the theory courses but also to offer as much practical exposure on IT aspects. The library schools may find lack of expert faculty and support staff specialised in computers, relevant computer and communication infrastructure etc. These can be overcome by seeking suitable help from computer specialists in the concerned University. A library professional should be trained on the utility of computers for diverse aspects of information work, and the training should encompass multiple skills desired to handle other jobs that may creep up in related environments, to improve the mobility of library trained for newly emerging information communication jobs.

2.4. CONCLUSION

Automation of library & information activities are happening in a slow but steady pace in our country too, with the penetration of computers and improvement in communication infrastructure. The research Institutions are also experiencing the benefits of Internet for R & D work. In such a scenario, much is to be done on the training and recruitment of library professionals for effective information work. The categorisation and recruitment formula followed for library staff should undergo appropriate changes to reflect the transition needed in accommodating the emerging information environment. There must be some sort of interaction between prospective employers and the library schools to attune the training programmes with potential job skills. Also, there is an urgent need of some organisation or a professional group to look into the characteristics of total and annual jobs in the library field, and to study the emerging human resource trends and requirements. There is a need for more studies on job opportunities in the profession by collecting data from regional as well as national newspapers and job portals. Only when results from such a large data set are available, conclusions can be drawn on the actual state of affairs regarding job opportunities in the library profession. Also needed is a study and assessment on the vacant positions in different libraries that are not being filled-up for a long time for various reasons. This will eventually help the professional forums and authorities concerned to initiate action on recruitment drives and to gather imminent new outlets for the professionally qualified. The results of more involved studies on the actual and advertised vacancies in the profession may further act as a word of caution for students enrolling in the professional courses in Library and Information science, as such courses are un/fortunately becoming very popular in the country.

REFERENCES

1. Anand, A. K. and Kapoor, Shabad, Manpower for the library and information field in India: a report on employment trends in 1981 and 1982, Annals of Library Science and Documentation, 30 (3-4), 1983, pp. 85-97.
2. Employment News, Publications Division, Ministry of Information and Broadcasting, India, 1998-1999.
3. India, Ministry of Labour, Director General of Employment and Training, Bulletin of Job Opportunities in India 1997, New Delhi, Dec 1999, p.73.
4. Jeevan, V K J, Distance or Distress Education for Librarianship, Herald of Library Science, 37(3-4), July-Oct 1998, pp. 196-204.
5. Jeevan, V K J, Open and Distance Learning for Library Science Professionals, University News, 40(16), 2002, pp. 3-9.
6. Kaula, P N, Education and Training of Library Personnel: The Indian Programme, Proceedings of ISLIC International Conference on Information Science, Tel Aviv, 29 Aug-3 Sept, 1971, National Centre for Scientific and Technical Information, Tel Aviv, 1972, vol. 2, pp. 491-507.
7. Nayar, B K et al, Demand for Information Scientists in India (An analysis of Advertised Vacancies), Handbook of Libraries, Archives and Information Centres in India,

Information Industry Publications, New Delhi, 1984-85, pp. 331-357.

8. Satija, Mohinder Partap, The plight of librarians: avenues for more jobs, Lucknow Librarian, 15(3), Sept 83, pp. 93-97.

9. S & T (Science & Technology) Pocket Data Book, Govt. of India, DSIR, New Delhi, 1992, pp. 114-115.

3

Publication in Journals from IIT Kharagpur

3.0. INTRODUCTION

Indian Institute of Technology, Kharagpur was set up in 1951 by the Government of India for furthering the growth of human resources in applied sciences and technology. It is a University level institute of national importance, offering offer 22 undergraduate and 50 postgraduate courses through its 18 departments, 5 centres and 2 schools of education in diverse branches of science and technology. On an average around 100 Ph.Ds and about 325 M. Tech dissertations are produced annually. The 500 faculty members and the research scholars registered under them conduct research with the assistance of scientific and technical staff. The Institute is getting support in the form of Research and Development (R&D) as well as Consultancy projects from international and national agencies and industries. In 1994-95, the Institute operated 79 sponsored projects worth Rs. 107 million and 179 consultancy projects for a total value of Rs. 9.5 million. In 1995-96, the Institute has secured more than 65 sponsored projects and 130 consultancy projects worth Rs. 100 million. Around 50 sponsored and 120 consultancy projects of value Rs. 170 million was secured in 1996-97. The Institute is very active in the frontier areas of technology as reflected in the publications originating from it.

The faculty and researchers publish their research results in national and international journals/conferences and so far special studies are not conducted about the publishing features of these papers. Some of the bibliographic databases subscribed at the Central Library of the Institute are searched to get an idea of how many of these papers are reported in such databases (see Table 3.1). However, due to the policies followed by each database producer and on account of the subject specialisations, a large number of papers from the Institute are not reported them. The authentic as well as exhaustive source to keep track of these publications is the Annual report of the Institute and the research publications from the Institute as reported there is shown in Table 3.2. These reports are compiled by collecting data from each department of the Institute based on a common format: author(s), title, and source, under different heads for research publications in journals/book chapters and conference presentations. Since the data for consecutive years are suffered by some overlap, and some of the multiple authored papers are entered as duplicates in different departments or in the same department, they are avoided and a cumulative list of the papers from different departments is summarised in Table 3.3.

Table 3.1: Papers from IIT, Kharagpur from Electronic Databases

Database	**Year**	**Papers**			**% of India to Total**	**% of IIT, Kharagpur to India**
		Total	**From India**	**From IIT, Kharagpur**		
INSPEC	1994	274238	5676	213	2.07	3.75
Compendex	1995	228555	4138	186	1.81	4.49
Compendex	1996	264272	4447	226	1.68	5.08
CCOD-ECT	1994			154		
CCOD-ECT	1995		3054	180		5.89
CCOD-ECT	1996		2242	127		5.66

Table 3.2: Publications from IIT Kharagpur (based on the Institute Annual Reports)

Year	***Journal Papers/ Book Chapters***	***Conference Papers***	***Total***
1994-95	505	427	932
1995-96	559	374	933
1996-97	541	504	1045
Total for 3 years	1605	1305	2910

1.1. Data Collection

The research publications as book chapters and those presented in conferences are excluded from the purview of this study. Though the Annual Report follow a standard format, since the data is supplied by individual researchers, some of them give the journal name in full, some as standard abbreviation, and a few others give the de-facto abbreviation. Tracing the correct journal name from this abbreviation has some times becomes very difficult. The electronic databases subscribed and the journals subscribed are consulted to trace out the full information for such partial data. Ulrich's International Periodicals Directory 1999 to properly identify the journals and their ISSNs. A database of research publications in journals from the different departments (as in Table 3.3) has been prepared after this data purification in MS Access with the structure shown in Table 3.4.

Table 3.3: Department wise List of Papers

#	***Department/ Centre/School (Code used in the paper)***	***1994-95***		***1995-96***		***1996-97***		***Total***	
		Journ-als (J)	***Pape-rs (P)***	***J***	***P***	***J***	***P***	***J***	***P***
1	Aerospace Engineering (AE)	8	13	7	15	13	15	28	43
2	Agriculture & Food Engineering (AG)	25	35	25	36	18	26	68	97
3	Architecture (AR)	3	4	3	5	3	3	9	12

#	Department/ Centre/School (Code used in the paper)	1994-95 Journals (J)	1994-95 Papers (P)	1995-96 J	1995-96 P	1996-97 J	1996-97 P	Total J	Total P
4	Chemical Engineering (CE)	11	15	11	14	8	11	30	40
5	Chemistry (CH)	38	55	30	53	24	34	92	142
6	Civil Engineering (CV)	15	28	13	20	12	18	40	66
7	Computer Science (CS)	17	20	13	14	19	22	49	56
8	Electrical Engineering (EE)	19	21	22	28	15	16	56	65
9	Electronics & Communication Engineering (EC)	24	32	28	30	27	34	79	96
10	Geology & Geophysics (GG)	8	13	10	12	9	10	27	35
11	Humanities & Social Sciences (HS)	3	3	3	3	5	5	11	11
12	Industrial Engineering (IE)	10	11	13	16	13	14	36	41
13	Mathematics (MA)	33	44	25	38	33	42	91	124
14	Mechanical Engineering (ME)	21	25	26	31	22	29	69	85
15	Metallurgy (MG)	22	34	22	28	28	35	72	97
16	Mining (MN)	9	10	4	5	13	16	26	31
17	Ocean Engineering & Naval Architecture (OE)	9	12	9	10	2	2	20	24
18	Physics & Meteorology (PH)	30	48	33	51	33	44	96	143
19	Biotechnology (BT)			9	11	5	5	14	16
20	Cryogenics (CY)	4	7	8	13	1	1	13	21
21	Materials Science (MS)	24	34	23	33	25	32	72	99
22	Reliability (RE)			11	13	3	3	14	16

#	Department/ Centre/School (Code used in the paper)	1994-95 Journals (J)	1994-95 Papers (P)	1995-96 J	1995-96 P	1996-97 J	1996-97 P	Total J	Total P
23	Rubber Technology (RT)	20	39	18	36	12	36	50	111
24	Rural Development (RD)	1	1	2	2	1	1	4	4
25	VG School of Management (VG)	2	3			1	1	3	4
	Total	356	507	368	517	345	455	1069	1479

Table 3.4: Database Structure

Field Name	***Data type***	***Size***	***Description***
Dept-Code	Text	2	Standard codes for the Departments of the Institute
Journal	Text	100	Name of the Journal
Publisher	Text	50	Name of the publisher
Country	Text	50	Country of Publication
ISSN	Text	10	Standard Number of the Journal
Year	Number	Long	Year of Publication
Papers	Number	Long	Number of Papers in a journal
Subscribed	Yes/No		Whether the journal is subscribed in the Central Library of the Institute
IF	Number	Long	Impact Factor of the Journal

1.2. Data Analysis

The data entered in the database and queried to assess the preferred journals, premier publishers, major countries of publication, bias towards subscribed journals and to assess the impact of these publications on future research. It was found that 1479 papers of the three year period from 1994 to 1996 are published in 568 journals as illustrated in Table 3.5. The top 16 (2.82%) journals account for over 302 (20.42%) papers or 10% of the journals published 40% of the papers. More than 50% of the journals publish only a single paper each.

The publisher characteristics of research papers in journals from IIT, Kharagpur are displayed in Table 3.6. Publishers of over 10% of the papers are not identified as the details given in the papers and verification with the reference sources does not yield much. About 27% of the papers from 23% of journals are published in Indian journals and 21.3% of the journals belonging to Research/Professional Societies published 15.55% of the papers. Commercial publishers publish a small portion of the journals (3.87%) and papers (2.57%) for Societies. Elsevier and Pergamon imprints of the Elsevier Science, Netherlands and associates stood top among publishers with 20.82% of papers in 17.41% of journals.

To categorise papers by country of publication was sometimes difficult as some of the major players have offices (for publishing and editing) in different countries like, Elsevier Science, Springer Verlag, Academic Press etc. Such publishers are clubbed together as International in Table 3.7 (33.06% of papers in 28.17% of journals). The countries in decreasing order of publication are India, USA, UK, Germany, and Netherlands.

The researchers in India publish their important research results in international journals for better visibility of their research output and due to the availability of specialized journals. Most of the researchers generally consult few journals in their subject specialisation and prefer to publish in such journals. To find out whether, subscription of a particular journal in one's library is influencing research publishing, the data relating to papers published in the subscribed and non-subscribed journals, such as journals with maximum papers, major countries of publication, and predominant publishers are listed in Tables 3.8-3.13. It was found that 39.61% of the subscribed journals published 51.72% of the papers whereas a considerably large number of Non-subscribed journals (60.39%) covered 48.28% of the papers.

Table 3.5: Journals

#	*Journal [Percentage] of 568*	*ISSN*	*Papers*	*Percentage*
1.	Journal of The Institution of Engineers (India) {6 of 18 Sections}	[0.17]	41	2.77
2.	Journal of Applied Polymer Science	0021-8995	39	2.64
3.	International Journal of Computers & Structures	0045-7949	33	2.23
4.	Journal of Materials Science	0022-2461	24	1.62
5.	Journal of Sound and Vibration	0022-460X	18	1.22
6.	IETE Technical Review	0256-4602	16	1.08
7.	Indian Journal of Pure and Applied Physics	0019-5596	16	1.08
8.	International Journal of Polymeric Materials	0091-4037	16	1.08
9.	Polymer	0032-3861	16	1.08
10.	Journal of Materials Science Letters	0261-8028	15	1.01
11.	Bulletin of Materials Science	0250-6327	14	0.95
12.	Plastics, Rubber and Composites-Processing and Applications	0959-8111	13	0.88
13.	Indian Chemical Engineer	0019-4506	11	0.74
14.	Applied Physics Letters	0003-6951	10	0.67
15.	The Journal of Fuzzy Mathematics	1066-8950	10	0.67
16.	Tetrahedron Letters	0040-4039	10	0.67
17-21.	5 Journals (9 articles each) [0.88]		45	3.04
22-30.	9 Journals (8 articles each) [1.58]		72	4.87
31-39.	9 Journals (7 articles each) [1.58]		63	4.26

#	Journal [Percentage]	ISSN	Papers	Percentage
40-55.	16 Journals (6 articles each) [2.82]		96	6.49
56-78.	23 Journals (5 articles each) [4.05]		115	7.77
79-106.	28 Journals (4 articles each) [4.93]		112	7.57
107-157.	51 Journals (3 articles each) [8.98]		153	10.34
158-267.	110 Journals (2 articles each) [19.36]		220	14.87
268-568.	301 Journals (1 article each) [52.99]		301	20.35
	Total Journals = 568	Total Papers = 1479		

Table 3.6: Publishers of Journals

#	Publisher	Journals		Papers	
		Number	Percentage	Number	Percentage
1.	Elsevier	62	10.92	178	12.04
2.	Pergamon	40	7.04	130	8.79
3.	Society Publications	55	9.68	73	4.94
4.	John Wiley	13	2.28	54	3.65
5.	IEEE, US	23	4.05	44	2.97
6.	Chapman & Hall, UK	4	0.70	41	2.77
7.	Society & Publisher Collaboration	22	3.87	38	2.57
8.	Academic Press	10	1.76	34	2.29
9.	American Institute of Physics,US	8	1.41	33	2.23
10.	Gordon & Breach	6	1.06	30	2.03
11.	Taylor & Francis	12	2.11	29	1.96
12.	Springer Verlag	10	1.76	26	1.76
13.	American Chemical Society, US	11	1.94	25	1.69
14.	Technomic, US	4	0.70	25	1.69

#	Publisher	Journals		Papers	
		Number	Percentage	Number	Percentage
15.	Institute of Materials, UK	3	0.53	18	1.22
16.	IOP, UK	8	1.41	16	1.08
17.	Plenum, US	3	0.52	13	0.88
18.	IEE, UK	7	1.23	11	0.74
19.	Kluwer	7	1.23	11	0.74
20.	Marcel Dekker, US	5	0.88	11	0.74
21.	Royal Society of Chemistry, UK	6	1.06	10	0.67
22.	Publishers, India	131	23.06	404	27.32
23.	Other 11 publishers	37	6.51	69	4.66
24.	Publishers not known	81	14.26	156	10.55
	Total	568		1479	

Table 3.7: Countries of Publication

#	Country	Journals		Papers	
		Number	Percentage	Number	Percentage
1.	International/ Multinational	160	28.17	489	33.06
2.	India	131	23.06	404	27.32
3.	U S	108	19.01	220	14.87
4.	U K	58	10.21	147	9.94
5.	Germany	19	3.35	42	2.84
6.	Netherlands	16	2.82	38	2.57
7.	Japan	7	1.23	11	0.74
8.	Denmark	1	0.17	9	0.61
9.	Singapore	6	1.06	9	0.61
10.	18 Other Countries	34	5.98	41	2.77
11.	Unknown	28	4.93	69	4.66
	Total	568		1479	

Table 3.8: Top Subscribed Journals

#	Journal	Country	Papers	
			Number	% (of 765)
1	Journal of Institution of Engineers (India)	India	41	5.36
2	Journal of Applied Polymer Science	U S	39	5.09
3	International Journal of Computers & Structures	U S	33	4.31
4	Journal of Materials Science	U K	24	3.14
5	Journal of Sound and Vibration	U K	18	2.35
6	IETE Technical Review	India	16	2.09
7	Indian Journal of Pure and Applied Physics	India	16	2.09
8	Journal of Materials Science Letters	U K	15	1.96
9	Bulletin of Materials Science	India	14	1.83
10	Plastics, Rubber and Composites-Processing & Applications	U K	13	1.70
11	Indian Chemical Engineer Section A	India	11	1.44
12	Applied Physics Letters	USA	10	1.31
13	Tetrahedron Letters	USA	10	1.31
	Total		260	33.99

Table 3.9: Countries Publishing Subscribed Journals

#	Country	Journals		Papers	
		Number	Percentage	Number	Percentage
1	U S	86	38.22	261	34.12
2	U K	61	27.11	194	25.36
3	India	31	13.78	180	23.53
4	Netherlands	28	12.44	85	11.11
5	Germany	7	3.11	18	2.35
6	Switzerland	5	2.22	15	1.96
7	Japan	3	1.33	6	0.78
8	Singapore	4	1.78	6	0.78
	Total	225.		765	

Table 3.10: Publishers of Subscribed Journals

#	Publisher	Journals		Papers	
		Number	Percentage	Number	Percentage
1	Elsevier	32	14.22	101	13.20
2	Pergamon	21	9.33	90	11.76
3	Society	41	18.22	84	10.98
4	IEEE, US	22	9.78	43	5.62
5	The Institution of Engineers, India	1	0.44	41	5.36
6	Chapman & Hall, UK	3	1.33	40	5.23
7	I. A. Sc., India	4	1.78	33	4.31
8	John Wiley, US	1	0.44	39	5.09
9	American Institute of Physics	5	2.22	27	3.53
10	Academic Press	5	2.22	25	3.27
11	Taylor & Francis	8	3.56	21	2.75
12	Society-Publisher	9	4.00	20	2.61
13	American Chemical Soc.	7	3.11	18	2.35
14	Publishers (India)	24	10.67	90	11.76
15	Other Publishers	42	18.67	93	12.16
	Total	225		765	

Table 3.11: Top Non-subscribed Journals

#	Journal	Country	Papers	
			Number	% (of 714)
1	International Journal of Polymeric Materials	UK	16	2.24
2	Polymer	UK	16	2.24
3	The Journal of Fuzzy Mathematics	US	10	1.40
4	Acta Crystallographica	Denmark	9	1.26
5	Bioprocess Engineering	Germany	9	1.26
6	Polymer Networks and Blends	US	8	1.12

#	Journal	Country	Papers	
			Number	% (of 714)
7	Chemical Physics Letters	Netherlands	7	0.98
8	Materials Research Bulletin	UK	7	0.98
9	Optimization	Germany	7	0.98
	Total		89	12.46

Table 3.12: Country of Publication of Non-subscribed Journals

#	Country	Journals		Papers	
		Number	Percentage	Number	Percentage
1	India	102	29.74	222	31.09
2	U K	61	17.78	145	20.31
3	U S	61	17.78	103	14.43
4	Netherlands	27	7.87	53	7.42
5	Germany	23	6.71	50	7.00
6	Switzerland	8	2.33	13	1.82
7	20 Countries	33	9.62	59	8.26
8	Unknown	28	8.16	69	9.66
	Total	343		714	

Table 3.13: Publishers of Non-subscribed Journals

#	Publisher	Journals		Papers	
		Number	Percentage	Number	Percentage
1	India	100	29.15	219	30.67
2	Society	55	16.03	81	11.34
3	Elsevier	31	9.04	77	10.78
5	Pergamon	19	5.54	40	5.60
6	Gordon & Breach	7	2.04	30	4.20
7	Springer, Germany	10	2.92	23	3.22
8	Society + Publisher	11	3.21	13	1.82
9	IEE, UK	7	2.04	11	1.54
10	Other Publishers	75	21.86	151	21.15
11	Unknown	28	8.16	69	9.66
	Total	343		714	

1.1. Quality Assessment of Papers

While verifying the journals in which the IIT, Kharagpur researchers published their papers, with Journal Citation Reports (JCR) of ISI, it was found that 431 of the 568 unique journals or 822 of the 1479 papers (55.58%) have Impact Factors (IFs) varying from 0.01 to 7.38. The classified data is presented in tables 3.14-3.16. It can be found that over 46% of the papers have IF values less than 0.5, 32% of the papers with IF between 0.5 and 1, and 18% of the papers possess IF between 1 and 2. There are about 8% of the papers for which IF vary from 2 to 4, and less than 1% of the papers have IF greater than 4. Over 75% of the papers from the departments of Chemistry, Cryogenics, Rubber Technology, Materials Science, and Management are published in journals with IF. In the case of papers from Reliability, Physics, Metallurgy, Electronics, Electrical, and Computer Science, 50-75% of papers was printed in journals with IF. However, may be due to the inherent features of the disciplines warrant publishing in Indian journals that are not well covered in JCR, none of the papers from Humanities and Rural Development figure in journals with IF. Only less than 15% of the papers from architecture, geology and mining are in IF journals. 6 papers from Chemistry and one each from Biotechnology and Agriculture had IF greater than 4. 40 papers from Chemistry, 13 from Physics, 5 from Electronics, 3 from Materials Science, 2 each from Biotechnology and Chemical, 1 each from Agriculture, Geology, Mechanical, and Cryogenics had IF between 2 and 4. 25 papers from Physics, 23 papers from Electronics, 19 papers each from Chemistry and Rubber Technology, 18 papers from Materials Science, 13 papers from Metallurgy, 7 papers from Cryogenics, 6 papers from Agriculture, 5 papers from Electrical, 4 papers from Mechanical, 3 papers each from Computer Science and Chemical, 2 papers each from Biotechnology and Civil, and 1 paper each from Industrial Engineering, Ocean Engineering and Mathematics, are with IF in between 1.01 and 2. In the case of 268 papers with IF between 0.51 and 1, departments and papers are as follows: Rubber Technology - 43, Chemistry - 30, Metallurgy - 26, Physics and Materials Science - 23 each, Computer Science - 20, Electronics - 12, Cryogenics - 11, Mathematics and Electrical - 10 each, Agriculture and Chemical - 9 each, Aerospace - 8, Management - 3, Biotechnology and Industrial - 2 each, and Geology and Ocean Engineering - 1 each.

Table 3.14: Journals and Papers with IF

No	Impact Factor	Journals		Papers	
		Number	Percentage	Number	Percentage
1.	7.385	1	0.23	2	0.24
2.	5.039	1	0.23	2	0.24
3.	4.609	1	0.23	3	0.36
4.	4.374	1	0.23	1	0.12
5.	3.001-4.000	21	4.87	32	3.89
6.	2.001-3.000	19	4.41	39	4.74
7.	1.501-2.000	28	6.49	44	5.35
8.	1.301-1.500	21	4.87	41	4.98
9.	1.101-1.300	20	4.64	35	4.26
10.	1.001-1.100	17	3.94	32	3.89
11.	0.901-1.000	24	5.57	49	5.96
12.	0.801-0.900	19	4.41	54	6.57
13.	0.701-0.800	31	7.19	65	7.91
14.	0.601-0.700	21	4.87	39	4.74
15.	0.501-0.600	27	6.26	61	7.42
16.	0.401-0.500	29	6.73	62	7.54
17.	0.301-0.400	47	10.91	73	8.88
18.	0.201-0.300	40	9.28	75	9.12
19.	0.101-0.200	39	9.05	81	9.85
20.	0.010-0.100	24	5.57	32	3.89
	Total	431		822	

Table 3.15: Journals and Papers with IF: Department/Year wise

Dept Code	IF Journals/Papers 1994 J	1994 P	1995 J	1995 P	1996 J	1996 P	Total with IF J	Total with IF P	Total Papers	Percentage of papers with IF to total
AE	2	3	3	7	6	8	11	18	43	41.86
AG	6	8	12	16	6	8	24	32	97	32.99
AR					1	1	1	1	12	8.33
CE	5	8	6	7	1	1	12	16	40	40
CH	28	46	24	49	20	29	72	124	142	87.32
CV	6	6	4	5	3	4	13	15	66	22.73
CS	12	14	8	9	12	15	32	38	56	67.86
EE	13	13	14	16	6	7	33	36	65	55.38
EC	18	23	19	21	15	21	52	65	96	67.71
GG	2	2	1	1	2	2	5	5	35	14.28
HS								0	11	0
IE	2	3	4	6	3	3	9	12	41	29.27
MA	17	22	13	19	16	20	46	61	124	49.19
ME	9	10	10	12	8	10	27	32	85	37.65
MG	13	21	15	20	12	17	40	58	97	59.79
MN	1	1	1	1	2	2	4	4	31	12.90
OE	5	6	3	3	1	1	9	10	24	41.67
PH	20	31	20	28	23	31	63	90	143	62.94
BT			3	6			3	6	16	37.50
CY	4	7	7	12			11	19	21	90.47
MS	17	24	18	28	17	24	52	76	99	76.77
RE			4	5	2	3	6	8	16	50
RT	12	29	14	32	9	32	35	93	111	83.78
RD								0	4	0
VG			1	2	1	1	2	3	4	75
Total	192	277	204	305	166	240	562	822	1479	55.58

Table 3.16: IF Classification of papers: Department/Year wise

No	Impact Factor	1994	1995	1996	Papers
1	7.385		AG-1 BT-1		2
2	5.039	CH-2			2
3	4.609	CH-3			3
4	4.374			CH-1	1
5	3.001-4.000	CE-1 EC-1 CH-4 PH-3 CY-1	EC-1 PH-3 MS-2 CH-5	EC-3 PH-1 MS-1 CH-4 MG-1 ME-1	32
6	2.001-3.000	MG-1 AG-1 CH-4 PH-1 GG-1	CE-1 BT-2 CH-16 PH-2	CH-7 PH-3	39
7	1.501-2.000	CH-3 EC-3 MG-4 PH-3 MS-1 AG-1	CH-5 PH-2 CS-1 IE-1 EC-3 MS-2 AG-2 BT-1 MG-1 CV-1	AG-1 CS-1 EC-2 PH-3 ME-1 MS-1 CH-1	44
8	1.301-1.500	CH-2 CV-1 MS-2 EC-1 RT-2 PH-1	CE-1 CH-2 MS-5 RT-4 PH-1 EE-1 CY-1	CH-1 MG-2 PH-2 RT-9 EC-2 MS-1	41
9	1.101-1.300	PH-2 CH-2 EE-2 EC-2 MS-1	AG-2 BT-1 EE-2 EC-3 ME-1 RT-1 CE-1 CY-2 MS-2 MG-2 PH-4 CH-1	MG-2 PH-1 CH-1	35
10	1.001-1.100	MS-1 EC-3 OE-1 MG-1 PH-1 CS-1 RT-3	PH-2 CY-4 MS-1 EC-2 CE-1 ME-1	ME-1 CH-1 EC-2 MA-1 PH-3 MS-1 MG-1	32
11	0.901-1.000	CH-2 AG-1 CS-2 RT-2 PH-2 MS-1	CH-4 EC-2 RT-2 PH-4 MG-2 MS-1 AG-1	PH-5 CS-2 MS-3 RT-10 MG-2 AG-1	49
12	0.801-0.900	EE-1 CE-3 CV-1 CH-8 CY-4 ME-1 CS-1 PH-3 MS-2 RT-10	EE-2 CH-2 MS-2 RT-8 MG-2	CS-2 PH-1 CH-1	54
13	0.701-0.800	CS-2 CH-4 CV-1 AG-2 MA-1 MG-2 PH-1	CV-1 CS-1 VG-2 CE-1 CH-3 MG-4 PH-2	EC-1 ME-3 EE-1 CE-1 IE-1 VG-1	65

No	Impact Factor	1994	1995	1996	Papers
		RT-1 CY-2 EC-2 CE-1	MS-2 RT-4	MS-5 RT-4 AG-2 CS-3 MG-3 PH-1	
14	0.601-0.700	MA-4 ME-4 CE-1 AE-1 CV-1 OE-1 PH-1 CS-1 EC-1 CH-1 MG-3	EE-1 MG-1 CS-2 IE-1 MA-1 EC-1	CS-4 EE-1 AE-3 ME-1 EC-1 MA-1 RT-2	39
15	0.501-0.600	MG-4 EE-1 ME-2 CH-2 MA-1 GG-1 MS-3 PH-1	CE-2 CV-3 BT-2 CY-5 ME-4 PH-3 EE-2 MS-1 AE-4 AG-2	EE-1 MA-2 CH-3 PH-2 MS-3 MG-3 EC-4	61
16	0.401-0.500	CS-1 EE-3 IE-1 CH-1 PH-3 AE-2 OE-2 RT-2 MA-3 EC-1 AG-1	MA-7 AE-3 CH-1 MG-3 PH-1 MS-2 RT-5 EC-3	MA-3 CH-5 IE-1 PH-3 AE-1 MN-1 RT-3	62
17	0.301-0.400	CV-2 MA-5 CH-4 CS-2 MG-2 IE-2 CE-1 RT-7 EC-1 PH-2 ME-1	AG-5 OE-1 GG-1 MA-5 RE-1 CH-4 MG-1 ME-1 MS-3	AG-4 OE-1 MS-2 MA-6 AE-2 CV-1 EC-3 CH-2 CS-1	73
18	0.201-0.300	EE-2 MA-2 AG-2 PH-7 MS-4 CH-1 ME-1 EC-2 OE-1 CS-1 MG-2	ME-1 MA-3 CH-3 EC-3 PH-1 EE-3 CS-4 IE-4 RE-1 MS-1 RT-4	EC-3 CE-1 RE-1 AR-1 GG-1 CV-1 CH-1 PH-6 CS-1 EE-1 RT-3 ME-1 MA-1	75
19	0.101-0.200	MA-5 EC-4 CS-2 CE-1 MS-8 CH-1 EE-2 ME-1 RT-2 MG-2	EC-1 ME-3 EE-3 MS-5 PH-3 RT-4 RE-3 CH-3 MG-2 CS-1 EC-1 MA-1	MA-4 GG-1 MS-5 RT-1 EE-2 RE-2 CV-2 IE-1 CH-1 ME-2 CS-1 AE-1	81

No	Impact Factor	1994	1995	1996	Papers
20	0.010-0.100	MA-1 EE-2 MN-1 EC-2 CH-2 OE-1 CS-1 AG-1	EE-3 ME-1 MN-1 MA-2 AG-2 OE-2 MG-1	MA-2 AE-1 CS-2 EE-1 MG-3	32
	Total	277	305	240	822

3.4. CONCLUSION

It was found that all the papers in journals from the Institute are not covered in the bibliographic databases, and the comprehensive source happen to be the Institute Annual Report, the data from the same is used for this study. The data thus collected is incorporated into a database and queried to assess the preferred journals, premier publishers, major countries of publication, bias towards subscribed journals and to assess the impact of these publications on future research. Around 1479 papers are published in 568 journals during 1994 to 1996. The top 16 (2.82%) journals account for over 302 (20.42%) papers. Only 10% of the journals published 40% of the papers whereas more than 50% of the journals publish only a single paper each. As far as publishers are concerned, about 27% of the papers from 23% of journals are published in Indian journals and 21% of the journals belonging to Research/ Professional Societies published 16% of the papers. Elsevier and Pergamon imprints of the Elsevier Science, Netherlands and associates stood top among publishers with 21% of papers in 17% of journals. A handful of international publishers with editorial/publishing offices in multiple countries accounted for 33% of papers in 28% of journals. The countries in descending order of publication are India, USA, UK, Germany, and Netherlands. It seems that whether subscribed or not, many researchers are interested to publish their important findings in such journals. Though 40% of the subscribed journals published 52% of the papers whereas 60% non-subscribed journals accounted for 48% of the papers.

As far as the quality of these publications is concerned, 431 of the 568 unique journals or 822 of the 1479 papers (56%) have Impact Factors (IFs). The IF values for these papers are: over 46% of the papers have less than 0.5, 32% of the papers between 0.5 and 1, 18% of the papers between 1 and 2, 8% of the papers between 2 and 4, and 1% of the papers have greater than 4. Over 75% of the papers from the departments of Chemistry, Cryogenics, Rubber Technology, Materials Science, and Management are published in journals with IF. In the case of papers from Reliability, Physics, Metallurgy, Electronics, Electrical, and Computer Science, 50-75% of papers was printed in journals with IF. 40 papers from Chemistry and 13 from Physics carried IF between 2 and 4. 25 papers from Physics, 23 papers from Electronics, 19 papers each from Chemistry and Rubber Technology, 18 papers from Materials Science, and 13 papers from Metallurgy are with IF in between 1.01 and 2. In the case of 268 papers with IF between 0.51 and 1, 43 are from Rubber Technology, 30 are from Chemistry, 26 are from Metallurgy, 23 each from Physics and Materials Science, and 20 from Computer Science.

A large number of conference papers are excluded from the purview of this study due to certain operational problems. They are to be included to get an exhaustive estimate of research dissemination from the Institute. Similar is the case with productivity mapping of each of the researchers by considering a whole set of parameters like number of research papers published, research and consultancy projects undertaken, patents and other IPR entities accumulated, visits to international facilities, etc. More rigorous studies as per the Science Citation Index data are required to assess the impact of individual papers on the ongoing research.

4
Quality in Library Services

4.0. INTRODUCTION

Quality is described in many different ways reflecting the complexity of the concept, its multidimensional nature and its numerous aspects as conformance to specifications, as fitness for use, as buyer satisfaction, as acceptability at an affordable price, as life benefits that are worth life costs [1]. Quality may be seen as "the total composite product and service characteristics of marketing, engineering, manufacturing, and maintenance thorough which the product and service in use will meet the expectations of the customer" [2]. Quality is something that is unique and of a higher standard than other similar products or services and has to be always aimed at satisfying expectations and demands of user through constant monitoring and continuous improvement. There are seven basic concerns in quality [3]:

* Psychology: people and human behaviour
* Statistics: variability and the effective use of quantitative data
* Management and supervision: directing human efforts toward specific goals
* Specialities: knowledge of a wide variety of subjects and ability to effectively use the know-how
* Time: trends, productivity, life cycle costs, delay and

synchronization

* Techniques: processes, methods, procedures, efficiency and operations
* Reliability: trustworthiness of performance, continuity of operations, and dependability of people and equipment

Thus each of these concerns needs to be addressed while attempting to maintain quality in library services. Library being a service institution and hence maintaining quality especially in library services must have a clear understanding of the peculiarities of a service institution. Rosander identified the peculiarities of a service institution as [1]:

* Direct transactions with masses of people
* Large volume of transactions, paper and paperwork movement
* Relatively small amounts of money per transaction
* An extremely large number of ways of making errors
* Not much machine and instrumental control, with the exception of computers
* Extremely large-scale operations may be involved
* Usually the customer does not prepare a formal specification of the type, amount and quality of service required
* Buying products is much more competitive than buying services

The last two items seem to be more critical as user does not have a clear understanding of what sort of service he is asking for and the library staff has no chance to estimate what type of service the user looks for; also there are few options to look for while seeking services in contrast to buying products. The major quality characteristics are error rates, time, cost, and buyer satisfaction [1]. Rowley [4] highlights different approaches to measuring quality:

* Complaints: the level of complaints is one indicator of quality, and provides some directions for potential improvements, whereas absence of dissatisfaction is not necessarily proof of customer satisfaction
* Customer surveys: these ask the customers for their assessment of the services offered
* Benchmarking: comparing the organisation with its competitors
* Employee surveys and suggestion boxes: can provide valuable information on the interfaces between teams and departments

While other researchers in the area of service quality have focused their qualitative inquiries upon the providers of service, LibQUAL+™ tool stresses on user judgement of service quality. LibQUAL+™ Surveys were conducted annually to assess service quality in research libraries in the US, and results of these surveys are followed up seriously to bridge the gap in access and services. However such serious and continuous studies in estimating service quality in libraries are yet to pickup in our country. In the absence of such studies, at best what we can do is to follow up the tool formulated in LibQUAL+™ to have an empirical estimate of where our libraries stand or how best the existing state of affairs can be improved by resorting to refined practices.

4.1. LibQUAL+™

LibQUAL+, a project undertaken by ARL in collaboration with Texas A&M University, is one of the instruments to assess service quality in the research library environment. Parasuraman, Berry, and Zeithaml proposed the SERVQUAL tool, the industry standard for measuring service quality in the private sector, to assess the gaps that emerge among perceived, desired, and minimum expectations to identify and address service quality issues [5] with the maxim that "only customers judge quality; all other judgments are essentially irrelevant" [6]. LibQUAL+ seems to have broken free from its SERVQUAL origins, and promises to more precisely measure the issues that the research library constituency deems important [7]. A diverse community of 12 ARL libraries piloted the first LibQUAL+TM instrument of 41 questions, incorporating 22 items from the original SERVQUAL instrument plus 19 items specific to the library community; to measure service quality across five dimensions: affect of service, reliability, library as place, provision of physical collections, and access to collections, in 2000 [8]. During 2001, the survey was conducted again with 43 libraries, including some non-ARL libraries and this time, the survey instrument consisted of 56 items designed to measure service quality across the following eight dimensions: assurance, empathy, library as place, reliability, responsiveness, tangibles, instruction, and self-reliance [8]. Construct-validity analyses of the 2001 data resulted in a reduced set of four dimensions that are measured in the 25-item 2002 survey: service affect, library as place, personal control, and information access [8]. The 25 items covered in this survey, measuring various aspects of the library's service quality from three perspectives (perceived, desired, and minimum) using one to nine scales, with provision to either rate all three columns or identify the item as N/A, are listed in Table 4.1 [9]. Here 'minimum' stands for the minimum level of service that one would find acceptable, 'desired' represents the level of service that one personally wants, and 'perceived' denotes the level of service that one believe his/her library currently provides.

Table 4.1: 25-items covered in the 2002 LibQUAL+^{TM} survey

#	*When it comes to...*	*My Minimum Service Level is low-high (1-9)*	*My Desired Service Levelis low-high (1-9)*	*Perceived Service Performance is low-high (1-9)*	*N/A*
1	Willingness to help users				
2	Space that facilitates quiet study				
3	Complete runs of journal titles				
4	Employees who are consistently courteous				
5	Making electronic resources accessible from my home or office				
6	Modern equipment that lets me easily access the information I need				
7	A library website enabling me to locate information on my own				
8	Timely document delivery/interlibrary loan				
9	Interdisciplinary library needs being addressed				
10	A haven for quiet and solitude				
11	Dependability in handling users' service problems				
12	Easy-to-use access tools that allow me to find things on my own				
13	A place for reflection and creativity				
14	Giving users individual attention				

15	Employees who deal with users in acaring fashion
16	Making information easily accessible for independent use
17	Employees who have the knowledge to answer user questions
18	Readiness to respond to users' questions
19	Convenient business hours
20	Employees who instill confidence in users
21	A comfortable and inviting location
22	Comprehensive print collections
23	A contemplative environment
24	Employees who understand the needs of their users
25	Convenient access to library Collections

Of these, seven items 1, 4, 14, 15, 17, 20 and 24 directly correspond to the professional skills and performance of the library staff. Are they helpful, courteous, caring and confident, or are they giving individual attention to users or do they understand the user needs and are they knowledgeable enough to tackle user queries. Items 2, 10, 13, 21, and 23 deal with the library environment and its aesthetics appeal and items 3, 9, and 22 relate to the collection and its interdisciplinary nature attuned to a research library environment. A large number of questions, 5, 6, 7, 8, 12, 16, 19, and 25 reflect upon the intricacies of library services, especially easy and fast end user access whereas fulfilling items 11 and 18 depend to a large extent on all the above aspects, in particular effective collection and efficient staff. In the light of this discussion, typically for a library in the country, the following may be vital parameters to ensure and judge quality in services, subject to the limitations on infrastructure in terms of space, collection, computer, and manpower:

Time: The library operations and services should be attempted with the least time lag as possible. The IT enabled information services and the onset of collaborative access through consortia, all this lead us to quantify time elapsed in information services. Often, it is the timely provision of few right sources to the right user that may lead to path breaking results, than delayed delivery of more resources which are either right/wrong.

Cost: Information, manpower and infrastructure are costly, and hence a library must work with judicious administrative and professional practices that can bring in a cost-effective and cost-benefit approach. If you have money, you can buy a lot and be rich in any or all of these aspects and still end up with poor services due to lack of coordination of the different components involved, poor targets and weak priorities set along with improper vision and unrealistic mission.

Availability: Availability should be considered both in terms of collection management and access management. The library may have some sources in its collection plus a wide range of access to other sources through resource sharing and ILL arrangements with other libraries as well as consortia based access from information providers. The acquisition profile of sources over the years can highlight the strengths and weaknesses of the collection. Studies are to be conducted to assess the sources that are left out of the acquisition process due to scarcity of funding, inability of vendors to supply, or the titles getting out-of-print etc. The established and informal collaboration might be carefully looked at to evaluate commonly requested sources to incorporate them in future acquisitions.

Extensibility: The services should be dynamic enough to accommodate the new techniques and tools in information handling. Are the services archaic and not influenced by the continuous changes occurring in the information-processing sphere? For example, how the library will be equipped to handle translating a source requested by a client? or whether reference services are restricted to in-house sources only?

4.2. STRATEGIES TO MAINTAIN QUALITY IN LIBRARY SERVICES

4.2.1. Acquisition

The acquisitions department has to regularly scan catalogues, book reviews, and cumulate such information to bring them to the attention of patrons. Users, especially in higher education and research institutions, bound by occupational pressures, will get hardly any time to seep through the flood of catalogues, brochures, and other promotional literature dealing with information products. It is imperative upon professionals to devise a mechanism to provide all relevant information from such sources to the target clientele before seeking their recommendations, as an important means to improve the quality of sources procured with a 'bit of money meant to buy a lot'. Regular scanning of publisher, author and vendor sites by acquisition librarians would help to collect information about a large set of sources not noticeable otherwise while dealing with local vendors. All aspects of procurement work should be automated and correspondences must be routed through electronic means to facilitate faster operations right from request collection, selection, approval, ordering, monitoring, and receipt to payment. The request system must be so intertwined with the library automation system that the requests for duplicates must be eliminated right at the request stage, barring textbooks. They also have to do a lot of public relations business with vendors and publishers to clinch best deals as far as commercial purchases are concerned. Constant evaluation of vendors might be conducted to fasten the supply of orders on the one hand and to instill a sense of competition among vendors and to seek better performance from them.

4.2.2. Processing

Authority manuals are to be maintained to deal with classification to avoid scattering of sources on same topic, and cataloguing to stick to consistent subject terms and keyword assigning. There are few choices to be made on the schemes for classifying, cataloguing, and subject indexing, but in most cases it is not the schemes per se, but their proficient practice that leads to drastic improvements in quality. Subject approach for information sources can be improved by identifying and incorporating proper terms from thesaurus, subject heading lists etc.

4.2.3. Circulation

The semi automated circulation system followed in many libraries leads to little improvement over manual processes. However disregarding signatures etc., totally may incur security issues. What is appropriate is to maintain a perfect balance by generating whatever reports required through computer and by optimizing time consumed in transactions. Reservations/ holds must be strictly maintained for making the books available in a democratic fashion to all needy users. Callback facility has to be followed for quick collection of reserved books from renew/default cases. There should be provision for a certain number of online renewals by patron without staff intervention or in cases that is not granted, provision to do so by staff without insisting the users to bring books to the counter. There may be drop boxes to receive issued books when the counter/library is closed. The staff mediated transactions may be altogether avoided by adopting self-check facility, easily possible now with the help of RF and electromagnetic/ electronic technology. Proper alerts and reminders are to be sent to avoid fines and different types of alerts can be configured on the server to warn those who attempt to do illegal transactions, to inform users about new additions to collection, and to update on changes in library rules. Some of these alerts can be configured on an interactive mode by incorporating email contacts of authors, publishers, vendors and members in to the library database. A member who is interested in contacting an author or publisher can do so as a result of this linkage. Similarly web site addresses of publishers and authors assist the user in browsing those sites to collect any further information required. Interfacing the system with administration servers of the institution may help in calculating and transferring fine information and any other fees related to library. The library automation system and catalogues should display the real time status of books such as, on shelf, issued, reserved, in bindery/processing, on order, etc. Many libraries follow separate cards for library and with the help of minor administrative coordination, the staff/student identity card may be used as the library identity card for availing library services.

4.2.4. Maintenance

Separating out collection in to 'active' and 'not so active' would be a good idea to practice in stack maintenance since better service of active collection could be provided to users by separating out not so active collection into closed stacks/ remote storage. Apart from the old and new books, if use studies are properly conducted, there may be a possibility of separating the collection into less used and used. There is no harm in separating out less used and old books to a large extent into remote storage. However such stack area should be readily available to those who are interested in using them at par with regular stacks. Proper labeling of stacks and spines, and keeping the place attractive will definitely gather more user attention. In an open access system, it is not advisable to ask the users to replace the books unless they are sensible enough to do so correctly. Thus placing shelves or trolleys marked 'to be arranged' in stacks and reading rooms is a good idea to discourage the practice of leaving books on tables.

4.2.5. Reference

In the emerging library and information-servicing

environment, information on demand services can be provided now, by including information existing in informal channels like web sites. Regular browsing of web to trace sites of interest to users should be added as a regular activity in the case of reference services. In some cases, prospective information not available in the library or in the established resource sharing programmes may be collected, by interacting with authors or libraries/institutions where such sources are present. Information consolidation work has been made easier in the post web era, as anybody with a web server will be able to collect information and host them. The bibliographies and documentation lists prepared earlier for one user can be hosted now on the web site, if the topic happens to be of interest to others too. Services like newspaper clipping can be transformed in to a value-added repository of information by scanning these pages (or linking to the paper's site) and by indexing them. Information sources may be taken from different sources, but how these contents can be put to augmented use of clientele by proper consolidation with better indexing and electronic availability, is the crucial question. The new information superhighways are opening the way to an enormous volume of cross-cultural communication and as a result they are inviting a variety of potential language problems in the process. The libraries must be amply equipped to contract translation services to bridge this language barrier.

4.2.6. Inter Library loan/ Document delivery Services (ILL/ DDS)

Increase in sources, users and research activity with inflation driven static budget force majority of the libraries to be more and more information poor over the years. However, it is one of the most important service implications of libraries to trace and track at least information about such information not available in its collection. And the libraries are doing so through bibliographic databases and information sharing arrangements with other libraries and agencies. Depending on the type of sources requested the nature of service changes. In the case of request to books, they are loaned out from other libraries through ILL whereas DDS is used to source photocopies/reprints of journal articles or conference papers not available in the collection from other libraries or through publishers or third party agencies. Some libraries attached to premier universities deliver DDS via the web, and users can retrieve the document requested by using login name and code number assigned during request in the case of MIT [10] and NUS [11].

4.2.7. Automation

With the help of a functional library automation package in a computer, the house keeping tasks can be performed faster with extra benefits like better inventory mechanisms, facility for generation of a number of reports which are unattainable so easily in the manual system. With automation, service information resided in the registers and manuals exclusively kept at the custodians of services in the manual system were now available to other stake holders. It is now easy to monitor the status of a request made for purchasing a book through the system by user and also able to know the status of a book of interest as issued/reserved and to find out issued to whom. Both users and staff have become more sensible and careful in dealing with their usage and work after the advent of the automation systems due to the feeling that 'someone's watching'. Many libraries follow a primitive automation culture where computer is kept on top of the desk and below that they still have the registers and manuals close to hand giving more emphasis to them than automation. Being largely deprived of chances to perform and shine unlike many other professions, some professionals feel that their only chance to project and protect their existence is through the untidy habit of binding users always to their assistance. The right automation system for our libraries should facilitate users to use the library resources and services with very little staff assistance. It is a good idea to give links to OPAC from new arrival list of books and journal issues. Providing options to view table of contents for books and searching up to article level for journals either through the same system or through links to other systems would help the user to search more relevant information in less time. Sirsi, introduced a new technological and business model for library automation with the release of iBistro, as an Internet access portal for library users with capacity to integrate related content into a unified display through simultaneous, broadcast searching. For example, searching the catalog displays not only holdings information but also additional content like reviews, tables of contents, synopses, and images of the book's cover jacket, as being done by Amazon.com is maintained on centralized servers at Sirsi's site [12].

4.2.8. Electronic Information Services

Day by day, the quality and quantity of contents in electronic form in the library is increasing through a wide variety of channels such as, web access of subscribed journals, resource sharing arrangements, consortia based access to full text and bibliographic resources etc. INDEST consortium for MHRD funded institutions has enabled libraries of IITs to increase their access to e-journals from 100 to 500 to more than 4000 journals which is comparable to world class institutions like MIT [13]. Instead of merely procuring electronic sources and assisting users to conduct their searches, the library could think of formulating different services like general and special current awareness and retrospective search services on demand or ahead of demand. Current Awareness Service (CAS) and Selective Dissemination of Information (SDI) are two established information services provided to meet different requirements of users in mind. Personalization is a process of gathering and storing information about site visitors, analyzing the information, and, based on the analysis, delivering the right information to each visitor at the right time [14]. Content Personalization in the perspective of a library comprise of dynamically scanning and delivering electronic contents selectively as per the interests of the individual user (expressed need as well as observed need), very similar to CAS and SDI, but a major difference here is the attempts to map and provide full text information rather than mere surrogates like indexes or abstracts. Apart from formal full text data bases for which the library has access rights, whatever formal/informal sources available free on web must be brought to the notice of users by keeping them updated regularly of such sources with the help of content personalization services.

4.2.9. Internet Information Services

The library's responsibility for internet information services should focus on two counts, to use the massive web contents for reference and other information services, and to create a web site as a forum to brief about library's activities as well as to interface some of the services with web. The site must act as a single window to brief about library's strengths, activities, rules and regulations, copyright warnings, details of contact persons to avail each and every service, and for interfacing the services. A library website enabling users to locate information on their own has been considered by LibQUAL+^{TM} as a quality feature [9]. Added electronic materials disseminated through web that supplement the printed information sources acquired in the library could be linked to the site for its easy notice and increased use by clients. Commercial databases subscribed in the library may be made accessible on the Intranet. Only a vigilant professional can sieve through the mass of resources on the web to track, trace and index those relevant to the key areas of interest of the Institution concerned. Care must be taken to look for prospective vendor sites, competitor sites, job sites for students, educational and professional sites, etc. If interested, the library can host courseware, exam papers, student/trainee assignment sheets, in-house publications etc., also on the Intranet. Different forms for recommending new books/journals, ILL/Photocopy requests, etc., to avail various services of library should be kept at the website.

4.2.10. Digital Library

Digital library comprised of electronic resources procured from vendors as well as digital sources created in-house such as theses and dissertations, proceedings of conferences hosted, e-prints archives of in-house publications, exam papers, course packs and other research and training resources generated internally. Creating virtual libraries out of links to useful web resources for various subjects is a good idea to profile web resources for easy consumption by users. There are different electronic resources sourced from vendors like web access to subscribed journals, consortia access to full text and bibliographic databases that form a major part of the local digital library on intranet. Thus efforts on digital library development should look at different avenues like, collaborating with others, special electronic access rights received out of subscriptions, digitization and access provision of local copyright owned contents like in-house journals, publications etc.

4.2.11. Ask a Librarian

Send simple questions to the library through this electronic form and the Librarian or authorized persons should respond to the questions in reasonable time. A reply can be expected in 1 hour or within 3 working days depending on the complexity of the query in the case of National University of Singapore Library [15]. Similarly users may be encouraged to submit their suggestions and comments for improving library services in writing and through email. Many libraries keep a suggestion box, but how many open them regularly and take corrective measures. Along with complaints and suggestions, it is always a good idea to conduct feedback and brainstorming sessions with different category of users, especially freshers along with their orientation session.

4.2.12. Off-Campus Access to Electronic Resources

Libraries are moving from on-library access of printed/ electronic resources to off-library on-campus access of printed/ electronic resources, and now considering off-campus access. This may also help a large number of learners who avail distance education and off campus courses. The vendors impose license restrictions which prevent from offering off-campus access to anyone outside the immediate user community. LibQUAL+^{TM}

counts accessibility to electronic resources from home or office as a quality aspect while assessing library services [9].

4.3. QUANTIFYING QUALITY

One way to count quality is to estimate the turnaround time for each of the library services and compare it with similar services offered by libraries in the developed countries. For example, Interlibrary Borrowing Service (ILB) to borrow materials not owned by MIT libraries take 4-7 days for articles and 1-2 weeks for books [10], and normal turn-around time for photocopies is 24 to 48 hours in the case of Caltech libraries with options to further rush up the services by paying extra charges [16]. LibQUAL+™ stipulate convenient business hours, convenient access to library collections and timely document delivery/interlibrary loan as quality concerns [9]. Some of the checklists to be considered while quantifying service quality in the case of libraries are shown in Table 4.2:

Table 4.2: Checklist of Parameters for Quantifying Library Service Quality

#	*Time elapsed in*
1	Request for new books getting consolidated
2	Approving requests
3	Ordering and supplying
4	Accessioning
5	Payment
6	Classification, cataloguing, labeling and releasing
7	Registering users and providing library identity cards
8	Issue, return, renewal, reservation of books
9	Calling back reserved books
10	Regular notification and collection of fines
11	Receipt of first issue of a new journal after request
12	Receipt of printed issues of journals in comparison to electronic release
13	Processing journal issues, Issuing reminders and follow up of missing issues
14	Answering reference queries

#	*Time elapsed in*
15	ILL requests for books
16	DDS for articles
17	Rectifying complaints regarding access of computer servers inside the library
18	Rectifying complaints regarding access of computer servers on Intranet
19	Rectifying complaints regarding access of computer servers on Internet
20	Rectifying complaints regarding access of terminals inside the library
21	Rectifying complaints regarding access of terminals on Intranet
22	Rectifying complaints regarding access of terminals on Internet
23	Rectifying complaints regarding access of e-resources inside library/intranet
24	Downtime of computer resources and network infrastructure
25	Number of days in which the library will be closed per year
26	Number of hours in which the circulation counter will work per day
27	Number of hours in which the library will work per day
28	Binding, accessioning and processing journal issues as bound volumes
29	Stack rectification-sorting and arranging issued books
30	Stack rectification-sorting and arranging books/journals on tables
31	Stack rectification-sorting and arranging books/journals from reprographic section
32	Stack rectification-identifying and arranging misplaced books/ journals

In Table 4.2, items 1 to 5 measure the fastness of acquisition operations, 6 counts the time involved in processing, 7 to 10 identifies the time factor in circulation operations which is a crucial area where direct user dealings are involved. Items 11 to 13 and 28 deal with the efficiency of journal section, and 14 to 16 that of the reference section. Items 17 to 24 measure the efficiency of computer and electronic infrastructure and operations in the library whereas items 29 to 33 are concerned with different aspects of stack maintenance. Along with circulation, these two are also very vital as both have a direct impact on user's approach towards libraries. The overall availability of library and its service against time is measured in 25 to 28. We have to admit that in each of these heads many libraries in the country have poor indices and that is the best way to admit that there are problems and to find out options for improving the quality of library services.

4.4. PROBLEMS IN ENSURING SERVICE QUALITY

4.4.1. Space

Many of the libraries attached to even the premier institutions were built without considering the functionalities and service aspects of a multidimensional service utility like library. Added to these, many are not getting recurring assistance to maintain and refurbish them. When the ambience is very poor, that will definitely discourage and sent back many users. The library buildings should have proper interior decoration and lighting that attracts people to visit and spent at least some time to avail their information needs. Institutions should earmark some part of the recurring budget to the daily upkeep of the building. As growing organisms with continued increase of collection and users, they need additional space and there should be futuristic planning to assess the space requirements periodically and subsequent action plan to construct new wings to the building. It is apt to note that LibQUAL+TM demands in library building a contemplative environment, comfortable and inviting location, place for reflection and creativity, space that facilitates quiet study, and haven for quiet and solitude [9].

4.4.2. Collection

Consortia based access may increase access rights for journals, but what about books and other resources. LibQUAL+TM identifies complete runs of journal titles, comprehensive print collections and addressing interdisciplinary library needs as quality features [9]. Budgets remain at best constant however the demands from users and books getting published are constantly rising. This needs libraries to devise some sort of arrangement on the lines of consortia for accessing and sharing books, but that will take at least some more time to have a sizeable number of books in electronic form. Libraries have to streamline their existing resource sharing channels and ILL pools and also have to lobby with publishers and book seller associations and Government to clinch low price editions and good deals in library purchases.

4.4.3. Computer and Communication Infrastructure

There is a mix of infrastructure in different libraries now, some have visibly poor and some possess reasonably good. LibQUAL+™ ask for modern equipment that lets user easily access the information needed as a feature to judge quality [9]. Hope the significant improvement in information and communication infrastructure and computer penetration now underway in the country may provide the desired infrastructure in libraries too.

4.4.4. Staff

LibQUAL+™ suggests some of the qualities of the library staff as their willingness to help users, a consistently courteous approach, giving users individual attention, dealing with users in a caring fashion, instilling confidence in users, understanding users needs, and having the knowledge to answer user questions [9]. It has identified staff as a key ingredient to consider while providing qualitative library services. This suggests that professional training requires to be constantly updated to include not only the new techniques and tools for information handling but also the behavioural science and social issues. Recruitments to library posts are to be fine tuned so that the best ones should be selected against fresh vacancies. Our role is to facilitate the best usage of library and its resources/services by users for whom it is collected since they are more knowledgeable than us to judge sources of relevance. LibQUAL+™ considered easy-to-use access tools that allow users to find things on their own and making information easily accessible for independent use as quality pointers [9]. We have to accept the fact that we are only good in identifying sources of interest, but subject specialization is required to judge their relevance and importance. The desired role of the staff is not to act as a hurdle between user and service but to step in only when there is a difficulty in availing the service by the user and to act as a catalyst in the efficient use of services by users. Continuous augmentation of old skills and constant accumulation of new skills are required to perform satisfactorily in an information service setup and that would be our motto. Thus professionals need to be periodically exposed to continuing education and informal learning programmes, attending professional meetings and conferences, and motivation in terms of rewards and recognitions, as well as promotion and other service benefits. Even though many fresh professionals are produced ever year, many of our libraries are facing acute staff shortage. It is high time to fill up the vacant posts including that of Librarians in many libraries to maintain at least the minimum healthy service level. The traditional employees' union mentality of leaving the job undone may lead to more recruitment is an exposed myth now. It is also difficult to quantify performance output in a service institution like library. In the coming days, a library can project for more posts by performing the existing jobs better and ask new posts for either improving the existing operations further or for starting altogether new services.

4.4.5. Copyright

Copyright is getting more wrong especially with regard to access and use of electronic resources. Some publishers may permit local hosting and electronic shelving on intranet of electronic resource subscribed singly or through consortia, while some may not. There are many fine prints in access rights document that may act as a hurdle even in the periphery of 'fair use' which requires constant follow up with providers at the individual and consortia level by libraries.

4.4.6. Policy

The first step to arrive at a quality culture is by adopting a policy resolution to achieve quality in library services. Web portals and online stores on the likes of Amazon.com delivers books faster than many of the traditional suppliers, sometimes at better discount rates and how to modify the library purchase rules to take advantage of such offers requires amendments in existing purchase and audit procedures. The library also has to keep a constant watch on products and services of relevance and must always be open to decide upon a multiple course of action, like dealing with publishers, vendors, or third party accumulators based on the merits on a case to case basis. Policy resolutions may be required to reserve a portion of the budget for document copy services from publishers or other non-library agencies.

4.4.7. Funds

Resources are many, demands for services are more, and however the funds are not always agreeable to meet the rising demands. The library should take a cue from their parent institutions to look for alternate funding from private sources, philanthropists, consultancy and research projects, generating revenues by selling services. Such avenues may not fetch substantial amount to begin with, but whatever little it may generate will add to the total budget with scope for increase in subsequent years.

4.4.8. Support

Libraries may not always get the required support from their parent institutions to modify the existing services or alter the prevalent practices. Support with policy, infrastructure and staff working as one unit will only ensure the features of dependability in handling users' service problems and readiness to respond to users' questions in LibQUAL+^{TM}.

4.4.9. Priority

Libraries are widely considered as traditional institutions to hold collection and render traditional services. Performance parameters are not at all considered while dealing with library and its services. Not only the library staff, but also the administration is equally responsible for this let down as they failed to open up avenues to instill confidence and sourcing professional performance of a higher quality from the library and its staff.

4.5. CONCLUSION

The first step in ensuring service quality in our libraries is to identify and ascertain the user satisfaction of existing services. Survey on the lines of LibQUAL+^{TM}, may be with modified indices to suit peculiar local conditions, need to be conducted on a national, regional and local level for various categories of libraries. Collection development and access management are identified as key areas of concern by many libraries; however they should also consider the importance of library ambience and the qualifications, expertise, continuing education, recognition, and motivation of library staff. Constant monitoring of new information products, services and what others are doing would always help to identify new areas to assign priority. Involving users in developing and conducting library services may enable them to be regular users of the service and this in turn helps to gather critical and useful comments which could be used to further improve the service. There should also be more feedback and brainstorming sessions with different category of users and constant monitoring of suggestions and complaints from users. The library authorities and staff have to admit and bring in a culture that there is always scope for improvement in whatever we do and users complain because they expect more from us and it is only by meeting their expectations that we should be able to survive and sustain in the skill intensive and highly competitive information service environment.

REFERENCES

1. Rosander, A C, Applications of Quality Control in the Service Industries, New York: Marcel Dekker, 1985, pp. 3-4.
2. Feigenbaum, Armand V., Total Quality Control. 3rd ed., New York, McGraw Hill, 1983, p. 7.

3. Op. cit. 1, pp. 231-232.
4. Rowley, Jennifer, Managing quality in information services, Information Today and Tomorrow, 16(1), January-March 1997, pp. 3-10.
5. Parasuraman, A., et al., "Alternative Scales for Measuring Service Quality: A Comparative Assessment Based on Psychometric and Diagnostic Criteria," Journal of Retailing, 70 (Fall 1994): 201-230.
6. Zeithaml, Valarie A., et al., Delivering Quality Service: Balancing Customer Perceptions and Expectations (New York: Free Press, 1990), 16.
7. Cook, Colleen and Thompson, Bruce, LibQUAL+: One Instrument in the New Measures Toolbox, http://www.arl.org/newsltr/212/libqual.html
8. Waller, Consuella Askew and Hipps, Kaylyn, Using LibQUAL+TM and Developing a Culture of Assessment in Libraries, http://www.arl.org/newsltr/221/libqarl.html
9. Waller, Consuella Askew, et al., LibQUAL+ Policies and Procedures Manual, Association of Research Libraries, Washington, D.C., 2003, http://www.libqual.org/documents/admin/procedures3.8.pdf
10. http://libraries.mit.edu/ordering/ilb.html
11. http://www.lib.nus.edu.sg/help/service/docdel.html and http://www.lib.nus.edu.sg/ guides/ddsnus.htm
12. Barry, Jeff, Automated System Marketplace 2001: Closing in on Content, Library Journal, April 1, 2001.
13. Arora, Jagdish, and Agrawal, Pawan, Indian Digital Library in Engineering Science and Technology (INDEST) Consortium: Consortia-Based Subscription to Electronic Resources for Technical Education System in India: A Government of India Initiative, International CALIBER 2003, Ahmedabad, 13-15 February 2003, Conference Volume - Mapping Technology on Libraries and People, Ahmedabad: INFLIBNET, 2003, pp. 271-290.

14. http://www-4.ibm.com/software/developer/library/personalization/
15. http://www.lib.nus.edu.sg/
16. http://library.caltech.edu/services/interlib.htm

5
Knowledge Management

5.0. INTRODUCTION

Libraries have been service driven repositories of knowledge from time immemorial and they rendered this role in a satisfactory manner with the help of tools like classification systems, cataloguing practices, indexing routines, subject heading and keyword assigning procedures, for effective library organization and efficient information services. With the onset of electronic sources and more focus on non-paper multimedia information resources, mere management of library and its collection was changed to encompass complex techniques of information processing and management. As a result, the libraries must be conversant with tracking not only locally hold collection owned by the libraries but also fee based access of electronic journals and other consortia information resources and free access of internet information. The arrival of Information Technology (IT) and the spread of Internet challenged the established roles of libraries and producers, consumers, and publishers of information. Thus the focus over the years in libraries changed from library management (more focus on form and sources) to information management (more focus on content) to knowledge management (value addition of information to knowledge).

Library Management is concerned with managing effectively human resources, finances, housekeeping, and planning in a library. The orientation is more towards a print based library holdings following predominantly manual operations to render organization of knowledge (or its documentary record) and provision of service as efficient as possible. Information management encompasses management of information that is traditional as well as nascent, print as well as electronic, locally hold as well as available on the network, and all aspects concerned with ownership and access of such information. It will also concentrate on identifying user needs and developing information products and services, and serving them for clients. Knowledge management is all concerned with the lofty goal of managing knowledge (that resides in the heads of people) by refining the practices of information management by arriving at more refined and structured user-specific information products and services that lead to better libraries and satisfactory clientele. In library and information management, we do things primarily for the customer whereas in knowledge management, the clients as well as libraries and librarians are beneficiaries. In other words, on the one hand we are planning to map the knowledge about libraries, its work practices, its user needs, qualifiers concerning collection and service details, special abilities of its professionals and other staff in 'synergy' into a system to substantially improve the library operations. This may seem something similar to the expert systems and artificial intelligence based techniques earlier, however the difference with knowledge management is that they are not meant to replace the human beings, but to aid their working with the expertise of other personnel working in the organization in a shared work environment. The more lofty ideals of knowledge management that directly benefit the user are concerned with rendering the information support role of preserving the organizational knowledge by the Institution, as Institutions are getting more brand conscious subsequent to globalization.

5.1. Knowledge Management

Knowledge resides in many different places such as,

databases, knowledge bases, filing cabinets and peoples' heads and distributed right across the enterprise [1]. An organization works with tacit knowledge (hands-on skills, special know-how, heuristics, intuitions, which are implicit), rule-based knowledge (explicit knowledge used to match actions to situations by invoking appropriate rules), and background knowledge (knowledge that is part of the organizational culture and is communicated through oral and verbal texts) [3]. Explicit knowledge consists of anything that can be documented, archived and codified, often with the help of IT whereas it is challenging to recognize, generate, share and manage tacit knowledge, or the know-how contained in people's heads [9]. The intelligent organization promotes the learning of tacit knowledge to increase the skill and creative capacity of its employees, takes advantage of rule-based knowledge to maximize efficiency and equability, and develops background knowledge to unify purpose and meaning in its community, and a fourth class of a higher order or meta-knowledge to create, integrate, and invigorate all its intellectual resources in order to achieve superior levels of performance [3]. At the strategic level the organisation needs to be able to analyse and plan its business in terms of the knowledge it currently has and the knowledge it needs for future; at the tactical level the organisation is concerned with identifying and formalising existing knowledge, acquiring new knowledge for future use, archiving it in organisational memories and creating systems that enable effective and efficient application of the knowledge within the organization; and at the operational level knowledge is used in everyday practice by professional personnel who need access to the right knowledge, at the right time, in the right location [1]. And libraries hold the repositories of different classes of knowledge for its users and work with different kinds of professional knowledge to ably perform their information support role.

Knowledge Management (also designated as organizational learning, organizational memory, and expertise management) is the collection of processes that govern the creation, organization, dissemination, and utilization of knowledge. Knowledge management is not only about managing the knowledge assets (knowledge regarding markets, products, technologies and organisations, a business owns or needs to own for its business processes to generate profits, add value, etc) but managing the processes (developing, preserving, using, and sharing knowledge) that act upon these assets [1]. Fundamental to the success of KM activities is the level of 'information literacy' skills throughout the organization, staff needs to be 'knowledge and information aware', and to understand the value of information within the context in which they are working and how quickly relevant knowledge can be used to make a decision or solve a problem [7].

5.1.1. Steps in Knowledge Management: Different knowledge management (KM) activities require investment of money or labour [4]:

- Knowledge capture, i.e., creation of documents and moving documents onto computer systems
- Adding value to knowledge through editing, packaging, and pruning
- Developing knowledge categorization approaches and categorizing new contributions to knowledge;
- Developing information technology infrastructures and applications for the distribution of knowledge;
- Educating employees on the creation, sharing, and use of knowledge.

5.1.2. Strategies for Knowledge Management: Kalseth identified the various strategies while implementing knowledge management as document management, improved access to information, use and reuse of information, access to people, learning by participation, networking/synergies, process orientation, human capital and management culture [6].

5.1.3. Tools and Technologies for Knowledge Management: Some of the tools and technologies that support KM include knowledge repositories, expertise access tools, elearning applications, discussion and chat technologies, synchronous interaction tools, and search and data mining tools [9].

5.1.4. Key ingredients of Knowledge Management: A useful framework for describing the key ingredients of KM success is the "8 Cs" framework: connectivity (adequate employee access to KM tools), content (user-friendly work-oriented content), community (communities of practice), culture (a culture of knowledge), capacity (learning capacity), cooperation (a spirit of cooperation), commerce (commercial and other incentives), and capital (carefully measured capital investments and returns) [8].

5.2. CORE COMPETENCIES OF KNOWLEDGE MANAGERS VS INFORMATION PROFESSIONALS

Few knowledge managers attempted to summarize the skill sets that keep them in firm wicket in the organization [7]:

Catalyst: To help the company understand the concept and value of effective knowledge creation, sharing and re-use.

Consultant: To help the company identify appropriate areas to apply KM principles for greatest gains with least pain in order to build a momentum for change.

Collaborator: To ensure the business role models KM through sharing of learning, successes and failures in the field of KM.

Business Acumen: Understand the strategy, the capabilities and knowledge vital to deliver the strategy and how to develop them.

Influencing: Selling of the concept and the value to businesses, individual and leaders in their words and their world.

Shaper and finisher: Help build the vision yet fanatical with detail and completion as transforming the current people, policy and processes will be long and demanding.

Stamina: A knowledge based Enterprise bigger than a family size unit is new, the transformations are demanding and there will be many highs and lows.

Credibility: Quickly establish a track record, familiarise with most operations and understand the issues faced and know many of the movers and shakers.

Encourage, facilitate, help projects and support teams in order to **capture those difficult to articulate but absolute little gems of learning** which are so easy to ignore or over-look.

'Thick skinned', and possess the patience of a saint - this is required to deal with the constant questions such as 'why should we share our knowledge'.

Mix of management competencies and professional skills relating to human resources, information technology, organisational development and information content.

Require skills which enable staff to assess their information requirements and to **find, share, use and create information**. The fifth skill is combining these into their core competence.

Curious, alert to the opportunity, no yes (wo)man, flexible and able to change pretty quickly, able to talk and listen, socialising, able to think quick and fast, keep your eyes in the middle so that you can see all of them, motivated, and focusing.

An Information Professional strategically uses information in his/her job to advance the mission of the organization through the development, deployment, and management of information resources and services [2]. Gorman and Corbitt [5] present a detailed list of core competencies for information professionals to deal with a set of four areas that encompass the basic knowledge base of present-day library science professionals: client needs and services, management of people and resources, technology utilisation, and organisation of knowledge. Information Professionals include, but are not limited to librarians, knowledge managers, chief information officers, web developers, information brokers, and consultants, require two types of competencies [2]:

- Professional Competencies relate to the knowledge of information resources, access, technology and management, and the ability to use this knowledge as a basis for providing the highest quality information services.
- Personal Competencies represent a set of attitudes, skills and values that enable to work effectively and contribute positively to their organizations, clients and profession. These competencies range from being strong communicators, to demonstrating the value-add of their contributions, to remaining flexible and positive in an ever-changing environment.

Apart from professional knowledge in traditional concepts of classification, cataloguing, indexing, the library professional must possess good computer skills to handle many of these concepts better implemented through computer. They should also have satisfactory exposure to networking, internet/web and information resources served on these platforms. Apart from this, they should possess better communication and interpersonal skills to perform in a very dynamic and undefined environment where library is often viewed as a very complex service centre and library professionals as master of many non-library tasks too.

5.3. KNOWLEDGE MANAGEMENT-A MISNOMER

Just as we eat food to satisfy our hunger, we consume information to satisfy our quest for knowledge and processing by the human body (some sort of mass to energy transformation) plays a major role in the first and that by the brain is essential in the second. Wilson opined that for the fields of information science and information systems, it is clearly necessary to distinguish between 'information' and 'knowledge' [10]. 'Knowledge' is defined as what we know, which involves the mental processes of comprehension, understanding and learning that go on in the mind and only in the mind, however much they involve interaction with the world outside the mind, and interaction with others. Whenever we wish to express what

we know, we can only do so by uttering messages of one kind or another - oral, written, graphic, gestural or even through 'body language'. Such messages do not carry 'knowledge', they constitute 'information', which a knowing mind may assimilate, understand, comprehend and incorporate into its own knowledge structures [10]. Therefore, the knowledge built from the messages can never be exactly the same as the knowledge base from which the messages were uttered. Everything outside the mind that can be manipulated in any way can be defined as 'data', if it consists of simple facts, or as 'information', if the data are embedded in a context of relevance to the recipient. Collections of messages, composed in various ways, may be considered as 'information resources'. Thus, data and information may be managed, and information resources may be managed, but knowledge (i.e., what we know) can never be managed, except by the individual knower and, even then, only imperfectly [10]. The fact is that we often do not know what we know: that we know something may only emerge when we need to employ the knowledge to accomplish something and we seem to have very little control over 'what we know'. In a sear on the ISI 'Web of Science' from 1981 to 2002 for papers the term 'knowledge management' in the title revealed th term did not occur until 1986, there were only a few occu in each year from 1986 to 1996, and the growth exponential from 1997 to 2001/2 [10].

The highly competitive industries, IT firm with very special information resources and they more complex and manipulative information not directly available elsewhere but may be by making summaries, comparisons and c sources. This work involves the collaborati IT and computer personnel, and infor these industries might have used th qualifier to designate the materia immediate needs to actively pe Though information resource structured information of a hi

comprehended and directly applied by the experts who are hard pressed for time in their busy schedule. There was also a need to record, document and preserve the different resources used as well as generated by different projects due to the repeatable nature of projects undertaken and reuse value of implemented solutions due to time bound projects, the high cost of human resources and their frequent switching of jobs.

5.4. ACTION PLAN FOR LIBRARIES

In the light of for and against views about managing knowledge, the different activities where libraries are engaged in shall be refined and optimized by using some of the tools and techniques suggested by knowledge management thinkers. KM activities, especially in a service institution such as library, must adopt a very pragmatic approach and attempt to transform the existing professional routines to the advantage of best practices in library management and information services. Collection-based, service-based and access-based models of library organization evolved at different times emphasizing on specific aspects of library functioning lead essentially to three aspects for adopting KM in libraries:

5.4.1. Documenting Library Procedures: Firstly, steps are taken to properly document the various activities in a library for improving the repeatability of decision making, tactical and operational procedures, irrespective of persons conducting the task. This is a very involving and tedious task as it involves not only the support of a responsive and encouraging management ut the wholehearted cooperation of library staff to share their periences and knowledge and even to examine, record and ort their responses, activities, in the day to day work. The lity management initiatives in many institutions entrated on streamlining different administrative, routine, keeping and professional procedures and compiling the tional manual which may tremendously help KM ies.

.4.2. Creating Knowledge Bases: Secondly, knowledge n various stakeholders in the library, such as users,

suppliers, and other business and operational partners are to be created for streamlined work procedures, better assessment of user needs and for placing services of interest to them. For this, proper inventory of users, their areas of interest, information seeking habits, information consumption abilities, etc., play a major role as knowledge assets concerned with improving collection development and information services. Detailed profiles about trade partners such as suppliers, publishers, distributors, database providers etc., shall help to identify the most suitable supplier for a product leading to its cost effective as well as fast supply. Similar knowledge bases about other libraries, their collection, and professionals working in those libraries act as better ingredients to network the library for various programmes concerned with consortia based access, information sharing, collaborative acquisitions, inter library loan and document delivery practices. Tools and techniques of knowledge management when carefully applied help the library to render new services as well as to refine the existing services.

5.4.3. Supporting Knowledge Management of Organization: The first two aspects in implementing KM concentrated more on improving library, its organization, services and above all the work and efficiency of its staff. The third aspect, very tedious but most important, is the use of knowledge management for preserving the organizational knowledge of the institution concerned. As the premier information repository to handle the different information requirements of an institution, the library is well placed to render the knowledge managerial role of the institution by revitalizing its procedures and services and by networking with the different information generating and information using entities of the institution. This role is now provided largely by non-library entities and has its own merits and limitations and involving library in this area must enable the institution to utilize the time tested information organization skills of the library in giving better visibility to intellectual property and in preserving the organizational knowledge. Aggressive 'information about information' services, refined repackaging of available information resources on and ahead of demand, periodic alerting of information access provisions (free and for fee) from publishers, efficient handling of user interests and their careful coupling with different information procurement and access activities, proper dissemination of institutional output, etc., are some of the key areas where libraries should venture for rendering the organizational knowledge managerial role.

The role of library in the institutional knowledge management is highlighted in figure 5.1. The library has to provide total information support for managing, generation and value addition of explicit knowledge but also to render special services in assisting institution's effort to record tacit and oral knowledge. The figure has another aspect, when we consider only the library and not the whole institution, of visualizing the tacit, oral and rule based knowledge of library professionals and their value addition through various professional activities.

5.4.4. Steps, Strategies, Ingredients

Let us do a brief evaluation of the present situation and preparedness of libraries in the context of discussion in section 2 of this paper.

Knowledge capture: Many libraries have presently bibliographic information about printed collection, bibliographic/full text electronic databases in standalone, networked or web access modes, online journals, and certain institute specific information on its Intranet.

Valued Adding knowledge: Libraries and librarians are doing a lot to improve the search, access, retrieval, use of different information resources in their collection or over which they have access rights by cataloguing, indexing, linking, repackaging etc.

Knowledge categorization: Periodically revised classification schemes, indexing lists, keyword assigning tools, subject heading lists etc., helps libraries to assign most relevant notations to categorize information resources. Cross-reference entries help to properly establish connection between old and new subject terms.

Information Technology infrastructure: Library Automation systems, web access of information, electronic information resources over Intranet, consortia based access to information resources, local digitization attempts, etc., are the major activities libraries are engaged in to realize at least partially some of these objectives.

Educating employees: Libraries can educate their staff on the creation, sharing, and use of knowledge. However, doing this for other staff in the institution will be difficult but the libraries can offer the required information support for them if they take it up as a priority.

Document Management: Libraries have demonstrated their skills and effectiveness in managing documents in different fields that come from of a wide variety of channels.

Improved access, use and reuse of information: Libraries strive hard to improve existing procedures and resorting to best practices for better access and enhanced use of information. However some of these activities may require the library to deviate from its common practice of placing more emphasis on content than client.

Access to people: There are front end jobs in the library that directly interacts with users and there are backend jobs that may or may not interact with clients. Professionals in different sections must be easily accessible to users. However this is impeded by the largely administrative nature of jobs dominant in many libraries, leaving less time for value addition, managing quality in operations, and for freely interacting with users, assessing their expectations, and educating them.

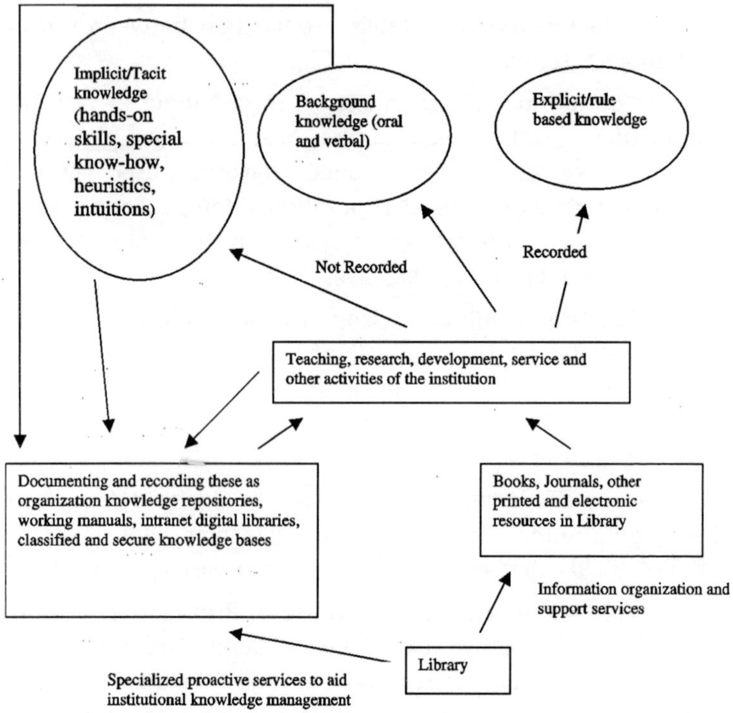

Figure 5.1: Role of Library in Institutional Knowledge Management

Learning by participation: Compartmentalization and hierarch is slowly sidelined in many institutions, especially service centres. Libraries should break the old management habits and create better performing functional entities to render different backend and front-end tasks. Similar types of problems may be faced in different sections and group discussions, brainstorming sessions and participatory learning helps to arrive at better solutions acceptable to different parties in less time.

Networking/synergies: Networking for resources, access, services, and professional goals are some of the key activities for present day performing libraries.

Process orientation: Libraries search, collect, connect, and serve information resources to help people learn and thereby enhance their knowledge and performance. Adopting better tools and techniques for information processing, organization, and services are central to the performance enhancement of libraries.

Human capital and management culture: Many play more emphasis to material assets and library management also gets proud of its collection, infrastructure, services, paying little attention to the staff. Identifying, selecting, recruiting, and retaining performing staff and sustaining their interest in the organization by providing them with a challenging work environment, better prospects for continuous learning, and suitable rewards are fundamental to the success of any institution.

Connectivity: Infrastructure is improving and the awareness of library staff is increasing and clients are now a days more demanding, and all these may contribute to better performance and visibility.

Content: Attempts by libraries to repackage and value add the contents definitely help to provide more useful information resources to users.

Community: It is more pragmatic to practice rather than preach. Conserve your resources and effort to create better information surrogates, access methods, and aggressive reference services, than spending time on products and services without much substance and blindly adopting expensive commercial solutions without any testing.

Culture: A high regard for learning and performance by the Institution will put emphasis on the employees to be more active in adopting a culture of knowledge.

Capacity: Evolving information solutions attuned to the learning standards and consumption styles of the different categories of clients.

Cooperation: One thread can spoil the whole carpet and hence equal emphasis on performance improvement of all departments and a spirit of cooperation among the different entities helps.

Commerce: Rewards and recognitions help sometimes to motivate people.

Capital: Performance audit of libraries are to be conducted periodically to carefully measure capital investments and returns.

5.5. CHALLENGES AND BENEFITS

Major challenges in practicing KM according to Santosus and Surmacz [9]:

* To identify and disseminate knowledge gems from a sea of information.
* Establishing a culture that recognizes tacit knowledge and encourages employees to share it
* Make KM decisions based on who (people), what (knowledge) and why (business objectives) by reserving the how (technology) for last
* Without a solid business case, KM is a futile exercise.
* Like product development, marketing and R&D, KM is a constantly evolving business practice.

The major challenge in the case of libraries and librarians is the lack of orientation, priorities and absence of role models. Libraries are not regarded as performing institutions and they are meant to showcase or even dump published resources largely expected to render the minimum role of a warehouse, bookstore or a leisure room. Separating out useful information from the mass of operational data to spruce up existing services and to plan new ones is a very crucial and challenging task. In the absence of better professional prospects and the presence of acute competition (poor mobility), it is extremely difficult to motivate professionals to share tacit knowledge and their special expertise. How to minimize the thrust in technology and IT gadgets and orient more towards librarianship, information organization and processing skills, collection and access management, best practices in qualitative library services, etc., are problematic areas requiring more discussion with all parties concerned and effective self and group learning by each one of them.

Santosus and Surmacz suggest the following benefits of KM [9]:

* Foster innovation by encouraging the free flow of ideas
* Improve customer service by streamlining response time
* Boost revenues by getting products and services to market faster
* Enhance employee retention rates by recognizing the value of employees' knowledge and rewarding them for it
* Streamline operations and reduce costs by eliminating redundant or unnecessary processes

Instead of the predominant user feeling of libraries as very passive institutions, knowledge management activities will spruce up professional work, organizational learning, apart from improved library organization and services. Information sources are always on the rise whereas resources available to procure them are declined or at best remained static, and hence libraries must be very careful about collection development and access procurement activities and details about users and their areas of interest act as useful pointers. The knowledge management activity in a library attempts to prepare very advanced structured knowledge bases about users and other stakeholders and hence library's collection, access, and services will get more visibility. Working professionals are suitably recognized in their day to day work and thus will be more motivated and become participative in rendering their professional responsibilities. Each person may also get a chance to identify his/her strength and weakness leading to reducing the weaknesses and furthering the strengths through invoking one's peers in the work place, problem specific group discussions, continuous education, etc.

5.6. CONCLUSION

Library and its importance in a performing institution constantly focused at improving the age old virtues of library profession and extending them to deal with electronic information on the network and their better access. Recorded information of very high relevance to the clients can be directly applied to the different information needs of users as not just information but as knowledge assets to effectively serve their needs. Not just the quantity of information resources, but their quality, better assessment of user interests, rendering efficient services to effectively realize the different expectations of users are some of the strategies libraries need to be adopted to play a vital information support role in managing the Institutional knowledge. But to engage in these activities require refinement, recording and resorting to standard procedures for different library practices as first the library has to manage its knowledge before acting as knowledge manager. The promises and expectations are many, but the challenges and constraints are also not few, and it is up to the individual institutions and libraries to pick up suitable role models, adopt pragmatic strategies and implement viable options for achieving some of the lofty goals of converting library from a passive printed library to a little active print plus electronic library to a very dynamic collection plus access plus service based knowledge repository. Even while pursuing these lofty goals, we shall not forget the ultimate fact that knowledge is managed in the brain and even on a very personal level we are unable to manage it outside the brain. And we are only creating better information products, properly connecting and linking it with various contexts and different users to aid and supplement the complex processes of the brain of converting information to knowledge.

REFERENCES

1. AIAI (Artificial Intelligence Applications Institute), http://www.aiai.ed.ac.uk/~alm/ kamlnks.html
2. Abels, Eileen et al, Competencies for Information Professionals of the 21st Century, Prepared for the Special

Libraries Association Board of Directors by the Special Committee on Competencies for Special Librarians, Revised edition, June 2003, www.sla.org/content/SLA/professional/ meaning/comp2003.cfm

3. Choo, Chun Wei, Information Management for the Intelligent Organization: Roles and Implications for the Information Professions, Digital Libraries Conference, March 27-28, 1995, Singapore, http://choo.fis.utoronto.ca/FIS/ResPub/DLC95.html
4. Davenport, Thomas H., Some Principles of Knowledge Management, http://www.itmweb.com/essay538.htm
5. Gorman, GE and Corbitt, BJ, Core competencies in information management education, New Library World, 103(1182/1183), pp. 436-445, 2002, www.decigi.ufpr.br/t_compete.pdf
6. Kalseth, Karl, Knowledge Management from a Business Strategy Perspective, FID Review, 1(1), 1999, pp. 37-41.
7. Keeble, John et al, Your Say, The rise and role of the Knowledge Manager, www.kmmagazine.com/xq/asp/sid.0/articleid.8FF1A428-6C4B-4966-ABF6-D172DB0B49A3/ qx/display.htm
8. Rao, Madanmohan, Eight C's of KM Success: Learn from the information technology sector's best knowledge enterprises, 2003, http://www.destinationkm.com/articles/ default.asp?ArticleID=1085
9. Santosus, Megan and Surmacz, Jon, The ABC's of Knowledge Management, http://www.cio.com/research/knowledge/edit/kmabcs.html
10. Wilson, T.D. (2002) "The nonsense of 'knowledge management" Information Research, 8(1), http://InformationR.net/ir/8-1/paper144.html

6
eLearning Library Science

6.0. INTRODUCTION

Libraries in the country, especially those attached to academic and research institutions, are experiencing the virtues of electronic information in different forms such as e-journals, e-books, bibliographic/full text electronic databases in CD/ through web access. Some of the libraries have even made it a point to prefer the electronic format over print for better access, efficient search mechanisms and effective retrieval, let alone the benefits of space. Other reasons for acquiring electronic sources may be economical; house keeping friendly, as they are easy to maintain, and are free from theft or mutilation when master/multiple copies are available; technical like access through standalone/intranet/internet. Due to publishers' electronic plus policies, libraries are able to access electronic versions of new files either free or by paying a nominal fee. It is quite natural in such a scenario that a library professional right from his first job is expected to be conversant with electronic apart from manual means of information collection, processing, management and servicing. Thus e-information management components found suitable inclusion in the curriculum for Library and Information Science (LIS) education, if not up to the desired extent in practice due to different problems like infrastructure and prevalent pedagogy. Development of courses in a recordable format, in the case of

LIS education started in the country under the aegis of Indira Gandhi National Open University (IGNOU) for its library science courses. The exact number of courses developed so far is not known, but there is no doubt that they are very small in number compared to courses in other disciplines beamed through Television. Personalization involves a process of gathering user-information during interaction with the user, which is then used to deliver appropriate content and services, tailor-made to the user's needs [1]. This in the context of education for LIS, it may be interpreted as attempts to provide a course in a manner in which the learner decides what to avail and how to avail subject to the restrictions of the broad curricular framework of the course concerned. Personalization can be seen as a technology that empowers the user to become more participative in the process [1]. The availability of computer and allied technology along with Internet enabled to adopt some of its virtues not only to supplement the conventional c(lassroom)Learning but in arriving at an altogether different learning delivery mechanism called eLearning. Despite its obvious advantages, the major irritants with respect to formal cLearning are: teacher as well as learner to assemble at one place at the same instant, the difficulties with respect to time available to dealt a subject in the class often leaving much information concerning the topic to be left out, the events are not recorded so that it will be difficult to go back in time and clarify doubts, much of the teacher's time is spent on lecturing and student's time in taking notes related to already available information leaving very little time for question answer sessions and in identifying new avenues for expanding knowledge.

6.1. PERSONALIZING COURSES

The 'Digital Portfolio Archives' (DPAs) project at the University of California, Los Angeles (UCLA) allows teachers to build a personalized information system or DPAs with the content and descriptions; and permit students to incorporate components of the teacher's DPA and additional project-related materials into their own DPAs [2]. Web databases have the potential to deliver personalized content to each individual in response to the individual's Web interactions [3]. Bradley discusses how the leading search engines offer personalized content in the form of 'My XYZ' (My Altavista, My Yahoo!, My Excite and My Lycos), in which subject content is arranged in broad headings, such as business, technology, news, sports, and so on [4]. NewsAgent for Libraries, a project funded by the Electronic Libraries Programme (eLib) in the UK (URL: http:/ /newsagent.ukoln.ac.uk), aims to create a user configurable electronic news and current awareness service for library and information professionals [5]. The Personal Digital Library (PDL) at De Montfort University, UK attempted to develop a personal information system that acts as a front end to other electronic library systems and manages all the users' information needs [6]. Hybrid Electronic Access and Delivery in the Library Networked Environment (Headline), project under the Electronic Libraries (eLib) programme of UK (URL: http://www.headline.ac.uk/) created the Headline Personal Information Environment (PIE) [7] to provide a tailored responsive service to its users. MyLibrary is a Cornell University Library initiative to provide personalized library services such as MyLinks, a tool for collecting and organizing resources for private use by a patron, and MyUpdates, a tool to help scholars stay informed of new resources provided by the library [8]. Another MyLibrary project is operational at the North Carolina State University (NCSU) Libraries to provide a user-centered front-end to collection of Internet and information resources [9].

Most of these initiatives primarily concentrate on personalizing contents in a library or information resources on Internet. In the conventional classroom setup, a course is dealt as per the syllabus according to the wishes of the teacher concerned. Thus the same course with the same syllabus may not be taught in the same fashion by the same teacher in two academic sessions, or by different teachers in the same department or in different departments. Also the emerging academic environment, need for the availability of teacher and learner to conduct a class, holidays etc., offer a bare minimum number of working days in a teaching department and doing justice to the curriculum through conventional classroom delivery often finds difficult. Here comes the benefit of offering courses in a personalized mode. The present practice in cLearning is that whatever teacher and student prepare for the course remains their private property (most of the teachers' still share lecture notes) and only printed materials are shared. Personalization will also offer encouraging possibilities to conserve and preserve the academic effort of teachers as well as learners, as hardly a small amount of academic input of a teacher will be delivered in a class, and no student has been able to present all what he prepares for a course in the conventional evaluation techniques of assignment, seminar or examination papers. Personalization argues to record and document in electronic form the academic efforts of teachers and learners, as per the individual's interest, for further academic exercises.

The Personalization consortium identified the purposes of personalization as to [10]:

* Better serve the customer by anticipating needs;
* Make the interaction efficient and satisfying for both parties;
* Build a relationship that encourages the customer to return for subsequent purchases.

Kramer et al suggest personalization as 'a toolbox of technologies and application features; from simple display of the end-user's name on a Web page, to complex catalog navigation and product customization based on deep models of users' needs and behaviors; used in the design of an end-user experience' [11].

6.1.1. How to Personalize

The basic reasons behind personalizing a course in the context of library & information science (LIS) education must include:

* Large amounts of knowledge concerning a discipline are not used in the classroom and never learned by learners
* Some part of the curriculum prescribed is not taught in class
* Some part of the curriculum taught is not studied by learners
* Difficult to satisfy the demands of job market otherwise
* Difficult to improve the quality of learners otherwise
* Educational technology, Internet and Web enable easy tools and techniques for custom delivery of courses
* Efficient learner centred teaching/learning methodology
* Improve the image of Library profession
* Properly record and archive teaching resources from teachers and learning resources from students such as assignments, project and seminar reports
* Learning experiences of individuals quickly get reflected in others who have access the e-content

Some of the major hurdles that hamper the acceptance of LIS course personalization include excuses like importance not felt; lack of infrastructure/cooperation from the university or regulatory bodies, inadequate funds/staff, and mindset.

Library science is not a discipline like, many other branches of science, languages, or social science where learning is imparted at different levels right from early schooling. Most of the learners are exposed afresh to the discipline after a Bachelor or Master degree in some other discipline. The separate courses of one year duration each at BLIS or MLIS or a two year combined MLIS leave very little time for imparting the basics and advanced portions concerning classification, cataloguing, indexing, subject heading, information management, information sources and retrieval. Added to this is the overload from computer side right from simple programming and database concepts to familiarizing with software packages to information products. All this leaves not much time in a 20 month training, and the teachers and learners somehow manage to perform as effective as possible. IIT Kharagpur has been able to install networked computers in all teacher's rooms and students are also encouraged to procure PCs in hostel rooms availing special deals, to adopt the virtues of computers and internet for teaching and research. It is too much to ask for such an infrastructure in the LIS teaching departments. But whatever little infrastructure available could be used for delivering courses and enhancing knowledge, rather than merely using them for conducting practical sessions on computer related topics. In the personalized environment, teachers don't need to be too linear and repetitive in their approach to teach a course. Also teachers can reuse the electronic materials they have prepared for earlier sessions. Thus a teacher teaching classification can go to any depth in covering not only CC and DDC, but also UDC and LC if he wants. He can also interlace his course delivery with materials available on these topics on the internet. As far as possible, students should be encouraged to prepare their entire seminar reports, self study materials, seminar reports, etc., in electronic so that they will easily get archived into personalizing and eLearning (P&E) servers (see figure 6.1) as resources of the department for later use.

6.2. ELEARNING LIS

In late 1999, John Chambers, CEO, Cisco Systems remarked that "The next big killer application for the Internet will be education. Education over the Internet is going to be so big it is going to make e-mail look like a rounding error." CISCO defines e-learning as "the overarching umbrella that encompasses education, information, communication, training, knowledge management, and performance management. It is the web-enabled system that makes information and knowledge accessible to those who need it, when they need it — anytime, anywhere" [12]. E-learning uses the power of the Internet's reach, scalability, and interactive potential to help people learn and describes a wide set of applications and processes, including computer-based training, web-based learning, virtual classrooms, and digital collaborations [13]. Though the 'e' in eLearning signifies electronic, Peterson et al define the "e" in e-Learning from the perspective of the user as [14]:

* **exploration:** e-Learners use the Web as an exploratory tool to access a plethora of information and resources.
* **experience:** The Web offers e-Learners a total learning experience, from synchronous learning to threaded discussions to self-paced study.
* **engagement:** The Web captivates learners by enabling creative approaches to learning that foster collaboration and a sense of community.
* **ease of use:** Not only is the Web easy to use for learners but to learning providers as well, as they can easily make content immediately available across all technical platforms (Windows, Unix, etc.).
* **empowerment:** The Web puts learners in the driver's seat with a set of tools that enables personalization of content and allows learners to choose the way in which they best learn.

E-learning also offers the ability to aggregate a large amount of learning material from numerous sources, giving learners access to a vast supply of courses and learning modules [13]. Some of the implied benefits of eLearning in contrast to the widespread and formal cLearning are [15]:

* *Personalized* – eLearning allows entire programs of study to be customized
* *Interactive* – eLearning can truly engage the learner in a give-and-take type of learning
* *Just-in-time* – eLearning moves training away from the "just-in-case" model where learning takes place outside of the context in which it will be used.
* *Current* – eLearning allows training providers to offer learners always up-to-date materials.
* *User-centric* – eLearning focuses primarily on the needs of the learner, instead of on the abilities of the instructor.

Some other benefits of e-learning include [13]:

* *Anywhere, Anytime, Anyone*: Learning is available 24 hours a day, around the globe.
* *Cost Reduction*: 'Training Magazine' estimates corporations save between 50-70% when replacing instructor-led training with electronic content delivery. Learners can improve productivity and use their time more efficiently.
* *Improved Collaboration and Interactivity among Students*: A number of tools, including case studies, role-playing, simulations, personalized coaching, discussion groups, etc., can be used to stimulate interaction and critical reasoning among learners, even those separated by physical distances.
* *Less Intimidating than Instructor-led Courses*: Online courses provide a risk-free environment where learners can try new things and eliminate the embarrassment of failure in front of a group.
* *Strengthens Traditional Classroom Learning*: E-learning does not fully replace instructor-led learning, but can provide a powerful supplement which maximizes the classroom experience.

To have strong eLearning initiatives, it is imperative to involve trainers to develop courseware, which is the focal point for receiving education and training at one's convenience.

6.2.1. Online Courseware in LIS

Regionally and professionally accredited (by ALA) courses at Master level are being offered at the Drexel University, Florida State University, Southern Connecticut State University, Syracuse University, Texas Woman's University, University of Arizona, University of Illinois-Urbana- Champaign, University of Missouri-Columbia, University of North Texas, University of Pittsburgh, University of Tennessee-Knoxville, University of Wisconsin-Milwaukee, and regionally accredited courses at Master level are conducted by East Carolina University and Mansfield University of Pennsylvania (all in US) [16]. All these courses are equivalent in curricula and training methodology to the cLearning courses offered in the concerned University, basically conducted by 56-256 K access speed using wide range of technologies like chat, threaded discussions, streaming video and audio, simulations and laboratories. Majority of them do not even require a visit to the University campus. Kentucky Virtual University offers online programs in 'Library Science Certification' and 'Master of Science in Library Media Education library science', and The Indiana State University offers Undergraduate/ Graduate Certificate in Library/Media Services [17].

6.2.2. Initiatives in the country

May be due to the prevalent network infrastructure and widespread availability of distance education options, our country is yet to experience the start of online courses in LIS. It is not known whether the video courses produced by IGNOU on LIS are converted into electronic form. The Centre for Educational Technology (CET) at IIT Kharagpur has been able to record over 30 courses (around 900 1 hour videocassettes) and some of these courses are also beamed on the Gyandarshan channel of Prasarbharti. The CET has also started to digitize these courses for distribution in CDs well as hosting on its servers through the campus LAN. Other IITs are also engaged in similar efforts on courseware development. UGC also supports Consortium for Educational Communication (CEC) and Universities in creating educational software.

National Centre for Science Information (NCSI), Bangalore conducted a corporate training for executives from Tata Infotech Ltd., during 10-13 July 2001 on "Webmaster/ Content Manager" and released a CD with PPT presentations of the courses, evaluation questionnaire used for evaluating the participants absorption, Lab exercises Scripts (PHP, ASP) and sample databases used for demonstration/presentation, for the personal use of NCSI-NET members (virtual community of present and previous staff and trainees of the NCSI), with the goal of knowledge sharing and professional advancement of the members. Dr. Rajashekar of NCSI also shared the papers presented by him at the June 2001"UNESCO-NISSAT-University of Mysore Workshop on Creation and Management of Digital Resources" with NCSI-NET members. The first NCSI-NET InfoWare CD-ROM containing presentations, lectures and training material contributed by alumni and staff of NCSI during January - August 2001was also distributed to NCSI-NET members at a nominal price. NCSI organized a NISSAT sponsored workshop on "Developing digital libraries using open source software" on 15-20 April 2002. The workshop focused on imparting practical skills in using Eprints Archive Software (EAS) and Greenstone Digital Library software (GSDL) for creating and managing digital collections and the workshop materials are kept at their web site (URL: http://144.16.72.189/opendl/). NCSI has also set up an eprints archive service (URL: http://eprints.iisc.ernet.in/) to support self archiving, improved visibility and access of research publications by IISc researchers on the Internet. Very recently, NCSI has created few sample digital library collections using the Greenstone Digital Library software (URL: http://144.16.72.189/cgi-bin/library.exe) with a few papers from the 4th International Conference of Asian Digital Libraries, held in Bangalore in December 2001, InfoWatch: Monthly electronic newsletter of NCSI, few project reports of NCSI trainees, etc.

The proceedings of the NISSAT Information Today and Tomorrow 2000 held at the National Aerospace Laboratories (NAL) were accessible from NAL website. Similarly the full text of papers presented at the XV Annual Conference of Asian Association of Open Universities (AAOU) on 'Access & Equity: Challenges for Open and Distance Learning' and the Pre-conference Seminar on 'Outreach Library Services for Distance Learners' were kept at the website of the host IGNOU. The Proceedings of the National Conference on Information Management in e-Libraries (IMeL), February 2002 has also been distributed in CD format along with the printed volume. Thus technology and tools to create and disseminate contents are with us, the initiatives to do so are also there, but there is a furthering need for more such initiatives.

6.3. TECHNOLOGIES AND TOOLS FOR ELEARNING

Barron assessed the technology trends for education and training on a five year basis as; the period from 1985-90 signifies stand-alone software, 1990-95 of client-server networks, 1995-2000 for Internet/Intranets, and 2000-05 efforts towards Wireless connectivity [18]. Our country's tryst with educational technology has largely been stuck up with videocassettes and CDs. Some of the technologies that are now in place for interactivity and simulate actual classroom environment for eLearning comprise of chat, threaded discussions, streaming video and audio, simulations and virtual laboratories. The minimum requirements in respect of an eLearning set up in the context of LIS education in the country must encompass:

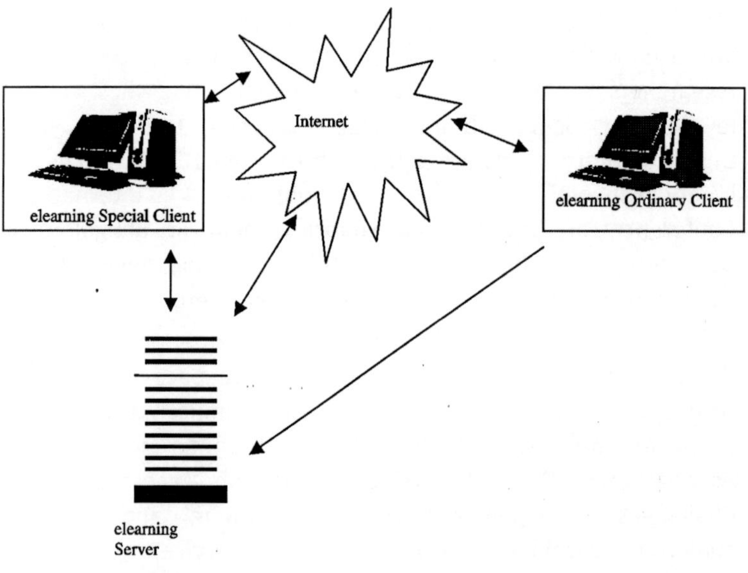

Fig. 6.1. Schematic of the eLearning System

6.3.1. Content Development: Courseware must be prepared using simple authoring tools such as HTML/XML with provision to layer materials in audio formats (WAV, real etc.) and video formats (AVI, MPG etc.). The course content may include text only materials such as reports or conference/

journal papers to PPT presentations or even live recordings of classroom teaching or lectures delivered in conferences by attending or through videoconferencing mode. This stage not only involves collection, conversion and formatting of content but also other tools required to access it such as development of user interfaces.

6.3.2. Content Serving: The contents created as per the earlier step must be either offered in CDs, loaded in standalone PCs, to serving through Intranet/Internet. The bandwidth availability may affect access speed and thus care should be taken to keep materials in such formats occupying less space.

6.3.3. Content Access: Learners access the courseware through standard Web browsers and Multimedia Players.

6.3.4. Database: Database of different lectures and indexes may be prepared for faster search and access to select materials. The database must also hold the profiles of teachers and learners to evolve personalized learning so that time as well as effort of both parties must be conserved.

The schematic for a P&E system out of the components discussed is shown in figure 6.1. The P&E server holds contents in electronic format, databases of profiles, and other programs for serving. The special client can add, delete, modify and access contents in the system are meant for teachers and staff of the department. The ordinary client can only search and access the resources, basically meant for students. However, students can add contents to the system under the supervision of those who have access to the special client. Though both clients can have access to the Internet, it is up to the department concerned to decide whether to keep their server on the Intranet or the Internet or both.

6.4. PROBLEMS AND PROSPECTS

Content Development: LIS teaching departments have to seriously engage in concrete action plans to record and preserve the class lectures and other academic output generated by teachers and learners as viable contents for future academic initiatives and their eLearning and personalizing endeavours.

Infrastructure improvement: The infrastructure at the teaching departments are not at all similar when comparing with science and engineering departments of a university or between different LIS departments. Some are reasonably good, but there is always scope for improvement. The digitization of academic efforts by teachers and learners requires further more client machines and comparatively good servers.

Continuing Education: As part of the continuing education and on-job training on latest technology tools for working professionals, many institutions and agencies are engaged in training in the form of short term courses, workshops, tutorials, etc. Most of these courses produce a printed volume even when it is prepared in DTP. The institutions organizing such courses and the funding agencies sponsoring the same should encourage preparing the course materials in electronic form to distribute it to participants and other interested professionals. There should be a professional body or government agency to co-ordinate the collection and distribution of such resources.

Conservation and optimization of teaching/learning resources: All teachers do not have the same skills to teach one or different topics. Recording and dissemination of course materials must allow learners to be exposed to lectures by faculty members of different institutions, giving them more chances to gather new ideas and insights on a particular topic. This will also enable the conservation and optimization of academic resources.

Professionals and Libraries in professional education: Many working professionals may not have teaching experience and skills to regularly teach LIS courses. However, most of them working in research and special libraries are exposed latest trends in the professional work, and sharing their experiences would benefit the students with a fresh insight unable to obtain via dry theoretical learning. Also some of the special libraries have better computer and network infrastructure as well as databases which could be used efficiently in delivering practical knowledge concerning IT intensive library work. The present difficulty in cLearning to use working professionals and libraries in LIS education concerns with availability of staff time and visits by students to the site. However, this constraint might be eliminated altogether through eLearning.

Archiving and Access Centres for Content: There are many conferences, workshops, short term courses, tutorials etc., conducted on different aspects of LIS. Also there are around 50-70 regular teaching departments and 15-20 distance education facilities in LIS in the country. All these activities generate a lot of content. It is up to the funding agencies to identify and sponsor institutions to electronically archive and provide network access to these resources.

Expert Databases and Student Directory: INFLIBNET has already been engaged in creating experts database of university researchers. There were similar projects earlier at NCSI and IIT Delhi on specialized areas like electronic engineering or biotechnology. The profiles and academic output of teachers in different institutions on a central P&E server must in turn act as an expert system to decide upon suitable consultants for awarding research & development projects, and in deciding upon experts for professional committees and keynote speakers for conferences. The student profiles may enable potential employers to shortlist suitable candidates for their future vacancies.

6.5. CONCLUSION

For personalization and eLearning to flourish in the country for the education and training of LIS, the first major deterrent we have to overcome is the lack of courseware and other educational contents in electronic format. Though professional events and contents are there in large numbers, but not many are properly recorded and archived in electronic format for future use. Technology is there and the initiatives are there in some corners, but what is lacking is the mindset to face challenges and in adopting technology to the advantage of profession and professionals. Whatever NCSI can do out of its limited training responsibilities, at least few of the teaching departments may be able to do the same or even more, on a limited scale to begin with. Personalization offers tremendous possibilities for the teacher and learner to stretch the limits of conventional education availing background materials in electronic format and self-study as per ones own convenience. The computer infrastructure in teaching departments, university and the availability and affordability of personal computers allow their use in teaching and learning to such an extent that boost the creation of more academic content in electronic form which could be easily shared among the different stakeholders in education. When the individual departments create and archive electronic contents related to teaching and research, and then only we can to think of using the virtues of personalizing and eLearning for education, research, and training in the country.

REFERENCES

1. Bonett, Monica. Personalization of Web Services: Opportunities and Challenges, Ariadne, Issue 28, http://www.ariadne.ac.uk /issue28/personalization/ intro.html
2. Gilliland-Swetland, A., The Digital Portfolio Archives project, California University at Los Angeles, Department of Library and Information Science, 1997.
3. Chard, S. M. Data management: the foundation for Web development in the retail and service industries, First Monday, 4 (9) Sep 1999, http://www.firstmonday.dk/ issues/ issue4—9/chard/ index.html
4. Bradley, P. Personalised news services: how personal, how much news?, Information World Review, (152), Nov 1999, pp. 47-8.
5. Tedd, L. A., Yeates, R. A personalised current awareness service for library and information services staff: an

overview of the NewsAgent for Libraries project, Program, 32(4), Oct 1998, pp. 373-390.

6. Zhao, D. The Personal Digital Library, ELINOR: Electronic Library Project. London: Bowker-Saur for British Library, 1998, pp. 97-103.
7. http://www.headline.ac.uk/public/diss/jp-PIE-HybLib-model/
8. Cohen, Suzanne et al. MyLibrary: Personalized Electronic Services in the Cornell University Library, D-Lib Magazine, 6(4), April 2000, http://www.dlib.org/dlib/april00/ mistlebauer/04mistlebauer.html.
9. http://my.lib.ncsu.edu
10. http://www.personalization.org/personalization.html
11. Kramer, Joseph et al., A User-Centered Design Approach to Personalization, Communications of the ACM, August 2000. 43(8), pp. 45-48.
12. Cisco E-Learning FAQ, August 2001
13. Tucker, Bill, E-Learning and the Nonprofit Sector: White Paper discussion of the potential of e-learning to improve nonprofit management training, June 2000, (accessed from http:// www.smarterorg.com)
14. USbancorp – Piper Jaffray, Helping Investors Climb the e-Learning Curve (report by Robert W. Peterson, Mark A. Marostica, and Lisa M. Callahan), Nov. 1999.
15. InterWise, Inc. and Keegan, Morgan, Live eLearning: Taking the First Steps, A Checklist to Choose a Live eLearning Solution That Suits Your Needs, (accessed from http://www.morgankeegan.com)
16. http://www.usnews.com/usnews/edu/elearning/rankings/lib_reg_prof.htm and http://www.usnews.com/usnews/edu/elearning/rankings/lib_reg.htm
17. http://www.worldwidelearn.com/library-science.htm
18. Barron, Tom, Evolving Business Models in eLearning, March 2002, http://www.sric-bi.com/LOD

7
Superconductivity Literature

7.0. INTRODUCTION

Evaluation of abstracts and abstracting services is of utmost importance to Library & Information personnel. This is being done to assess the output and coverage of relevant primary literature, contribution of a particular country, satisfactory working of indexes, identify significant journals etc. The present study adopts the tools of bibliometrics in studying or observing the coverage of superconductivity abstracts of Physics Abstracts. Physics Abstracts is the most widely used English language abstracting service of Physics community and superconductivity is one thrust area of current research.

The information explosion and the flood of interdisciplinary and multidisciplinary research activities stressed the urgency of bibliometric studies to concentrate on specialised subdivisions of a subject rather than on a main subject or discipline. Emphasis should be given to such areas were tremendous research activity is involved. Superconductivity is such a field where a lot of current enthusiasm is involved. Distinction of physics and other branches of science as well as materials technology and other branches of technology is never felt as before due to the advancements coming up in this field. Abstracts come under bibliographical type of secondary sources which aid in finding out what and where primary information has been published on a given topic. A well written informative abstract helps the user to save a lot of time in reading the originals whereas an indicative abstract acts as a torch to decide upon the relevant documents. The Institution of Electrical Engineers (IEE), UK and Institution of Electrical and Electronics Engineers (IEEE), USA collaborate in INSPEC whose major activity is to provide various information services in physics and related applied sciences.

Physics Abstracts, a semi-monthly abstracting product is one of the services which records around 1,50,000 entries per year under 2,000 subject headings. The information is culled from a wide range of sources including journals, reports, books, dissertations and conference papers published in all countries and languages of the world. Around 3,000 journals and corresponding number of other sources are regularly scanned for the semi-monthly service. The abstracts are arranged by a special classification scheme called 'Subject Guide'. Around 21 headings and an equal number of 'see' and 'see also' references related to superconductivity were provided. 4498 out of 1,55,000 abstracts of 1991 deals with superconductivity (approx. 2.9%).

7.1. OBJECTIVES

Superconductivity abstracts of Physics Abstracts is analysed in this study to identify the inner and outer forms of material; to trace out significant journals; to ascertain time-lag; to calculate geographical scattering in terms of author as well as publisher; to estimate subject dispersion; to analyse combined and single author work; to emphasize the coverage of Indian contribution; and to evaluate the format of abstracts and indexes.

7.2. NEED

Information explosion gave way to another trend of information drought due to stagnating funds where many users from developing countries are starved of their information needs though information is available in plenty in a multiplicity of sources and forms. Thus strict monitoring mechanism is the need of the hour in acqisition of information sources. Citation studies offer some means to achieve this. But the unethical citation habits and comparative shoot up of self citations reduces its efficacy.

Another channel available is to critically evaluate international abstracting services which economize time to scan the recent and relevant literature in any area of activity under a discipline. They are important also due to the fact that 'today's literature' becomes 'tomorrow's citations'. It is the duty of library personnel to furnish researchers with more useful, nascent and standard literature in their fields of interest. In this venture, studies of the present sort is the only resort for library personnel to deliver their best results.

7.3. METHODOLOGY

Though the total number of superconductivity abstracts of the entire 1991 issues of Physics Abstracts is counted, and as time factor is dominant in abstracting, only three issues at a gap of five months viz. January 2, July 1, and December 2 (roughly 10 % of the total annual output) is included as sample for the detailed study. Abstracts on superconductivity from those issues are carefully examined and the following details are noted on small slips: entry number, subject, number of authors, country, source and date of publication etc. The entry number is recorded as an identification number for the individual abstract. When the title of the item is not clear, the whole abstract is examined to trace the inherent subject; where preference is given to identify the particular material involved. Care is given to count the number of authors mainly to search whether solo or team research is prevalent in the field. The format of the abstract discloses whether it is from a journal, book, research report, conference proceeding etc. In the case of conference proceedings, the publisher details specify whether it is published in a journal or as a separate book. The date of publication attached in the abstract compared with the issue of the abstract helps in assessing the time-lag. The author affiliation of the significant author reveal the country where the work is pursued. Abstracts generally indicate if it is a non-English one, which is eventually used in language analysis. No evaluative study of an abstract is complete unless the format of abstracts for various forms of documents and usefulness of its indexes is critically examined.

7.4. MAJOR FINDINGS

Abstracts are classified as whether it is from a journal or book in the outer form study and found that about 83.37 % belongs to the former. As a flexible and fast medium of dissemination, the dominance of the journal is justifiable. Though books and journals are print-on-paper forms, their striking and remarkable difference compelled to classify them separately. Investigation is also made to get an idea of the intention for which the article is written, whether to address a conference or as a traditional journal article. The latter account for 68.74 % of the abstracts. Since journals are an established medium for reporting nascent information, effort is being made to identify the significant journals publishing superconductivity literature- 6 among the top 10 are published in USA and 2 from UK.

There is no doubt to confirm that the service is biased to English language articles from North America and UK. This accounts for the poor coverage of other languages. Abstracting journals provides clues of whether to go for translation of an alien language material. The English language abstracting services face a lot of problem in controlling other language publications due to the bulk of literature coming out in English and the poor bibliographic control apart from the troubled state of information services in other languages. One reason for the omission of other language publications may be the comparatively late receipt of them and the creeping up of similar work in English by that time. Non-English abstracts are indicated with the corresponding languages and this facilitated to distinguish the languages involved. Around 79.6 % of the abstracts originate from English language publications. Russian (15.96%) and Japanese (3.10 %) follow soon. The data available is also gathered to assess the time taken for translation. Though cover -to-cover translation is in progress, most of the Russian articles take 4-9 months in the process. Around 13.88 % of Russian articles were translated within 6 months and another 26.39 % in 9 months. A language spectrum of different journals identified is also estimated.

The subject headings in a comparatively young and narrow area like superconductivity in Physics Abstracts gives an idea of the vastness in growth of scientific subjects. These subject divisions are closely watched in the present study to identify the areas which gathered enough momentum and to identify the significant superconducting compositions. Apart from the subject headings provided in the abstracts, new ones are identified from the title and abstracts. This has been done to cover up the inherent weakness of printed headings and due to their characteristic exclusion of significant material compositions. Around 31.93 % studied 'YBCO' sample and 15.74 % were on 'tunneling'.

Users prefer fast and sound abstracts which is next to impossible to materialize. Abstracting services have a smooth sailing due to the mechanization of all operations except the intellectual one of abstracting by a person proficient in the techniques of abstracting and having satisfactory knowledge of the discipline in question. Still then a time-delay of 3-4 months is suffered in a print-on-paper output. This much time is perhaps elapsed due to the policy of inclusion in 'materials to be abstracted' only after their publication, due to copyright and other formalities involved. No article is abstracted in Physics Abstracts within 1 or 2 months of publication. Around 29.71 % of articles fetch an abstract after 3 months; and 26.83 % after 4 months. At least 3.33 % of the articles belongs to material published an year ago. This is due to the least importance given to them or due to their late receipt.

Mission oriented and problem oriented research of today stress more on 'what to find' and 'how to find' rather than on 'whom to find'. This gave birth to an unprecedented hike in combined or team work. Only 17.29 % of abstracts falls under single authored work whereas 19.07 % and 18.85 % were attributed to two and three author articles respectively.

Apart from the inner form study discussed earlier to stress conference proceedings, country of location of the various conferences, time-lag in publication of proceedings etc., were also revealed. The recent tendency of inculcating proceedings in journals have to be appreciated in the poor plight of a major share of such literature never find a publisher. Around 26.38 % of articles were from conferences of which 14.63 % were published in journals.

The present study views the country aspect from two directions: one in terms of research activity and the other by publishing activity. Another off-shoot of this study is the plot on the publishing habits of authors which reveals the tendency of them to publish inside or outside their home country. USSR accounts for 23.06 % of authorship USA 46.78 % of publishing.

India stood seventh in authorship (around 3.5 % of the total output) and ninth in publishing. The subject and institution wise scatter of Indian work is also made. As done elsewhere, 'YBCO'is the most sought-after material by Indian researchers too. Some of the institutions which produced significant amount of work include I.I.Sc, TIFR etc.Indians prefer combined work to single authored. While scanning abstracts of work done in USA, Indian authors were also found as co-authors. Such works were identified separately to trace the Indian contribution from 'brain-drain'. Percentage of Indian authorship and subject scattering of such contributions is also estimated.

The format of abstracts as well as issue and cumulative indexes of Physics Abstracts are also critically evaluated to point out their utility and effectiveness. Each article, identified by its entry number, is provided with the necessary details to go for original, as and when needed. All authors and affiliation of the first or primary author are listed. Those publications received late were shown both date of publication and date of reception. Informative abstracts provided were brief and unsigned. The number of references is also shown which may help in the compilation of subject bibliographies. The bibliographical details at the head of abstract vary according to type of the original source; viz. a report refers to the name of the report series and number while a conference proceeding presents title, place and date of the conference. Indexes effect considerable time-saving in scanning only relevant abstracts and they also offer a means of cumulation of related abstracts scattered under different subject headings or issues. Physics Abstracts provides Author Index and subsidiary indexes like Bibliography Index, Book Index, Corporate Author Index and Conference Index in each semimonthly issue. The simplicity of the indexes has to be appreciated. Indexes are cumulated every six months. A special addition is that of a Subject Index. This provides an alphabetical subject key to the abstracts. Such major concepts appearing in each paper is indexed under headings drawn from the INSPEC Thesaurus. Author Index is sufficiently modified with the addition of names of all authors and title with main author and cross references were provided to collaborating authors.

7.5. SUGGESTIONS

As innovations in printing technology reduced their time-lag, some of the recent books are more helpful than review articles coming up in journals. Thus abstracting services should adopt measures for better bibliographic control of such books. It is also felt necessary to include at least month of official release or data of receipt of them in their abstracts.

Conference proceedings received new impetus in publishing through journals. This has to be appreciated as it brings out continuous and unending supply of proceedings from various conferences.

As a step to increase the coverage of non-English literature, the English language abstracting services should maintain close coordination with the various translation pools like NTC, ETC, ITC etc. Those articles translated may have some nascent information to convey and hence should find place in abstracting services. The cover-to-cover translation which now exists with Russian should be extended to such languages with considerable literature output like Japanese, Chinese, German, French, Spanish etc.

The national documentation centres like NISCAIR can provide English language abstracts of all primary literature produced in its territory in all languages to the International abstracting services to step up their country's coverage in a fast and comfortable manner.

No international abstracting service can alone conserve the primary literature explosion. The national and regional feeder services like 'Indian Science Abstracts' (ISA) and the erstwhile UNESCO's 'Bibliography of scientific publications in South Asia' has a significant role to play in areas where international services failed. Such services should be started in developing countries with significant research activities and can act thereby in collaboration with international services.

An article abstracted very late has of little or no use and it wastes a lot of time spent on duplicating the same. The existing practice of abstracting after publication will not resolve this time delay. The publisher can provide at least galley proofs to the international and national abstracting services, as the case may be, to report their turn out in the most opportune time. The developments in copying technology permit even to supply a copy of the revised version of the accepted article to the service and thereby help in printing abstracts as well as articles simultaneously. The present study concentrated on Physics Abstracts in print form only and thus, the electronic options which further reduce the time delay, are beyond the purview of this study.

The English language services originating from USA (north America) and UK are selling their products throughout the world due to the internationality of their language. But they never give importance to even the English language material produced elsewhere. An Indian author can find his/her articles abstracted easily when published in such countries and face no representation or late abstracting for even a better article published at home. This tendency has to change. The international services have to follow the true international spirit. 'What produced' should be the deciding factor for inclusion than 'where produced'.

Some of the abstracts were found to be of indicative nature and even informative ones were found to be too brief. This tendency should be repealed. The Physics Abstracts service has to look more into the information value of articles rather than on the handy final product. Though research activities in physics and chemistry were more or less of equal level, the two weekly issues of 'Chemical Abstracts' coming up during one issue of 'Physics Abstracts' reveals this fact. This may be one reason for migration to other sources like reprints, preprints, and research reports by Physicists.

The library clientele constitutes different category of persons and they have varied times at disposal to consult. Thus instead of just keeping the Abstracts in the racks, libraries should offer a bunch of support services and provide unique help in the literature survey and collection activities of them. The ultimate aim of the library or information centre should be to disseminate maximum information out of abstracts in the minimum time according to the needs and demands of the clientele. They can also abstract relevant articles available in its collection not reported by abstracting services on thrust areas of research by competent reference staff and can make it available to researchers. This will serve the twin purpose of not only saving the time of researchers but also increases the use of libraries.

Japan, Russian Republics, China and some other non-English speaking countries have significant contributions in new areas like superconductivity , lasers, materials etc. The library can initiate translation services from such languages either on demand or on established criteria set out for the purpose.

Library & Information Science studies literature of other disciplines mainly with a view to maintain a well balanced collection on them. Also studies at the local level have more importance as the results of such studies found faster application in libraries where they were carried out. The outcome from the experiment can be safely watched by others and hence followed, if need exists.

PART 2: BOOK ACQUISITION

8

Book Acquisition to Access Management

8.0. INTRODUCTION

Book is the most omnipresent mode of disseminating information and knowledge the world over since the advent of printing and they still form a significant portion of the resources in many of our libraries. Also they are heavily used due to the content and style of information dealt in them, their finite size and easy loan procedures followed in the library. A book is defined as a "document other than a periodical publication - that is it has been completed or has been intended to be completed in one volume or a finite number of volumes" [11]. The most obvious limitation of book is the currency of contents due to the time involved in its publication despite improvements as a result of computer aided publication procedures. There is also a general feeling that books are not primary and they are largely secondary or tertiary sources which is fast changing these days as a result of the publication in book form of increasing number of conference proceedings and edited volumes covering state of the art information. Together with the ISBN system, the trade and national bibliographies, and the publishers' catalogues, books have an efficient system for bibliographic control and the individual library access catalogues ensure their easy retrieval. In continuation with the importance of books in libraries coupled with advances in computer technology, several libraries are streamlining their activities concerning procurement of books from passive acquisition systems to result oriented collection development and exploring options for dynamic access management systems.

8.1. BOOK ACQUISITION

Acquisition or book procurement section in a library is primarily concerned with a set of professional and administrative activities concerning:

* dissemination of new book information to users
* arranging book fairs and book displays to facilitate users have a look and feel of latest books in the field
* liaising with vendors to source new books through approval system
* collection of requests for procuring new books from users
* checking requests with catalogue to eliminate purchasing multiple copies unless the demand is for frequently used books and text books
* consolidating the requests as per budget allocation and priority
* seeking sanction for purchase from appropriate authorities
* satisfying the administrative, purchase, and accounts rules of the institution to proceed with the purchase
* identifying a suitable supplier to supply the book at the best prices in the least possible time
* interfacing with the purchase unit of the institution to release the orders
* monitoring the progress of supply with the supplier
* verifying the supplied books for correct edition, publication year and other bibliographic indicators as in the request and order, and assuring that the book is free from missing pages or other physical faults

* ensuring that the bills are as per publishers prices and applicable discounts are granted
* accessioning the books and forwarding the bills for payment to the accounts section of the institution
* forwarding the accessioned book to the processing section for completing classification, cataloguing and database entry operations
* receiving gift books and forwarding to the processing section after accessioning
* interfacing with the circulation section to accept replacement copies for lost books
* updating accession register for missing, withdrawal and replacement cases

The stakeholders in the Acquisition operation are primarily:

* users, who always ask for new books and expect the section will procure them apart from refreshing the collection with new books and updated editions of old volumes
* suppliers and publishers, who accept the orders and arrange for supplying the books in the earliest possible time
* library staff, in different sections who are formally/ informally and directly/indirectly involved with the book procurement operations. Staff of not only the acquisition section but the processing, stack and circulation sections also play vital role in taking the new books to the users
* administration sections of the Institution, especially the purchase and accounts section who release the purchase orders and disburse the bills respectively

Primary challenges faced by the Acquisition operations are:

* Vendors are always interested in filling the libraries with whatever they have in stock. Many of these warehouse

titles may not be of interest to library or only of secondary importance.

* Users would always like to have a book they consider as most important to suit their needs. Many such books have either become out of print, or not available with normal trade channels.
* Time involved in pre-acquisition and post-acquisition stage in the Acquisition section and the processing and new arrival sections for a book to reach the circulation section for its final handing to the recommended user and how to optimize these operations by arriving at appropriate and user-friendly turn out time for each of these operations in the best and worst cases.

The arrival of library automation systems made all the routine operations in the Acquisition section handled more efficiently and significantly faster than the manual operations. Even then, the administrative and routine jobs in the section gets piled up in a typical library depending on the size of the library, budget for book purchase, number of users and their demand. In many libraries due to the intricacies of many of the operations listed above plus the 'always urgent' demand of users reduced this section to a mere unit spending its whole time in satisfying the administrative tasks rather than contributing professionally to the growth of library and in effectively improving the quality of its collection. The professional importance is further subverted as many libraries entrusted the task of selecting books exclusively to the users reducing the Acquisition staff to administrative tasks of collecting and consolidating user requests rather than providing any professional evaluation of new books added to the collection.

8.2. BOOK SELECTION

Dewey suggested the principle of book selection as "the best reading for the largest number at the least cost". In today's scenario where books are becoming costlier day by day and the demand for books are rising without any substantial increase in the budget allocated for their purchase, it is more justifiable the need for arriving at a selective and service oriented library collection. The library differs from the bookshop not just due to the classified arrangement but also due to the importance it pays to arrive at a functional and lively collection carefully selected satisfying the diverse needs of in-depth research, cross-migratory studies, inter/intra-disciplinary interests etc. Drury stated that the purpose of book selection is "to provide the right reader with the right book at the right time".

8.2.1. Role of Library Professionals

Some categories of users have special needs and interests that require targeted collection assessment and management and libraries should involve their clientele in collection management to ensure that the materials satisfy the clients' needs and that the clients are aware of the materials and services available to them [1]. Many libraries used to get more than one copy of the book earlier, even though it is not a text book or frequently consulted due to lesser number of books and their lower prices, better money outlay, and a strong rupee over foreign currencies. All these are things of the forgotten past and hence every rupee spent on book purchase must be suitably evaluated and justified. Duplicate purchases are avoided at the screening and consolidation of request itself by checking with the library catalogue. Library automation systems and OPAC facilitate easy execution of this task. More publishers, large number of authors and greater number of books are the order of the day and along with this users demand on the library for books of diverse nature in divergent numbers are rising. There is no doubt to highlight that in today's frontier areas of research and higher studies, researcher is more competent to identify the good titles from the heap published. Hence user requests carry ample weight than the professional techniques adopted by librarians for book selection. And many librarians are liaising with users to fine tune the selection of new books. Liaison work is the process by which librarians involve the library's clientele in the assessment and satisfaction of collection needs which includes identifying user needs, evaluating existing collections, removing extraneous materials, and locating resources that will enhance the collections [1]. A user recommends a book based on his/her expertise in the subject concerned to satisfy current, continuous or future requirements. S/he may or may not consider the interests of other user community in the book and the operational constraints like budget, difficulty to procure the book, etc., were totally disregarded in their approach. It is a topic of useful study to assess the percentage of user requests thus ordered but not supplied by the suppliers due to the title getting out of print. Users may not take the pains to gather the full bibliographic details in the requisitions which facilitate and fasten the acquisition operations. And the acquisition staff fails even with standard trade bibliographies and publisher catalogues to elicit the required details for some such requests due to the wrong rendering of bibliographic information in those requests. Users, especially in a compelling environment bound by occupational pressures, will get hardly any time to seep through the flood of catalogues, brochures, and other promotional literature dealing with information products. It is imperative upon professionals to devise a mechanism to provide all relevant information from such sources to the target clientele before seeking their recommendations, as an important means to improve the quality of sources procured with a 'bit of money meant to buy a lot'. Regular scanning of publisher, author and vendor sites is required from acquisition librarians to collect information about a large set of sources not noticeable otherwise when dealing only through local vendors.

Since they lack the premier advantage of sufficient subject knowledge of the user, the library professional adopts a totally different approach in selecting suitable books for library. The library/information management papers in BLIS and MLIS advocates the need, purpose, procedure, and tools of book selection. The professional selection is free from personal bias and it opts to maintain a balance between a single user need with that of the collective need of the user community. Since not a subject specialist, they are supposed to utilize book selection tools and especially book reviews from experts in the field to validate a book. The more divergent opinions are being considered, and when properly adopted, the selection from library professionals may bring in more variety. However, it needs more analytical studies with the usage of titles bought as per user request and professional selection to confirm the basic merits and inherent limitations of the two approaches. It may so happen that the book recommended by a person may not be consulted even by that person and the selection from the professional was also gathering dust as inferior tools were applied to assess its suitability. It may so happen that both parties were fallen pray to the repeated persuasion by the local supplier. It is also of professional honesty to assess how many of the professionals get free time from their routine tasks and have interest to consult book selection tools to refine the book selection process. When the emerging assessment parameter for the success of acquisition operation considers only the turnout of more books in less time as the key indicator, there is no doubt to gather elsewhere the reason for the widespread absence of a truly professional approach in the acquisition operations.

8.2.2. Professional Aspects of Book Section

Even if the onus of book selection is getting transferred to the users, a library professional has ample role to make the user selections more refined. This requires certain programmes from the Acquisition unit of the library to maintain the right balance between the conflicting aspects of professional concerns of library staff, information needs of users and commercial interests of publishers and suppliers. Users generally get new information from their peers, citations from reading other books and journals, book reviews, library and the easiest channel of suppliers. Suppliers are more interested primarily to grab orders for whatever they have in stock rather than what the library needs. So it is more important to relegate the supplier leads, and to follow a user focused action plan by the Acquisition unit to supply users with as much information as possible regarding latest books in their fields of importance.

Thus the Acquisition unit has to constantly gather publisher catalogues and circulate the important ones of interest as per the interests of the Institution to users. Users, most often busy with their regular activities may not take it sympathetically to browse thick catalogues to make recommendations for few books. Hence based on the book reviews and the author profile, the professionals may reduce the number of books in the catalogues and brochures to few titles matching the important needs and comparable to the budget of the library, so that users can be easily attracted to provide comments based on their subject expertise. The availability of many book related information in catalogues, brochures, reviews etc., in electronic form and new book email alerts from publishers/online book stores like Amazon, barnesandnoble, etc., facilitate their easy manipulation as per the subject interests of the library and proper dissemination on selective basis to target clientele.

8.3. COLLECTION DEVELOPMENT

To inculcate the emerging challenges in book acquisition process in library, a new term collection development is slowly getting popularity to designate the dynamic and streamlined information procurement processes. This paper mainly concentrates on the collection development aspects of books or monographs. Libraries should have detailed collection development policies, which should be available to staff and constituent users, that define the parameters of resources and services provided and describe the mechanisms for amending the policies [1]. Instead of single request acquisition process, the acquisition work is handled in this approach over a set of parameters like existing collection and concerns at improving its functionality, potential needs of clients, research, academic and development activities of the institution, refining the erstwhile processes for request collection, selection and ordering, and above all adopting a policy for future collection additions. Academic and library-related listservs, collection development sites, review sources, online catalogs, and sites for publishers, vendors, and bookstores offer librarians new and efficient methods for performing traditional tasks [5].

Collection management involves the key functions of planning and policymaking, collection analysis, materials selection, collection maintenance, fiscal management, user liaison, resource sharing, and program evaluation [3]. Academic libraries should follow a formula for allocating collection development funds and the policy and the budget should be available to faculty, staff, students, and other service populations [1]. As more libraries put their catalogs online and as technology improves, it should become easier to compare the holdings of two libraries [5] to evaluate how your collection matches with others or to evolve collaborative acquisitions with other libraries.

The whole gamut of book procurement gets more dynamic, evaluative, result driven, and responsible in the collection development regime, as:

* A collection development policy is framed to vouch for the efficacy of new titles procured. This policy gets constant evaluation in the light of deliverables and user demands. Even though a written policy is not in vogue, many libraries now evaluate the requests for new books in terms of the net resultant the procurement of the said book would bring in the present and future programmes of the Institution.

* A book is purchased not as a single entity but on the overall effect it has on the servicing of the total collection. It is another way to satisfy the second and third laws of library science in one go. Emphasis is put not only on buying latest and more number of books in core areas but also on penumbral and alien areas to satisfy the inter, intra and multi-disciplinary information needs. To bring in more variety and to provide a balanced approach to the diverse interests of users, books on a subject looking at its different aspects are most important. Similar is the case with emerging subjects and books on disciplines covering more than one subject.

* More active participation and involvement of users are

encouraged in the book selection process so that they feel involved like a party to collection development rather than a mere receiver of services. Even senior members of the user community who are often busy with their regular activities are now paying more attention to the book selection process to bring in more authenticity and transparency to the process. Usage is one major criteria that will justify the performance of library collection development, and there is no doubt that user recommended titles will lead to increased use of the collection.

* Suppliers and publishers are treated as responsible agents in the collection development process to inform and update the library on new publications, good deals and above all as prompt provider of services. As libraries put more emphasis on the quality of its collection along with other factors like cost benefit and cost effective collection at a quicker pace of supply, publishers and suppliers are also becoming more disciplined to attune to the needs of library.
* Interest to mature beyond traditional book purchase systems to information access systems. There are commercial interests coming on the way even though technological feasibility is demonstrated for such systems.
* The present status of many of our libraries forces to look ahead of single library physical collection setup to a collaboration and networking of different libraries concentrating more on global information access rather than local physical holding.

According to Hunsucker [5], many of the traditional jobs attempted in the book acquisition section could be enhanced with the help of computers, web and email, such as:

* Passive (discussion lists, newsletters via e-mail, etc.) and active (searching publishers' catalogues on the Net) current awareness possibilities

* looking in the reviews and "books received" sections of professional journals on the WWW
* checking out the archives of discussion lists
* Using online library catalogues, union catalogues and cataloguing systems on the Internet to find out necessary further bibliographic information for user requisitions
* querying appropriate specialist discussion list for descriptive or evaluative information on some publication
* browsing online cataloguing system to profit from what colleagues elsewhere have acquired or ordered
* use of multi-tasking with downloading, cut-and paste, etc., while working with computerized ordering system

8.4. ACCESS MANAGEMENT

There is a perceptible shift from ownership to access based library model: i.e., from physically browsable locally stored traditional print collections to access to electronically browsable networked resources, from value on size of the collection to value on availability and deliverability, from 'just in case' physical resource acquisition and archival collection to 'just in time' document delivery centred collection management [13]. Due to limited staff resources, preference will often be given to products provided by connecting to a publisher's or vendor's server and the need to archive the information is an additional consideration in making choices regarding digital resources [7]. Just as ejournals and electronic information resources, though there are ebooks, but their concerted access in our libraries are still a long way to go.

8.4.1. ebooks vs ejournals

An ebook is the contents of a book made available to the reader in electronic form [4]. Hawkins also made a distinction with online bookstores that provide a means of ordering a copy of a printed book electronically [4]. A digital book is a large structured collection of bits transported on a storage media or delivered over a network connection, and is designed to be viewed on some combination of hardware and software ranging from dumb terminals to personal computers to the new book reading appliances [6]. Each and every facet of the book production system has been steadily changing for many years with each major advance in printing technology and to a large extent in recent years due to advances and affordability of computerized printing, word processing, storage and network delivery systems.

In contrast to monographs or books that are self-contained in a volume, publications that continue to occur in different pieces are called by names of periodicals, serials or journals. A periodical is "published at regular intervals longer than a day, as weekly, monthly etc." or "a magazine or miscellany, the successive numbers of which are published at regular intervals" [8] whereas a journal deals with "matters of current interest in any particular sphere" [9]. ALA Glossary of Library Terms defined a serial as "a publication issued in successive parts, usually at regular intervals, and as a rule, intended to be continued indefinitely". Ranganathan defined periodicals as documents with the attributes periodicity, distinguishing number and continuity [12]. In this paper, we stick to the term journal to designate all its variants. The electronic form of such publications is designated as ejournals. Being predominant carrier of primary information, increasing importance in scholarly research and higher education, comparatively smaller page lengths than books along with their advance subscription made it possible for almost all journals from international publishers now available in full text electronic form. Though there are attempts to keep alive an alternative electronic book delivery mode with informal contents, such an electronic boom was altogether absent initially in the case of books, may be because of:

* Large number of books and more pages to electronically convert and deliver
* Electronic access problems due to delivery and receipt of such huge files on the network; can be reduced to some extent by distribution through magnetic/optical media

* Journals are not consulted from cover to cover by a user, but only for one or few articles making them an affordable electronic delivery model, where as users consult a book may be full, or for more number of pages than an article or few in a journal issue/volume
* Subscription cost of journals with/out additional fee for electronic access made a profitable business model for publishers and affordable access model for libraries through library consortia. Such mechanisms are totally absent in the case of ebooks for operational, managerial, and technical reasons plus profit motives of publishers.

Seeing the electronic advantages brought to the age-old book by portals and free initiatives, many publishers including major international names are slowly waking up to the potentialities of this medium. Society publishers have made a major boost to this initiative by collaborating with ebook portals and by offering their books through web sites. Though there are different readers (the three most dominant ones being Adobe eBook Reader for desktop/laptop, Microsoft Reader for desktop/laptop/Pocket PC, and Mobi Pocket Reader for handheld devices) and formats, the ebook technology is slowly finding acceptance with major publishers. Conventional publishers put outlandish price-tags on their e-books (to avoid cannibalising their paper sales) and insisted on burdensome security systems to try to prevent copying [10]. McGraw Hill is offering 50% discount on their ebooks. Many of the publishers are on the path towards electronic offering of books as they have started doing what they used to do earlier with journals, such as offering information about table of contents and sample chapters etc., from their websites. Table 8.1 attempts to provide a quantitative estimate of electronic books from a publisher, an online bookstore and few ebook portals. Table 8.2 presents some of the major ebook portals and their diverse access modes. The data in both tables support the inertia on the part of significant commercial publishers to engage in an aggressive manner in this medium. Almost all have opened their accounts, but still are very selective and cautious in their approach. It appears that the ebook market is still thriving due to informal content, books from society and university presses, and selective or very popular or e-friendly/marketable books from commercial publishers. As far as access modes are concerned, some are charging access fees, some subscriptions, some free access. Though very few permit downloading and storing at the client site, many provide limited access from their site for onsite viewing and printing or copying of few pages.

Table 8.1: Quantitative Estimate of ebooks

Publisher/ Portal	***Subject***	***Printed Books***	***Ebooks (%Pbooks)***
McGraw-Hill	Architecture	191	8 (4.19%)
	Business & Economics	945	368 (38.94)
	Technology & Engineering	878	118 (13.44)
	All subjects		561
Barnes and Noble		750,000	12,557 (1.67)
netLibrary			45,000
onlinebooks			19,000
lightningsource	All subjects		200,000+ OR (Tens of thousands)
Project Gutenberg	Literature, References		10000
Questia	Humanities & social sciences		70000
Books24x7	IT and business		3734
ebrary	All Subjects		20,000

Table 8.2: Some Major ebook Portals and Access Mode

Service	**Year (Coverage)**	**Website**	**Publishers**	**Access mode**
netLibrary	August 1998 (All subjects)	www. netlibrary. com/	Total-309 Society/Univ- 114Popular publishers- 27	purchasing titles just as print titles from their eBooks servers
Safari Tech Books Online	July 2002 (IT)	proquest. safaribooks online. com/	"best IT books from the best authors and publishers"	monthly subscription service (a license, not a sale)
FirstPrint	(fiction, non-fiction, and short stories)	www. firstprint. com/	Works directly with authors	Author sets the price, Minimum is $2.00
lightning source	(All subjects)	www. lightning source. com/	1800+ publishers	Access fee
online originals	January 1997	www. online originals. com/	No conventional publishers	Claims low prices. Books can be downloaded to client machines
Online Book Initiative (OBI)	(Spirituality, novels, poetry, standards documents)	http://ftp. std.com/ obi/		freely redistri- butable
Project Gutenberg	1971 (Classics, Literature and References)	www. promo. net/pg/ history. html	Copyright free contents	Available free

Service	*Year (Coverage)*	*Website*	*Publishers*	*Access mode*
Questia	(humanities and social sciences)	www. questia. com/	Total-235 Society/ Univ-108 Popular publishers- 10	Monthly, quarterly and annual subscription
Books24x7	(IT and business)	www. books 24x7. com	"world's top IT and business publishers"	Annual subscription
ebrary	(All Subjects)	www. ebrary. com/	"150 leading academic, trade and professional publishers"	subscription pricing

8.4.2. ejournal delivery model through consortia

The Central Library of IIT Kharagpur has been able to access in electronic form more than 4000 journals with printed subscription for just 1100 journals as a result of:

* **MHRD INDEST Consortia**

Before the start of consortium, the access to electronic journals remained at 60% of subscribed titles. The full text resources covered in the Consortia include IEL Online (journals of IEE and IEEE), Science Direct and IDEAL (of Academic Press) from Elsevier Science, Link from Springer Verlag, ABI/INFORM for full text management journals, ACM Digital Library, and Applied Science & Technology Plus (collection of full text journals from HW Wilson/UMI). The rates offered to the consortium are lower by 50% to 90% depending upon the category of institution and the consortium paid only Rs. 18.60 crores to access resources worth Rs. 164 crores as per their list price [2].

* **Free web access with print subscription**

Many publishers permit electronic access through web without paying any extra fee. Some of the journals not considered by the INDEST consortium continued to be accessed by the publishers' policy of free web access to valid print subscribers.

Such an electronic advantage is totally lacking in the case of books, and so far the Central Library has been able to electronically aid the following in the case of books:

* CDs and Floppies that come as supplements to printed books are being accessed through stand alone PCs and intranet servers. But the contents of these electronic alternatives are not an electronic full text of the original, but only some demo programs of exercises, and can only be put to effective use with the help of the printed book.
* Free ebooks from web portals, virtual libraries and secondary sources

8.5. CONSTRAINTS AND PROSPECTS

Library Automation Systems: Many software packages are available to match the varied demands of libraries. However, the options provided by many of them may not satisfy the immediate requirements of a particular library. No software package is functional enough to satisfy all the wide-ranging requirements of a library; only we can adapt the general options to somehow match the local requirements with the aid of continuous customizations and constant monitoring. Selecting suitable software for library automation will significantly reduce the manual operations and enable the professionals to dedicate more time for professional jobs. In the case of book acquisition work, the library automation software should be able to handle all the activities concerning receiving, checking for duplicates and consolidating requests, generating sanction letters, ordering with the appropriate vendor, monitoring the status of orders, accessioning books on receipt and making arrangements for payment. Most important requirements of the package are to electronically communicate with the stakeholders and generate whatever manual reports needed in the section and demanded by the library authorities.

Proactive role in book selection: Don't get disheartened by the user's dominant role in book selection, since information professionals have a key role to supplement, aid and refine the user selection by providing pin-pointed information about new books that matches the interest of the person concerned.

Resource Sharing and ILL initiatives: Since many books are available on a particular topic by different authors, it has become extremely difficult for even libraries with sufficient budget to hold all of them in their collection. This warrants collaborative arrangements with other libraries. Most of the libraries now encourage to loan out books to collaborating libraries, and hence presence of a book in a collaborating library is as good as having it in own premises, provided faster follow up and delivery mechanism is put in place to honour ILL requests. The participating libraries should also form suitable policy especially with respect to duplicating costly books, shared purchasing of costly books, and balanced collection in individual premises.

What is required?: Access system like journals for electronic access of purchased books through local serving or remote accessing from publisher/intermediary site with single/ multiple access depending on the number of copies procured.

Digital Library: Digital library of books can be set up on the Intranet by

* Local archiving of free and paid e-books available
* Local serving of e-supplements of locally purchased books
* In-house digitization of copyright owned and copyright free printed books in the collection. This is especially viable for libraries whose communities still cherish old books (many of them are copyright exhausted) as part of teaching, research and study purposes. There are also many publications from the Institution for which it holds copyright and may be digitized.

8.6. CONCLUSION

From a mere administrative and manual section engrossed in more like a warehousing activity, the book procurement and acquisition units in libraries are undergoing rapid strides in routine operations with the help of library automation systems and book related information such as publisher catalogues, online bookstores, library OPACs etc., on internet. Though libraries are putting into good use the said book related information for the quick purchase of printed books, they are facing different challenges and difficult hurdles in respect of moving from book acquisition and collection development systems to ebook access systems. Like libraries in the developed countries and institutions where research and development on a high pedestal are attempted, our libraries also, especially those attached to higher education and research institutions, will have to involve in different activities like outright purchase, lease, subscription, loan, cooperative ventures with data producers, shared purchase arrangements through consortia with other institutions, direct remote free/ fee on-line access to significantly integrate ebooks as part of their ever changing collection development strategy. This needs constant counseling with users to perceive their demands and communicating the same in the right perspective to suppliers, intermediaries and publishers of books. An alert acquisition unit must be able to identify the available e-resources, good deals, correct prices and arriving at electronic alternatives to the traditional products. A continuous survey as well as evaluation of products and solutions in the information market pertaining to ebooks along with budgetary provision to avail such products and infrastructure improvement to effectively serve them would be the initial steps to progress towards an access management strategy from printed books to electronic books.

REFERENCES

1. ALA,http://www.ala.org/Template.cfm? Section= Collection_Development&template=/Content Management/ContentDisplay. cfm& ContentID =26942

2. Arora, Jagdish and Agrawal, Pawan, Indian Digital Library in Engineering Science and Technology (INDEST) Consortium: Consortia-Based Subscription to Electronic Resources for Technical Education System in India: A Government of India Initiative, International CALIBER 2003, Ahmedabad, 13-15 February 2003, Conference Volume - Mapping Technology on Libraries and People, Ahmedabad: INFLIBNET, 2003, pp. 271-290.
3. Cogswell, J, The organization of collection management functions in academic research libraries, Journal of Academic Librarianship, 13, 1987, pp. 268-276.
4. Hawkins, Donald T., Electronic books: a major publishing revolution. Part 1: General considerations and issues, Online, 24 (4) Jul/Aug 2000, p.14-18, 20-22, 24-26, 28.
5. http://www.loc.gov/acq/colldev/handbook.html
6. Lynch, Clifford, The Battle to Define the Future of the Book in the Digital World, First Monday, 6(6), http://firstmonday.org/issues/issue6_6/lynch/index.html, June 2001.
7. http://macfadden.mit.edu:9500/networked/policy.html
8. The Oxford English Dictionary, 2nd ed., Clarendon: Oxford, 1989, vol. XI, p. 560.
9. Op. Cit., vol. VII, p. 280.
10. Onlineoriginals, see faq at www.onlineoriginals.com/
11. Ranganathan, S R, Prolegomena to Library Classification, vol. 1, 3rd ed., Bangalore: Sarada Ranganathan Endowment for Library Science, Reprint 1994, p. 490.
12. Op. Cit., p. 501.
13. Seetharama S, Collection Development/Management in an Information Technology-Based Environment: Current Initiatives and Issues, DESIDOC Bulletin of Information Technology, 17(1), January 1997, pp. 11-20.

9
Good Offices Committee

9.0. INTRODUCTION

The Good Offices Committee (GOC) is a voluntary organization formed to establish uniform terms of book supplies to libraries, and to ensure a fair working margin to booksellers and an efficient service to the library [2]. The GOC no doubt offered a fair working margin to the sellers as mostly the rates arrived at were higher than the prevailing bank rates, which otherwise the libraries would have followed. However, the publishers, importers, resellers originated at various times, a large number of them without a serious professional approach to the demands of libraries and challenges of a vocation that demands enough social commitment like book trade, forced many of our libraries to suffer with their time taking, costly and not so efficient services. The GOC has been in existence for more than 30 years [2] whereas Indian Library Chronology describes about rates active from 15th February 1984 [3]. The Committee meets at regular intervals and after taking to consideration the fluctuations in the currency rates decides on the rates of conversion governing sale of books and periodicals [2]. These rates are widely circulated amongst the libraries all over India either directly or through booksellers [2]. This helped to dispense with the need for a cumbersome procedure of inviting tenders for a diverse product like Books [2]. This argument is not clear and confusing as dispensing with tenders for book purchase was made possible not by GOC exchange rates but due to the Ministry of Finance letter No. F.23(7).EII(A)/83 dated 7th February 1984 amending the General Financial Rules (GFR). Even if, GOC rates are not in place, the libraries have the popular option of bank rates already being applied for purchases of other international products. The libraries that still follow GOC rate for purchasing books are very cautious about remitting subscriptions for journals in bank rates because of the huge amount involved and easy nature of one time payment. There have not been many studies on the impact of trends in book trade influencing library collection development. Samuel illustrated that the devaluation of the rupee has been beneficial to book importers with examples of exploitation of libraries by the GOC, a non-statutory body dominated by the book trade and warned that the death of libraries demands an investigation into the operations of the book trade [5]. Another study suggested the interrelation of author, publisher, bookseller and librarian in the book trade, looking at the individual role of each in building responsive library collections, with emphasis on sharing and the application of information technology in library resource management [1].

9.1. GENERAL FINANCIAL RULES (GFR)

Traders used to confuse even library professionals with the argument that the relaxation in GFR by Govt. of India for calling quotations must work only with GOC. The GFR Rule 99 granted exemption for "books, publications, periodicals, etc., in a library" from the term 'stores'. Rule 116 permits that "Librarian (not below the rank of Deputy Secretary to Government of India) subject to the powers delegated under Delegation of Financial Power Rules, 1978, may purchase books, etc., from the reputed and standard book sellers on the prevalent terms and conditions. Tenders need not be called for this purpose". Thus it is evident that even without following the GOC exchange rates, libraries can buy books without violating the GFR norms. When a library finds that there is more than one supplier willing to offer a title, or there is a tie with more than one supplier for a particular title after a book fair/display, there is no harm in negotiating with or collecting quotations from the parties concerned to arrive at a suitable decision. Though title wise quotation may call for lot of paperwork and administrative routines, one viable alternative is to negotiate with suppliers for arriving at specific discount rates based on publishers. GOC rates have made it convenient for libraries to buy books at 10% discount at the exchange rates announced in their circular. Seeing the huge margin different players receive from their principals, it is high time for libraries and librarians to rethink about the prevailing norms of book purchase and to negotiate for higher discount than the GOC stipulated 10%. The present day librarians exposed to the virtues of technology and aggressive work environment do not hesitate to take challenges to deal with publishers and suppliers to arrive at a cost effective and budget optimized efficient procurement option of books in their libraries. With RBI website displaying the bank rates for foreign currencies in their Website (www.rbi.org.in), it is not difficult for libraries to ascertain these rates. The same may also be obtained from the local bank. This practice does not violate any Government rules as libraries are getting higher discount (interestingly GFR does not stipulate any standard discount rate for buying books) and paying less exchange when compared with GOC norms, which lead to cost effective and optimum utilization of budget earmarked for procuring books.

9.2. PARTICIPATION OF LIBRARY ASSOCIATIONS, LIBRARIES, AND LIBRARIANS IN GOC

The GOC, in 1985 had members from major library professional associations such as Government of India Library Association (GILA) and Indian Library Association (ILA); major libraries in Delhi like Delhi University Library, Jawaharlal Nehru University Library, Jamia Milia University Library, National Medical Library; information centres INSDOC (now NISCAIR) and DESIDOC; institutions/councils/commissions such as UGC, CSIR, ICAR and IIT Delhi; Publishers and book trade associations like FPBAI, Federation of Indian Publishers, Delhi

State Book Sellers and Publishers Association, Akhil Bharatiya Hindi Prakashak Sangh; and Integrated Finance Cell and Books Promotion Division, both of Ministry of Education as Associate Members. In 1996, it had in addition to the trade members listed earlier, another trade body, Federation of Educational Publishers in India, apart from ILA and GILA (now AGLIS); the professional bodies were represented by IASLIC and MLAI; libraries included Central Secretariat Library, Delhi Public Library, and IARI library; institutions such as National Physical Laboratory, Planning Commission, representatives of book trade, representatives of librarians from states, one representative from BHEL and one from IOCL; whereas INSDOC (now NISCAIR), DESIDOC, CSIR, UGC, and ICAR ceased to be its members. In both cases, the membership over such a long period included the major stakeholders in the book trade and consumer chain of trade representatives, libraries, government institutions and professional associations of librarians. However the present GOC comprises of members from book trade only and there is no reason why libraries accept recommendations of such a one sided body. In view of the persisting difficulty with the ILA committee, and pending resolution of the issue with the librarians, the Federation, in consultation with the affiliated associations as also important members of the trade, is presently announcing the book trade's own conversion rates [2]. Thus it should not be proper to call it GOC rates and in the best case it may be taken as the Trade Associations' rates. Though the trade bodies were very vocal about resurrecting the activities of GOC by putting in place the old membership pattern, there has been silence from the professional associations, libraries and institutions and since there are not any published information about the "persisting difficulty", only the senior professionals served in the GOC can give a professional picture of the strained relationship or the events that lead to the one sided membership of GOC.

9.3. GOC RATE, BANK RATE AND CUSHION IN EXCHANGE RATES

GOC Rates and Bank Rates (as on date of GOC and the average for the month) from 2001 March to 2004 March are displayed along with difference in exchange rate for the current month (D1) and last month (D2), percentage of difference to the bank rate for current month (P1) and percentage of difference to the bank rate for last month (P2) for US Dollar is presented in Table 9.1. Similar information for the currencies UK Pound and Euro for the same period are provided in Tables 9.2 and 9.3 respectively. GOC has not so far disclosed the procedure followed to arrive at exchange rates periodically. What an ideal GOC would have been? May be we can follow the average of bank rates for a month to avoid the hassles of verifying the bank rate every day, even though the rates can be easily ascertained from the RBI web site (www.rbi.org.in) or from the local branch of any nationalized or scheduled bank. 'Cushion' is the trade term used to decorate the higher exchange rate followed by GOC, which varied over the three years period in terms of difference in Rupees from 0.33 to 6.67 (there is only one case during the study period, for Euro, where the GOC rate was lower than RBI rate) and in terms of percentage over bank rate from as low as 0.61 to as high as 9.52, as illustrated in Table 9.4. Table 9.4 also reveals that Dollar shows less fluctuations in Rupee exchange rate in comparison to Euro and Pound, where the latter shows more variations. In March 1998 when the previous team of Indian library Association (ILA) took over, the GOC was passing through crises and resolved by agreeing to a lower 'cushion' in exchange rates [2]. However, there has been a crisis in the Good offices Committee since a new team of Office-bearers of ILA took over from April 2000. The new ILA committee tried to give their version why the exchange rate should not have a 'cushion' which has indeed been in effect for about 25 years [2]. ILA and professionals must have rightly expressed the growing concerns of the library profession: budgets are always limited; currency is every time weak, whereas sources, users and demands are consistently increasing. However, the trade body has the following justifications in always putting a cushioned exchange rate:

* long history of its existence
* since there is constant devaluation of the Indian Rupee against the foreign currencies, to protect against the loss during the period that the sale is made and the time it takes to realize bills and payment to source
* increase in landed cost in recent years (Air freight charges, wharf rents, customs, bank charges, etc.)

History of existence for last 25 years alone can not be cited for the continuation of an old practice that is being constantly challenged by emerging social and consumer needs. There is justification in the traders' concern of reducing the time lag in selecting, ordering and making payments. At the same time, it seems that the so called losses during the intermittent period are projected wrongly in an exploding manner. If the trade wants it to be sustainable and strong, then it should not look for such concessions from the consumers, but instead work for agreements with their principals to absolve or share any losses. Also, libraries should take proper mechanism to disburse the bills in reasonable time and expedite payments quickly. In many cases, payments are delayed due to the lack of compliance from suppliers for price proof, price certificate, book ordered does not match with the supplied one, and copy supplied is defective and normally get exchanged only after much persuasion. Sometimes, though the library forwards the bill in time, the final payment may get delayed due to clerical operations in the Payment unit of the Administrative section. Every library must consult their respective administrative units and by taking them into confidence can usher in a time bound approach in disbursing payments related to library purchase. There is an increase in landed cost, but there is also an increase in margins passed on by publishers, especially the international ones, to traders. This may be one reason for the high prices of books, though there are some justifications on account of raw material and production costs.

Table. 9.1: GOC and Bank Rates for US Dollar from 2001 March to 2004 March

Year	Month	Date	GOC	Bank Rate Date	Bank Rate Average	D1	P1	D2	P2
2004	March	1	47.80	45.24	45.02	2.78	6.18	2.53	5.59
	February	2	48.00		45.27	2.73	6.03	2.55	5.61
	January	1	48.10		45.45	2.65	5.83	2.51	5.51
2003	December	1	48.10	45.78	45.59	2.51	5.51	2.58	5.67
	November	1	48.00		45.52	2.48	5.45	2.61	5.75
	October	3	48.40	45.46	45.39	3.01	6.63	2.55	5.56
	September	1	48.50	45.83	45.85	2.65	5.78	2.56	5.57
	August	1	48.80	46.16	45.94	2.86	6.23	2.57	5.56
	July	1	49.40	46.48	46.23	3.17	6.86	2.69	5.76
	June	2	49.70	47.16	46.71	2.99	6.40	2.62	5.56
	May	1	50.00		47.08	2.92	6.20	2.62	5.53
	April	1	50.20		47.38	2.82	5.95	2.56	5.37
	March	3	50.40	47.66	47.64	2.76	5.79	2.67	5.59
	February	1	50.70		47.73	2.97	6.22	2.72	5.67
	January	1	50.80	47.99	47.98	2.82	5.88	2.66	5.53
2002	December	2	50.90	48.32	48.14	2.76	5.73	2.64	5.47
	November	1	51.00	48.34	48.26	2.74	5.68	2.57	5.31
	October	1	51.10	48.36	48.43	2.67	5.51	2.61	5.38
	September	2	51.30	48.48	48.49	2.81	5.80	2.71	5.58
	August	1	51.40	48.67	48.59	2.81	5.78	2.64	5.41
	July	1	51.70	48.84	48.76	2.94	6.03	2.82	5.77
	June	1	51.70		48.88	2.82	5.77	2.70	5.51
	May	1	51.60		49.00	2.60	5.31	2.68	5.48
	April	1	51.40		48.92	2.48	5.07	2.66	5.46
	March	1	51.40	48.75	48.74	2.66	5.46	3.71	7.78
	February	1	51.10	48.53	47.69	3.41	7.15	2.77	5.73
	January	1	50.70	48.24	48.33	2.37	4.90	2.78	5.80
2001	December				47.92				
	November	1	50.70	48.00	48.00	2.70	5.63	2.68	5.58
	October	1	50.20	47.93	48.02	2.18	4.54	2.55	5.35

Year	Month	Date	GOC	Bank Rate Date	Bank Rate Average	D1	P1	D2	P2
	September	3	49.80	47.13	47.65	2.15	4.51	2.67	5.67
	August	1	49.80	47.13	47.13	2.67	5.67	2.63	5.58
	July	2	49.60	47.07	47.17	2.43	5.15	2.59	5.51
	June	1	49.50	47.05	47.01	2.49	5.30	2.58	5.50
	May				46.92				
	April	4	49.20	46.63	46.79	2.41	5.15	2.58	5.53
	March	1	47.90	46.53	46.62	1.28	2.75	1.38	2.97

Table 9.2: GOC and Bank Rates for UK Pound from 2001 March to 2004 March

Year	Month	Date	GOC	Bank Rate Date	Bank Rate Average	D1	P1	D2	P2
2004	March	1	88.90	84.68	82.28	6.62	8.05	4.37	5.17
	February	2	87.20		84.53	2.67	3.16	4.45	5.38
	January	1	84.30		82.75	1.55	1.87	4.54	5.69
2003	December	1	81.40	78.83	79.76	1.64	2.06	4.51	5.87
	November	1	80.50		76.89	3.61	4.70	4.40	5.78
	October	3	78.00	75.92	76.10	1.90	2.50	4.29	5.82
	September	1	77.30	72.41	73.71	3.59	4.87	3.09	4.22
	August	1	79.50	74.21	73.22	6.28	8.58	4.37	5.82
	July	1	81.80	76.94	75.13	6.67	8.88	4.27	5.51
	June	2	80.90	76.96	77.53	3.37	4.35	4.48	5.86
	May	1	78.80		76.42	2.38	3.11	4.19	5.62
	April	1	79.60		74.61	4.99	6.69	4.17	5.53
	March	3	81.40	75.07	75.43	5.97	7.92	4.58	5.96
	February	1	82.10		76.82	5.28	6.87	4.62	5.96
	January	1	80.40	77.34	77.48	2.92	3.77	4.07	5.33
2002	December	2	80.10	75.19	76.33	3.77	4.94	4.23	5.58
	November	1	79.50	75.62	75.87	3.63	4.78	4.17	5.54
	October	1	79.50	76.10	75.33	4.17	5.54	4.20	5.58
	September	2	79.50	74.99	75.30	4.20	5.58	4.76	6.37

Year	Month	Date	GOC	Bank Rate		D1	P1	D2	P2
				Date	Average				
	August	1	80.10	76.00	74.74	5.36	7.17	4.25	5.60
	July	1	76.50	74.83	75.85	0.65	0.86	3.92	5.40
	June	1	75.40		72.58	2.82	3.89	3.88	5.43
	May	1	74.60		71.52	3.08	4.31	4.06	5.76
	April	1	73.30		70.54	2.76	3.91	3.94	5.68
	March	1	73.10	69.10	69.36	3.74	5.39	3.81	5.50
	February	1	73.10	68.47	69.29	3.81	5.50	3.72	5.36
	January	1	72.80	70.18	69.38	3.42	4.93	3.81	5.52
2001	December				68.99				
	November	1	73.90	69.79	68.98	4.92	7.13	4.16	5.97
	October	1	73.30	70.54	69.74	3.56	5.11	3.65	5.24
	September	3	71.60	68.49	69.65	1.95	2.80	3.93	5.81
	August	1	70.40	67.35	67.67	2.73	4.03	3.58	5.36
	July	2	69.40	66.50	66.82	2.58	3.86	3.55	5.39
	June	1	70.70	66.85	65.85	4.85	7.37	3.77	5.63
	May				66.93				
	April	4	71.30	66.76	67.22	4.08	6.07	3.91	5.80
	March	1	70.00	67.26	67.39	2.61	3.87	2.31	3.41

Table 9.3: GOC and Bank Rates for Euro from 2001 March to 2004 March

Year	Month	Date	GOC	Bank Rate		D1	P1	D2	P2
				Date	Average				
2004	March	1	60.50	56.65	55.24	5.26	9.52	3.28	5.73
	February	2	60.50		57.22	3.28	5.73	3.17	5.53
	January	1	59.50		57.33	2.17	3.79	3.54	6.33
2003	December	1	56.30	54.82	55.96	0.34	0.61	3.04	5.71
	November	1	56.20		53.26	2.94	5.52	3.10	5.84
	October	3	54.00	53.16	53.10	0.90	1.69	2.62	5.10
	September	1	54.10	50.44	51.38	2.72	5.29	2.90	5.66
	August	1	55.60	51.78	51.20	4.40	8.59	3.00	5.70

Year	*Month*	*Date*	*GOC*	*Bank Rate*		*D1*	*P1*	*D2*	*P2*
				Date	*Average*				
	July	1	57.40	53.57	52.60	4.80	9.13	2.86	5.24
	June	2	57.50	55.26	54.54	2.96	5.43	2.98	5.47
	May	1	54.50		54.52	-0.02	-0.04	2.97	5.76
	April	1	54.50		51.53	2.97	5.76	3.00	5.83
	March	3	54.60	51.38	51.50	3.10	6.02	3.16	6.14
	February	1	53.80		51.44	2.36	4.59	2.92	5.74
	January	1	52.00	50.31	50.88	1.12	2.20	2.96	6.04
2002	December	2	51.10	47.97	49.04	2.06	4.20	2.79	5.78
	November	1	50.20	47.87	48.31	1.89	3.91	2.75	5.80
	October	1	50.40	47.76	47.45	2.95	6.22	2.92	6.15
	September	2	50.30	47.56	47.48	2.82	5.94	2.78	5.85
	August	1	51.50	47.55	47.52	3.98	8.38	3.01	6.21
	July	1	49.10	48.55	48.49	0.61	1.26	2.36	5.05
	June	1	47.10		46.74	0.36	0.78	2.17	4.83
	May	1	46.00		44.93	1.07	2.38	2.70	6.24
	April	1	45.00		43.30	1.70	3.93	2.31	5.41
	March	1	44.70	42.27	42.69	2.01	4.71	2.34	5.52
	February	1	45.10	41.68	42.36	2.74	6.47	2.24	5.23
	January	1	45.10	42.90	42.86	2.24	5.23	2.35	5.50
2001	December				42.75				
	November	1	46.10	43.24	42.66	3.44	8.06	2.55	5.86
	October	1	45.60	43.61	43.55	2.05	4.71	2.19	5.05
	September	3	44.80	42.87	43.41	1.39	3.20	2.43	5.74
	August	1	42.70	41.52	42.37	0.33	0.78	1.99	4.89
	July	2	42.50	39.87	40.71	1.79	4.40	2.33	5.80
	June	1	43.50	39.87	40.17	3.33	8.29	2.44	5.94
	May				41.06				
	April	4	44.70	41.73	41.83	2.87	6.86	2.25	5.30
	March	1	44.30	42.95	42.45	1.85	4.36	1.34	3.12

Table 9.4: Cushion in Exchange Rates in terms of difference in Rupees and Percentage

Cushion	U S Dollar				U K Pound				Euro			
Range	D1	P1	D2	P2	D1	P1	D2	P2	D1	P1	D2	P2
9.51-10.00										1		
9.01-9.50										1		
8.51-9.00						2				1		
8.01-8.50						1				3		
7.51-8.00				1		1						
7.01-7.50		1				3						
6.51-7.00		2			2	2				1		
6.01-6.50		7			1	1		1		3		6
5.51-6.00		14		24	1	2		22		4		17
5.01-5.50		7		9	2	3		10	1	3		9
4.51-5.00		3			3	5	5		1	3		2
4.01-4.50					3	3	16	1	1	3		
3.51-4.00			1		7	5	12	1	1	3	1	
3.01-3.50	3				3	2	1		4	1	6	1
2.51-3.00	23	1	33	1	7	1			8		15	
2.01-2.50	8				1	2	1		6	2	11	
1.51-2.00	1		1		4	1			4	1	1	
1.01-1.50									3	1	1	
0.51-1.00					1	1			2	3		
0.01-0.50									3			
-0.01- -0.50									1	1		

9.4. GOC TERMS FOR SUPPLY OF BOOKS VS LIBRARY INTERESTS

* "In order to bring about a uniformity of GOC recommended conversion rates, library discount and standardization in the terms of supply, the Librarians are advised to deal only with the members of state and national level book trade associations and federation."

How this is going to benefit libraries is difficult to explain as by paying the membership fee, anybody can be a member of such associations and libraries bewilder that their best and worst suppliers are members of the same trade body. Moreover, to enroll a supplier in a trade association is exclusively under the purview of the association concerned, and libraries have no say in these matters. What is required is based on the objective evaluation by libraries and library associations, the trade bodies should be bold enough to remove suppliers with poor performance indices, doubtful motives and those entering into malpractices and pursuing bad business interests from their membership.

* "Books on approval should be finalized/returned within 30 days. The payment for the books approved should be made within 60 days of the receipt of the bill. The bill to be raised by the supplier at the conversion rate prevailing on the date when the books are finally selected by the librarians for purchase. Payment of outstation suppliers should preferably be made through bank drafts, after deducting bank charges."

Sometimes, libraries were forced to get the book examined by different users some of them very busy with their professional work, especially in a special/research/academic institution, forcing it difficult to make a decision within a month. But the Suppliers used to compensate by claiming for a higher exchange on the date of bill. The clause that 'the bill to be raised by the supplier at the conversion rate prevailing on the date when the books are finally selected by the librarians for purchase' clearly indicates that the supplier should bill as per the exchange rate based on date of order or even a day before it, but almost all the suppliers prepare the bill based on the exchange rate prevailing on the date of bill, and some suppliers even wait for a suitable date to quote the higher rate by comparing 2-3 GOC circulars/bank rates. Traders may be given freedom to raise a bill on a convenient date as the libraries have the freedom to order a book on any date, however the trader must quote the exchange rates valid for the order date. Libraries never look for a convenient date as per exchange rate to release orders but there are many instances to point out that the supplier billed on a date with the maximum rate for a particular currency. Thus leaving what rate to quote for a purchase totally on the supplier may not be in the best interests of libraries. The trade bodies should formulate clear policy regarding these norms with punitive action (may be in the form of fines, foregoing membership temporarily, etc.) against members violating them. There may be difficulties on the part of libraries to remit payment as drafts and traders must be accommodative enough to accept cheques.

* "The supplier shall append the following declaration on the bills. Only latest editions have been supplied and these are not remainder titles."

There should be enough information on the part of libraries to identify what are remaindered titles and then only they can verify the genuineness of declaration by suppliers, many of them smart enough to fool even the smarter libraries. There are cases the suppliers tampering with the title and back of title pages, getting the books bound in the country after bringing the unbound books, etc. There are also cases where the supplier may not inform the libraries about special prices and discounts or special offers for the titles procured. The libraries can escape from these unhealthy trade practices only with the co-operation of genuine suppliers, distributors, publishers and trade associations with statistics and relevant information concerning book trade and import.

* "Income tax permanent account no. (PAN) of the supplier must be provided."

Required proof regarding PAN is submitted by all the suppliers.

* "The prices have been correctly charged in accordance with the publisher's/ Importer's/ Distributors' invoices and Publishers' catalogues."

Most of the publishers never print prices in the books concerned and it is quite common to revise the prices frequently. Suppliers in many cases do not enclose the original import invoices and in some cases claim the revised price even though they got the book at the relatively lower earlier price. As there are different prices in different catalogues/web sites, rather than blindly certifying on the bills, they should attach sufficient proof like import invoices to justify their case and to enhance their image.

* "The order placed by the libraries will be usually valid for six months unless otherwise mutually agreed upon by the librarian and the supplier."

In a time when air mail and international couriers used to deliver foreign books direct from the publisher within a couple of weeks, why this extra time be given to suppliers basically to collect books through sea mail only to further save on their operating cost. In a research library, researchers are hard pressed for information and most often they will be provided with the required information as timely, efficient, effective and fast as possible. Also, in highly competitive disciplines where research activity is rampant, most often books get obsolete immediately after its publication and the earlier they are supplied to clients, the more they are used for the little time in which they will be in demand.

In this premise, it is very reasonable to demand the supplier to deliver the Indian books within a month and foreign book within 2-3 months. Extra time for supply in exceptional cases may be granted by the librarian seeing the merit, on a case to case basis.

* "Discount: All books in English, Hindi and other Regional languages, whether of Indian origin with the exception of those conversed by the following special categories, will carry a uniform discount of 10% of the published prices in respect of Indian or converted into Rupee prices in the case of imported titles."

As per the price proof submitted by suppliers along with bills to a library, it was found that the direct importers used to get foreign books at different discount from the publisher and in a similar manner the books are transferred from the importer to the supplier (see Table 9.5). Why it is then that library should only live with 10% discount and why not more as the importers and suppliers in some cases earn huge margins? In the present trends of pricing of books, the importers and suppliers should each satisfy with a minimum 10% for books priced up to $100 and must subsequently reduce their margins for costlier books. Whatever money saved by libraries in each purchase may lead to more purchases and this when happen in multiple libraries will lead to a proliferation of increased commercial activity in the book trade in the country benefiting both the traders (more volumes generate more profit) and libraries.

* "Special Categories: Central and State Government publications - no discount. Short/No discount titles procured from abroad against specific order or Indian publications. The importer or the library supplier is expected to work on the margin of 15% on net landed cost. The invoice is to be prepared on the following terms. Published price minus (-) discount earned plus (+) 15% handling charges plus (+) actual freight, clearance, bank and postal charges, documentary evidence to be submitted by the supplier to the library on demand."

Table 9.5: Suppliers' margin

% of discount received by Supplier	*Number of books* 2001-2002	2002-2003
20	23	
25	268	1
27.50	14	
28.75	25	2
30	414	135
33.33	10	13
35	36	
40	157	
42	4	3
45	103	
55	39	
	1093	154

If a rule is to be framed for the smooth operation of a business relation between two parties, it should not be biased to one party and should be of benefit to both. The rule on special categories says that when a supplier is not getting enough margins, he should get 15% profit by charging extra. Whereas a large number of normal discount titles are imported at huge margins and the distributor/supplier is granting only 10% to the Library. Why should the library be satisfied with a fixed discount? What is needed is a variable discount based on the publisher, type of book etc. Many libraries are not resorting to a variable discount regime due to the difficulties involved in operating such a setup, especially in the context of falling budgets and less manpower. The importer or the library supplier must agree to work on a maximum margin of 10% on net landed cost in the case of 'Short/No discount' titles.

* "Terms of supply of Journals: No discount. Conversion rates as per latest GOC Circular."

Even before the advent of following bank rates for book purchase, many libraries used to remit journal subscriptions to subscription agents only by bank rates due to the huge sum involved. Many subscription agents have an open mind and accepted this and the same supplier while dealing with book purchase found it inconvenient to accept payment as per bank rate, which is another example of the double standards and acute profit motive on the part of suppliers. The subscription agents who bag sizeable amount of subscriptions must think of either giving some discount or granting few free subscriptions to popular journals.

* "Bills to remain valid for 60 days from the date of invoice. All payments not made within the 60 days validity of the bills will be subject to change as per the new conversion rates prevailing on the date of receipt of payment."

This deadline should be flexible and accommodative enough considering the nature, type and administrative set up of libraries. Suppliers and libraries can fix a time bound approach discussed earlier to disburse payments.

9.5. LIBRARY VS BOOK TRADE INTERACTION - NEW ROLE OF GOC

Describing booksellers and libraries as "partners in progress," FPBAI expects the revived GOC to have an expanded role, going well beyond the routine work of fixing of rates. Those libraries trying to disregard GOC rates for exchange rate of foreign currencies have to face a tough time due to the difficulties they had to convince the suppliers. Some suppliers agreed due to the margins they get or the interest to spread the volume of their business. One common argument propounded by many unwilling suppliers was that they get the books from distributors who import books on three-month credit on GOC rates only. It is a simple management policy the libraries should adopt that in a business deal those who earn profit must bear the losses also and the library need not be a party to compensate for the losses. Seeing the margins the middlemen involved in book trade earn, difference in exchange rates must be compensated by the suppliers and distributors as they are the parties who earn profit in the deal. Also why should the importers ask the suppliers to pay the exchange rate as per GOC rates as they themselves are paying in bank rates to the publishers? One reason for the lack of professionalism in the book trade unlike other trades which are constantly challenged by imports and international trends is due to these sort of accommodative measures built in the trade and the silent suffering or lack of opposition of the parties seeking their services. Libraries have to be very vigilant, watchful, and reactive regarding supply time, prices, discount, etc., to survive in the coming days where budget is always short of demand and information products are always growing. Book trade is not like other trades and hence commercial interests must be pursued with a social commitment as traders are one of the important links in the scholarly information communication chain and they must render this role in the larger interests of nation's progress.

The acceptance of GOC as an agency to periodically fix the exchange rates of foreign currencies must be very much in doubt as the very purpose for which it was set has become more biased towards the traders and the importance of such unilateral agencies will no doubt slowly recede. However as the representative of almost all the major traders associations in the national and state level, the GOC can work in a library friendly mode even while pursuing activities for the benefit of book trade. Libraries and Book Trade must be equal partners in social issues like spreading education and literacy, information support for research and development initiatives, ensuring the emergence of information and knowledge age, archiving country's publishing output, etc. Some of the crucial areas where traders and GOC can pursue in the interests of trade as well as for the benefits of libraries and the country must include:

9.5.1. Textbooks

The publishing community should be sensitive enough to assess the needs of libraries, especially in the case of textbooks. Only affordable Indian reprints of books in popular disciplines like computer science and management are available right now. The Publishers should assess the statistics available with trade channels, and strive for either publishing reprints of textbooks in all disciplines in the country or try to get special prices for imports of such books.

9.5.2. Trade-Library Interaction

Joint consultations between libraries and book trade are always welcome. There should be at least one session on vendor-professional interaction in library conferences. Similar programmes may also be planned in connection with book fairs, book displays, and book exhibitions.

9.5.3. Digital Books

It is doubtful that our book trade is comfortable in dealing with new technology products like digital or ebooks. Only exception is that the CD-ROMs accompanying books are getting distributed with them. In recent days, international publishers provide contents, sample chapters, reviews, etc., of books published and it is up to the distributors to inform the libraries about the availability of such material and there must be mirror sites in the country for easily accessing these information. There are not any attempts in the country for leasing and accessing ebooks, which must be pursued as a major resource pool for the traders in the coming years.

9.5.4. Smart Warehousing

Instead of luring libraries to buy whatever they stock, the traders should move on to the practice of arranging to supply whatever libraries demand. They have to adhere to the practices of smart warehousing followed by computer makers like DELL.

9.5.5. Sponsored Studies

Each distributor should donate a percentage of their profit to the Federation to sponsor studies by a team comprising representatives from the trade, library profession and policy makers on importing, marketing, and trading books, ebook distribution, information needs of libraries, etc.

9.5.6. Public Library

To save their warehouse space, the trade can think of donating old, remaindered, and books in poor demand to the public libraries of the country.

9.5.7. Archiving and Digitization

Either through few important libraries or under the aegis of the federation, copyright free books may be digitized to ensure archiving and to preserve the country's cultural heritage.

9.5.8. Remaindered Books

Remainder books accounted for some 40 per cent of the total book imports by India of Rs. 1,200 crore [4]. If the trade community is sensible, they may not bother to import remaindered books, but try to collect the requisitions of individual libraries and procure only such books. This may in turn vouch for the quality of foreign books available in the country.

9.5.9. Photocopying

The large scale photocopying of books, if present, are not happening at the behest of libraries. Such cases to a large extent for textbooks can be prevented effectively by making these books available at affordable rates.

9.5.10. Portals

It is high time for the Government and Libraries to make necessary changes in their purchase procedures to ensure speedy receipt of latest books through portals like Amazon.com. There are some small startups in this area in the country too. It is up to the book trade to devise similar portals for Indian books and foreign books with options to pay after the receipt of books. Variable discounts and fast supply could be achieved through web enabled ordering and supply of books.

9.5.11. Shipping Region

Since Dollar is more stable to rupee, it has been observed that publishers and their allies would like to quote prices in Pound and Euro even for books published in USA by citing shipping region decided by publisher or that they imported the books through UK or other European countries. Librarians are familiar with the recent practice of selling books from CRC Press, USA and Taylor & Francis, USA in Pound in the country. Traders and GOC can work for countering such practices by liaising with their counterparts and publishers abroad insisting for pricing books in the currency of the country in which the book is published.

9.6. STEPS FOR POSSIBLE IMPROVEMENT OF BOOK PURCHASE OPERATIONS

9.6.1. Difficulties to buy book from publishers

Some publishers insist to deal through their agents. Many publishers work in a hierarchical manner through sales/information offices, agents, distributors, and suppliers. Generally the agents/importers/distributors import books from the publishers and want the libraries to procure the books from suppliers/book sellers. Even if a library attempts to break this chain, it may not get high discount since the distributor may not offer higher discount than the seller and may not give the same discount to the library what they offer to the bookseller.

Some publishers may accept orders directly, but in the case of international publishers, the library has to arrange for customs 'duty exemption certificate' or arrange for paying duties. This may turn out to be costly and needs interaction with customs departments and clearing agents, which may further delay the purchase process and take more time of professional staff in administrative matters. In some cases, for such direct orders with publishers, sometimes the library may not get any discount.

9.6.2. Possible to purchase from Direct importers

Most suppliers used to source books from importers at higher discount. However, it is not known whether the importers offer the same discount to a library, when placing orders directly with them. Perhaps the libraries can initiate a dialogue with some importers to assess the possibilities of working with them and explore the possibilities of the prevailing over the library-unfriendly book trade and breaking its unhealthy hierarchy.

9.6.3. Supplier Evaluation

Evaluation of suppliers must be very much required especially when GFR suggests to deal with "reputed and standard book sellers" and leaving this matter to trade bodies alone will not do much benefit to libraries. As is common in quality circles, the best way to assess the performance is through the users of the service and hence libraries and librarians are more competent to objectively evaluate the performance of book suppliers. Though many libraries are doing this at a confidential level, results of such studies are not disclosed to avoid hampering business interests of suppliers. However, library associations may take necessary steps to shortlist at least problematic suppliers and spread the warning message to those with doubtful motives. The trade bodies must also respond positively to such evaluation and take appropriate action to expel problematic suppliers from their membership. Another feature rampant in the trade is to float more than one company by one person and care should be taken that a closed firm will not be resurrected in another name with the same set of persons in the vanguard.

Over the years, any library has certain authorized suppliers and there are always enthusiastic new suppliers who want to enroll as a registered supplier and different libraries follow different procedures for registering suppliers. In most cases, a library normally looks for the supplier's standing in the field, other clients and may be their feedback, publishers represented, infrastructure etc., before enrolling a new supplier. It is in the interest of libraries in the emerging trade scenario to always keep the number of suppliers to a sizeable number and to continuously evaluate their performance and by keeping the list as dynamic and functional as possible by constantly avoiding non-performing suppliers and adding new ones with good track record. Thus libraries should conduct performance evaluation of suppliers of books with respect to the time involved in supply, prices quoted, copies supplied in good condition, fastness in responding to various queries, etc., which will help in identifying good suppliers and avoiding bad suppliers. All new suppliers get registered must be kept on probation for a period of one year to evaluate their performance before enrolling them as registered suppliers. The evaluation must be pursued, if not continuous, at least as an annual event to keep an always-active supplier list. The supplier should realize that library is not a charity and libraries must expect quick, efficient, and effective services with good deals.

9.6.4. Prices

In many cases, libraries consider the price of the book at the request/order stage only as an approximation to assess the budget availability. The actual price of the book will be checked at the time of supply with publisher's prices. The correct price of the book can be decided only from the publisher's sources. This was done earlier with the help of publisher's catalogue or publisher's invoice to importers/suppliers. Though prices of online bookstores like Amazon, Baranesandnoble differ from the publisher's price; our experience shows that many of the publishers display the correct price on their site. Their sites also contain special offer prices for pre-publication, seasonal discount, etc. One way to resolve price problems quickly and in accepting ordered books in a faster manner is by considering the price information on the publisher site as the authentic price. However, there is a catch here also. Not only international, now even many Indian publishers do not display the price of the book in the book and the price may be assessed from the publicity material such as catalogues, brochures, price lists, web site, etc. Many publishers are of the habit of revising their prices monthly, quarterly, semi-annually or annually to recover a part of their warehouse and operating costs. This may sometimes help distributors and suppliers to claim higher price for a book sourced at the lesser price by providing a copy of the revised price list from the publisher. This practice is also possible with proof of price as copies of purchase/import invoices from the Publisher. Trade parties always express difficulties to submit originals of such invoices. Perhaps Publishers must mark copy number in all books and print this number in their purchase invoices to eliminate any exploitation of one invoice for multiple deals by distributors/sellers/ suppliers. It is difficult to eliminate such bad trade practices, but can be prevented to some extent by always insisting for import invoice from the publisher. This may also help to weed out books brought to the country through bad trade channels without proper import documents. Another way to eliminate the burden of price revisions in between requisition, order and supply stages is by entering into a contract with the supplier, taking the publisher price at the time of ordering as authentic and issue the orders with a condition that 'no further increase of the price acceptable hereafter'. But the library will be a loser in few cases where the publisher reduces the price of a book due to the unpopularity or overpricing of a particular title. Being social service institutions and as active partners in the scholarly information communication, it is not that difficult to involve suppliers as partners in this pious role of libraries by taking them into confidence and asking them to work in 'no more price increases in between but reductions always welcome' approach.

9.6.5. Difficulty of collecting quotations for Book Purchase

It would be difficult each time to call for quotations in the case of purchasing books, due to the specific features of book purchase (there can be only one book with a particular title on a specific subject by a particular author published (edition) in a particular year by a specific publisher), the large volume of purchase spread over an year in many libraries and library being more a professional service institution rather than an administrative stores department. Calling for quotations and other administrative hassles involved may further delay the already delayed process (due to the peculiar problems of book trade involving publishers, importers, and suppliers, many of them still following the sea mail and cheaper shipping options due to profit motives, and the availability or not of a particular title at the time of ordering) of book procurement. Since there are more books than publishers, one way to realize at least partially the 'virtues' of quotation system in book purchase is by seeking discount rates for each and every publisher (since there are many publishers, the pragmatic approach must be to identify the major publishers of interest to a library) from the registered suppliers and by placing order for books from a particular publisher to the supplier who quoted the maximum discount and the least time for supply for that publisher. Books from new publishers and those who are not frequent may be ordered by negotiating with all or best suppliers on a case to case basis.

9.6.6. E-negotiation System

With advances in computer and information technology and its increased applications in library and information work, it is not difficult to develop an e-negotiation system to electronically call for 'offer price' and 'supply time' from different suppliers for identifying the best supplier for a specific book. There is no doubt that the system will be faster than a manual quotation collection system as electronic communication using email and web access that are more fast and efficient will be used for its working. However, the system should build enough security measures to prevent a supplier from seeing offers from other suppliers.

9.6.7. Purchases from Online stores

Online stores and web portals offer special deals for some titles for a specific period. There are also 'combined' deals like special offers and discount prices for procuring a group of titles. Depending on the need and interests of a particular library, if not as a regular feature, once in a while these offers may be tried and converted to the advantage of library by procuring few books through this mode. This requires the library to get a credit card for international money transactions and by reserving a portion of their budget for purchases through credit card.

9.6.8. Book selection and purchase committees

Book selection role is now in the hands of researchers, teachers and users in many institutions and in many places there are committees to advice the library professionals in book selection, screening and purchase. Such committees may in place of/in addition to examine requisitions and deciding upon individual purchases should instead take up the crucial responsibilities of: supplier evaluation and interviewing, possibilities of dealing with importers, arriving at better discount rates for books from important publishers, and any other policy and operational matter concerning book purchases.

9.6.9. Releasing the Purchase Order from Purchase Section

There are not many studies on this aspect of book purchase in the country due to the difficulty in collecting reliable data from many institutions and libraries. There are two models in operation to name; one is the popular and predominant practice of purchase through the library and another through the purchase section of the institution, especially in the case of small libraries. The effectiveness of either and their relative merits are not known. It is not possible to avoid the library in the second case also as the library basically receives requisitions for books and do the background job for ordering and is the final receiver of books. Like the responsibility of selecting books being taken from library professionals in many institutions, removing the purchase responsibility may further erode the morale and importance of the library staff. As library professionals are trained in the intricacies of book purchase, just because book is not a commodity procured in stores, entrusting the task of purchasing with the library professionals instill in them the importance of their role, ensure smooth follow-up of pending orders, and avoid the time delay in releasing orders and any other issues that may crop-up from sharing this responsibility with administrative units.

9.6.10. Electronic information and digital sources

Though the traders are very good in dealing with printed books and journals, many are averse to the idea of providing electronic products to the benefit of libraries and their users. There are very few members in the trade who are actually comfortable and conversant with and are attuned with the desired infrastructure and expertise in disseminating information concerning and in distributing digital sources. As enabling electronic information will have an increased presence in the coming years, the trade associations and their members must undergo drastic changes in their mode of working with predominantly printed sources to exploit the digital virtues for the benefit of libraries.

9.7. CONCLUSION

Why only the book suppliers need protection when all other trade suffers stiff international competition in the wake of trade reforms in the country after the establishment of WTO in the era of globalization. It is not through protecting mediocre local trade and industry that we are going to excel and become a developed country in the future but by creating an environment in which the local players understand the pulse of the world market and thereby improving their products, processes and services to face the aggressive competition. The traders need libraries for their business and libraries need traders to procure their books. Apart from this, the libraries have time tested skills in storage, preservation and dissemination of information from a wide variety of sources. Since the archiving of the country's publishing output is not conducted in an organized manner either by the trade associations or by individual publishers and is now restricted (?) to the handful of 'Depository libraries', there should be enough space for both these parties to work for the preservation of intellectual as well as information heritage of the country. Only with a strong information repository, education and research in the country would excel and this requires augmentation and availability of important books in all areas of knowledge through fruitful interaction and dealings by book trade and libraries. Fixing exchange rates of foreign currencies are minor issues and has to be abandoned for larger issues concerning information production, publishing, and knowledge advancement and even to fight for the cause of country against converting it as a free and silent market for continuous exploitation by foreign publishers.

REFERENCES

1. Deshpande, K. S., The librarian, the book trade and collection development: random reflections, Library Science with a Slant to Documentation and Information Studies, 36 (4) Dec 1999, pp.249-56.
2. FPBAI, The Federation of Publishers & Booksellers Associations in India, http://www.fpbai.org
3. Kumar, P S G, Indian Library Chronology, Mumbai: Allied, 2nd ed., 2000, p. 679.
4. Padmanabhan, Mohan, Awareness campaign launched to tackle book piracy, plagiarism, http://www.thehindubusinessline.com/bline/2002/08/10/stories/2002081002 500200.htm
5. Samuel T., Booking the book importers, Herald of Library Science, 30 (3-4) Jul-Oct 91, pp. 232-4.

PART 3: IT ENABLING

10
IT enabling Public Libraries

10.0. INTRODUCTION

The UNESCO Public Library Manifesto defines the public library as "the local gateway to knowledge, provides a basic condition for lifelong learning, independent decision- making and cultural development of the individual and social groups" [1]. It also emphasized that the public library services should be formulated with certain objectives that relate to information, literacy, education and culture in mind [1]:

* creating and strengthening reading habits in children from an early age;
* supporting both individual and self conducted education as well as formal education at all levels;
* providing opportunities for personal creative development;
* stimulating the imagination and creativity of children and young people;
* promoting awareness of cultural heritage, appreciation of the arts, scientific achievements and innovations;
* providing access to cultural expressions of all performing arts;
* fostering inter-cultural dialogue and favouring cultural diversity;

* supporting the oral tradition;
* ensuring access for citizens to all sorts of community information;
* providing adequate information services to local enterprises, associations and interest groups;
* facilitating the development of information and computer literacy skills;
* supporting and participating in literacy activities and programmes for all age groups, and initiating such activities if necessary

Ranganathan formulated an integrated five-tier public library system comprising primary service library, secondary service library (city central and district central libraries), tertiary service library (state central library), national library and the futuristic world grid of public libraries [6]. This largely acted as the guiding principle in evolving public library system in the country. Depending on whether the Public Library Act is in vogue and based on the interests of the State Government or the level of public movement behind this cause, there may be variations between different states on the penetration and services of public library network. Some of the predominant services offered by our public libraries to the community are lending out collection of light reading and fiction, reading room facility of newspapers and popular magazines, as a distribution network for government information like gazettes. Some of them also hold reference collection and engage in reference services. The problems and constraints faced by the public library system to effectively disseminate information are manifold in the country, essentially as a result of:

* A considerable percentage of the population is illiterate or functionally literate forcing library to be of minimal use to them
* Poor allocation for the infrastructure improvement and collection development for public libraries
* Lack of enough sanctioned posts, forcing most of the

services to be operated by voluntary non-professional staff, causing sufficient deterioration on information organisation and servicing

* There is also a problem of educated professionals preferring to work in special and academic libraries than public libraries
* Little emphasis on adoption Information Technology for public library systems and services

Being a State responsibility as per the Constitution, states are vested with the mandate to set up public libraries at different levels. The state governments have departments/directorates/ councils of public libraries to start, maintain and operate public libraries under its jurisdiction. But due to the difference in the level of state-wise development, the Department of Culture, Government of India has set up Raja Rammohun Roy Library Foundation (RRRLF) to act as a nodal agency for development of public libraries in India. Since all the States have not passed the requisite library legislation, RRRLF is working towards a model Public Library Bill. The RRRLF has also been given the responsibility of resource mobilization for modernisation of the state and district central libraries, the development of infrastructure and training of personnel [9]. Public libraries are considered more as entertaining institutions and the collection predominantly in book form meant for light reading, caused the absence of any concrete mechanisms for either automating them or networking them. 'Reach' refers to the physical or geographic areas to which service is provided that is a function of the communications components of an information system and 'range' stands for the types of services available once connectivity is provided [5]. This paper will explore the possibility of considering IT as a valuable cost-effective tool for spreading, improving and enlarging public library systems and services.

10.1. HOW BIG IS OUR PUBLIC LIBRARY SYSTEM?

It has been difficult to collect authorised statistics on public libraries in the country, as the same happens to be under the purview of different agencies that never disclose such information on a national scale for various reasons. So we are forced to depend on published ones which are unfortunately quite dated. Sen put the number of libraries in the country as 5400 in 1951 [11]. IASLIC's old directory put the number of special and research libraries as 173 [12] whereas BLA estimated around 3980 libraries in the sate of West Bengal only [13]. The country presently comprises of 28 states, 6 union territories and the national capital region, which together account for approximately 550 districts. The number of inhabited villages in the country is around 568558 [14]. These figures force us to estimate the number of public libraries to be more than a lakh and there is no doubt to imagine the difficulties of facilitating information and library support to the mass of over a billion population, spread over 32 lakhs sq. km.

10.1.1. Constraints for Public Library Services

Gardner estimated the use patterns of the Central Library of Delhi Public Library and found that 28.89% of the users have less than 16 years of age, 26.67% in between 17-20 years, 30.35% around 21-29 years, 9.65% about 30-45 years and only 2.47% have above 45 years. The educational attributes are 21.27% users primary, 18.36% middle school, 28.59% matriculation, 10.54% intermediate, 10.14% graduate, 1.81% post graduate and 2.05% professionals. Out of these only 31.28% of the users reside farther than 1.5 miles from the library [15]. The constraints that are significant are the ones suggested by the World Information Report, 1997-98, quoted by Dasgupta [10]:

* The bulk of the population is not information-dependent in day-to-day work and living.
* A large proportion of the population cannot consume information in written form.
* The vast majority of the population does not have the means to access information.
* People in general are not accustomed to pay, cannot pay or are unwilling to pay for information as it does not figure in their list of wants.

* The existing pattern of economic activities does not favour a growth in information consumption.
* The countries do not have sufficient capacity to invest in infrastructure development

The second point raises enough justification for the necessity of information in non-written forms like audio, video, and multimedia. The advent of computer and information technology has yielded the availability of all these forms into one computer amenable form. Perhaps that is the reason why we should explore the adoption of these new technologies for delivering public library services to a large mass of illiterate and semiliterate populace, apart from improving the services presently provided to the reading public.

10.2. IT APPLICATIONS IN LIBRARIES: NATIONAL STATUS

The special, research and academic libraries attached to premier institutions were the forerunners of adopting computer and communication technology (or information technology (IT)) for revamping library administration and services in the country. It is almost a decade since the spread of such activities on a large scale, concentrating essentially on three counts. The primary interest is in computerising the routine house keeping aspects of library work like acquisition and processing of reading materials, and their lending to clients. Similarly the specialised journals generally bought at an exorbitant price are properly managed with the help of programs termed as library automation packages. Such packages are now available not only from private firms (for ex. TLMS, LibSys, Librarian, PALMS, etc.,) but also from not-for-profit institutions (for ex. SOUL, Sanjay, CDS/ISIS, etc.,) at affordable prices with pick and choose options. The electronic delivery of information promoted the arrival of online information hosts (which unfortunately have not made the desired impact as they are expensive and due to telecommunication problems and charges) and CD-ROM databases. Secondary databases and reference books were disseminated predominantly in CD-ROM forced a large number of libraries to subscribe and service them.

Some libraries made their frequently used CD-ROM databases available on the local network with the help of CD Towers, juke boxes or software tailor made to copy CD data into high capacity hard disc servers. The last five years has been significant for IT services in the country as a result of the spread of Internet and web culture for all areas of human endeavour and librarians were next to none in exploiting the virtues of net for information processing and servicing. The net with its enormous information contents provided the first landing point for reference librarians whenever they have a query not answerable with the local resources. Primary publishers force libraries to receive web editions of journals and other information sources, as an alternative or supplement of print subscriptions. Creating web sites and keeping Online Public Access Catalogues (OPACs) accessible through the site facilitated efficient networking of libraries and resource sharing among them. Though the networking of libraries like CALIBNET (Kolkata), DELNET (Delhi), networks in few other cities, INFLIBNET (national and educational) and other means of resource sharing like Inter Library Loan (ILL) started before the spread of Internet, the net fastened meeting most of the objectives with its vital tools and techniques. The special, research and academic libraries were forced to migrate to new technology initiatives for the following reasons:

* Retrieval of subject based information has become very crucial and the manual means of handling the constantly growing collection found more demanding on time and other resources
* Cost Vs allocation gap forced many libraries to cut subscriptions and acquisitions demanding them to network and collaborate
* Electronic information preferred over print due to the widely competing work environment and ease of use

10.3. IT INTRINSIC PUBLIC LIBRARY SERVICES

Hennen's American Public Library Ratings (HAPLR) consider the following 15 attributes with different weighted measures: expenditure per capita – 3, percent budget to materials – 2, materials expenditure per capita – 2, full time employed (FTE) staff per 1,000 population – 2, periodicals per 1000 residents – 1, volumes per capita – 1, cost per circulation (low to high) – 3, visits per capita – 3, collection turnover – 2, circulation per FTE Staff Hour – 2, circulation per capita – 2, reference per capita – 2, circulation per hour – 2, visits per hour – 1, circulation per visit – 1. Internet, electronic services and audiovisual services are excluded because there is simply not enough data from enough libraries for meaningful comparison [17]. By May 1998, approximately 86% of public libraries in U.S. will have an Internet connection (of varying speeds from 28.8 kbps (kilo bits per second) to 1.54 Mbps), which serve approximately 97% of the population with an average annual expenditure of $32,104 [16]. In April-June 1991, John Smith conducted a survey on the state of networking in UK Public Libraries, and 99 out of 167 replied of which 92 used computers or some form of information technology and 51 used CD-ROMs. Of the 70 that used a mini or mainframe computer used it for cataloguing (67) or issue systems (64) and over half (37) used it for OPAC. 24 claimed to use a Local Area Network (LAN) and three respondents claimed use of a private Wide Area Network (WAN). Of the 50 where the local authority had a WAN only 37 made use of it for access to financial information (18), mainframe access (12), and general intersite communication (11). Although there were a wide range of modem speeds indicated two preferred ones were 1200/2400 and 9600. A very high fraction (81) had access to a Fax machine, 53 were using electronic mail, and over half (49) of the respondents indicated they had definite plans for introducing new telecommunications or networking in the next few years [18].

Internet connectivity can be achieved in three ways viz., low-speed (2400 bps – 28.8 kbps) dial-up access using a modem through an ordinary phone line, Integrated Services Digital Network (ISDN) high-speed dial access with 128 kbps data transfer rates, and leased access with leased point-to-point circuits connecting the user with the Internet provider's network. Three services associated with dial-up access are [5]:

* Terminal Access (VT-100 shell account): Accesses a vendor-provided host computer connected to the Internet. As the protocol TCP/IP stops at the host, the terminal will not be able to use graphical browsers such as Netscape or Explorer but can use the Web through text-based browsers like Lynx and can also use electronic mail, telnet, and ftp.
* Workstation SLIP (Serial Line Internet Protocol) or PPP (Point to Point Protocol) Access: Allows to use graphical Internet tools such as packet video teleconferencing and multimedia access to the WWW.
* Internet Gateway Access: Some commercial on-line services like America Online offer users a graphical interface in front of a terminal connection to the Internet. Thus packet video and other applications requiring TCP/IP will not work in this configuration.

In contrast to dial-up access, leased line connectivity will always include TCP/IP, facilitating library to run sophisticated software, access packet video, and execute Web enabled services [5]. Depending on the resources and infrastructure of library, there can be two levels of Internet involvement [5]:

* Internet Access: How the library will be connected to/can access the Internet. Costs include the purchase of workstations/terminals, modems/cabling/e-mail accounts, monthly access fees, and telecommunications charges.
* Internet Service: Internet services like setting up Web servers, preparing and making available library-specific resources such as local databases and images on the Internet. Costs include that for research and development, staff, and technology in support of such services.

10.3.1. Saga of American Center and British Council

Though on a limited scale, the country can boast of the

presence of few libraries practicing state of the art public library work, two such institutions that are operating on the national level being the American Center and British Council. The American Information Resource Centers (AIRCs) provide information about the United States, its people, and its policies to promote mutual understanding, culture and information exchange with India. These libraries (located in Calcutta, Chennai, Mumbai, and New Delhi) are open to people from all walks of life for reference, research and borrowing facilities. Generally, four types of memberships: individual, temporary, distance (for people residing in adjoining areas where the library is located), and institutional are offered. The collections consist of multidisciplinary American books, journals and reference materials, U.S. government publications, and think tank reports. The four libraries together have a collection of about 82,721 books, 586 print periodicals with over a 1,000 journals in electronic format, 2,425 videocassettes, and subscriptions to a few leading American newspapers. Apart from print, information is available in several electronic formats like, CD-ROMs, online databases and Internet-based databases; and reference queries are answered through telephone, fax, mail, or e-mail. The OPAC allows sharing resources amongst the four libraries. Several commercial and government online services such as, Dialog (over 500 databases), OCLC First Search (more than 55 databases), ProQuest Direct (over 400 full-text periodicals and bibliographic data for about 1600 periodicals and newspapers) etc., are being used for value-added information access [7].

The British Council is Britain's international network for education, science and technology, culture and development services by harnessing information and knowledge initiatives, industries and networks for mutual benefit. It also aims to promote information about the UK to other countries on the core subject areas of education, English language teaching, arts, science, governance and civil society. The British Council operates in the country a network of thirteen libraries (in Ahmedabad, Bangalore, Bhopal, Chandigarh, Chennai,

Hyderabad, Kolkata, Lucknow, Mumbai, New Delhi, Patna, Pune, and Thiruvananthapuram), which is the Council's largest operation in the world and run jointly with the Indian Council for Cultural Relations (ICCR). These libraries provide access to British information and culture to a large body of professionals and students. Besides books, journals and training videos, most of the libraries also stock children's books, home videos and electronic information resources like CD-ROMs, multimedia and on-line subscriptions. Some of the important services offered include, lending books/journals/videos, reference, information about Britain, Internet access, indev (Development Network for NGOs), BLDSC International Book Loan, educational counselling, information about British examinations, book promotion, business Information Centre, proactive information to opinion formers and decision makers, photocopying, library orientations, video screenings, interlibrary loans, renewal of items over the telephone/e-mail, programmes for members and children, sale of withdrawn books, electronic 'Current Awareness Service', and Internet awareness programme for members. Most of these libraries work from 11 AM to 7 PM and possess variable number of collection (only one has over 60000, five of them with about 30000, three with approximately 25000, and the remaining in between 6000-15000) [8].

The American Center and British Council libraries falling in the genre of public libraries in the country would be able to provide such distinctive services as a result of:

* Assimilation of the state of the art practices and technology for information work
* Result oriented and service driven management
* Their clientele, being the upper crust of the Indian society who are able to pay slightly higher service charges and more responsive to access the sophisticated facilities
* Continuous weeding out of collection (though the total collection being small) ensures relevance and higher use rate

* Better pay and service conditions lure the best professionals in India to work for them

10.4. PRAGMATIC APPLICATION OF IT FOR PUBLIC LIBRARY WORK

The Department of Culture through the Central Secretariat Library (CSL) has laid down standards for library development software and networking as well as for bibliographic description to ensure standardization both in infrastructural development as well as retro-conversion of library catalogue in machine-readable format [9]. Similar exercises were also conducted by several library networks mentioned earlier, and perhaps the public library movement can seriously think of accepting one or many such systems for their in-house data management. The onus of creating and maintaining databases can be assigned first to the vast spectrum of public libraries, may be first up to taluka level and later on can be passed on to all the individual libraries depending on the penetration of technology and staff expertise to them. Since the collection and other resources are duplicating, data management at any level will not be a problem, if efforts will be put on formulating guidelines on authority control and data validation. May be all libraries in one taluka can host the same union catalogue with proper identification of the individual holdings guiding even the user of a title demanded in the near proximity. CD-ROM titles in Indian languages have not picked up the desired number, barring few attempts on tourist and business information [2], but there exists chances for such procurement for international reference sources like dictionaries, encyclopaedias, etc. During the television boom, there was a programme to provide public libraries with TV sets to disseminate government information with entertainment. It can be thought of in this computer crazy time, to provide public libraries with multimedia PCs. Significant attempts are underway to improve the telephone density in the country and it is a good deed to provide telephones in public libraries. Not only these phones act as community telephones where such provisions lack; they can also be used for dial-up Internet connection. There are also certain untapped networks, which can be explored for public library networking like the satellite based network of National Informatics Centre (NIC) which connects all the districts, network of Videsh Sanchar Nigam Limited (VSNL), and those of private Internet Service Providers (ISPs) like Satyam. RRRLF is having matching grant schemes for "assistance to state, central and district Libraries to acquire TV-cum-VCR sets and cassettes for educational purposes, and assistance to libraries below the district level for increasing accommodation" [3]. Some of these schemes could be extended or modified to frame similar schemes for computer and communications infrastructure in public libraries. In 1998-99, our country exported $2.6 billion or Rs. 10940 crores of IT software and services to 91 countries.... IT industry has a potential of providing 2 million jobs and $50 billion in the next 10 years [4]. There is no doubt about the constructive work, assistance and support this industry can offer in wiring our public libraries to systematically upgrade the literacy, information consumption of a large chunk of the population, especially in rural and semi-urban areas. Some of the sate governments like Andhra Pradesh, Tamil Nadu, Karnataka, Maharashtra, etc. are pursuing an enthusiastic agenda towards migrating to e-governance and making the administration and welfare measures more open, deep and transparent. Public libraries restructured as network kiosks to deliver and access a whole lot of information facilities and support services can go a long way in reassuring such initiatives.

The approximate cost elements incurred to set up some of the IT based facilities in the public library system include:

A Local Library

A1 Non-Recurring

* **Hardware:** Mutimedia PCs @ Rs. 35000 (The number of PCs to be bought required must be based on the population served by the library. But it should be nothing less than at least one for 10 users visiting the library at one point of time. 2-3 for the village library, 10 for the

Taluk library, 20-30 or a mini server with enough terminals for the district and state libraries is a safe bet to begin with.) @ Rs 105000

* **Communications Hardware:** Telephone connection and Modem @ Rs. 10000
* Training and Education for library staff/volunteers @ Rs. 10000

A2 Recurring

* Communication and Internet Access Fees @ Rs. 25000 per annum
* Facilities Upgrades and Maintenance @ Rs. 25000 per annum

Total for one Local Library for both recurring and nonrecurring: Rs. 175000

Total for approximately one lakh Local Library for both recurring and nonrecurring:

Rs. 1750 crores

B Taluka Library

B1 Non-Recurring

* Hardware: Mutimedia PCs @ Rs. 35000 (The number of PCs to be bought required must be based on the population served by the library. But it should be nothing less than at least one for 10 users visiting the library at one point of time. 2-3 for the village library, 10 for the Taluk library, 20-30 or a mini server with enough terminals for the district and state libraries is a safe bet to begin with.) @ Rs 350000
* Library Automation and other Software @ Rs. 50000 (this may be required only up to District/Taluk level)
* Communications Hardware: Telephone connection and Modem @ Rs. 20000
* Training and Education for library staff/volunteers @ Rs. 20000

B2 Recurring

* Communication and Internet Access Fees @ Rs. 40000 per annum
* Facilities Upgrades and Maintenance @ Rs. 40000 per annum

Total for Taluka Library for both recurring and nonrecurring: Rs. 420000

Total for approximately 5000 Taluk Library for both recurring and nonrecurring:

Rs. 210 crores

C District Library

Similarly by considering 2-3 times increase for the District Library, total for both recurring and nonrecurring: Rs. 840000 to Rs. 1260000

Total for approximately 550 District Library for both recurring and nonrecurring:

Rs. 70 crores

D State Library

Similarly by considering 2-3 times increase for the State Library, total for both recurring and nonrecurring: Rs. 2-4 crores

Total for the state libraries: Rs. (29X4 + 6X2)= Rs. 123 crores

D 1 Special Expenses needed at the State level:

* **Content and Resource Development:** State level digital information facilities can be formulated in phases by derived from copyright free/copyright paid contents reflecting the literature, culture, educational and government information pertaining to the state. Since this will be a continuous process, considerable resources need to be spent and earmarking few crores of rupees at the state level from government's concerned departments might be a good beginning (@Rs. 10 crores by each state, Rs. 2 crores by each union territory, Total @ Rs. 302 crores).

* **Program Planning, Management, and Staffing:** Recruitment of specialists well versed in information and communication is required to efficiently administer and ably pursue IT enabled public library system and services. Such personnel can be recruited in the entry level officer grade of state @ Rs. 1.5 -2 lakhs, up to district level forcing them to supervise the operations to certain viable decentralised mode (Total @ Rs. 11 Crores).

  Total for all in A, B, C & D: Rs. 2466 Crores

Since the exact number of libraries in different levels is not known, the amount assessed may be arbitrary, as it has been difficult to cumulate the expenses for the required number. Considering the bulk of resources the central, state and local governments used to spend for social welfare, education, health and family welfare, resources can be easily mobilised to spend on these lines.

10.5. CONCLUSION

Information, Communication and Entertainment (ICE) and convergence are the buzzwords in computer, communications and information technology nowadays. Since public libraries being the nerve centres for spreading sociocultural information that can be used for improving the quality of life, much needs to be done in restructuring the programmes and plans for upgrading the public library system in the country. Our public libraries can be turned to better public libraries if they examine the management, staffing, and performance of special libraries in the country and libraries run by the British council and American Center. Some of these objectives can be better realised if bodies like RRRLF can commission some software development firms and network providers to evolve an action plan to improve the range of public library services and reach of public library system using such a cost effective tool as IT to enable the information age in the country.

REFERENCES

1. UNESCO Public Library Manifesto, www.ifla.org/documents/libraries/policies/ unesco.htm
2. Arun Kumar Chakraborty, Publishing on CD-ROM: Indian Potential, Desidoc Bulletin of Information Technology, 15 (7), Sept 1997, pp. 23-30.
3. Raja Rammohan Roy Library Foundation, Calcutta, http://216.87.26.241/en/org/ raja%20 ram.htm
4. Dewang Mehta, Software Policy: The New Mantra, The Hindu Survey of Indian Industry 1999, Chennai, Kasturi & Sons, January 2000, pp. 321-323.
5. Charles R. McClure et al., Internet Costs and Cost Models for Public Libraries: Final Report, http://istweb.syr.edu/~mcclure/nclis/FinalReport.html
6. S R Ranganathan, Integrated Public Library System, pp. 208-212, in Public Library System, ed. by S R Ranganathan and A Neelameghan.
7. http://americanlibrary.in.library.net
8. http://www.britishcouncil.org/india/
9. Kalpana Dasgupta, Libraries and librarians in India on the threshold of the 3rd millennium: challenges and risks, 66th IFLA Council and General Conference, Jerusalem, Israel, 13-18 August, http://www.ifla.org/IV/ifla66/papers/039-120e.htm
10. World Information Report 1997/98, Paris: UNESCO, 1997.
11. N B Sen (ed.), Indian Book Trade and Library Directory 1950-51, Delhi, New Book Society of India.
12. IASLIC, Directory of Special and Research Libraries in India, Calcutta, IASLIC, 1962.
13. Bengal Library Association, West Bengal Library Directory, Calcutta, BLA, 1963.
14. Manorama Year Book 1999, Kottayam, Malayala Manorama, p. 635.
15. Frank M. Gardner, The Delhi Public Library: An

Evaluation Report, Zurich, UNESCO, 1957, pp. 26-29.

16. John Carlo Bertot et al, The 1997 National Survey of U.S. Public Libraries and the Internet: Final Report, www.research.umbc.edu/~bertot/ala97.html
17. Thomas J. Hennen Jr., Hennen's American Public Library Ratings (HAPLR), www.haplr-index.com/rating_methods.htm
18. John Smith, Summary of Public Libraries Survey, 1991, www.ukoln.ac.uk/services/ ukoln/smith-1999-01.

11
Information Oriented Rural Development

11.0. INTRODUCTION

Since a large percentage of our population lives in villages and hence these villages are to be developed as the overall progress of the nation depends to a large extent on the welfare of the rural areas and its people. Thus rural development is one of the aggressively pursued activities of the central and state Governments and NGOs and a major concern for development experts as half a century of planned development still fails to make a constructive change in our rural areas. The prevailing rural scenario is characterized by unemployment, migration of population, social and environmental degradation in rural mass, illiteracy and lack of health awareness, non-compatibility in agricultural, environmental, and macroeconomic policy and absence of appropriate planning in management of land resources [1]. Majority of these problems can be resolved only by programmes and action plans supported by motivated local people, performing and conscious government agencies and dynamic NGOs. The parameters that are to be integrated for rural development are rural population; social milieu; production, conservation and appropriate utilization of human and natural resources; rural environment upkeep; equality and solidarity; agricultural perspectives; state of art of the existing rural economy vis-à-vis its development; available technology and possibility of developing indigenous technology without dependence on high-technology transfer; ethical mindset for pursuing development policy with scientific temper; application of the concept of networking [1]. Therefore rural development requires tremendous extent of money and labour and the very little resources available can only be optimized by judicious application of technology and information. There are also concerns that very little portion of the budget earmarked reaching the target population due to the flawed development policies aided by the prevailing implementation mechanism. The prevailing rural development scenario has very limited scope for the participation of information professionals and this can be easily changed by strengthening the existing public and school library system so that there should be more consolidation of information that is lost in the present broadcasting model, especially with the aid of rural digital libraries and digital library for rural development.

11.1. INFORMATION FOR RURAL DEVELOPMENT

11.1.1. Types, Sources and Channels of Information

Rural development requires a variable mix of information generated by government, media, NGOs, rural development practitioners and experts, oral and written indigenous rural knowledge passed on to generations through largely informal means, statistical information, implementation data from previous projects and schemes, etc. The sources include published and unpublished, formal and informal, print and non-print etc. The significant constraints of facilitating information to rural people, according to the World Information Report, 1997-98, quoted by Dasgupta [2] are:

* The bulk of the population is not information-dependent in day-to-day work and living.
* A large proportion of the population cannot consume information in written form.
* The vast majority of the population does not have the means to access information.

* People in general are not accustomed to pay, cannot pay or are unwilling to pay for information as it does not figure in their list of wants.
* The existing pattern of economic activities does not favour a growth in information consumption.
* The countries do not have sufficient capacity to invest in infrastructure development

The second constraint raises enough justification (in a society with over 45% are illiterate) for the necessity of information in non-written forms like audio, video, and multimedia. The advent of computer and information technology has yielded the availability of all these divergent forms into one computer amenable format. The coverage of subject matter must be of easy assimilation to people with less education and poor knowledge in the subject concerned.

11.1.2. Impediments for accessing information

The major impediments of rural population with respect to accessing the information resources are:

* **Information Drought:** Lack of availability of information resources in their level and style of interest
* **Literacy:** Literacy rate and educational background are poor.
* **Time:** They are so busy with household and livelihood, so that they don't get time for entertainment, reading, or accessing information.
* **Language:** There are many languages and even in one place more than one language is spoken. More over, the information required might not be available in the language in which one is proficient. We need good translation mechanisms to get over this problem.
* **Culture:** Due to the prevailing mindset and cultural barriers, rural people are unable to seek and gather information for their livelihood unlike their counterparts in urban areas. The situation will be more volatile in the case of those termed inferior in caste and creed,

minorities, women and children.

* **Bad shape of public libraries and their alienation from the development model:** Developing countries would have progressed more, if they had the means to supplement the broadcasting oriented development paradigm to a broadcasting plus library centred community information dissemination mechanism and resources to transform their public libraries at least to the level of infrastructure prevailing in their research and higher education libraries.
* **Poor use of ICT:** Infrastructure limitations prevent the required information to reach the needy. Cable, television are not used to the desired extent for community welfare and development programmes (radio is an exception up to some extent) as the popular media are too biased towards sports and movie/serial based entertainment, which gather more advertisement revenues.

11.1.3. Information Enabling Technologies

In many cases it is not the technology which is important, but how the technology is being used for positive and pragmatic applications. There are also cases where the bad applications of good technology which lead to more problems than solutions. The technologies that are to be harnessed (of course after printing) and strengthened especially in connection with the dissemination of information for rural development include:

Radio: Apart from programmes meant for agriculture and news, there should be more programmes on rural welfare, health, rural vocation, options for government funding and subsidies, motivating case studies on how other villages created better infrastructure and houses using local materials and voluntary labour, question answer sessions with government officials, rural development experts, NGOs on specific problems of rural people, information about what sort of help is available where on specific tasks, etc.

TV & Cable: Visual media is stronger than radio as images speak more louder than words. The present fair of advertisement and emotional entertainment needs to be pruned to find space for viewer friendly programmes.

Computer & IT: Electronic information, locally created as well as purchased from publishers and providers, of interest to rural people may be disseminated through the application of computer, communication and information technologies. Some of the major tools and techniques for disseminating information in the computerized environment include Web sites, email, Listservers, chat forums, etc., as they provide wide variety of options to store, display, interact and communicate information of interest to single or multiple users.

Mobile Phones: Information at your fingertips is slowly being replaced from the desk to your hand with major improvements in mobile technology and the arrival of economical products and solutions from wide variety of providers. Seeing the penetration of this technology than other technologies such as TV and PC, it appears that we have to base on accessing information through mobile technologies rather than through the desktop PC to take the benefits of information in electronic form to a large mass of population. This becomes especially significant for rural areas with no electricity and land lines where mobile technology through wireless mode enable us to reach those not reached otherwise.

11.2. BROADCASTING ORIENTED RURAL DEVELOPMENT

The present model for disseminating information to the rural population and the practitioners of rural development is through the broadcasting model which involves the different departments and offices of government, press, publications, radio, TV and cable. This model has advantages and limitations of serving a country as evident through its prevalence for more than 50 years. In a country with over 45% illiterates, there is no doubt the Government has considered the broadcasting model more viable than a library oriented model for taking its programmes to the people. But the major limitation with the broadcasting approach, especially in the context of rural communities, though the programmes on radio and TV meant for the rural people are aired at such times convenient for them to listen and watch, are the lack of options to record and utilize the programmes later. The case is something like if you are not in front of the broadcasting media, you definitely miss the fare. Same difficulties also exist in the case of print media such as newspapers, magazines, brochures and publicity materials from government and NGOs, as there is no concrete mechanism to document, archive, and disseminate them. Apart from the administrative officers and specialists (journalists, social scientists, technologists, doctors, lawyers etc.) in different departments, the present set of professionals involved with rural development activities are the volunteers of rural community, representatives of NGOs and politicians. Unfortunately library professionals have no say in these matters as they find it difficult to get involved in the existing setup. There is no doubt that library and information professionals in research and educational institutions for rural development (National Institute of Rural Development (NIRD) at Hyderabad and its regional centre at Guwahati, Council for Advancement of People's Action & Rural Technology (CAPART), 25 State Institutes of Rural Development (SIRDs)), are doing a good job, but it is still to see a major shift in the government policies to base rural development on an information oriented model.

11.3. INFORMATION ORIENTED RURAL DEVELOPMENT

Apart from NIRD, CAPART and its 14 technology resource centres, and SIRDs, there are many other institutions involved in training and research in rural development such as, 87 Extension Training Centres (ETCs) at district/block/village levels, many Krishi Vigyan Kendras, 442 community polytechnics, training centres under TRYSEM, 52 rural technology demonstration cum training centres under the National Research & Development Corporation (NRDC), and training as well as research institutions under the Khadi and Village Industries Commission (KVIC). But it is not clear about the availability of library and information facilities in these institutions. Since rural development activities work in the present in a totally distributed manner by involving diverse players with diverging interests, it would be difficult to create and sustain a library system or network of libraries exclusively for rural development activities. Thus a pragmatic approach could be to involve the public library system and those of educational institutions such as schools (at least secondary/ higher secondary) in rural areas to document, preserve and disseminate a wide variety of information of interest to rural development practitioners as well as rural people to stimulate and strengthen the existing and emerging initiatives.

Quality of infrastructure, collection, information technology use, manpower, etc., in public libraries and school libraries are very poor, barring few facilities in cities. It is practically impossible to replicate the comparatively better indices of research, higher education and special libraries in public libraries and school libraries due to the large number of such libraries and hence the enormous investment required. The Central and state governments spend considerable amount on rural development which is normally distributed through local bodies. Perhaps one way to effectively place and conduct these programmes concerned with socioeconomic progress might be to include the public library-school library systems in these programmes. Thus these libraries should get minimum professional manpower, collection, building, computer, and communication infrastructure. During the television boom, there was a programme to provide public libraries with TV sets to disseminate government information with entertainment. It can be thought of in the present context where a computer is more a necessity than luxury, to provide public libraries with computers and networking facilities. Significant attempts are underway to improve the telephone density in the country and it is a good feat to provide telephones in public libraries. Not only these phones act as community telephones where such provisions lack; they can also be used for dial-up Internet connection. There are also certain untapped networks, which can be explored for public library networking like the satellite based network of National Informatics Centre (NIC) which connects all the districts, network of Videsh Sanchar Nigam Limited (VSNL), and those of private Internet Service Providers (ISPs) like Satyam, Reliance, etc. Public libraries restructured as network kiosks to deliver and access a whole lot of information facilities and support services can go a long way in reassuring rural development initiatives.

11.3.1. Public and School Libraries Collaborative for Rural Information Services

The country presently has 28 states, 6 union territories and the national capital region, which together account for approximately 550 districts. The number of inhabited villages in the country is around 580781 [14]. These figures force us to imagine the difficulties of facilitating information and library support to the mass of over a billion population (of which over 73% are rural), spread over 32 lakhs sq. km. During the last 28 years, the Raja Rammohun Roy Library Foundation (RRRLF) has covered, out of 60000 public libraries located in the country in a scattered way, more than 31000 libraries at different levels [15]. But many of these 60000 libraries (see Table 11.1) are mere reading rooms without much books or good infrastructure or trained full time staff. According to International Federation of Library Associations & Institutions (IFLA) standards, there should be one public library for every 3000 people [15], and with over 1 billion people, our country needs more than 343000 public library units which means there may not be even one public library for 8-10 of rural villages.

Table 11.1: Public Library System

Public Libraries	***Covered by RRRLF [15]***	***Total (Approximate)***
State Central Libraries	28	35
Divisional and District Libraries	451	597
Sub-Divisional/Taluka/Tehsil Libraries	501	2300
Town & Rural Libraries	29820	Town- 15000 Rural-42000
Nehru Yuvak Kendras	272	500

Public Libraries	*Covered by RRRLF [15]*	*Total (Approximate)*
Jawahar Bal Bhavans	49	120
Others	128	
	31249	60000

Table 11.2: School Libraries

Schools, as per 1995-96 data [14]	*Number*
Primary Schools	590421
Upper Primary Schools	171216
Higher Secondary Schools	98134

The number of schools at the primary, upper primary, and higher secondary levels are listed in Table 11.2. It is difficult to have libraries in each of these schools, considering the ground realities of our education setup, but at least a name sake of library exists in the higher secondary schools and if the school has no librarian, a person with dual responsibilities of school plus village public librarian may be able to sustain that post by sharing the revenue from the concerned departments. This may also give the professional necessary job satisfaction as s/he can spare time and render social services by taking additional role as librarian of the village public library with a host of services discussed in the later part of this paper. Thus using the existing public and secondary school libraries, we are left with at least one library for 3-4 of the rural villages which is a viable setup considering the geographical terrain of the country, the prevailing infrastructure and the current budgetary allocation. These libraries with the aid of information and communication technology can function as rural digital libraries and information kiosks to take the virtues of rural development programmes to the rural people.

11.4. RURAL DIGITAL LIBRARIES

Digital libraries aim at unhindered access to content over

computer and communication networks. Libraries in India are also getting engaged in the development of prototypes of digital information resources, as influenced by developments in the developed countries. There are certain types of content which lie inaccessible or less used in its present physical form that can be put to more visible and enhanced use, to overcome the limitations of few number of copies in the case of heavily used content, to provide a hypertext approach and multimedia features, to simulate learning by doing, to sustain attention and interest of the user for long duration etc., as a result of digitization. The static content in printed sources fails to attract users who are increasingly exposed to the widely appealing features of new broadcasting technologies and IT intensive presentation tools. Multimedia enabled digital information will also make it consumable to a large percentage of illiterate and old population. With a comparatively strong IT workforce and the emerging development oriented governance, it is not difficult to set up rural digital libraries to create, collect and host information of interest to the rural community as a major initiative to improve the rural livelihood.

An illustrative list of some projects of importance to develop a rural digital library comprise of:

E-governance initiatives in states:

* eSeva [5] of the Government of Andhra Pradesh provides 'One-stop-shop' for over 66 citizen services using state-of-the-art technologies. It builds on the success of the TWINS pilot project launched in December 1999 and now has over 46 service centres in the twin cities of Hyderabad and Secunderabad, and the adjoining Rangareddy District. Major services on offer include payment of utilities Bills like electricity bills, water and sewerage bills, telephone bills (BSNL & TATA Tele Services), property tax, sales tax and issue of certificates of births/ deaths, Caste/Nativity, etc.
* A similar project FRIENDS (Fast Reliable Instant Efficient Network for Disbursement of Services) has been

launched in all 14 district headquarters by the Government of Kerala through its Dept. of IT in association with the local bodies and seven other Departments as an integrated Services center with a view to enable a smooth and transparent Citizen to Government (C2G) interface. These centers accept all utility bills, taxes and fees pertaining to the participating departments and offer quality services to the citizens [6]. Akshaya Kendras (information kiosks) are also launched in the most backward district of the state to leverage more on the benefits of IT for more transparent and people friendly governance.

* Bhoomi project launched by the Karnataka government attempts to digitise rural land revenue records seems to have opened up new vistas of e-governance that could become a model for other states [7].

* Community Information Centre (with one server machine, five client systems, one each of a VSAT, Laser Printer, Dot Matrix Printer, modem, LAN hub, TV, Webcam and two UPS (1KVA, 2 KVA)) has been set up in 457 blocks of North-East, as a joint effort by Ministry of Communications and Information Technology (MCIT), National Informatics Centre (NIC) and the State Governments of the North-Eastern states, to provide Internet access and Email, printing, data entry and word processing and training for the local populace. Several citizen-centric or Government to Citizen (G2C) services, such as birth and death registration, e-Suvidha where different types of certificates issued by Block and District administrations like SC/ST, Marriage etc., prices and other market information of agricultural produce, information on educational opportunities, and job portals are also delivered from the CICs [8].

* Citizen Information Centre (Lokmitra Soochna Kendra) implemented as a pilot project in Hamirpur district by the Government of Himachal Pradesh attempts to achieve easy access to Government Information at the

remotest corners of the State; redressal of complaints without physically visiting the Government offices; transparency in the working of the Government; responsive and responsible Administration etc. Services offered include lodging complaints, questions/ grievances, downloadable forms, job opportunities and tenders, information about government schemes, contact details of government departments and offices, market rates, networked rural market for purchase/sale of goods, matrimonial services, rural news, notice board, children corner and village email [9]. Jan Mitra is an integrated e-platform through which the rural population of Rajasthan can get desired information and avail services related to various government departments at kiosks near their doorsteps [10]. Mahiti Shakti Kendras (MSKs) project of Gujarat envisions a portal providing a single window to all relevant information and services [11]. NAI-DISHA is a web portal to provide about 25 Government-to-Citizens (G2C), Citizens-to-Government (C2G), Government-to-Government (G2G), Citizens-to-Citizens (C2C) services by the Government of Haryana [12].

Information Village/Village Information Projects:

* Gyandoot is an intranet in Dhar district connecting rural cybercafes catering to the everyday needs of the masses [13]. Some of the services on offer include Commodity/ Mandi Marketing Information System, various certificates issued by government departments, Landholder's passbook of land rights and loans, rural Hindi email, forms of various Government Schemes, rural matrimonial, rural market, rural News Paper, E-education etc.
* M S Swaminathan Research Foundation (MSSRF) established this project in some villages of Pondicherry to demonstrate the pragmatic applications of information and communications technology for the welfare of rural community [16].

* Village Information Centre (VIC) at Kuzhumani in Tiruchi district, set up two years ago as a pilot project by the Tamil Nadu Veterinary and Animal Sciences University (TANUVAS) to take information technology (IT) to rural people, has been successfully transferred to the local community [17].
* Sustainable Access in Rural India (SARI) project, a collaborative and interactive research agenda drawing on the expertise of Harvard's Centre for International Development, IIT Madras and the MIT Media Laboratory, works for a shared platform to deliver a variety of high quality services, allowing Internet access to be financially self-sustaining or profitable while reaching the rural poor, in all the villages and small towns in Madurai District (except the city of Madurai) [18].
* Dairy Information Services Kiosk (DISK) makes it possible for co-operatives and farmers to manage a database of all milch cattle and access a dairy portal with information about valued services [19].

Project Gutenberg: Project Gutenberg is the oldest producer of free electronic books (eBooks or etexts) on the Internet. Most of the Project Gutenberg eBooks (more than 12000 eBooks produced by hundreds of volunteers) are older literary works that are in the public domain in the United States and may be freely downloaded and read, and redistributed for non-commercial use [3].

Traditional Knowledge Digital Library: National development in an increasingly technology intensive social order requires efficient mechanisms for properly recording and fruitfully preserving the traditional knowledge and ongoing research and development activities of a country. As a nation with centuries of intellectual growth and demonstrated progress like ours with not so ordered forms of knowledge recording and distribution, this has achieved growing concern. We have seen not one but many encroachments on the traditional knowledge of the country through patenting by multinationals. Though the Post World Trade Organization (WTO) world order expressed increasing concern for preserving the intellectual property rights (IPRs) of a country in a properly documented and preserved format, the main reason for these infringements are largely due to the apathy towards constructive organization of such knowledge and making it available in an easily disseminating format. The problems with traditional knowledge are that they are not available in a properly written form, transmitted through generations predominantly in vocal form and are not tested and validated scientifically in many cases. The Council of Scientific and Industrial Research (CSIR) of India is thus proceeding with a major project to map the traditional knowledge of the country with the Traditional Knowledge Digital Library (TKDL) [4]. When many of the new technology oriented development model fails to conserve the water level, ensuring food security, etc., traditional and indigenous knowledge have been found inspiring and successful at the village level in different parts of the country.

Mobile Digital Library of popular books from C-DAC: C-DAC developed an Internet enabled Mobile Digital Library (DDGS) for common citizen, for promoting literacy and for making books available to schools in villages and remote areas using Mobile Van with satellite connection for connectivity to Internet and fitted with printer, scorer, cutter and binding machine for providing bound books to the end user from a single point. 105 books are listed on the site in August 2004 [20].

Digital Library of India: Digital Library of India is a collaborative project between Indian Institute of Science, Bangalore and Carnegie Mellon University with partners from Government, Academia and Religious Institutions. The main objective of the project is to digitize all the significant literary, artistic, and scientific works of mankind and making them freely available, in every corner of the world, for our education, study and appreciation and for all our future generations. Over 50000 books are scanned and out of which around 30000 are accessible over Web [21]. This project is part of the Universal (Digital)

Library initiative of Carnegie Mellon in which National Science Foundation of USA is providing funding for Scanners, Computers, Servers, and Software and augmented by manpower (about 2,000 man years of effort each, over a five year period) from China and India to digitize 1 million books (less than 1% of all books in all languages ever published) by 2005.

American Memory: American Memory of Library of Congress is a gateway to rich primary source materials relating to the history and culture of the United States. The site offers more than 7.5 million digital items from more than 100 historical collections, mainly multimedia collections of digitized documents, photographs, recorded sound, moving pictures, and text. The American Memory pilot project was initiated in 1990 well before the World Wide Web, in which CD-ROMs were distributed to 44 schools and libraries across the country to assess interest in accessing important materials relating to American history from its collections [22]. Time has come for a similar project on the country's history and culture by involving the National Library, State Central Libraries and other Institutions having good collection in these areas.

Each of the above projects illustrates viable application of information communication technologies. Some of these initiatives give enough hints about what are the components of a digital library facility of use to rural people. A rural digital library must essentially facilitate to provide easy and convenient access to:

* Single window system to provide and seek different G2C, C2G, G2G, C2C services
* Facility for computer or other mode of archiving and retrieving programmes on rural development aired on radio and beamed on television and broadcasted through other channels
* access to electronic books, electronic periodicals and electronic databases

* information about government schemes, rural market, etc.
* e-learning facilities of rural children and continuing education facilities for rural adults
* Subject gateways and virtual libraries
* Born digital in-house publications from the village
* Written or voice communication through local language email inside the village or among nearby villages
* Government publications, spiritual, heritage and folklore resources, etc.

In addition to functioning as a digital library, it should also replicate itself as a village information kiosk and communication facility in an interactive mode as a one stop point to satisfy all the practical information needs of rural population.

11.5. DIGITAL LIBRARY FOR RURAL DEVELOPMENT

In contrast to rural digital library for the primary use of rural people, a subject specific digital library for rural development could be set up as is being done in other subject areas for the benefit of institutions and people engaged in rural development. Such a digital library needs to involve the different stakeholders in a multi-institution framework and must include the following components:

* Electronic books, electronic journals and electronic databases related to rural development
* Subject gateways and virtual libraries
* access to bibliographic and full text databases, and CD publications
* In-house digitization of copyright owned and copyright free printed books (including classics and spiritual books)
* Born digital in-house publications such as research and status reports, programme evaluation and implementation reports, annual reports, teaching and research materials, theses and dissertations, in-house

journals, and proceedings of conferences, seminars, workshops, etc.

* Preprints and Post-prints of research papers, especially in the perspective of Open Archives initiative gaining ground to further access to published research and to make the results of public funded research available to those who need them.
* Publications in the public domain such as government publications, publications from non-profit institutions, etc.

A schematic of the distributed digital library for rural development in the existing and emerging information support scenario in the country is shown in figure 11.1. All the arrows indicating information flow are two sided as each and every entity will supply as well as receive information. Various databases and information sources are to be created with the help of a varied category of people for providing different services to help the rural development practitioners to perform effectively.

Databases: Database on different attributes and areas of rural development are to be developed. They should not just map the agencies, programmes, and technologies but also cover live details of projects completed earlier which may lead to better cost utilization and optimization of other projects. Raw materials and commonly available materials in each and every region of the country must be mapped along with climatic conditions and weather chart to work out ideal time for initiation of construction projects. Collecting and compiling information about social, ethnic, community and cultural characteristics of people in different parts of the country will also help to take appropriate decisions about overall development of rural areas. While deciding about rural employment and industry, commonly available materials, skills and artisanship of the people must be considered. Also the implementing agencies of the various rural development schemes from central and state governments or NGOs should have complete details of funds received, item-wise expenditure of money spent, social, technical and management aspects of projects undertaken, groundwork for the project, schedule, beneficiaries, etc. Thus devising databases requires formally published sources, government publications and records, as well as practical experience of persons engaged in implementation of development schemes and informal knowledge of the local people.

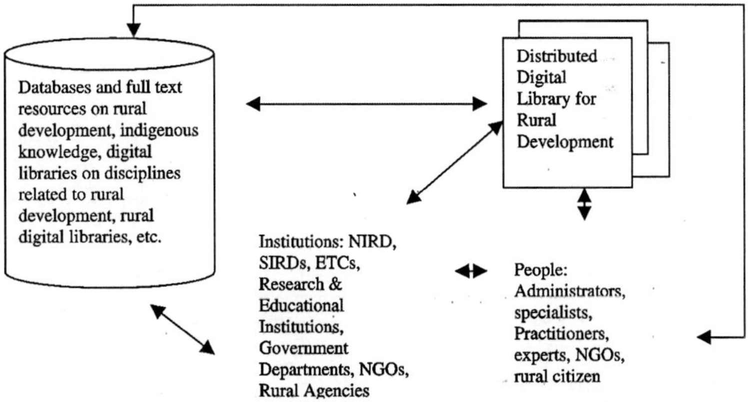

Fig. 11.1: Schematic of Digital Library for Rural Development

Information: It is of utmost importance that different rural development programmes are properly implemented and misutilization, project overruns and other irregularities are minimized to the least possible. Thus there is an urgent need to have greater transparency and increased public participation in their implementation at various levels. This requires that implementers and beneficiaries should have access to information about implementation and various aspects of these programmes. Compiling bibliographic information and attempt to create very functional databases on different aspects related to improve the rural infrastructure, self employment and entrepreneurship with rural goods as raw materials, and any other aspects concerned with the improvement of rural life and well being of rural folk. The digital library for rural development must include not only relevant information from published sources such as books, journals, research/progress/ annual reports, but also survey the technologies developed and implemented by various agencies in rural development projects. It should also collect information concerning new research projects, development works undertaken, technologies developed as well as implemented, skilled manpower, local resources, etc., and these will be incorporated in the suitable databases and information systems. Adding full text information, creating digital libraries on rural technology and rural development, as well as facility to link to experts will be attempted after the completion of bibliographic databases. Statistical information concerning completed and live rural development projects may be incorporated to guide new projects being undertaken in less time avoiding cost overruns. There must be resource sharing arrangements with other institutions to collect full text resources on demand.

Stakeholders: The different stakeholders in the rural development initiatives include Central and State Government, Rural Development Agencies, NGOs, private entrepreneurs, professional associations, autonomous institutions and corporate bodies including public sector agencies. The digital information facility must keep up to date information about contact addresses of these stakeholders, publications from them, and profiles and contact details of officials and experts attached to these entities.

Services: Database search services, referral services, document delivery, electronic information services, digital reference services, identifying and contacting experts, virtual community of specialists, etc., as a one stop centre for information support for rural development.

11.6. CONCLUSION

Five decades of broadcasting oriented rural development initiatives have confirmed the wide spread prevalence of information gap among practitioners and beneficiaries of rural development. By replicating the limited information infrastructure created for information village projects and e-governance examples, the wide spread network of public libraries and school libraries would be able to spread better awareness about rural development schemes, and as a rural information kiosk to provide various citizen services and for serving the local information and communication needs. Information and communication technologies has a major say in improving the quality of information services among the rural population by creating rural digital libraries. Similarly a multidisciplinary area of the practice and implementation of rural development needs a functional distributed digital library for providing effective information support to undertake various projects and complete them in time. Librarians and libraries have an influential role in realizing many of these objectives to convince government, rural community, and other stakeholders about the overall necessity of a library and information oriented rural development setup.

REFERENCES

1. Mukhopadhyay, Ananda Deb, Integrated Rural Development (IRD) and Information Support System (ISS), IASLIC Bulletin, 48(3), September 2003, pp. 131-140.
2. World Information Report 1997/98, Paris: UNESCO, 1997 (quoted in Dasgupta, Kalpana, Libraries and librarians in India on the threshold of the 3rd millennium: challenges and risks, 66th IFLA Council and General Conference, http://www.ifla.org/ IV/ifla66/papers/039-120e.htm).
3. http://www.gutenberg.net/
4. Traditional Knowledge Digital Library, Information Today & Tomorrow, 20 (3), September 2001, pp. 16-17, http://itt.nissat.tripod.com/itt0103/tkdl.htm
5. http://www.esevaonline.com/
6. http://www.keralaitmission.org/content/egovernance/

7. http://www.revdept-01.kar.nic.in/Bhoomi/web-page/ Karnatakas%20Bhoomi%20Proje ct.htm
8. http://www.cic.nic.in/mainblocks1.htm
9. http://www.himachal.nic.in/lokmitra.htm
10. http://rajasthan.gov.in/it/eg/Janmitra.shtm
11. http://www.mahitishakti.net/
12. http://web1.hry.nic.in/naidisha/aboutus.asp
13. Rajora, Rajesh. Bridging the digital divide Gyandoot: The model for community networks, Tata McGraw-Hill, New Delhi, 2002, XXV, 319 p.
14. Manorama Year Book 1999, Kottayam, Malayala Manorama.
15. Bhattacharjee, R., Public Library Services in India: Systems and Deficiencies, Country Report: India, http://www.ifla.org/VII/s8/annual/cr02-in.htm
16. Balaji, V et al., The Information Village Experiment in Pondicherry, Information Today & Tomorrow, 19 (4), December 2000, p.3-p.7 & p.10, http://itt.nissat.tripod.com/ itt20004/infovill.htm
17. http://www.hindu.com/2004/04/05/stories/2004040504780600.htm
18. http://www.tenet.res.in/sari/
19. http://www1.worldbank.org/publicsector/egov/diskcs.htm#
20. http://mobilelibrary.cdacnoida.com/
21. http://www.dli.ernet.in/
22. http://memory.loc.gov/

12
Decentralized Digital National Library System

12.0. INTRODUCTION

The National Library designated to collect, disseminate and preserve the printed material produced in the country and its cultural heritage, is the largest (and even the mightiest and holiest) library in the country. It was established with many lofty aims such as, acquisition and conservation of all significant printed material published in the country and on the country, acquisition and conservation of foreign material required by the country, rendering of bibliographical and documents services and acting as a referral centre purveying full and accurate knowledge [9]. It has an impeccable collection of over 22 lakhs (17,530 current periodicals) spread over a shelf space of more than 45 Km., in buildings of about 2.5 lakhs sq. ft., and no doubt is one of the proud possessions of the country [12]. The Library is not a mute spectator to the technological advances as it has also tried like other libraries in the country to practice computer applications, library automation, electronic databases, digitization, etc., as part of its efforts to interface information technology to usher in better collection development, functional information organization, and finer information services. The Computer Division was established in 1988 to augment the modernization activities with a Mini

Computer- HP 3000 and MINISIS and switched over to Client-Server Environment in 2001 with SUN E450 server and the campus LAN is being developed with 98 HP Pentium III PCs as nodes [4]. The scanning and archiving of rare and brittle books and other documents on compact disc are under taken, especially earmarking a target to digitize English books and documents published before 1900 and Indian publications of pre 1920. However, due to various reasons, so far only 6,600 selected books (over 25 lakhs pages) in Indian and English languages have been scanned and stored on 548 CDs. These statistics are not very impressive when compared with the massive collection of the library and the computer enabling achieved by many of the research and higher education libraries in the country. An institution with its roots going back to more than a century, this is the right time to introspect its activities and consolidate on the benefits of technology and good practices elsewhere to prepare and execute an aggressive as well as pragmatic action plan for preserving the cultural heritage of the country more oriented towards electronic and digital modes. As far as the National Library is concerned, the Delivery of Books Act is very important and efforts must be made to streamline this Act in the changing perspective to guarantee the availability of out of print books on the one hand and to include electronic books produced in the country.

12.1. DELIVERY OF BOOKS ACT

The Delivery of Books (Public Libraries) Act, 1954: No. 27 of 1954, as amended by the Delivery of Books (Public Libraries) Amendment Act, 1956: No. 99 of 1956, defines a "book" as every volume, part or division of a volume and pamphlet, in any language, and every sheet of music, map, chart or plan separately printed or lithographed, but does not include a newspaper published in conformity with the provisions of Section 5 of the Press and Registration of Books Act, 1867 (XXV of 1867); and "public libraries" as the National Library at Calcutta (now Kolkata) and any three other libraries which may be specified by the Central Government in this behalf by notification in the Official Gazette. The Act directs the Publisher to deliver at his own expense a copy of the book (copy of the whole book with all maps and illustrations finished, coloured and produced as the best copies of the same) to the National Library at Calcutta and one such copy (on the paper on which the largest number of copies of the book is printed for sale) to each of the other three public libraries within thirty days from the date of its publication. The Act also calls for "the publisher of every newspaper to deliver at his own expense one copy of each issue of the newspaper as soon as it is published to each such public library as may be notified in this behalf by the Central Government in the Official Gazette." Normally reprints and unrevised editions are relaxed (though there is no discretion on the part of any publisher to decide what to be deposited) whereas Government Publications other than those "meant for official use only" are included. Any publisher who violates the Act shall be punishable with fine, which may extend to fifty rupees or the value of the book. By virtue of this Act, the National Library receives books and periodicals in almost all the Indian languages and English books published in the country [10].

The National Library's collection has grown so huge as a result of the operation of the D.B. Act, as more than 40% of its total collection of books is accounted through this channel. However, it is not correct to assume that the country published only 9 lakhs books in the last 50 years as many publishers are defaulting on this count and many titles are not reaching this august repository, as evident from the Director's letter to Publishers about defaulters [10]. Apart from the legal obligation, the Director also talks about the advantage of giving widest possible publicity to their publications not only in this country but virtually all over the world also through the Indian National Bibliography. Thus the National Library must make Indian National Bibliography (INB) as up-to-date as possible and disseminate it as farther and fuller as feasible attracting the publishers to deposit their publications in the National Library as a better and stronger publicity option apart from the responsibility of preserving cultural heritage and the liability of the Act. This is evident from the fact that a lot of publishers send their publications free of cost to Newspapers like 'The Hindu' to get a bibliographic list/review in their paper. To every copy deposited freely, the National Library (other public libraries) must explore to buy a copy also to lure in the defaulters. Stringent enforcement of the Act, the National Library may also be directly/indirectly involved with publisher registration, institutional member in publishers and trade associations, etc., would also help for better follow up and effective tracking of defaulters.

12.2. DECENTRALIZATION OF NATIONAL LIBRARY SYSTEM

In a country like India with such a vast area; huge population; linguistic, cultural and racial diversity; a monolithic structure may not yield the desired benefits and centenary is the right time for an unbiased introspection for overcoming the hurdles and consolidating on the strengths. Just as we have many universities, IITs, IIMs, research and cultural institutions, there is need to have a decentralized national library system too with the National Library at the national level not as a centralized repository but as a national service and co-ordination unit, 5/6 Regional/Zonal National Libraries (in each of the four metros, one for the north east and another for the less privileged smaller states in the north) and 28 or more State National Libraries for the different states and union territories, as illustrated in figure 12.1. The union territories depending on their population may have a separate library or can be clubbed to a nearest state. In order to meet the aspirations of the people in different parts of the country, states and cities, and to serve them more closely, the State National Libraries for those states with a metro as capital may opt for another city in that state (for example, the Regional National Library of East Zone may be at Bhubaneswar, Ranchi or Patna instead of Kolkata, the State National Library of Maharashtra may be at Pune or Nagpur instead of Mumbai, etc.). This can be done without much monetary involvement by converting the existing State Central Libraries to the State National Libraries by bringing them under direct Central Government control. The overall responsibility of collecting and archiving the regional language materials will be left with the individual State National Library and English publications from the state will be collected in two copies, one each for the State National Library and the Regional National Library. The responsibility of bringing out regional language bibliographies may be handed over to the State National Library and the responsibility of bringing out English publications may be done by the National Library by coordinating the task with the help of Regional National Libraries. As far as collection development is concerned, National Library will only acquire foreign publications on India and other foreign material required by the country. It should act as a referral centre by coordinating bibliographical and documents services for purveying full and accurate knowledge with the aid of its collection and the help and collection of Regional and State National Libraries by involving them. There has to be a very functional and smooth resource sharing/ILL/document delivery system by employing traditional (involving special couriers) and nascent (fax, electronic, etc.) tools and techniques so that any user from any part of the country will get a publication from one's State National Library itself. If this arrangement could be extended to other members in the Public Library System like district, taluka, city, town and village level public libraries, it may also play a vital role to revamp the fund starved and collection scarce public library system. By decentralizing the national library system, we are not lessening the national spirit but by creating a group of more manageable libraries, we are trying to refine and make it speedier the diverging roles and responsibilities of the national library system. If configuring a single repository may hamper the loss of cultural heritage in the case of accidents like fire and natural hazards, the regional libraries can also archive language materials in that region and similarly the national library can archive English language materials from all parts of the country, so that two copies of the materials were available at different destinations. The primary advantage as a result of this decentralization is that the National Library is spared of many of the routine jobs about managing a huge collection leaving it time and resources for planning, developing, and launching digitization activities at a high pitch not just alone but involving and directing other Libraries in the National Library System and other educational and research Institutions and voluntary organizations who are interested in digitizing publications. The digital information services by the national libraries of UK and US may give suitable pointers to examine and identify what is possible with digital technology in the Indian setup. Since both of these libraries have very functional OPAC and bibliographic information systems, the discussion gets largely restricted to their attempts at providing full text digital information resources.

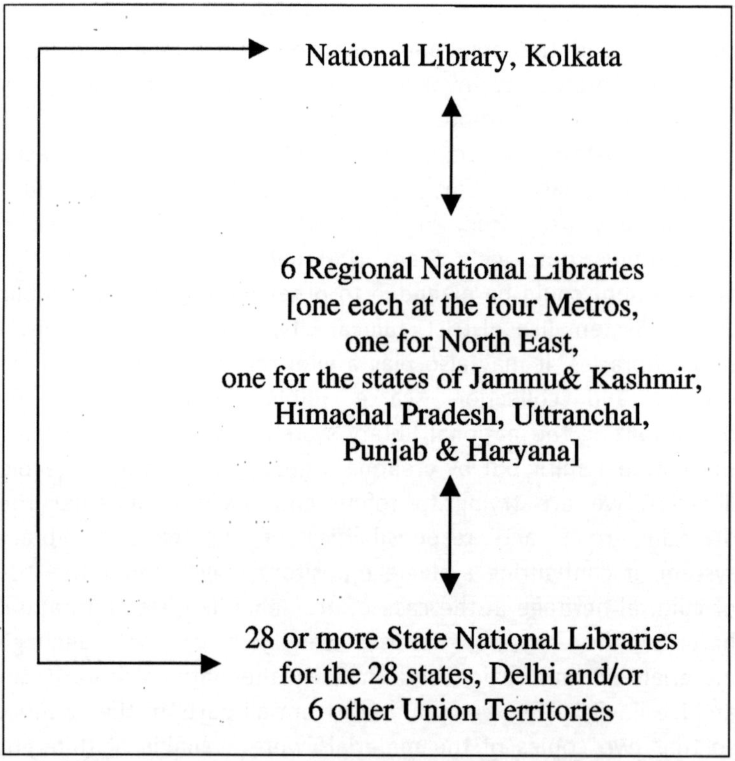

Fig. 12.1: Proposed Decentralized National Library System

12.3. DIGITAL INFORMATION SERVICES FROM US LIBRARY OF CONGRESS <HTTP://WWW.LOC.GOV/LIBRARY/LIBARCH-DIGITAL.HTML>

The Library of Congress National Digital Library Program (NDLP), initiated in 1995, was one of the first large-scale efforts to disseminate high-quality educational and cultural content—digital versions of manuscripts, maps, films, photographs, sound recordings, and printed material—over the Internet [1]. Realizing that "digital is rapidly becoming a principal medium to create, distribute and store content, and increasingly, digital content embodies much of the nation's intellectual, social and cultural history", the National Library of US, Library of Congress is engaged in a series of activities related to providing full text information through its website. Since the preservation of digital content has become a major challenge for society, in 1998 the Library of Congress began to develop a digital strategy. At the same time, the National Academy of Sciences (NAS) commissioned study report also recommended that the Library should work with other federal and nonfederal institutions and take the lead in a national, cooperative effort to archive and preserve digital information. In December 2000, $100 million was given to the Library to lead a national digital-strategy effort called the National Digital Information Infrastructure and Preservation Program to provide a national focus on important policy, standards and technical components necessary to preserve digital content [2]. In early 2001 the Library established a National Digital Strategy Advisory Board of experts from the technology, publishing, Internet, library and intellectual-property communities as well as government to help guide it through the planning process. As the Library is the home of the U.S. Copyright Office, it is already engaged in issues relating to copyright in a digital environment.

The major digital initiatives of the Library are:

American Memory <http://memory.loc.gov/> is a gateway to rich primary source materials relating to the history and culture of the United States. The site offers more than 7.5 million digital items from more than 100 historical collections, mainly multimedia collections of digitized documents, photographs, recorded sound, moving pictures, and text. The American Memory pilot project was initiated in 1990 well before the World Wide Web, in which CD-ROMs were distributed to 44 schools and libraries across the country to assess interest in accessing important materials relating to American history from its collections.

Thomas <http://thomas.loc.gov/> contains US legislative information on Internet. Under the directive of the Congress to make Federal legislative information freely available to the Internet public, the Library of Congress brought the THOMAS World Wide Web system online in January 1995. Searching capabilities were built on the InQuery information retrieval system, developed by the Center for Intelligent Information Retrieval, University of Massachusetts, Amherst. The first database made available was Bill Text, followed shortly by Congressional Record Text, Bill Summary & Status, Hot Bills, the Congressional Record Index, and the Constitution. Enhancements in the types of legislative data available, as well as in search and display capabilities, have been continuously added. THOMAS currently offers the following databases: House Floor This Week, House Floor Now, Quick Search of Text of Bills, Bill Summary & Status, Bill Text, Public Laws by Law Number, House Roll Call Votes, Senate Roll Call Votes, Congressional Record Text, Congressional Record Index, Committee Reports, Committee Home Pages, House Committees, Senate Committees, etc.

Mapping the INternet Electronic Resources Virtual Archive (MINERVA) <http://www.loc.gov/minerva/> Web Preservation Project was established to initiate a broad program to collect and preserve primary "born digital" source materials created in digital formats and does not exist in any physical form, including open access materials on the World Wide Web.

Country Studies <http://lcweb2.loc.gov/frd/cs/> contains the on-line versions of books published (between1988 and 1998) in hard copy by the Federal Research Division of the Library under the Country Studies/Area Handbook Program sponsored by the U.S. Department of Army. At present, 101 countries and regions including India are covered. The contents cover a description and analysis of the historical setting and the social, economic, political, and national security systems and institutions of countries throughout the world and examine the interrelationships of those systems and how they are shaped by cultural factors. As the information provided is not copyrighted, this digital collection is available for free and unrestricted use.

Global Legal Information (GLIN) <http://www.loc.gov/law/glin/> collects digitized laws, regulations, and other complementary legal sources.

Apart from these, the Library also offers [3]:

* The Library's 21 reading rooms provide access to unparalleled global information
* Selected items of international, cultural or historic importance from the Library's collections
* International Exhibitions: Many exhibits on international themes are accessible through the Library's Exhibitions Web site
* Portals to the World: Electronic resources on the nations of the world selected by Library of Congress subject experts
* International Cybercasts: Videos of many public programs on international issues are available through the Cyber LC Web site

12.4. DIGITAL INFORMATION SERVICES FROM BRITISH LIBRARY <HTTP://WWW.BL.UK/>

The British Library, the National Library of UK, now holds the following digital materials [7]:

* Digital publications via Voluntary Deposit agreements, such as journals and interactive multimedia on CD-ROM
* Disks accompanying print publications
* Networked/online publications sent by email or ftp

* Special collections material such as manuscript collections containing email, disks, tapes etc.
* Digitisation and in-house projects producing images and structured products, for example 'Turning the Pages'
* Web sites
* Audio
* Geographic information system data (GIS)
* "Initiatives for Access" programme demonstrated technology assisted access to information such as, digitisation of old manuscript, and the establishment of a digital storage, ordering, and transmission system for patents in electronic form.
* Turning the Pages is an interactive display system so that Visitors can virtually 'turn' the pages of rare books or manuscripts in a highly realistic way, using touch-screen technology and animation. They can zoom in on the high-quality digitised images and read or listen to notes explaining the significance of each page from four priceless manuscripts currently available online through web: Leonardo Notebook, Sultan Baybars' Qur'an, The Sherborne Missal, and The Lindisfarne Gospels [8].
* An electronic storage and retrieval system in 1999-2000 for access to more than nine hundred major science serial titles in the reading rooms and by document supply.

As far as future plans are concerned, the Library would [5]:

* Hold more electronic works.
* Develop a digitisation policy to facilitate access and preserve collection items.
* Establish a collaborative approach to the digitisation of heritage items in its collection.
* Specify the digital library infrastructure it needs and begin the procurement process
* Seek public sector funding for the hardware and software development required.

* Seek private sector alliances to maximise income from value-added service areas
* Assess the burden on publishers of an extension of legal deposit to digital and other non-print forms of publication, as the Library through Government tries for extending the existing legal deposit legislation beyond print to include digital and other non-print forms of publication [6].

12.5. DIGITAL ACTION PLAN FOR INDIA'S NATIONAL LIBRARY

Library of Congress has also to shoulder the multiple roles of the National Library, Congress Library and Copyright office. Similarly the British Library is also a very premier center for science and technology information especially for Document delivery services. However our National Library has many other Institutions and Libraries to shoulder some of these roles leaving it to be more focused and streamlined in its vital task of preserving, maintaining and servicing information and publications concerning the nation's cultural heritage. Some of the activities that need to be taken on a high priority are as follows and as in figure 12.2.

12.5.1. Web OPAC: Indications are that the library is seriously trying to create a database of its collection and make it available through a computerized information retrieval system. But seeing the massive and burgeoning collection and the existing output, the completion of this task may take more time unless some concrete action plans like the decentralization mentioned above, creating better infrastructure and recruiting more computer proficient manpower, or subcontracting the work to private concerns etc., are taken. The Library should place on its action plan as the highest priority to practice automating its housekeeping operations through a functional library automation system. It has to look for a good package that has demonstrated capacity to serve such a huge collection. And this package should support searching and selective retrieval of collection through a web enabled interface for permitting access to any person from any part of India (and even across globe).

12.5.2. Digital services from its non-digital collection: A researcher from a far off place may be often interested in a reference from a book or few pages from an old journal and these can be sent to the person through a totally digital mode without investing much labour and money. The Library has to seriously revamp its reference wing with the minimum infrastructure required for such services (it seems this is already in place) and by identifying manpower with potential skills from its rolls and deploying them for this sort of services.

12.5.3. Digital Conservation and Preservation: The National Library has very strong facilities for traditional and conventional conservation and preservation facilities and it has separate divisions for physical, chemical (treatment and fumigation), reprographic (microfilming) and digital conservations [11]. However as the quantum of digitization achieved so far (only 6600 books [11]) is very meager compared to the collection, the Library has to gear up very seriously about making a visible impact on digital conservation and preservation activities.

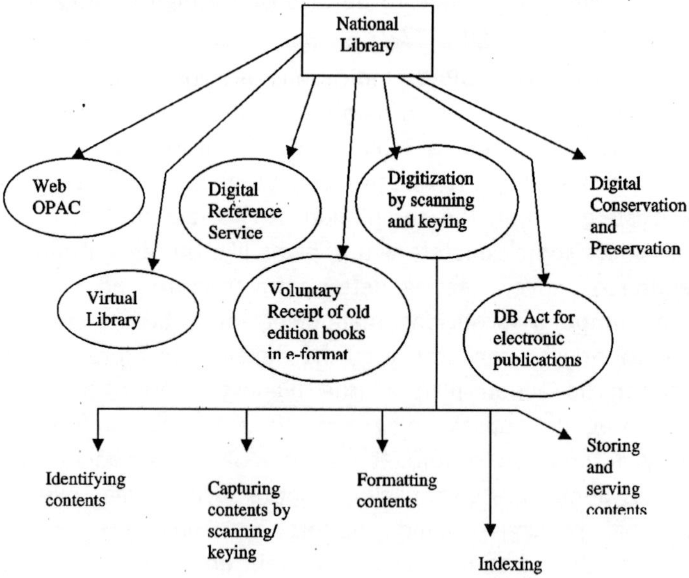

Fig. 12.2: Digital Action Plan for National Library

12.5.4. Decentralization and Parallel Development Effort: When the National Library alone can digitize 6600 books in a short span of time, the proposed network of National Libraries can achieve more through decentralization and parallel development. Digitization of our cultural heritage should be teamwork involving as many interested institutions and people as possible. There are many educational and research institutions, libraries, professionals, publishers and people at large who would be more than willing to offer their expertise, time, and money to act as participants in such a mammoth and onus task. As print to digital conversion through on-site keying and scanning takes more time, the Library must first explore alternate modes like DB Act for electronic books and publications and receipt of electronic book/files from publishers/authors.

12.5.5. DB Act for electronic publications: Like the BL's effort to extend the existing 'legal deposit' beyond print to include digital and other non-print forms of publication, the National Library may also try through Government to include electronic books and other information sources produced only in electronic form (electronic supplements of printed books are expected to be sent by the Publishers as per the existing Act itself). This should facilitate the National Library System to have more digital documents in its collection without spending time and resources for the complex operations of converting the printed sources digital. Moreover as electronic gadgets are widely being used in all spheres of human activity and the quantum of electronic publications is also increasing in the country, this will help to make our cultural heritage deposit system more exhaustive and functional.

12.5.6. Voluntary Receipt of old edition books in e-format: Many of the books published in regional languages and even in English are published only once as either the publisher finds it worthwhile not to go for another edition as the first edition itself took so much time to sell or the author is not healthy or interested enough to update the contents to get it accepted by the same or another publisher. It remains to be seen whether the publisher or author has any apprehensions about offering a digital access to such out of print books, when such an initiative comes from a respectable institution like the National Library. When the small aberrations in following legal deposit will be bridged by more public relations exercises and mutually beneficial talks with the trade bodies, many of them will voluntarily offer their electronic files of such books (as Desktop Publishing (DTP) is very cost effective, even small publishers create an electronic version of the book before going for its final printing) for serving by the National Library System. However, the Library has to procure/develop functional information retrieval systems (hardware as well as software) to host these contents. A mechanism must be created for publishers to send these files in multiple media and formats to the Library with a provision even for the publisher to upload the files to the Library's servers through login and password authentication.

12.5.7. Virtual Library: Attracted towards the virtues of electronic information, Internet and digital libraries, many institutions and libraries are making many of their publications accessible through their websites. The National Library may compile a list of such sites and create virtual library for enhancing the visibility of these sites and as a comprehensive source of digital information produced and hosted in the country. The Library may also motivate these institutions to convert and make available other in-house publications too.

12.6. DIGITIZING CULTURAL HERITAGE

12.6.1. Identifying contents: Since digitization from the printed text involves equipments, manpower, consumables and other operational expenditure, a careful selection by experts in the field, opinion of frequent users, and expressed user demand is very much essential before selecting a particular source for digitization. However electronic surrogates of printed materials, and electronic only sources received directly from the publishers and other channels may be hosted depending on the applicability of the retrieval software and availability of hardware storage. Also the Library must honour the legal rights of publishers to encourage their business interests. Hence care must be taken to provide only full text information of those publications having either the copyrights expired, or those for which the publisher/author expressed their willingness for providing digital access by the National Library.

12.6.2. e-nabling (capturing, formatting, storing, etc.) contents: Late starters of technology have certain advantages especially for IT applications as technology gets more advanced at lesser and affordable prices. We have to make certain administrative and technical decisions; administrative decisions such as whether the collections are stored centrally or distributed and the technical decisions such as what magnetic media and hardware platforms, refreshing or replacement of storage media, etc.

Conversion of printed information into digital form is widely attempted either through scanning or keying in data. In the case of largely textual library resources in printed form, a pragmatic approach is to scan full-text part and key in index and abstract for efficient selective retrieval. Storing electronic files in a particular format also needs decision making since there are many formats to choose from (PDF for text and image pages, Word/html for text only, jpg, tiff, gif etc., for images, to name a few). Compression techniques may be used not only for saving space at the server side but also to effect fast transfer and client retrieval over limited bandwidth.

12.6.3. Indexing contents: What aspects of the scanned/ keyed in contents are to be indexed (author, subject, keywords, phrases, etc.), usage of stop words, vocabulary control, proximity searches, language and period limiting, exhaustive or sparse selection of potential keywords, etc.? The search engine dominated internet indexing environment calls for machine indexing and formats like XML enable the whole text to be searchable leaving little to be decided manually about the index terms. However the primary drawbacks of this approach are lack of context in retrievals, attempting more recall, too many results for even a very specific search, too much noise in retrievals, etc.

12.6.4. Serving contents: A database system must keep an inventory of the digitized collection especially because we expect to provide selective access to the data. Necessary front end to accept search queries and display matched results would be developed. We should also attempt for seamless access of metadata and contents over same or different servers permitting users to search the Library OPAC first and thereafter a smooth traverse to the different identified full text links.

12.6.5. Configuration for digitization: In the least guess, the Library must have a host of servers (with terabytes and terabytes of storage) with all the wares supporting digital information storage and serving using Internet tools. However as better technology will be available tomorrow at lesser rates, the specifications are not very important at this stage. What is important is to start seriously scanning, keying, collecting and serving more and more of cultural heritage information in electronic form through web, discouraging proprietary tools to the utmost extent. We also need very functional scanners permitting continuous scanning of books of different sizes and condition, many PCs connected to the LAN and server for data entry and uploading information to servers.

12.7. CONSTRAINTS AND OPPORTUNITIES

12.7.1. Access management

Managing secure access is not a problem in the context of national library as we are trying to provide non-profitable access from copyright free or copyright transferred items. However there is still the threat from hackers of defacing the websites by either deleting the authentic files or replacing the contents with doubtful contents of propagandist nature. Hence the system personnel should be watchful in monitoring the contents served on a regular basis on the one hand and enforce strict technical controls such as firewalls and upload/modify/save restrictions on files stored. Enforcing foolproof access to servers of the National Library from unauthorized quarters through commonly employed technical restrictions such as IP validations of client, login and password verified access etc., will be difficult as we are not aware of the profiles of clients. Precautions must also be taken from operational perils like virus and other server access problems.

12.7.2. Technology and Standardization Issues

Like other technologies, computer technology has many ills apart from its projected virtues. How perfect is technology and how quickly is it transforming? Very new things (especially software) have a habit of not working properly for quite a while [13] and migration to new storage systems is expensive, apart from concerns about the loss of data or data transfer quality [16]. Even if the media are preserved intact, digital materials (susceptible to loss and destruction since stored on fragile magnetic and optical media that deteriorate rapidly and can fail suddenly from exposure to heat, humidity, or airborne contaminants) become unreadable if the devices to retrieve information from the media become obsolete or if the software that translates digital information to human-readable form is no longer available [14]. The electronic products are vulnerable to the same enemies that threaten paper, viz. natural threats such as light, moisture, and heat; organic threats such as rodents and insects; and chemical threats such as acid content, air pollution, and plastic, they face new problems like obsolescence, data degradation and the ease with which a document can be changed, either deliberately or by accident [15]. Unlike printed information that can be read anytime anywhere any posture when you had the original/copy of the material, "access to hardware and software, access to telephone connections, and knowledge of protocols can limit access to online information [18]. Since computers and allied technology are embedded in proprietary developments from many firms, it is always important to stress for interoperability and the need for standards and standardization.

12.7.3. Optical Character Recognition

Optical character recognition is widely used to identify

the characters in the document after scanning especially for full text search and retrieval. OCR conversion is not an exact science and considering an accuracy rate of 99.7% (three characters in 1000 are wrong leaving every 67th word with a spelling mistake on average) when indexed leads to confusion and can be a monumental task to correct [13]. Another problem is the development of OCRs for Indian language materials and the solutions are still either at the nascent stage for some languages and not available for many.

12.7.4. Infrastructure

The significant human labour required for editing, inspecting, correcting, and metadata adding digital objects inhibit libraries from initiating large-scale digitization efforts [17]. The actual costs of retrospective conversion will vary according to the condition, formats, content, and volume of the original collections; the choice of scanning technologies; scanning in-house versus contracting; the level of metadata needed to provide basic access; and the range of searching/ processing functions to be supported [19]. Funds are always on the decline or being kept steady or enhanced only to counter the price increase and/or inflation. Since a large part of the library budget will be spend on staff with conventional skills and printed collection, there is very little left for creating required computer infrastructure and recruiting proficient manpower.

12.7.5. Sources

In the context of National Library and digitization of cultural heritage, copyrights are not a major issue as many a time copyrights are either expired or the copyright owners are willing to ease their rights to such a virtuous task by an eminent institution like the National Library system.

12.8. CONCLUSION

The last fifty years of the National Library has been so exciting on many counts especially as it transformed itself from what is left by the empire to serve a buoyant and vibrant young democracy with a rich cultural, ethnic and linguistic diversity.

This is the right time to evaluate the collection, departments, programmes and services of the Library to make the collection more comprehensive and the services more up to date. It is highly required for the library to conduct all its house keeping operations through computer with a web OPAC and online reading room with provision for fast document delivery and electronic browsing of few pages on request. The proposed decentralized system must liberate the National Library from doing the menial routines and concentrate on more serious activities related to preservation and dissemination of the country's cultural heritage and publishing output and give the well desired leadership to other libraries in the National Library system and the Public Library system. Digitization on a massive scale is to be taken up for copyright free and copyright owned publications by sourcing electronic files from publishers, collaborative effort by other institutions and libraries, apart from local digitization by the National Library either using its staff by giving the work to outside agencies. And the digital components must be so vast in the years to come so that the Library site must be able to gather few thousands of hits per day to reflect the transformation and its leadership in preserving and disseminating the cultural heritage of the country through digital mode.

REFERENCES

1. http://www.loc.gov/rr/digital.html
2. http://www.digitalpreservation.gov/index.php?nav=1
3. http://international.loc.gov/intldl/intldlhome.html
4. http://www.nlindia.org/modernisation.html
5. http://www.bl.uk/pdf/stplan.pdf
6. http://www.bl.uk/pdf/strat-bs.pdf
7. http://www.bl.uk/about/collectioncare/digpresintro.html
8. http://www.bl.uk/collections/treasures/about.html
9. http://www.nlindia.org/index2.html

10. http://www.nlindia.org/for-publishers.html
11. http://www.nlindia.org/conservation.html
12. http://www.nlindia.org/useful_info.html
13. Noerr, Peter, The Digital Library Toolkit, 2nd ed., March 2000, Palo Alto: Sun Microsystems, http://www.sun.com/products-n-solutions/edu/libraries/digitaltoolkit.html
14. Hedstrom, Margaret and Montgomery, Sheon, Digital Preservation Needs and Requirements in RLG Member Institutions, A study commissioned by the Research Libraries Group, December 1998, http://www.rlg.org/preserv/digpres.html
15. Beebe, Linda and Meyers, Barbara, The Unsettled State of Archiving, The Journal of Electronic Publishing, 4(4), June 1999, http://www.press.umich.edu/jep/04-04/beebe.html
16. Hodge, Gail M., An Information Life-Cycle Approach: Best Practices for Digital Archiving, The Journal of Electronic Publishing, 5(4), June 2000, http://www.press.umich.edu/jep/05-04/hodge.html
17. Choudhury, G. Sayeed, et al., Digital Workflow Management: The Lester S. Levy Digitized Collection of Sheet Music. First Monday, 5(6), June 2000, http://www.firstmonday.org/issues/ issue5_6/choudhury/
18. Weisser, Christian R. and Walker, Janice R., Electronic Theses and Dissertations: Digitizing Scholarship for Its Own Sake, The Journal of Electronic Publishing, 3(2), December 1997, http://www.press.umich.edu/jep/03-02/etd.html
19. Chapman, Stephen and Kenney, Anne R., Digital Conversion of Research Library Materials: A Case for Full Informational Capture, D-Lib Magazine, October 1996, http://www.dlib.org/dlib/october96/cornell/10chapman.html

PART 4: ELECTRONIC CONTENTS

13
Bioinformatics and Internet

13.0. INTRODUCTION

Bioinformatics can be loosely defined as the application of computer technology to collect, analyze, organise and merge biological and genetic information which can be used for gene-based drug discovery and development. The need for Bioinformatics capabilities has been precipitated by the explosion of genomic information resulting from the Human Genome Project. The discipline of bioinformatics, a hybrid of molecular biology with computer science, is essential to the use of genomic information in understanding human diseases and for drug discovery. Thus, many universities, government institutions and pharmaceutical firms have formed bioinformatics groups, consisting of (computational) biologists and (bioinformatics) computer scientists. Such groups will be key to unravelling massive information generated by large scale sequencing efforts underway in laboratories around the world.

Internet is a virtual library of resources in all branches of human activity. This can be easily confirmed by searching for any term in search engines like yahoo, google etc. But like any other decentralised human endeavour, the diversity of resources available, the non-availablity of proper inventories, infinitely extended (hypertensing) hypertexts etc. are all creating a havoc, and can easily disturb the enthusiastic researcher to navigate the cyberspace. Few of the resources on internet related to bioinformatics are presented for interested researchers.

13.1. INTERNET RESOURCES

In recent times, remarkable progress has been made in the application of hypertext over Internet, and this splendid progress has resulted in a virtual on-slaught of web (WWW) sites over other protocols like gopher, wais etc. Most of the institutions, organisations, and companies have their web presence, and these home pages are used for serving different functions. The simple applications identified by most of them are as publicity/ promotion aspects, and some others have gone to the extent of integrating other contents, like publications, databases etc., to their web pages.

Some of the Biolinks - Sources of Sources, or links to informatics resources on the net which act as an inventory (don't take it for granted that they are exhaustive) of other sites are listed in Table 13.1. Information on research activites and resources available in few academic institutes and other organisations can be traced out by accessing the home page (see Table 13.2) of the Institution concerned.

Table 13.1: Bioinformatics Links on the Web

Yahoo!:Bioinformatic Servers http://www.yahoo.com/Science/Biology/Molecular_Biology/ Bioinformatic_Servers/index.html
Yahoo! UK & Ireland - Bioinformatic Servers http://www.yahoo.ie/Science/Biology/Molecular_Biology/ Bioinformatic_Servers/
World Bioinformation Sites : 2,000 biology-relevant websites http://moon2.cicams.ac.cn/biosites/bioinforg97.htm
List of BioInformatics centres on the Human (or other species) Genome http://www.hgmp.mrc.ac.uk/Public/Data/genome-centres.data
DiscoveryBase: Public Databases and Analysis Engines for Reliable, Secure Sequence Analysis etc. http://www.pathfinder.com/money/latest/press/BU/1998Feb09/1505.html
CatoSource Directory of products and services in biotechnology http://www.catosource.com/
Links to bioinformatics servers on the Web compiled by: Inge Jonassen. http://www.cs.city.ac.uk/~drg/research/bioinformatics-list.html

Bioinformatics Hot Links General Site. UTMDACC Sequence Analysis Users Information, Pedro's BioMolecular Research Tools http://odin.mda.uth.tmc.edu/seqan/molec.html

Home page of the company, Bioplanet http://www.bioplanet.com/links/links.html

BioSpace — links to biotech companies http://www.biospace.com/

BioValley — European biotech companies http://www.biovalley.com/

BioView Information, employment and links for the Biosciences http://bioview.com/BioWeb

Information Resource for Biologists http://www.bioweb.com/

BIOINFORMATICs Biota - Bioinformation: an annotated directory of molecuar biology tools and hypertext-based search tools http://www.tradenet.it/links/sc/bioinformatic.html

Links to Molecular Biology information servers, sequence databases, etc. http://listeria.nwfsc.noaa.gov/bioinformatics.html

McGuire, Woods, Battle & Boothe http://www.mwbb.com

WWW Virtual Library : Biotechnology http://vlib.stanford.edu/Overview.html

World Wide Web Servers & Gophers for bioinfomatics http://sg2.sbc.man.ac.uk/gradschool/bioinf/biogop1.html

---

Table 13.2: Institutional Websites (Bioinformatics)

Agricultural Biotechnology Center (ABC), Hungary http://www.abc.hu/

American Society for Clinical Pharmacology and Therapeutics (ASCPT), US http://www.ascpt.org/

Australian National University (ANU) Bioinformatics Facility http://life.anu.edu.au/bioinf.html

Baylor Human Genome Center, Baylor College of Medicine http://gc.bcm.tmc.edu:8088/

Laboratory for Biological Informatics and Theoretical Medicine (BITMED), US http://bitmed.ucsd.edu/

Biocomputing Shared Resource, Fred Hutchinson Cancer Research Center http://www.fhcrc.org/biocomp/

Bioinformatics Centre, Indian Institute of Science, Bangalore http://physics.iisc.ernet.in/bioinf.html/

Bioinformatics Centre, University of Pune http://bioinfo.ernet.in

Bioinformatics, King's College, UK http://www.kcl.ac.uk/kis/support/cc/bioinfo/top.html

Bioinformatics Server, UCL, USA http://www.biochem.ucl.ac.uk/bsm/dbbrowser/

Bioinformatics, Section on Medical Informatics, Stanford University, USA http://smi-web.stanford.edu/ http://camis.stanford.edu/smi/academics/bioinformaticssupplement. html

BioInformatics, Trinity College, Dublin, Ireland http://biotech.bio.tcd.ie/

Bioinformatics Resource (BR), School of Medicine, Stanford University, USA http://cmgm.stanford.edu/br.html

BioServe, Universities of Colorado and Kansas State & NASA, USA http://stripe.colarado.edu/~bioserve/

BioTech (educational & scientific information), University of Indiana, USA http://biotech.chem.indiana.edu

Biotech Information Center, USDA National Agricultural Library, University of Maryland, USA http://www.inform.umd.edu/EdRes/Topic/AgrEnv/Biotech

Biotechnology Law Web Server (Foley & Lardner) http://biotechlaw.ari.net

CCP11 - Biosequences and Structure Analysis, USA http://gserv1.dl.ac.uk/CCP/CCP11/

CMELUN lab, Department of Genetics, University of Nottingham, UK http://evol.nott.ac.uk/cmelun/links.html

Canadian Genome Analysis and Technology Program http://cgat.bch.umontreal.ca/

Cambridge Crystallographic Data Centre, UK http://www.ccdc.cam.uk/about

Center for Bioinformatics, Pennsylvania University, USA http://cbil.humgen.upenn.edu/cbiweb/

Center for Biological Sequence Analysis, Technical University of Denmark http://www.cbs.dtu.dk/welcome.html

Center for Computational Biology, CalTech, USA http://www.compbio.caltech.edu

Center for Computational and Experimental Genomics, USC, Los Angeles,USA http://www-hto.usc.edu

Center for Drug Development Sciences, Georgetown University, USA http://www.dml.georgetown.edu/pharmacology/cdds

Center for Neuroscientific Databases, University of Minnesota, USA http://www.cs.umn.edu/neural/index.html

Computational Biology and Informatics Laboratory, University of Penn, US http://cbil.humgen.upenn.edu/

Computational Biology Center, University of Minnesota, Minneapolis, USA http://www.cbc.med.umn.edu

Computational Biology Group, University of California, Santa Cruz, USA http://www.cse.ucsc.edu/research/compbio

Computational Bioscience and Engineering Laboratory, NIH,Washington D.C. http://cbel.dcrt.nih.gov/

Cooperative Human Linkage Center http://www.chlc.org

DDBJ DNA Databank of Japan http://www.ddbj.nig.ac.jp

DKFZ's FTP Server, EMBL, Germany http://www.dkfz-heidelberg.de/tbi/people/yuan/bioinfo.html

DNASYSTEM Home Page Sequence Analysis Site, UCSD, La Jolla, USA http://glamdring.ucsd.edu/others/dsmith/dnasys.html

Drosophila Genome Center, University of California, Berkeley, USA http://fly2.berkeley.edu

E. coli Genome Center, University of Wisconsin, USA http://www.genetics.wisc.edu

European Bioinformatics Institute (EBI), Cambridge, UK http://www.ebi.ac.uk/ebi_home.html

European Union Drug Regulatory Authorities Network, EudraNet http://www.eudra.org/

European Molecular Biology Laboratory (EMBL), Germany http://www.embl-heidelberg.de

ExPASy Molecular Biology Server http://www.expasy.ch

Food Animal Biotechnology Center (FAB), University of Minnesota, USA http://fabctr.umn.edu/

Genome Sequencing Center, School of Medicine, Washington University, US http://genome.wustl.edu/gsc/gschmpg.html

The Genome Sequence Database, BCM Search Launcher http://taipan.nmsu.edu/neurolab/bioinfo.html

Genetics and Genomics Collection, UCI http://www.oac.uci.edu/indiv/wiedeman/genome.html

HUJI - Genomic and BioInformatics Server for Computational biology, Biotechnology, Genetics, Bioinformatics , Israel http://gene.md.huji.ac.il/gene/index.html

Human Genome Project Information, LBNL Human Genome Center,

DOE,US http://www-hgc.lbl.gov/BioSrver.html

Human Genome Mapping Project Resource Centre, UK http://www.hgmp.mrc.ac.uk

Human genome project, USA http://info.mcc.ac.uk/hpctec/courses/Biocomputing/tools/ InetToolsBio_27.html

Institute for Biomedical Computing, University of Washington, St. Louis, Missouri, USA http://www.ibc.wustl.edu/

International Center For Cooperation in Bioinformatics (ICCB) UNESCO http://dapsas.weizmann.ac.il/bcd/bcd_parent/ICCB/more_info.html

International Pharmaceutical Federation, FIP http://www.mcc.ac.uk/pwmirror/pw9/fip/pharmweb92.html

Irish National Centre for BioInformatics, Ireland http://acer.gen.tcd.ie

Johns Hopkins Bioninformatics Web Server, USA http://www.gdb.org/hopkins.html

Laboratory of Experimental and Computational Biology, NIH, USA http://www-lmmb.ncifcrf.gov/

National Biotechnology Information Facility (NBIF), USA http://www.nbif.org

National Center for Biotechnology Information (NCBI), NIH, USA http://www.ncbi.nlm.nih.gov

National Center for Genome Resources (NCGR), USA http://www.ncgr.org National Library of Medicine, USA http://www.nlm.nih.gov/current_news.dir/biomed.html

Patents STO Internet Patent Search System http://sunsite.unc.edu/patents/intropat.html

Sanger Centre, UK http://staffa.sanger.ac.uk/

Software archives for Bioinformatics, National University of Singapore http://mbisg2.sbc.man.ac.uk/soft2.html

Stanford Human Genome Center, Stanford University, USA http://shgc.stanford.edu/

Stanford University DNA Sequence and Technology Center, USA http://genome-www.stanford.edu/SDSATC

The Institute for Genomic Research (TIGR) http://www.tigr.org

Vitual School of Natural Sciences (VSNS), Bielefeld University Bioinformatics Server

http://bibiserv.techfak.uni-bielefeld.de/

Weizmann Institute Genome and Bioinformatics, Israel http://bioinformatics.weizmann.ac.il/

Apart from the Institutional level, sections, departments or groups are also reachable through www. Some such groups are listed in Table 13.3. By contacting their websites, researchers can identify and communicate with specialists working in other parts of the world. This will fructify research collaboration with distant colleagues, and may further lead to the establishment of strong 'invisible colleges'.

Table 13.3: Academic Research Groups (Bioinformatics)

3D modelling / BioComputing Unit, EMBL, Germany http://www.sander.embl-heidelberg.de/future/members.html

Artificial Intelligence Laboratory, University of Illinois, Chicago, USA http://www.ai.uic.edu/

Bayesian Bioinformatics Program, Wadsworth Center, Albany,NY, US http://www.wadsworth.org/resnres/bioinfo/

Bioinformatics Research Group, University of Bergen, Norway http://www.ii.uib.no/bio/

Bioinformation Systems Group, Oak Ridge N.L., Tennessee, USA http://grail.lsd.ornl.gov/section/bioinfo/index.shtml

Biomolecular Modelling Laboratory, ICRF, UK http://bonsai.lif.icnet.uk/

Brutlag Bioinformatics Group, Stanford University, Palo Alto, USA http://motif.stanford.edu/

Computational Genomics Group, Sanger Centre, UK http://genomic.sanger.ac.uk/

Computational Protein Structure Group, Oak Ridge N.L., USA http://grail.lsd.ornl.gov/section/structure/index.shtml

Computation and Biology group, MIT, Boston, USA http://theory.lcs.mit.edu/groups/biology.html

CSI Bioinformatics Group, George Mason University, D.C., USA http://www.science.gmu.edu/~michaels/Bioinformatics/gateway.html

Drug Design Group, University of Cambridge, UK http://www.phar.cam.ac.uk/DDG/

Glycoprotein Structure/Function Group, UCL, UK http://www.biochem.ucl.ac.uk/bsm/gpg/index.html

Helix Group, Stanford University, Palo Alto, USA http://smi-web.stanford.edu/projects/helix/

Image Processing Section, LECB / NIH, D.C., USA http://www-lmmb.ncifcrf.gov/index-ips.html

Informatics Group, Sanger Centre, UK http://www.sanger.ac.uk/Teams/Informatics/

LBNL Human Genome Informatics Group,Lawrence Berkeley NL, US http://www-hgc.lbl.gov/inf/informatics-home.html

LICR/UCL Joint NMR Laboratory, UK http://www.biochem.ucl.ac.uk/bsm/nmr/index.html

Machine Learning Group, University of Wisconsin, USA

http://www.cs.wisc.edu/~shvalik/uwml.html

Molecular Design Laboratory, Peking University, China http://162.105.177.12/moldes.lab.html

Molecular Information Theory Group, LECB / NIH, D.C., USA http://www-lmmb.ncifcrf.gov/~toms

Molecular Structure Section, LECB / NIH, D.C., USA http://www-lmmb.ncifcrf.gov/~durell

NCSA Computational Biology Group,University of Illinois,Urbana,US http://bioweb.ncsa.uiuc.edu/

Protein Design Group, Centro Nacional de Biotecnologma, Spain http://gredos.cnb.uam.es/

Protein Sequence Analysis Group, UCL, UK http://www.biochem.ucl.ac.uk/bsm/dbbrowser/index/

Protein Structure Group, University of York, UK http://www.yorvic.york.ac.uk/

Sequence Analysis Service, EMBL, Germany http://www.embl-heidelberg.de/~seqanal

Simulation Group, Birkbeck College, London, UK http://www.cryst.bbk.ac.uk/research/simulation/simulation.html

Software Engineering Group, Birkbeck College, London, UK http://www.cryst.bbk.ac.uk/~classlib/

Structural Glycobiology Section, LECB / NIH, D.C., USA http://www-lmmb.ncifcrf.gov/~qasba/

Structure and Modelling Group, UCL, UK http://www.biochem.ucl.ac.uk/bsm/biocomp/index.html

Theoretical Biology and Biophysics Group, Los Alamos NL, New Mexico,US

http://www.t10.lanl.gov/

Theoretical Biology / Bioinformatics Group, Utrecht University, Netherlands http://binf.biol.rnu.nl/

Theoretical Biophysics Group, University of Illinois, Urbana Champaign, US
http://www.ks.uiuc.edu/

UCLA Biocybernetics Research Laboratory, UCLA, Los Angeles, USA
http://www.cs.ucla.edu/labs/biocyber/

UCL Protein Crystallography Group, UCL, UK http://www.biochem.ucl.ac.uk/bsm/xtal/index.html

---

Another web resource is the personal homepages of scientists, like Susan Davidson's Home Page, Associate Professor, CIS Co-Director, Center for Bioinformatics, Department of Computer and Information Science, University of Pennsylvania, http://www.cis.upenn.edu/~susan or Homepage of Dr. Michael Rebhan, Weizmann Institute of Science Genome Center, Rehovot, Israel, who is active in the study of data mining for functional genomics, http://bioinformatics.weizmann.ac.il/cards/ rebhan.html

The quick application of bioinformatics research in pharmaceutical industry resulted to the rousing interest in this area by MNCs like SmithKline Beecham, Glaxo Wellcome and Johnson & Johnson. Apart from them, a host of other small players are also active in the field, as shown in Table 13.4.

Table 13.4: Company/Industry Sites (Bioinformatics)

Antibody Resources Page (ARP)http://www.antibodyresource.com/

Base4 Bioinformatics http://www.base4.com/

Biotechnology and Gene Therapy (B&GT) http://www.natx.com

BIAweb by Bio Sensor Biomolecular interaction analysis http://www.pharmacia.se/biosensor/

BioCentury Analysis http://www.biocentury.com

BioData Navigator http://www.biodata.com/

BioInformatics Services (BIS) http://www.webcom.com/rphair/

BioMedNet (Internet club) http://www.BioMednet.com/

BIO-Online http://cns.bio.com/bio.html

Bioportfolio Information http://www.bioportfolio.com/

BioSupplyNet (Research Products Sources) http://www.biosupplynet.com

Biotech Company Web Registry http://www.data-transport.com

Canadian Biotech.com http://canadianbiotech.com/

Centerwatch Clinical trial http://www.centerwatch.com

DNA Vaccine Web http://www.genweb.com/Dnavax/dnavax.html

European Bioinformatics Institute — Industry Support Programme http://industry.ebi.ac.uk/

http://sol2.ebi.ac.uk/index.html

Institute for Biotechnology Information (IBI) — Strategic business information for biotechnology http://www.biotechinfo.com/

Structural Bioinformatics, Inc. (SBI), San Diego, USA http://www.strubix.com/~sbi/Intro.html

OxMol PR: Oxford Molecular and Genetics Computer Group Connect http://www.oxmol.com/news/4191.html

---

Apart from (un)published or informal information, Internet also contains two types of published information. One set of them contains a copy of the printed original document. The identification and recognition of Internet as an alternate medium for information communication was responsible for the second type of sources. Some publications in the field of bioinformatics, available on the net are listed in Table 13.5.

Table 13.5: Publications/News Letters/Journals etc. on Web (Bioinformatics)

Bioline Publications: various biosciences publications by BDT the Tropical Database (Brazil) http://www.bdt.org.br/bioline/

BioAccess Monthly: online newsletter with a business bent on human biotechnology http://biomednet.com/gateways/bac

The BioInformer newsletter http://lsr.ebi.ac.uk/newsletter/archives/1/about.html

Biotechnology Today: Daily news service, jobs/meetings databases http://biotech.mond.org/

The British Medical Journal (BMJ) http://www.bmj.com/bmj

Canadian Biotech News http://www.biotech.ca

China Medipharm Insights: electronic journal on China's medical & pharmaceutical R&D, industry and market http://www.asiawind.com/pub/cmi

CMS Business Intelligence Service: Catalogue of business intelligence newsletters http://www.textor.com/cms

CORE Biosciences magazine on the Web http://www.core.co.uk/core

BioInform: biweekly on the practice & business of bioinformatics http://www.bioinform.com/forms/trialrequest.html

De Montfort University Biotechnology Directory http://helios.dmn.ac.uk/~pka/guides/biotechnology.html

Journal of Chemical Technology and Biotechnology http://sci.mond.org/pubs/jctb.html

European Molecular Biology Network (EMBNet) Newsletter http://www.cbi.pku.edu.cn/

Bioinformatics From Theory to Application: about user-friendly interfaces for finding promising therapeutic targets, databases and access http://nmhcc.org/event2.cfm/BB730

Publications Index - Molecular Bioinformatics of Gene Regulation Papers (peer-reviewed):. Heinemeyer, T., Wingender, E., Reuter, I., Hermjakob, H., Kel, A. E., Kel, O. V., Ignatieva, E. V., Ananko, E. A., Podkolodnaya, O. A., Kolpakov, F. A., ... http://transfac.gbf-braunschweig.de/Publications.html

NetSci's Science Center - Bioinformatics: The Web journal of computers in pharmaceutical R&D http://www.netsci.org/Science/Bioinform/top.html

Page de Philippe Laffaire Les liens de Philippe Laffaire Version style sheets Bioinformatique, Biologie, Sciences Les Sciences en Vrac Etude DNA CHIPS- document researched and written by Ph. Laffaire. http://www2.smart.net/~msears/phil.html

Bioinformatics: C.D. Nager, H.A. Moser, T. Nyffenegger http://www.fmi.ch/reports/nager.htm

Robert J. Robbins: Challenges in the Human Genome Project (reprint of original paper published in IEEE Engineering in Medicine and Biology, March 1992, pages 25-34.) http://www.gdb.org/rjr/umdnj.pdf

Robert J. Robbins: Biological Databases: A New Scientific Literature (text of presentation first given as the keynote address to the 37th Annual Meeting of the Council of Biology Editors,San Diego, California, 8-11 May 1993, later published in Publishing Research Quarterly, Spring 1994, pp. 3-27) http://www.gdb.org/rjr/pub-rq.pdf

Robert J. Robbins: An Information Infrastructure for the Human Genome Project (preprint of the paper appeared in IEEE Engineering in Medicine and Biology, Nov 1995) http://www.gdb.org/rjr/ieee-1.pdf

Robert J. Robbins: Comparative Genomics: A New Integrative (preprint of the paper presented at the First International Workshop on Integrative Approaches to Molecular Biology, Cuernavaca, Mexico, 2024 February 1994.) http://www.gdb.org/rjr/cg.pdf

Robert J. Robbins: Informatics and the Human Genome Project (preprint of original paper co-authored with David Benton and Jay Snoddy, appeared in IEEE Engineering in Medicine and Biology, November 1995) http://www.gdb.org/rjr/ ieee-2.pdf

Robert J. Robbins: BioInformatics: Essential Infrastructure for Global Biology (A special report prepared for consideration by

the Organization for Economic Coordination and Development (OECD), Paris, France) http://www.gdb.org/rjr/oecd.pdf

Robert J. Robbins: Towards a Federated Information Infrastructure for Biology: Electronic Publishing on the Global Information Highway (Seminar Presentation at School of Library and Information Studies, University of Michigan, Ann Arbor, Michigan, 1 November 1994.) http:/ /www.gdb.org/rjr/sls.pdf

Robert J. Robbins: Genome Informatics, the Sine Qua Non of Genomic Research (paper presented in the Fourth International Conference on Bioinformatics & Genome Research,5-7 June 1995, San Francisco, California.) http://www.gdb.org/rjr/chi.pdf

Robert J. Robbins: Growth of GenBank, bar graph showing the content of GenBank (in numbers of base pairs) for every release from Release 1 through Release 88, http://www.gdb.org/rjr/genbank.pdf

The BioInformer: a quarterly newsletter that provides bioinformatics scientists with news & information about the European BioInformatics Institute, and other bioinformatics resources http:// bioinformer.ebi.ac.uk/newsletter/

For interactive communication between subject specialists, Internet has got Newsgroups/Discussion Forums/ List Servers/Chat etc. Few such facilities in bioinformatics include:

BIOSCI: a set of electronic communication forums - the bionet USENET newsgroups and parallel e-mail lists - used by biological scientists worldwide http://www.bio.net/

Bioinf - Bioinformatics Interest List owner-new-list@LISTSERV.NODAK.EDU

bioinf : The Bioinformatics Mailing List Subscription Address: bioinf-request@vei.co.uk

Owner: Barry Hardy <bioinforg@vei.co.uk>

Clinical Trials mailing list: contact LISTSERV@SHRSYS.HSLC.ORG with body of message:SUBSCRIBE CLINICAL-TRIALS yourfirstname yourlastname

Bulletin Board of the IMG, The Institute of Molecular Genetics: Teaching, Research, Organization http://www.img.bio.uni-goettingen.de/www/img_bul.htm

Further, there are 18 Newsgroups in the sci.bio Hierarchy, like sci.bio.botany — the scientific study of plants, sci.bio.ecology — ecological research, sci.bio.food-science — topics related to food science & technology sci.bio.immunocytochem — immuno-labelling of biological material sci.bio.systematics — systematics, taxonomy, and the tree of life, sci.bio.technology — any topic relating to biotechnology. Several databases can also be accessed through web and few of them are given in Table 13.6.

Table 13.6: Bioinformatics Databases on Web

Medline http://www.ncbi.nlm.nih.gov
BioMedical Strategies : Global database of pharmaceutical & biotechnology news and business research http://biomed.securities.com
Bioinformatics: Gene and Protein Sequence Databases http://www.hslib.washington.edu/hsl/liaisons/yarfitz/Meded530/index.htm
Johns Hopkins University BioInformatics Web Server: Databases and electronic publications for biology http://www.bis.med.jhmi.edu/
Ovid Technologies: Platform-independent access to bibliographic & full text databases for academic, biomedical and scientific research http://www.ovid.com/
Knight-Ridder ScienceBase http://krscience.dailog.com/
UCL's Database Browser: OWL composite sequence & database of fingerprints, PRINTS http://bsmcha1.biochem.ucl.ac.uk/bsm/dbbrowser/
EMBL Nucleotide Sequence Database Geneva, European Bioinformatics Institute (EBI) http://www.mpiem.gwdg.de/Extern/database.html

UCL Special Node of EMBnet DbBrowser, UCL's Bioinformatics Server: in-house databases

and sequence & structure analysis software http://www.biochem.ucl.ac.uk/bsm/dbbrowser/embnet.html

Molecular Bioinformatics of Gene Regulation TRANSFAC - The Transcription Factor Database http://transfac.gbf.de/

Bioinformatics links - Databases over Databases and Tools. SRS Sequence Retrieval System: Network Browser for Databanks http://www.cbs.dtu.dk/janhan/protlink.html

---

Internet was formulated for better communication among research groups in academic & research institutions, and the present day science & technology (S&T) research necessitates still faster communication and sharing of information. Thus the academics put considerable amount of educational information on the internet (Table 13.7). In the case of jobs, individual institutions/companies put wanted notices on their homepages and there also exist feeder services dedicated for career info (Table 13.8).

Table 13.7: Educational resources

BioTech: Bioinformatics - Academic Programs, Conferences, Courses, Documents, Grant Sources, Medical Informatics, CS Disciplines, Research Institutes, Research Issues, Tools. http://biotech.chem.indiana.edu/pages/bioinfo5.html

Cambridge Healthtech Institute (CHI), USA http://cato.com/crl/fyi.html

MSc Molecular Modelling & Bioinformatics: Fourier Analysis, Diffraction Theory, & Image Processing, Dept. of Crystallography http://gordon.cryst.bbk.ac.uk/www/times/year97/model_image.htm

Welcome to Students on Bioinformatics Tools (BIOTOOLS) http://ala.vsms.nottingham.ac.uk/vsms/biotools/welcome21.html

BIOTOOLS96: Frequently Asked Questions. What is the purpose of the course? To show the use of Java-based software tools for Bioinformatics software http://ala.vsms.nottingham.ac.uk/vsms/biotools/faq.html

Bioinformatics Courses World-Wide in the field of Bioinformatics (compiled by the Bioinformatics Unit at the Weizmann Institute) http://bioinfo.weizmann.ac.il/cards/bioinfo_courses.html

archive: BIOTOOLS96-a virtual course using Java http://www.ch.ic.ac.uk/hypermail/chemime/0215.html

New Niches-Resources: Resources for Starting a Career in Bioinformatics, Academic Programs for Training in Bioinformatics, The W. M. Keck Center in Pittsburgh, Pennsylvania http://www.edoc.com/nextwave/niches-bio/resources.html

Activities in Bioinformatics Education, Department of Computer Science and Biotechnology at Bielefeld University, Germany Computer Applications in Molecular Biology at Stanford Representations and Algorithms http://sequoia.techfak.uni-bielefeld.de/ intro/bioinfedu.html

New Undergraduate Major in Bioinformatics http://www.rpi.edu/dept/NewsComm/Review/sept97/sept_19/bioinfo.html

The Virtual School of Molecular Sciences (http://www.nottingham.ac.uk/vsms/) at Nottingham University, UK ad/course/Virtual - Bioinformatics tools virtual course http://sunsite.doc.ic.ac.uk/public/packages/javarc/ad/course/Virtual/

Materials used in a short course on computational biology, Computer Science Department, Johns Hopkins University:

a) Course Syllabus http://www.gdb.org/rjr/syllabus.pdf

b) Molecular Biology Fundamentals (overhead transparencies presenting some basic concepts in molecular biology) http://www.gdb.org/rjr/mol-bio.pdf

c) DNA as a Mass Storage Device (overhead transparencies presenting DNA in its role as a biological mass storage device) http://www.gdb.org/rjr/dna.pdf

d) Database Fundamentals (overhead transparencies discussing some fundamental aspects of database theory and design) http://www.gdb.org/rjr/db-fund.pdf

Bioinformatics Academic Programs, CMS Molecular Biology Resource listing of cources in bioinformatics http://www.unl.edu/stc-95/ResTools/biotools/biotools.htm#Part5

Biocomputing Course Resource List, Virtual School of Natural Sciences (VSNS) BioComputing Division: syllabi of on- and off-line bioinformatics courses http://www.techfak.uni-bielefeld.de/bcd/Curric/syllabi.html

Biocomputing Course Resource List : Course Syllabi — developed for the VSNS-BCD BioComputing Courses, aimed at a mixed audience of biologists, computer scientists, and students + researchers ... http://www.biotech.ist.unige.it/bcd/Curric/syllabi.html

Introduction to Bioinformatics: Chapter 1 of the Hypertext lecture notes at the GenZentrum http://www.lmb.uni-muenchen.de/groups/bioinformatics/ch1/chap-1.html

Resources for starting a career in bioinformatics, Science's Nextwave list of graduate programs in bioinformatics http://www.nextwave.org/nextwave/niches-bio/resources.html

Amjad-Ali Khoja: Career Advice for Computational Biology at University of Texas, Austin, USA http://www.utexas.edu/students/compbio/html/c.htm#7

How to become a bioinformatics expert, with a listing of European opportunities, Virtual School of Natural Sciences, BioComputing Divisionhttp://www.Techfak.Uni-bielefeld.DE/bcd/ForAll/Econom/study.html

Lists of on- & off-line bioinformatics programs can also be found at: http://www.nextwave.org/server-java/SAM/virtual.htm http://www.techfak.uni-bielefeld.de/bcd/Curric/syllabi.html

Table 13.8: Career Information (Bioinformatics)

Bioplanet Employers: links to homepages of corporate biotech, big pharma and other bioinformatics employers http://www.bioplanet.com/employlinks.htm

Bio Online Career Centre: information and job postings in biotechnology and pharmaceutical research http://bio.com/hr/job/

BioSpace Career Center: employment opportunities and career resources in the bioscience industry

http://www.biospace.com/career/

BioView: life sciences/biotech jobs, career resources, and information on job fairs http://www.bioview.com

Bioinformatics job opportunities, SmithKline Beecham http://www.bioinformatics.com/

Jobs in Bioinformatics at Yale: Post-doc Postion or Summer Job in Bioinformatics at Yale http://bioinfo.csb.yale.edu/jobs/

Wyeth Ayerst Job Postings - BIOINFORMATICS: Wyeth Ayerst Philadelphia Pennsylvania http://cns.bio.com/hr/job/wyeth_3.html

Internet also host information on different scientific meetings on bioinformatics, some have even gone to the extent of putting proceedings and working papers on their website. Few conference sites gathered are listed in Table 13.9.

Table 13.9: Conference Information (Bioinformatics)

Alan Robinson's Home Page: Frontiers in Visualisation and Human Computer Interaction '97, December 10th and 11th, 1997 http://industry.ebi.ac.uk/~alan/
Bioinformatics :IBC's Third International Symposium, September 29October 1, 1997, San Diego, CA. http://home.ican.net/~ibc/bioinfo/index.html
7th Annual Bioinformatics Conference http://www.pslgroup.com/dg/3900e.htm
MIMBD 96: Java and CORBA for Bioinformatics: Third annual MIMBD (Meeting on the Interconnection of Molecular Biology Databases), St.Louis, June 16-17, 1996. http://info.gdb.org/~letovsky/jcws.html
EU Work Shop: CORBA in Bioinformatics: Seminar & Discussion Day Wednesday, 10th September 1997 EMBL Outstation - EBI http://industry.ebi.ac.uk/~slidel/eu-corba-workshop/discussions.html
Virtual Environments International (VEI)-Bioinformatics Conference (BIOINF IEC1) : The First Internet-Extended Bioinformatics Virtual Conference http://www.vei.co.uk/bioinfiec1/entry/bioinfiec1.html
Bioinformatics: Biotechnology Enters the Information Age: Drug & Market Development Reports, Published by IBC USA Conferences, Inc. http://www.ibcusa.com/pub/bioinfo/
ITSE96- ANGIS, The Internet and Your Future Computers and the Internet in Biology & Medicine-Bioinformatics http://www.angis.su.oz.au/Education/itse96/index.html
Graham Kemp, Conferences Conferences, Abstracts, etc.. 1997. Molecular Graphics and Modelling Society meeting on Bioinformatics and Drug Discovery, Manchester, April 2-4 1997 http://www.csd.abdn.ac.uk/~gjlk/conferences.html
Bioinformatics — previous meetings: Previous bioinformatics (and related) meetings. Bioinformatics and Genome Research, San Francisco, June 5-7 1995. CPM 95, Helsinki, July 1995. ISMB 95, Cambridge, July 1995 http://www.ii.uib.no/~inge/list-old.html

13.2. BIOINFORMATICS: INDIAN SCENARIO

The Department of Biotechnology, Governement of India (http://btic. dbt.ernet.in) has been successfully operating a Biotechnology Information System (BTIS) in the country. The nine Distributed Information Centres (DICs) are set up for disseminating subject/discipline oriented information to interested users. These nodes are also called Bioinformatics Centres and are located at:

1. Indian Institute of Science, Bangalore
2. Madurai Kamaraj Univeristy, Madurai
3. Bose Institute, Calcutta
4. Jawaharlal Nehru Univeristy, New Delhi (all the four specialising on different aspects of Genetic Engineering)
5. Univerisity of Poona, Pune (Animal Biotechnology and Virology)
6. Indian Agricultural Research Institute, New Delhi (Plant Tissue Culture and Plant Biotechnoloigy)
7. Centre for Cellular & Molecular Biology, Hyderabad (Oncogenes, Nucleic Acid and Protein Sequences)
8. National Institute of Immunology, New Delhi (Immunology)
9. Institute of Microbial Technology, Chandigarh (Enzyme and Bioprocess Engineering)

Though tremendous opportunities are available for pursuing courses at different levels in Biotechnology (In IIT, Kharagpur, the Biotechnology Centre is offering Integrated M.Tech. (provision to leave after 8 semesters with B.Tech) in Biotechnology as well as a 3 semester M.Tech. in Biotechnology and Biochemical Engineering, and Ph.D Programme. In 1997, IIT, Kharagpur and Gregor Mendel Biotechnological Research and Engineering Foundation (BREF) have jointly launched IIT-BREF-Biotek for contractual research/ teaching/training in biotechnology). Institute of Bioinformatics and Applied Biotechnology (IBAB), Bangalore offers a course in bioinformatics covering the latest trends. There are also short term courses in Bioinformatics at Madurai Kamaraj University, University of Pune, Jawaharlal Nehru University, Jadavpur University, etc.

The characteristics dominant on the Internet are continuous change and unsteady and undirected growth, and in such a perspective, ensuring the exhaustiveness and authenticity of resources is a difficult task. Another feature is the dynamism of resources on the net resulted out of modification of information on sites or due to change in their hosts. But few resources identified are submitted for testing and verification by Indian researchers, and perhaps such activities in a vigorous way will lead to more and more net resources, coupled with hosting of in-house information on the net (web), may end up one day in an Indian Digital Library on Bioinformatics. Library science degree holders with bioscience background can be very well entrenched in this new and very active stream of bioresearch and pursue bright careers by fine tuning their already learned skills.

14
Personalizing Electronic Contents

14.0. INTRODUCTION

Applied Sciences, Engineering or Technology as designated by different terms pertain to the pragmatic and effective transformation of the results of scientific research to products and processes to improve the quality of life and for the betterment of society. Technical Institute Libraries are in the forefront of better technology assimilation and in formulating new and path breaking information organization and services in the country, of which those attached to IITs were the pioneers in designing and developing fresh initiatives. The Central Libraries of IITs spend few crores of Rupees at each site every year to procure a plenty of costly international information sources to deliver the requisite information support for the faculty, researchers, and students engaged in teaching and research activities. Due to various reasons such as increase in price and wide currency fluctuations, the number of sources procured in IIT libraries are either depleting or they are being forced to increase the budget substantially to arrest this erosion. Mere increase in budget for continuing the existing subscription may not be entertained for a long period, as that alone will not contribute in any way to substantial research or academic outputs. To get over this crisis, the IIT libraries have already devised certain collaborating arrangements to share resources among their libraries or with other important national ones, through IT enabled information sharing as well as consortia based subscriptions. There is also a need to look into the question of information use in technical libraries, as the users always demand for information not available in the library, but at the same time never pay much attention to some of the high quality resources that are lying on the stacks. Perhaps one way to get rid of this misfits or information under-use is to carefully instill the user interest patterns in acquisitions and effectively filter and personalize the contents procured to the notice of interested clients.

14.1. CONTENT PERSONALIZATION

The term content though widely designated as the subject matter of a document in the old library parlance, here it is used to designate any pertinent source of information that can be of use to the clientele. It has to take a wider connotation in the emerging digital environment as it encompasses both formal (published sources) as well as informal (meant for private distribution in academic circles), irrespective of the physical form (in floppy, on CD-ROM, or as web pages) occurring in different modes (like ASCII/scanned text, voice, images, pictures etc.). Content management includes basically the operations of collection, processing, organization, query based retrieval etc. *Content Personalization may be loosely defined as all set of actions resorted by the library to dynamically scan and deliver its collection (especially the newly added ones at regular intervals through electronic means) based on the interests of the individual user (expressed need as well as observed need through use patterns, apart from intelligently learning about the patron's interest).* This may be taken as very similar to the activities performed by the library for Current Awareness Services (CAS) or Selective Dissemination of Information (SDI) services, but a major difference in the case of personalization is the attempts to map and provide full text information rather than mere surrogates like indexes or abstracts. The Personalization consortium (http://www.personalization.org/personalization.

html) identified the purposes of personalization as to:

* Better serve the customer by anticipating needs;
* Make the interaction efficient and satisfying for both parties;
* Build a relationship that encourages the customer to return for subsequent purchases.

The basic reasons behind content personalization in a library must be:

* Large amounts of contents procured are unused
* A small part of contents acquired are not being used properly
* Difficult to satisfy the user demands otherwise
* Difficult to attract the users otherwise
* Electronic contents available can be easily personalized
* Efficient Collection Management
* Improve the image of Library

Still excuses like importance not felt, lack of infrastructure/cooperation from the Management, and inadequate funds/staff may prevent personalizing library contents to users. Not many involved studies are conducted on the actual use of sources procured in libraries using national resources by investing significant amount of professional time. The two laws of library science argue for putting into enhanced use the sources acquired on the one hand and for providing the right source demanded by users on the other. In the absence of intensive personal information support, users (especially researchers who work under extreme pressure to deliver solutions with regard to various consultancy and research projects) will be left to fend for themselves to scan the information overload through library OPACs (Online Public Access Catalogues) and commercial electronic databases. Most of the time, this may lead to information under-use which will have a drastic impact on the research and development output, as right sources may not reach the right person at the right time. However, there are certain attempts from portals, libraries and information suppliers to personalize their content repository to individual users.

14.2. CONTENTS PERSONALIZATION ATTEMPTS

Though the technology was primitive, to counter the problems of mammoth increase in information sources forcing it difficult for users to track, identify, and use the relevant ones, Bush dreamed of a sophisticated personalization system, "Memex" that would allow a user to organize information in an efficient but personal manner. [1]. Cuadra discusses the personalized system brought out by US online hosts, in which, for instance, the language of the user-system dialogue is tailored to individual user requirements [2].

The enormous growth of online services, particularly those on the Internet and Web, has encouraged many publishers to consider how best to deliver real time access as users come to expect personalization of the information and greater management of the content delivery [3]. Web databases have the potential to deliver personalized content to each individual in response to the individual's Web interactions [4]. Bradley discusses the popular trend with many of the leading search engines, to offer personalized content in the form of 'My XYZ' (My Altavista, My Yahoo!, My Excite and My Lycos), in which subject content is arranged in broad headings, such as business, technology, world news, sports, etc. [5]. Significant improvements in general content search engine retrieval and ranking performance may not be possible, and are probably not worth the effort, although search engine providers have introduced some rudimentary attempts at personalization, summarisation, and query expansion [6]. New technologies coupled to the WWW enable web sites to serve the needs of their visitors better by gauging users' unique needs and customizing the delivery of the information content [7]. PointCast, is a service that delivers scrolling personalized news via the Internet to users' desktops through a screen saver whose contents can be customized [8].

NewsAgent for Libraries, a project funded by the

Electronic Libraries Programme (eLib) in the UK, (URL: http:/ /newsagent.ukoln.ac.uk) aims to create a user configurable electronic news and current awareness service for library and information professionals. Users' interests are specified by profiles, which are then matched with incoming records and users are alerted through electronic mail about items of potential interest [9]. The Personal Digital Library (PDL), from the Electronic Library Project at De Montfort University, Leicester, UK (ELINOR) attempted to develop a personal information system which acts as a front end to other electronic library systems and manages all the users' information needs [10]. The 'Digital Portfolio Archives' (DPAs) project at University of California, Los Angeles (UCLA) allows teachers to build a personalized information system or DPAs with the content and descriptions; and enable students to incorporate components of the teacher's DPA and additional project-related materials into their own DPAs [11]. Hybrid Electronic Access and Delivery in the Library Networked Environment (Headline), project under the Electronic Libraries (eLib) programme of UK (URL: http://www.headline.ac.uk/) created the Headline Personal Information Environment (PIE) [12] to provide a tailored responsive service to its users. The user has a 'My PIE' page where he or she can group favourite or most used resources from the other pages and the content can also be customised at institutional level. MyLibrary is a Cornell University Library initiative to provide personalized library services such as MyLinks, a tool for collecting and organizing resources for private use by a patron, and MyUpdates, a tool to help scholars stay informed of new resources provided by the library [13]. Another MyLibrary (URL: http://my.lib.ncsu.edu/) project is operational at the North Carolina State University (NCSU) Libraries which is a user-centered front-end to collection of Internet and information resources and provides a customisable interface to several types of information. French and Viles brief about a Personalized Information Environment or "PIE" as a conceptual architecture that allows unified, highly customizable access to distributed information resources by providing users the tools to compose personalized collections from a palette of information resources. In contrast to a typical Internet search, where control of which resources are searched is in the search engine, a PIE places the control in the user as descriptions of resources are made available to users and they decide which resources to include in a search [14]. Interspace of Illinois Digital Library builds a world of connected information units where each unit is highly tuned to a particular community or set of individuals where the community is responsible for the maintenance and evolution of the unit [15]. PrePRINT Alerts, a new personalized alert service for the PrePRINT Network (http://www.osti.gov/preprint) allows its patrons to register, create one or more personalized search profiles, and automatically receive notifications of new preprint information matching the profile. The ScienceDirect service (http://www.sciencedirect .com) from Elsevier Science offers personalized access options such as setting up of personal profiles, customizing search features and receipt of email alerts of new articles etc. Similarly, the Current Contents Connect (http://connect.isihost.com), the web version of the wide acclaimed Current Contents database permits creation of personalized search profiles which can be modified, edited or saved for future use.

14.3. STATE OF THE ART

Now itself, libraries attached to academic and research institutions in general and technical libraries in particular are experiencing the virtues of electronic information in the form of e-journals, e-books, bibliographic/full text electronic databases in CD/through web access, and so on. Some of the libraries have even made it a point to prefer the electronic format for better access, efficient search mechanisms and effective services, let alone the benefits of space. Other reasons for acquiring electronic sources may be economical; house keeping friendly, as they are easy to maintain, and are free from theft or mutilation when master/multiple copies are available; technical like access through standalone/intranet/internet. Due to publishers' electronic plus policies, libraries are able to access electronic versions of new files either free or by paying a nominal fee. However accessing back files, may not be an easy proposition in many cases. Many of the technical libraries have some sort of CAS/SDI either based on new journal issues or updates of bibliographic databases and comprehensive search based on back issues of electronic databases. Even in cases, where full text databases are present, the CAS/SDI services have not included the outputs from these databases as most often, the full text information is handled in separate formats making it difficult to include the full text files in alerting services. Another difficulty is technical limitation incorporated by providers as most of the full text files can only be printed and can not be copied easily like bibliographic data.

Personalization involves a process of gathering user-information during interaction with the user, which is then used to deliver appropriate content and services, tailor-made to the user's needs [16]. As far as user interest management is concerned, they are not taken up in an integrated fashion so far. The user database in the library automation system is only for keeping the inventory of books issued, returned, renewed, reserved, or fine incurred by a person. Some libraries may have added few keywords in the user database to run CAS/SDI of books added to the library. The CAS/SDI services in its true sense essentially operated with the help of electronic bibliographic database hold detailed profiles about users or user groups in the proprietary software of the database. Recommendations from individual users are seriously sought and considered for procuring books, and such recommendations on a departmental/group of departments basis definitely influence addition or deletion of journals. But most of these recommendations and user preferences, as in other cases now stand only in the concerned automation software modules and does not give us a concrete picture of user interests. Three dominant modes of collecting user interests are input through printed forms, submitting electronic forms through email and filling up of forms kept on the web site. How continuously the user interests are modified in the

CAS/SDI profiles to reflect the continuous subject change of users is another area of concern. In many cases, either feedback mechanism will not work as interactively as desired since library professionals attempt to be as 'recall' as possible whereas the users want it to be as 'precise' as possible. Apart from the expressed needs, many are not considering it important, most probably due to difficulty in implementation, the usage statistics and use behaviour from library databases, or records kept at ILL/Resource Sharing unit, Reprography Section etc., in the construction of user profiles. Artificial Intelligence (AI) techniques are not at all used for dynamic modification and optimization of profiles using filtering agents, intelligent agents, etc., in the light of estimated use behavior. The only data mining application engaged by most of the libraries is to devise and update a bibliographic database of their collection of books and mere volume and issue inventory for journals.

14.4. DESIGN AND DEVELOPMENT

Personalization can be seen as a technology that empowers the user to become more participative in the process; it can be employed by the intermediaries as an assistive tool in the selection and filtering of information to provide the users with what they need most [17]. MyLibrary used a formal design process and adopted certain standards for a web-based application with a database back end. It uses Java servlets for implementing access to the database and providing dynamic web content which allowed the use of the JDBC standard for querying, inserting, and modifying records in the database. Oracle is the database technology used for storing information about users and the Kerberos Authentication mechanism provides user id and password authentication. For those without/unable to use e-mail, the most recent reports generated for a search profile can be viewed through the MyUpdates Web interface [18]. There are four central conceptual requirements of customizability, effective search, sharability, and security that embody the Personalized Information Environment (PIE) [19]. Each of these parameters should influence the design of a library content personalization system. The key elements of a Content Personalization System (CPS) comprise of user interest management systems, electronic content servers, and network or medium to access the tailored contents.

14.4.1. User Interest Management Subsystem

Bonett [20] identified some of the technologies to determine and deliver 'appropriate content' that match the users needs as:

a) **Fill-in Profile:** A profile is built through active involvement of the user, typically through fill-in forms.

b) **Click-stream Analysis/ Web Usage Mining Systems:** Used to record a track of the links visited. Click-stream analysis can become part of a process where rule-based systems are built to determine what content to offer.

c) **Collaborative Filtering:** This technique compares a user's tastes with those of other users to build up a picture of like-minded people. It may be less important when categories of users and preferences are already well defined.

d) **Cookies:** The cookie, a small data packet sent by a web site and stored on the browser can form the link to profile-specific information stored on the server side.

Each one of these techniques, especially the second and fourth offered by Internet engineering, and the first and second improved by Internet technology can be used as per the individual library's satisfaction to elicit user preferences. The user has attributes, interests, desires, needs – some or all of which need to be captured and processed and the techniques used to complete the picture of the user are varied and may engage the user to different degrees, directly or indirectly [21]. And the curious fact is that some of the needs are expressed, while some of them have to be assessed and captured through:

***Online/offline forms*:** Printed forms are circulated erstwhile to elicit the subject specialization of users before venturing into SDI Service. Nowadays, the same information can be collected from web forms, and the process can be made interactive by enabling the user to modify terms based on the results retrieved.

Library Usage History: The usage by individual user can be explored to refine their subject profiles such as what kind of books or journals they are referring, and placing resource sharing/database search requests for which information.

Artificial Intelligence: AI techniques may be employed to auto-learn and intelligently refine the subject specialization of individual client.

The user interests collected are to be incorporated into a suitable database engine and access may be provided to users in a restrictive fashion so that a person can modify his/her profile as and when needed without professional intervention. However, care should be taken about not disclosing other's profile to a user and what they can browse is only some schematic or patterns of group interests. Profiles are to be constructed at an individual and group level to render different types of services. This may go through different iterations and refinements based both on feedback as well as outputs of searches with respect to profile. Since information retrieval works based on the search terms selected, and for profile based matching, it is required to identify the essential concepts of the subject specialization of the users and there should be correspondence with the key words used to index resources. While mechanisms to generate information continue to grow in number and sophistication, tools and techniques to manage, filter, and search lag behind [22]. An efficient user interest management system will interface with one or more content servers in a distributed environment to extract contents of interest and concern to individual users.

14.4.2. Electronic Content Server Subsystem

The contents for personalization must include easily available electronic information such as e-journals and electronic databases, but must also use full text databases, book floppies/CDs, Internet/Web resources, and scanned/digitized printed text. Information in electronic form currently resides in different servers in the library like bibliographic data of holdings in the library automation server for house keeping operations, CD-ROM servers for access of electronic databases in CD form, web servers for intranet/internet information, etc. Since many libraries are planning for digital libraries in the near future, planning a distributed approach will yield better results than a unitary system. Internet, web, database technology and their interfacing is leading to interesting experiences of data storage, organization and demand based retrieval.

14.4.3. Network/Delivery Subsystem

Output of personalized contents might be delivered as email attachments or through logging into web sites. This subsystem may get less attention due to the wide application of intranet/internet technology in our institutions. In a well-connected campus, users can log into the systems and browse and manipulate the required results. As in the case of MyLibrary, separate areas can be provided on the CPS for users to manage their outputs.

14.5. PROBLEMS AND PROSPECTS

Users have different needs, desires, and operational modes and to recognize that relevance means different things in different situations [23]. Because much of personalization entails intensive collection and use of personal information there are implications for the respect of user privacy and protection of information supplied by users [24]. Since the system will have an automatic work-environment, only electronic resources may be brought under its purview, to begin with. As the users in an technical institute like IITs are largely students who are a floating population, this experiment will first attempt to map only the interests of faculty and researchers to have a substantial length of interaction between users and resources. User profiles are constructed from keywords collected from the users themselves and will be suffered from problems of proper representation of information requirements of need, want etc. as most of the time, whatever expressed is not the actual need. Since information needs of users is always hazy, we need to develop general models for organising literature by identifying the new concepts emerging in various subject of studies, updating and sharpening technical tools such as classification schemes, subject heading lists, thesauri etc. Though the library automation system will return results of whatever sources issued by users, so far it is difficult to quantify what sort of books are being read in the halls, and to assess which articles are photocopied. Further, when artificial intelligence techniques are being used to auto modify profiles, the success of constructive representation of user interests will be further suffered by limitations of machine intelligence. It is also required to avoid the previous problems with push technologies of information overload [25].

As a result of content personalization, the library is in a position to significantly utilise the interest profiles of its users in all decision making with regard to information selection, collection, organization and servicing. The present information environment in libraries is one in which there is little money to satisfy the highly demanding client base, refinement and fine-tuning acquisitions itself will improve the confidence of users in libraries. There will be a positive outlook on library professionals with respect to their day-to-day work, as well as efficiency and productivity as a result of personalization when satisfied customers keep on putting library to increased use which envisage enough confidence to staff in rendering their services. The content personalization will attempt, pinpointed information supply to users, exposing users to highly relevant contents, requiring users to scan only a portion of the collection, better use of the library collection, improvement of collection development policies, and enhanced use of library contents. The inherent benefits are 'more use/rs for contents' and 'apt contents for users' apart from timesaving as implied in the fundamental laws of library & information science. Also any attempt towards Information filtering is always welcome as information explosion and its aftermath of a flood of sources are indirectly alienating a large number of users from a considerable chunk of core resources.

14.6. CONCLUSION

In short, how the library will go to user or the user can receive relevant and pinpointed information without even visiting library is the critical and arduous task of personalization. The success of personalization efforts intertwines with how effectively and intelligently the Content Personalization System can capture the user preferences based on the books issued to them, as per the books they have requested, articles they referred etc. The CPS should be able to take input from users as well as capture information based on self-learning from evolved use patterns. This can be better realized only through integrated application of the tools and techniques of library & information science (use characteristics, user interest management, data mining, knowledge management, metadata) and artificial intelligence (machine learning, natural language systems, filtering/intelligent agents). This should also require some sort of symbiosis in managing documents and users, in contrast to what is practiced now, where user interests are handled only in an isolated fashion for procuring sources or for rendering CAS/SDI services. The library service databases should keep dynamic user profiles to deal with all aspects of selection, organisation, management and dissemination of information sources. The availability of more and more full text information in libraries and the significant application of Web and Internet engineering evolved options for augmenting CAS and SDI services to full text digital contents. Perhaps one way to meet the two imperatives of 'books for users' and 'users for books' in the emerging IT intensive library and information scenario is through 'personalization', which correctly maps the information requirements of users and considers the expressed as well as intrinsic/intuitive use before delving into information processing and management. How to evolve and continuously monitor and modify a dynamic user interest database is a vital issue that requires introspection from operational, professional and technical angles. It is not that procured contents are personalized but contents with some personal interest are only procured and this will go a long way in refining the collection development and enhance the library usage. Also the CPS must adopt the push mechanism (of delivering ahead of request) rather than the common pull mechanism (on demand) of information services. Research and work in the technical field is a highly competitive one and any attempt to selectively deliver information resources from the information flood will undoubtedly enhance use and boost output leading to the improvement of technical scene in the country.

REFERENCES

1. Bush. V, As We May Think, Atlantic Monthly, 176(1), 1945, pp. 101-108.
2. Cuadra, Carlos A., Commercially funded on-line retrieval services-past, present and future, Aslib Proceedings, 30 (1) Jan 78, p. 2-15.
3. Clayton, J, A step by step guide to content management, Digital Publishing Strategies, 2 (3) Nov 97, p.9.
4. Chard, S. M., Data management: the foundation for Web development in the retail and service industries, First Monday, 4 (9) Sep 1999, <http://www.firstmonday.dk/ issues/ issue4—9/chard/ index.html>
5. Bradley, P, Personalised news services: how personal, how much news?, Information World Review, (152), Nov 1999, pp. 47-8.
6. Schwartz, C, Web search engines, Journal of the American Society for Information Science, 49 (11) Sep 1998, pp. 973-82.
7. Robertson, N, A personalized Web, Internet World, 8 (4) Apr 97, p. 32, 34.
8. Ubois, J., Hassett, C, Cast system, Internet World, 7 (10) Oct 96, pp. 94-8, 100.
9. Tedd, L. A., Yeates, R, A personalised current awareness

service for library and information services staff: an overview of the NewsAgent for Libraries project, Program, 32 (4) Oct 1998, pp. 373-90.

10. Zhao, D, The Personal Digital Library, ELINOR: Electronic Library Project. London: Bowker-Saur for British Library, 1998, pp. 97-103.
11. Gilliland-Swetland, A., The Digital Portfolio Archives project, California University at Los Angeles, Department of Library and Information Science, 1997.
12. http://www.headline.ac.uk/public/diss/jp-PIE-HybLib-model/
13. Cohen, Suzanne et al., MyLibrary: Personalized Electronic Services in the Cornell University Library, D-Lib Magazine, 6(4), April 2000, http://www.dlib.org/dlib/april00/ mistlebauer/04mistlebauer.html.
14. French, James C., Viles, Charles L, Personalized Information Environments: An Architecture for Customizable Access to Distributed Digital Libraries, D-Lib Magazine, 5(6), June 1999, http://www.dlib.org/dlib/june99/french/06french.html.
15. Schatz, B. R., Building the Interspace: The Illinois Digital Library Project, Communications of the ACM, 38(4), 1995, pp. 62-63.
16. Bonett, Monica, Personalization of Web Services: Opportunities and Challenges, Ariadne, Issue 28, http://www.ariadne.ac.uk /issue28/personalization/intro.html
17. Bonett, Monica, op. cit. 16
18. Cohen, Suzanne et al., op. cit. 13
19. French, James C., Viles, Charles L., op. cit. 14
20. Bonett, Monica, op. cit. 16
21. Bonett, Monica, op. cit. 16
22. French, James C., Viles, Charles L., op. cit. 14
23. French, James C., Viles, Charles L., op. cit. 14
24. Bonett, Monica, op. cit. 16
25. Cohen, Suzanne et al., op. cit. 13

15
Edutainment Centres

15.0. INTRODUCTION

There was a time when we were compelled to believe that education and learning can be conducted only by the strict rules of classroom teaching and homework, all done basically through printed books. But as in other areas of human activity, technology has brought in tremendous changes in the way learning and teaching is delivered. Infotainment and edutainment are the new buzzwords today to denote information and education achieved through entertainment, essentially realized through good applications of computers and information technology. This can be easily adopted in schools and colleges as our country has made significant strides in viable applications of these technologies. There is no doubt that our computer proficiency and software talent is being recognized widely the world over. We can now make significant contribution to usher in a major revolution in the way education and learning is offered in this country, as demonstrated by our excellence in software and computer technology in other areas.

15.1. RADIO AND TELEVISION TECHNOLOGY

Our country has already taken advantage of technology to aid education with radio and television acting as effective catalysts in educational activities. Even now we have various programmes in these media dealing with general and specific aspects of education. Television and cable channels are offering a variety of programmes with the aim of educating the viewers. Then there are channels totally dedicated to educational aspects such as Discovery, National Geographic, Animal Planet, History Channel etc., apart from a host of channels dealing with morals, ethics and spirituality. But the basic limitation with these programmes is the difficulty in watching them when you are not in front of the TV or near the radio when they are delivered. However, with the aid of computer technology, functional archiving of these programmes is possible so that they can be reused more often. Though recording could be done by the old cassette recorder or VCR as well, this has not been done so far before the arrival of multimedia PCs due to the cost and diverse formatting problems of those media.

15.2. COMPUTERS, INFORMATION AND COMMUNICATION TECHNOLOGY

Perhaps the most significant asset of these technologies is that they can support multiple formats, for example you can type a letter or even this essay using a computer, you can listen to a good song by Rafi on it or see a good Amitabh movie on it, and you can even hear and watch the sound and images recorded out of radio or TV on a CD or any other computer readable media. Communication technology is so dominant that you cannot think now about a PC lying idle at home or school, and not connected to a communication network. There are networks by VSNL and private providers such as Satyam to connect your computer to the Internet (a network of networks, connecting essentially all the computers in the world), and this helps you to access Web sites (basic details about a person, company, or institution and kept on a computer system for others to see), or correspond to different persons through email. This has immense utility to students like us as we can see sites of different schools, colleges and other educational institutions and even communicate with students and teachers there. The Internet also helps us to gather a great amount of general knowledge by browsing and identifying useful information from the lakhs and crores of sites located in a distributed manner in different computer systems in different countries of the world.

But there is a catch here, as people of doubtful intentions have configured many sites with malicious information which are very detrimental to students and young people like us. Thus we should be safeguarded by parents and teachers about what sort of sites would be useful to us and care should be exerted right from the beginning to not get addicted to the habit of browsing such sites. Since the network line we use to access these sites is chargeable, instead of every student accessing the same site again and again, each one of us must make the habit of storing useful information so that others can access the same without consuming the network again. These technologies have a lot of potential to contain illiteracy and aid the neo-literate in becoming more literate as persons without much ability to read books can increase their awareness by taking advantage of multimedia resources as per the saying that "seeing is believing".

15.3. EDUTAINMENT CENTRES

In the backdrop of this discussion, a good and functional edutainment center in schools and colleges could be set up by making use of the following:

1. Creating a multimedia library/computer center with a few multimedia PCs
2. Collecting CDs or other media containing reference sources such as dictionaries, encyclopedias, atlases, teaching aids, and course materials
3. Recording educational programmes from radio and TV in computer readable media
4. Copying various science fair exhibits, cultural festivals etc. in computer readable media
5. Preparing classroom lectures, and student homework assignments in these media so that students can take advantage of the lectures later and can be benefited by well prepared homework tasks

6. Buying books and other learning materials for school syllabus in computer format

Once we start, who knows one day we may be able to add many more resources to this list. Schools and colleges should have the facility and slot in the class schedule for conveniently accessing these resources so that studies become less stressful and more painless. They should also issue out these materials like books so that interested students can watch them at home either through computer/VCP and thus utilize the time otherwise wasted on watching serials in a better manner. With significant and pragmatic application of computer aided learning, we shall be able to make learning more absorbing and interactive in times to come. And no doubt students would be far more comfortable stepping into an edutainment center than to a classroom or library.

16
Licensing Models and Repackaging Electronic Content

16.0. INTRODUCTION

Libraries in the country, especially those in research and higher education, as they have to depend largely on international sources, suffer very severely due to the unfriendly trends in the emerging information market. The annual cost to maintain information access is still rising faster than either inflation or library budgets and publishers continue to ask libraries to invest in new publishing initiatives while still maintaining or expanding the existing publications [1]. Also the new information marketing techniques like consortia based pricing and possibilities of delivering and accessing electronic information in diverse channels force libraries to be very vigilant and cautious in their approach towards information acquisition and services. The consortia wish to achieve greater value for money by purchasing the titles that receive actual use, by discontinuing purchase of low-use or unused titles and to arrive at more cost- effective or more accessible models [1]. Nowadays libraries have to deal not only with conventional sources in electronic form but new information that is available only in electronic form. Though professionals have justification to share resources, the publishing fraternity has a different opinion as that reduces their market. Recent years saw the widespread practice of consortia based subscriptions to balance the conflicting interests of suppliers (publishers, vendors, agents) and consumers (libraries, users).

The very predominant form of scholarly information, the electronic journals are made available through the Web at varying price models, in some cases free with printed counterparts or priced at a fixed percentage over the print subscriptions or it may also be offered in electronic only format. Publishers generally view a site as a single, geographically contiguous office building, complex, or campus location—plus dial-in access via the Licensee's secure network. Unlike many single site universities and research facilities in developed countries with more users, most of our Institutions of higher education and research were with less users and such a definition of a site may how far benefit our country will be a matter of introspection. Also the per capita consumption of information will be less and at the same time, the cost will be more.

Libraries conversant in electronic form have been experiencing the dangers of repackaging the same content in different products either by the same vendor or by different vendors through mutual agreements. Libraries tolerate duplication of information in secondary sources due to multidisciplinary subject specialization and for the comparatively cheap cost involved. However, such duplications with full text information may indirectly rob the library of spending its hard-earned money in procuring very less fresh content. Publishers may engage in such cross platform migrations and mergers with the idea of improving and enhancing the utility of their product, however libraries are a major looser as a result of this increased emphasis on the part of publishers to repackage content.

Since publishers have overheads to design search engines to supplement the data, the electronic product would normally be costlier than the printed equivalents unless large numbers of copies are sold [8]. Another argument is that a part of the savings from printed production costs are more than sufficient to account for electronic product development. Though libraries have their justification to share resources, the publishers/vendors have a different opinion about the whole issue. This forced them to devise options to give some acceptance to resource sharing channels by formulating consortia level pricing schemes for information products. As a result, few libraries can form a consortium and bargain with the vendor for special prices and for library friendly licensing models.

16.1. ELECTRONIC INFORMATION PROCURING ALONE OR THROUGH CONSORTIA

Libraries are able to achieve significant gains by entering into collaborations with other like minded libraries and form consortia to bargain library-friendly deals rather than leasing contents on their own as a single institution. The usage rights and other facilities offered by publishers when libraries procure single or consortia site license as suggested by Licensingmodels.com [2, 3] are listed in Table 16.1. As an emerging concept, the 'library consortia' is applied to different collaborative arrangements between libraries. Library consortia networks have existed for a long time, particularly in the USA, but their main aim of sharing printed material, has changed to providing common access to electronic resources via the Internet [4]. However the term is slowly establishing to designate library groupings to negotiate access rights of (print and) electronic information with publishers and vendors to arrive at enhanced access to more resources at better pricing. Due to consortia arrangements, libraries are in a position to have access to sources which hitherto have been impossible at existing budget allocations. On the plus side, 'consortia can be a means to introduce products to a previously untapped market' for vendors and 'consortia provide shared expertise, access to new electronic and print resources, professional development, new sources of funds, and safety in numbers' for libraries [5]. They 'increase the buying power of individual libraries over the short term' and 'maximize opportunities for cooperative collection building and for resource sharing over the long term' [6]. May be due to the wide variation in electronic information consumption by different libraries, the consortia based library acquisitions have not so far reached the desired level in our country. The consortia initiatives did not work in the country so far because of [7]:

* Lack of understanding of the concept of consortia
* Paucity of funds, as libraries needs to pay additional charges for buying electronic access
* Consortia need to have a legal entity, involved in collecting subscription amount from the participating libraries and make payments in foreign exchange
* Problems in transfer of funds from various participating libraries to the consortia due to administrative problems
* Co-ordination amongst the participating libraries becomes difficult due to geographical distances

Table 16.1: Electronic Information Usage Rights

Feature	***Single Site***	***Consortium***
Authorised Users	Current members of the staff (permanent, temporary, contract or visiting basis) and individuals who are currently studying at the individual/ Member's institution, who are permitted to access the Secure Network from within the Library Premises or from such other places where Authorised Users work or study (including but not limited to Authorised Users' offices and homes, halls of residence and student dormitories) and who have been issued with a password or other authentication [together with other persons who are permitted to use the library or information service and access the Secure Network but only from computer terminals within the Library Premises].	
Serving	Library's server	Consortium's server
Back-up copies	Permitted as are reasonably necessary	Permitted as are reasonably necessary

Feature	*Single Site*	*Consortium*
Mirroring	through cacheing or mirrored storage of all or part of the Licensed Materials to ensure efficient use by Authorised Users and not to make available duplicate copies	through cacheing or mirrored storage of all or part of the Licensed Materials to ensure efficient use by Members and Authorised Users and not to make available duplicate copies
Provision of copies	single printed or electronic copies of single articles on request from a user permitted	
Display, download or print	for the purpose of internal marketing or testing or for training permitted	
Authorised User rights subject to copyright laws	Search, view, retrieve and display the Licensed Materials. Electronically save individual articles or items for personal use. Print off a copy of parts of the Licensed Materials. Distribute a copy of individual articles or items of the Licensed Materials in print or electronic form to other Authorised Users.	
Supply of Copies to other Libraries	Permitted to supply to an Authorised User of another library {within the same country} (whether by post or fax or electronic transmission via the Internet or otherwise, [or secure transmission, whereby the electronic file is deleted immediately after printing]), for the purposes of research or private study and not for Commercial Use, a single paper copy of an electronic original of an individual document being part of the Licensed Materials.	
Course Packs and Electronic Reserve	Permitted to incorporate parts of the Licensed Materials, with acknowledgement of the source, in printed Course Packs (A collection or compilation of materials (e.g. book chapters, journal articles) assembled by staff for use by students in a class for the purposes of instruction.) [and Electronic Reserve collections- Electronic copies of materials (e.g. book chapters, journal articles) made and stored on the Secure Network for use by students in connection with specific courses of instruction] for the use of authorised Users in the course of instruction at the Licensee's/a Member's institution, but not for	

Feature	*Single Site*	*Consortium*
	Commercial Use (Use for the purposes of monetary reward by means of sale, resale, loan, transfer, hire or other form of exploitation). Course packs in non-electronic non-print perceptible form, such as audio or Braille, may also be offered to visually impaired Authorised Users.	
Prohibited Uses	Remove or alter the authors' names or the Publisher's copyright notices or other means of identification or disclaimers in the Licensed Materials; systematically make print or electronic copies of multiple extracts of the Licensed Materials for any purpose [other than back-up copies permitted; mount or distribute any part of the Licensed Material on any electronic network, other than the Secure Network of the Licensee; no alteration of the words or their order is permitted.	
The Publisher's explicit written permission must be obtained to	Use all or any part of the Licensed Materials for any Commercial Use; systematically distribute the whole or any part of the Licensed Materials to anyone other than Authorised Users; publish, distribute or make available the Licensed Materials, works based on the Licensed Materials or works which combine them with any other material, other than as permitted in the Licence; alter, abridge, adapt or modify the Licensed Materials, except to the extent necessary to make them perceptible on a computer screen to Authorised Users.	
Licensee's/ Consortium's Undertakings	use all reasonable endeavours to ensure that all Authorised Users are appropriately notified of: the importance of respecting the intellectual property rights in the Licensed Materials and of the sanctions which the Licensee/each Member imposes for failing to do so; the terms and conditions of the Licence and take steps to protect the Licensed Materials from unauthorised use or other breach of this License. Monitor compliance and immediately upon becoming aware of any unauthorised use or other breach, inform the Publisher and take all reasonable and appropriate steps, including disciplinary action, both to ensure that such activity	

Feature	*Single Site*	*Consortium*
		ceases and to prevent any recurrence; issue passwords or other access information only to Authorised Users and use all reasonable endeavours to ensure that Authorised Users do not divulge their passwords or other access information to any third party; keep full and up-to-date records of all [Authorised Users and their access details][IP addresses] and provide the Publisher with details of such additions, deletions or other alterations to such records as are necessary to enable the Publisher to provide Authorised Users with Access

Due to the consistent efforts made by libraries in premier institutions and the generous support received from MHRD, the first and foremost library consortia in the country is all set to unveil from January 2003. MHRD consortia for electronic access to databases (full-text & bibliographic) for Institutes under the MHRD, such as seven IITs, six IIMs, IISc, seventeen NITs/RECs, SLIET, NERIST, and NIFFT will be operational from 2003 January as trial access started from late 2002. The e-resources identified for web subscription are IEL online, ScienceDirect, IDEAL, ABI/Inform (On CD with Web Access), ACM Digital Library [all full-text], Web of Science, Compendex, SciFinder Scholar, MathSciNet, JCCC, J-GATE etc., [all bibliographic with links to full-text in some cases]. The Central Library of IIT Kharagpur has been able to save over 14 % of journal budget due to this initiative, and a portion of which may be spent for subscribing to new journals. It is not in this mere saving, but the wider access achieved (till 2002 IIT Kharagpur had subscriptions and access rights to only 90 journals of Elsevier Science where as from 2003, it has electronic access rights to over 1100 more journals from the same publisher) as a result of this consortia which is mind boggling.

16.2. LICENSING MODELS

Librarians are pushed into consortia and consortial licensing by university administrators, who like to see them share and reduce costs [9]. However, librarians are confused by the lack of precedence in consortial licensing, and are faced with rising costs and the increasing tendency to look at information as a commodity and not as scholarly information [9]. International Coalition of Library Consortia (ICOLC) suggests that libraries should have the option to purchase the electronic product without the paper subscription, and the electronic product should cost less than the printed subscription price, and to offer multiple and flexible economic models for electronic information [10]. The electronic journals are made available through the Web at varying price models, in most of the cases linked to printed counterparts, i.e. it may be offered free with print subscription (e.g. publications of American Physical Society and American Society of Civil Engineers) or priced at a fixed percentage over the print subscriptions (e.g. journals of Elsevier Science, Springer Verlag and IEEE) or it may also be offered exclusively in electronic media [7]. The different options provided by publishers to access electronic information site wide [a single, geographically contiguous office building, complex, or campus location—plus dial-in access via the secure network (not a mailing address and may include more than one library)] by libraries, as described on their Web sites is presented in Table 16.2. ICOLC outlines the different content purchase models [1]:

Title-by-title subscription model: The practice followed in most of the libraries to subscribe print journals. The only concession library may get by this model is the special rates if one subscribes few (Physical Reviews package from American Physical Society/AIP) or all publications (ASPP from IEEE) from the publisher, regarded as set price schemes.

"Print Plus" Model: The pricing of the electronic journal product is expressed as an "add-on" to the price of the print product, or the price quoted is linked to a "no-print cancellation" clause in the contract.

"Electronic Plus" Model: The electronic journal content supplied for a base price and the price for print copies added to that base price. ICOLC argues for keeping the purchase of the print copies as optional, and the base price for the electronic content is not more than 80% of the price for the electronic-plus-print and the combined electronic and print price is no more than current print-only prices.

"All-You-Can-Eat" Model: Some publishers offer their total content for the price that a library might have paid for a limited number of print journal subscriptions.

"Pay-by-the-drink" Model: Provision to purchase blocks of journal articles, or may pay only for the delivery of the articles that are actually used.

Through consortia, most often the libraries are paying for subscriptions, access, and lease of information, thus a careful examination of the different clauses in the contracts with publishers and vendors required to assess the different rights vested in the library and its users, not only for the subscription period but for archival use thereafter.

Table 16.2: Licensing option for Electronic Content

Publisher	Licensing option for Electronic Content through Consortia
American Physical Society	Subscriptions include institutional online access via IP registration. Online only subscription at 15% below the price for print plus online (print only is not available). Average price increase: 7-9%. Electronic copies of subscriptions on the library's servers as a permanent record ("electronic shelving"). A PDF collection of all articles published each year, which can be mounted on local servers and accessed using internet browsers, distributed in CD-ROMs at $50 per disc extra.
American Institute of Physics (AIP)	The systematic making of print or electronic copies for transmission to non-subscribers or non-subscribing institutions (such as in "interlibrary loan") are prohibited. Online only costs 28-50% of Print+Online for members and 70-75% of Print+Online for others.

MCB Press (Emerald Consortia)	Price predictability and discount for additional paper (up to 70%) and electronic resources (full text articles from 1994, with an abstract archive from 1989). Unlimited site licence (IP and/or password) so that many users (including remote) can simultaneously access the material. Free TOC alerting service e-mails the contents pages of journals and free document delivery (150 articles provided free of charge per annum). An archive of the material subscribed will be available as SGML tagged data and PDF formats. Usage statistics provided for each institution at article as well as journal level. Copies of online articles may be used in course packs, reserves or offprint collections.
Institute of Physics Publishing (IOP)	Institutional rate subscriptions include online access to journals at no extra cost. Electronic access to subscribed journals covers the subscribing site only, and may be networked to all physical sites that are legally part of a single educational institution. Organizations that wish to network subscribed journals to sites in other cities/ countries must obtain a/n national/ international Network License.
Wiley InterScience	For print subscription or electronic access (via IP authentication), only a base subscription price is to be paid, and 5% extra for both. Basic Access License (BAL) for single site customers and Enhanced Access License for those with multiple sites. Choice to have titles in print and electronic, or some in print only, or some in electronic format only. In BAL, any number of authorized users can browse and search tables of contents, whereas access to full text limited to one simultaneous user per subscription. Customers activated BAL before 31.12.2001 are entitled to access back volumes from 1996 whereas others have to pay an additional one-time fee (10-15% for print subscribers and 20-40% for others). If not renewed,

	customers continue to have access rights to the titles for the year(s) paid. Usage data is not available for BAL while monthly reports are provided for Enhanced Access License.
American Mathematical Society (AMS)	Sites may be academic or nonacademic. For academic institutions, different campuses are considered different sites even if they are within the same city whereas departments or libraries of the same campus are considered part of the same site. Access to MathSciNet for all subscribers is sitewide, via IP authentication with no limits on simultaneous users or length of time connected. The annual subscription price for *Mathematical Reviews* (MR) products is based on the database or content and the product(s) used to view the MR database. The Database Fee (DAF), or "content fee", reflects the cost of creating and maintaining the MR database, is based on the number of previous subscribers (DAF-holders) in the group with no additional DAF amount required for new subscribers in the consortium. Consortia MathSciNet fees are calculated per site based on "Mathematical Activity" (MA), the number of papers from that site reviewed in MR in a three-year period. The formula for the MathSciNet fee is MA x $20 + $250, with a minimum fee of $250 and a maximum fee of $1000.
Institute of Electrical and Electronics Engineers (IEEE)	Online access not free with the print subscription. Same subscription price for print and online while back volumes up to 1998 are available with online. Prices discounted by 39% if all journals are opted for, and approximately 24% more amount is to be paid when online and print are simultaneously required. IEEE / IEE Electronic Library (IEL) (full text of IEEE and IEE publications from 1988 claims more than $850,000 of content as per IEEE's and IEE's 2001 print prices) Online pricing is based on the number and location of user sites and

	user population. The standard license is for 15 simultaneous users at a single site. But the IEL CD ROM pricing is based on a single site with one simultaneous user. Started to digitize select content from 1952 to 1987. One-time access to articles may be purchased using a credit card for US$35 (US$13 for IEEE members).
Elsevier Science Science Direct	Relationship pricing by setting a fixed increase (5% cap) based on the total value of the print and electronic journal collections and not on the individual journals, for ScienceDirect customers. With the inclusion of 335 prestigious Academic Press journals (IDEAL articles back to 1993), ScienceDirect provides access to over 1,500 academic journals having more than 2 million articles, search over 50 million abstracts from scientific articles and link out to articles from over 120 other publishers. ScienceDirect Web Editions offers existing print subscribers electronic access to the last 12 months of journal issues, at no additional cost. ScienceDirect OnSite offers local loading onto the institution's Intranet.
Springer Verlag LINK	Basic institutional licence for electronic access up to three simultaneous users included in the price for the print subscription, can be made accessible to staff and other authorized users of the institution. Unlimited institutional licence for access for an unlimited number of simultaneous users can be obtained at an extra 25% for Academic and 30% for Corporate users. Access at most institutions is set up with authentication via the IP address.
American Chemical Society	SciFinder is a desktop tool to explore CAS Databases by author, keyword, (sub)structure, sequence, and more with capability to analyze, sort and visualize results. SciFinder Scholar similar to SciFinder, but for academic institutions only.

Institute for Scientific Information (ISI)	Web of Science provides sitewide access through Internet and Intranet to the ISI Citation Indexes to search current and retrospective multidisciplinary information from nearly 8,500 high impact research journals (over 1.1 million records and more than 23 million cited references per year from more than 230 disciplines). Updated weekly and coverage include: Science Citation Index Expanded (from 1945, with author abstracts from 1991), Social Sciences Citation Index (from 1956, with author abstracts from 1992), Arts & Humanities Citation Index (from 1975, with author abstracts from 2000), with provision for ordering full-text documents directly on the Web and delivery through ISI Document Solution.

16.3. REPACKAGING CONTENT

It is not only the tough legal clauses concerning easily manipulatable electronic information that libraries have to bear with in the changing environment. Apart from professional skills to process, organize and service electronic sources, they should also amass awareness about these legal clauses. Like acquisition and mergers in the commercial and business circles to strengthen and consolidate business interests and to improve market share, scholarly publishers are also entering into mergers or make arrangements for content sharing. Over the years, Elsevier Science has become an amalgam of 5-6 publishing houses, the latest acquisition being that of Academic Press. Institute of Scientific Information (ISI) has become a part of The Thomson Corporation. Whether through acquisitions or not, publishers have arrangements to lease content or to link to full text of other publishers. ICOLC guidelines demand that 'publishers should curtail the practice of repurposing or repackaging content (such as republication of articles in multiple electronic journals) in ways that require libraries to pay for the same content multiple times' [1]. Libraries are the severe victims of this acute commercialism as they are forced to spend their hard-earned money in duplicate content whereas the users always demand for fresh content. Libraries tolerate duplication of information in secondary sources due to the interdisciplinary and multidisciplinary subject specialization and the cost for such sources are comparatively smaller than for full text primary sources. Repackaging may benefit the publishers to advance their products to fresh markets, however it may hamper established libraries interests, and this has to be addressed by mutual consultations between trade and professional librarians. To have an illustration of the amount of repackaging in the vogue, three products, ScienceDirect from Elsevier Science, Scifinder from the Chemical Abstracts Service of the American Chemical Society, and The Web of Knowledge from Thomson-ISI, are listed. Only in-depth studies through an exhaustive survey of all the available electronic information products must be able to ascertain and bring to light the present level of content duplication.

16.3.1. ScienceDirect

The ScienceDirect [URL http://www.sciencedirect.com/], launched in 1999 as a web database of Elsevier Science journals, today offers multiple content sources including research journals, bibliographic databases and reference works. Claimed as the world's largest full-text journals database with more than 1700 scientific, technical and medical peer-reviewed journals, over 59 million abstract and over two million full-text scientific journal articles. It also has a repackaged suite of bibliographic databases (covers around 10000 journals) and linking to another one million full-text articles from 110 other publishers (American Institute of Chemical Engineers (AIChE), American Psychological Association, ASM International, Gauthier-Villars, CRC Press, TMS, to name a few). Some of the bibliographic databases available are Beilstein Abstracts, FLUIDEX, BIOSIS Previews, GEOBASE, BIOTECHNOBASE, INSPEC, Compendex, MEDLINE, EconLit, OceanBase, EMBASE, World Textiles, Elsevier BIOBASE, and PsycINFO.

16.3.2. SCIFINDER

SCIFINDER is the web version of Chemical Abstracts delivered as value added service by American Chemical Society [URL http://www.cas.org/SCIFINDER/]. SciFinder provides full-text capability via the ChemPort Connection. SciFinder lists the references in reverse chronological order, with provision to see the cited and citing references, which was hitherto a feature of the citation indexes from ISI.

16.3.3. ISI Web of Knowledge

Web of Knowledge from ISI [URL http://www.isinet.com/webofknowledge/] repackages their erstwhile citation and current awareness products and bibliographic products from other publishers with arrangements to access full text in some cases. The individual entities include:

* Web of Science — Nearly 8,500 authoritative, high impact journals covered by ISI Citation Indexes.
* ISI Current Contents Connect — Tables of contents from about 7,600 journals and 2,000 books; with links to more than 3,600 ISI-evaluated Web sites and over 170,000 searchable, full-text Web documents.
* Derwent Innovations Index — Coverage of 20 million patents from 40 international patent-issuing authorities
* ISI Proceedings — Global coverage of proceedings from the most prestigious conferences and meetings
* ISI Chemistry — High quality, synthetic chemical information with precise query capabilities
* BIOSIS Previews — Renowned life science and biomedical research index
* CAB ABSTRACTS — Coverage of international applied life sciences research
* INSPEC — A comprehensive index to literature in physics, electrical/electronic engineering, computing, control engineering, and information technology
* ISI Journal Citation Reports on the Web — A unique and

powerful resource that enables highly focused analysis and evaluation of nearly 7,000 science and social sciences journals

16.4. CONCLUSION

Like their counterparts in the developed world, libraries in the country are experiencing the virtues of electronic information. Whether electronic information resources are costlier than printed or difficult to put into proper service by the existing infrastructure are issues to be addressed considering an integrated view of the emerging information market and the role of libraries in the post web academic environment. Libraries can procure and serve electronic information just as single entities, however it would be judicious to frame networks with like-minded libraries in one's city, state or country. The significant progress made by the MHRD to form a consortia for front ranking institutions in the country has elevated the information base in these institutions and transformed the term 'consortia' from a mere buzz word or theoretical concept. Many such initiatives may follow in the coming years such as consortia for university libraries, research libraries under DRDO/CSIR etc. Since repackaging, cross platform content migration, duplication of information in multiple product etc., by one publisher or different publishers has become the marketing slogan these days to enrich a product and take it to fresh customers. Evaluation of electronic products before original procurement will be the librarian's forte to counter such library and consumer unfriendly tactics for widening the information base in our libraries.

REFERENCES

1. International Coalition Of Library Consortia (ICOLC), Statement of Current Perspective and Preferred Practices for the Selection and Purchase of Electronic Information, Update No. 1; New Developments In E-Journal Licensing, (December 2001 update to March 1998 Statement), http://www.library.yale.edu/consortia/ 2001 currentpractices.htm

2. Academic Single Institution License, http://www.licensingmodels.com/academic.htm
3. Academic Consortia License, http:// www.licensingmodels.com/consortia.htm
4. Emerald Consortia, http://www.emeraldinsight.com/consortia/
5. Helmer, John F., Editorial: Epidemiology of the Consortial Spore, Information Technology and Libraries, 18 (3), Sept 1999.
6. Landesman, M. and van Reenen, J., Consortia vs. reform: creating congruence, JEP: the Journal of Electronic Publishing, 6(2), Dec 2000, http://www.press.umich.edu/ jep/06-02/landesman.html
7. Arora, Jagdish, Indian National Digital Library in Engineering Science and Technology (INDEST): A Proposal for Strategic Co-operation for Consortia-based Access to Electronic Resources, International Information & Library Review, 33, pp. 149-165, 2001
8. Will Science Publishing Perish? The Paradox of Contemporary Science Journals, American Chemical Society, Washington, D.C, p. 2.
9. Binder, Michael B., Licensing Models: Information as a Commodity, The Journal of Electronic Publishing, 3(3), March 1998, http://www.press.umich.edu/jep/03-03/binder.html
10. Hirshon, Arnold et al., International Coalition of Library Consortia (ICOLC) Statement of Current Perspective and Preferred Practices for the Selection and Purchase of Electronic Information, http://www.library.yale.edu/consortia/statement. html

17
Electronic Libraries and Users

17.0. INTRODUCTION

Libraries across the country are facing sweeping changes on account of the very nature in which information is generated, transmitted, disseminated and archived due to the increasing presence of information in non-print form. There is no doubt that information in the electronic form is a potential asset that can be vigorously applied to any information-requiring environment without any hassle. There is a major difference in the information processing as well as service environment in our libraries due to the advent and spread of electronic forms, especially after the emergence of Internet and web as a dominant pathway and repository of electronic information resources. In an increasingly wired world, it is possible that universities may be able to take back control of scholarly information, it doesn't necessarily help libraries, as they may risk being cut out of the author-publisher-dissemination loop [7]. There is also a question about relevance of information services, what we perceive from a professional angle, and how does it affect the user response and in any way contribute to a reduced interest to use the library is a crucial matter to be evaluated. It is equally important like quantifying use to assess the qualitative attributes of implicit and explicit use and examine the difficulties of users to properly frame their requests. The limitations on the part of library professionals to perceive and represent what is demanded by users in information systems, and the dilemmas of information organization and retrieval to handle these vexed issues are also emphasized. In the absence of sufficient data to justify the subjective patterns of library use, attempt will be made to draw some inferences on the emergence of Internet as a beyond library information repository demonstrated by enhanced citations of web resources. In one way library acquisitions are falling, sources are increasing, and a single site library satisfying user needs is a doubtful proposition forcing users to look ahead of the library for their information needs. It is to be debated in professional circles and user meets the reason for a waning interest (?) in libraries either due to electronic access options elsewhere or due to not so satisfactory user services. Thus the only option for the libraries is to enter into collaborations, networking and consortia and to reorient their role as information service and access centres rather as information warehouses. Also the extra time that is required in adapting the printed information is considerably reduced or totally absent with electronic information in the case of computer intensive research, development, professional and service environment what the society is engaged in. The technical advances as a result of enhanced research in science and technology made it possible to reduce drastically the time involved in information collection and identification.

17.1. TECHNICAL ADVANCES

The first major technical breakthrough, of course after paper and printing, in the information distribution chain is that of microforms. They helped to preserve less used information in compact space on one hand and as a delivery option for voluminous sources on the other. The librarians have their unchallenged role even in the microform era as a sophisticated technology like microfilms and microfiche required costly and special purpose readers that are exclusively housed in the library. Due to the inherent features of the technology, the cost involved in readers/printers, the patience involved on the part of users/professionals to search, identify and use relevant sources, this technology has not picked up much especially after advances in affordable computer technology. A number of microfilms and readers housed in our libraries may throng up as a counter argument. When we say about consulting time, where facility for printing was provided, one can say that the user has spent less time in library for using the microforms than for printed sources. The primary disadvantage of microform is that the readers are single purpose and involve considerable sum for maintenance and operation. Next came the significant advancement we still experience that of photocopying. The cheap and affordable copying technology revolutionised the concept of information use as it spearheaded the trend of owning copies of library resources. Consultation most often earlier involves the user to patiently sit in the library and take notes to create at least a distant original. The copying technology has freed the users from sitting in the library for longer duration for reading, since one can simply copy in a minute and leave. Then came the biggest revolution so far regarded, that of computer and communications, as these technologies are major enablers in the information dissemination chain, they are not stand-alone unlike earlier technologies and can be networked and integrated with other devices and technologies. They not only perfected the manual technologies of print and microform production, but also gave us online and CD-ROM databases, electronic information resources, Internet and digital revolution. With electronic information services, a user can copy or access in a second, and for some Internet/Intranet resources, the user does not have to visit the library at all. This time saving on the part of library services has come as a blessing in disguise and works as a straight illustration of validating the fourth law of library science. Though our libraries are progressing well on the automation and information access front, there is a definite case of depleting user presence due to many reasons. The real question is whether our electronic services have any way affected the user interests or are the users found more confidence in a beyond library information superhighway that forced them to bypass formal libraries.

17.2. MANUAL VS ELECTRONIC INFORMATION SERVICES

In the largely print dominated manual environment, a library was regarded as a dominant player in the information processing-dissemination chain as the age old techniques of classification, cataloguing and documentation was largely applied to the printed sources by the librarian. One can assign fixed responsibilities in the print world as producers and consumers of information for researchers; producers of physical volumes assuring the quality of the intellectual content for academic presses; and the responsibility for purchasing, organizing, preserving, and providing access for academic libraries [7]. Only when the library professional processes the resources as per the content covered in them or any other attribute that does matter, the user may be able to retrieve the relevant ones and able to consult a few in the time available. The printed indexing and abstracting services that flourished then helped to extend the information consolidation work attempted at individual libraries with some exhaustivity to a subject or discipline level. The library tools as well as the indexing/abstracting tools most likely give only indicative or informative surrogates about the original source and one has to consult the original source for their exact information requirements.

The manual services rendered exclusively by library professionals in our libraries fall under processing of printed sources to generate catalogue cards, documentation and bibliography lists with or without indicative or informative abstract about the original, and reference, current awareness or selective dissemination services. Most of these services, though library centred, were offered after considerable time and effort put by library staff, and most often each of the libraries have to 'reinvent the wheel' as the chances of collaboration in such a manual environment were rather primitive. These library centred services got some refinement when international professional associations and commercial publishers started offering discipline centred information surrogates of indexing and abstracting services. It is difficult to trace out the satisfaction of information needs of users in a totally manual environment when we are increasingly exposed of the benefits of commercial information products and electronic tools. Also manual information search required more time as well as rigorous knowledge about indexing techniques, and researchers find it tedious to spend their valuable time on these routine chores, forcing them to entrust this task to library professionals. One thing is sure, though the exhaustiveness and relevance of manual information services offered by libraries were poor, the users have a strong dependence on libraries and professionals as they need their services to trace, examine and consolidate the print resources.

The application of computers for information work progressed in two ways, to refine the techniques in generating printed information products and to arrive at electronic only information products. The benefits of computer application both at the pre and post-production stages for printed information resources had been manifold. This significantly reduced the time lag in production and remarkably improved the format and presentation of information in these sources. However, the vital step in the application of computer and allied technology in the information dissemination chain is the arrival of viable non-print delivery means such as online, floppy, and CD-ROM databases of electronic information. Initially started for bibliographic information only, slowly with significant advances in computer and memory technology, these started to amass numeric, full text/image, and other types of information. The Internet and its dominant protocol Web demonstrated, outside the library networking and formal resource sharing channels, that large amount of electronic information can be hosted in a decentralised fashion, across the globe in a cost effective manner. Since 1990s the Internet has changed the dissemination of information such as electronic copies of traditional paper-based journals and conference proceedings accessible through subscription or pay per view, free electronic-only refereed journals, haphazard copies of all kinds of material on the home pages, and a handful of electronic pre-prints archives [4]. Libraries and librarians like commercial publishers were soon to feel the virtues of Web and started using it as a carrier for disseminating information resources. What distinguishes current networked resource discovery from the traditional library model is the limited, if almost non-existent, role of surrogates in the process [6].

17.3. MANUAL VS ELECTRONIC SEARCH

Search for manual sources required scanning of catalogue cards or indexing and abstracting sources. As cross-references often increase the number of cards or pages, there was a difficulty in being very exhaustive. Conducting selective dissemination of information (SDI) services had been extremely difficult as the document profiles are to be matched with user profiles often achieved with the aid of semi-mechanical systems. Most of these limitations are easily bypassed in the electronic environment due to the very nature of information processing and organisation in electronic form. The inherent advantages of indexing electronic information help to search for any or all the fields in a time saving manner. Since document profiles are already stored in the database and the search software supports creation of user profiles, the current awareness services (CAS) and SDI services would be achieved easier. The concern for end-user search was very dominant right from the beginning of early CD-ROM database systems as the time spent for search was not chargeable. Also the universe of knowledge getting complex as a result of continued advanced research in intra and inter-disciplinary areas, often the search conducted by a generalist like librarian may not understand either the information requirements completely or has not achieved the desired results from the user point of view. The convoluted information requirements of present day researchers require sufficient knowledge of the discipline and since the users are increasingly exposed to the computerised work environment, they feel very convenient to conduct information search on electronic systems. The professional ethos and egos also played its part as users found more satisfactory results in a relatively easy and convenient way than manual systems. The librarians should recognise the confidence and maturity of users to conduct searches on their own as they have better knowledge of the discipline, different keywords and their relationships and for the inherent advantages of locating related sources by browsing or serendipity. There should be closer interaction and effective communication between library professionals and users to understand each others views about information needs and use.

17.4. INFORMATION USE

Justifying one's own mistakes might also work to doubt the efficacy of professional searches. It is difficult to tell what is needed and information services attempted by a library are primarily based on this subjective input and hence quite justifying for users to comment about misses or noise in SDI/CAS outputs. Information need is what an individual *ought* to have; want is what an individual *would* like to have; demand is what an individual *asks* for; use is what an individual actually *uses*; and requirement denotes what is needed, what is wanted or what is demanded [9]. Information needs are affected by a variety of factors such as the range of sources available, the uses to which information will be put, individual characteristics of the user, social, political and economic systems surrounding the user, and the consequences of information use [11]. Scientists spend 50-60% of their time communicating [4]. Computerised environment has no doubt increased the quantum of information available at one's reach, but it has in no way enhanced a person's information consumption skills. Though the user is exposed to more microfilms, xerox copies, and electronic information on desktop/ Intranet/Web ready to display at the touch of a button, the more time one spends in searching and collecting information, the less time s/he gets to use it. Scholarly articles are identified for reading in five basic ways: browsing, automated searches, citations found in the literature, mentions by other people, and current-awareness tools [13]. How much information one can use to work on a particular problem is also subjective as human beings observe the 'principle of least effort'. Accessibility of information resources is usually assumed to depend on a range of cognitive, social, and physical factors, such as whether a person is aware of a resource, has the knowledge and skills needed to access it, and has the resource close at hand [3]. Perhaps one may easily tide over an information crisis by identifying only 20% of the total references and even by using only 20% what is identified. Our own experience in professional research suggests that in many cases there is always impossible to collect all the information sources available on a particular topic and absolutely no need of all of them to work with. There is a burden of effort in information storage and retrieval that may be shifted from shoulder to shoulder, from author, to indexer, to index language designer, to searcher, to user [2].

17.5. INFORMATION ORGANIZATION AND RETRIEVAL

Some of the problems were to strike the perfect balance and to optimize the conflicting information retrieval (IR) parameters of recall (measure of retrieval of relevant sources) and precision (quantification of the avoidance of irrelevant documents). And simple Boolean intersection of natural language terms can produce imprecise results when two or more terms are present in a record, but without the semantic association expected by the user, though proximity searching can overcome this problem to some extent [2]. Most of the available systems support logical Boolean operators of AND, NOT and OR, which has a perennial problem as it tells only whether a source is relevant or not relevant as per the presence/ absence of a particular search term. No chance to rank or identify relative importance when one is working with Boolean logic. This disadvantage can be overcome by other information retrieval models like, probabilistic, fuzzy set, vector retrieval etc. [1], but we are yet to see them getting prominence. Since writers are not consistent in their use of all the words to describe topics, the searcher must plan very carefully to include all synonyms and all necessary levels of specificity in searching [2]. How to significantly embody the various terms, their relations, their order, proximity etc., which an actual user expect and work with, using the IR tools is the crucial issue. Another perennial problem is to transform the user needs to workable and efficient profiles to run the different information services in a personalized fashion, as there is always difficulty on the part of user to express exact information requirements. The personalization attempts and the means of electronic information delivery received a tremendous boost after the dominance of Internet and Web as even library databases and electronic database systems mimic a web like front end and search features.

17.6. WEB MODEL FOR ELECTRONIC INFORMATION DELIVERY

Increasingly, electronic information providers are using hypertext techniques to navigate their files, both within a file and across files, even for ephemeral information like daily news extracts [2]. While the Web is undeniably valuable as an information resource, any suggestion that it supplants the role of a library is foolhardy as a library is not just a repository of information, but a rich collection of services including selection, preservation, categorization, location, and reference [6]. There are also concerns like 'either the information wanted is not available on the Internet, or not found it, or not have enough confidence in its accuracy and completeness to rely on it for scholarly purposes' [10]. The problems with information organisation on web are largely attributed to the distributed location of sources and the huge numbers of such sources. The technology behind web indexing has four notable problems: scalability – difficult to scale as Web-crawlers have to download resources to the indexing location; accessibility – primitive domain-based access control lists; retrieval technology - only relevant for textual resources, but a significant amount of the resources over the Internet are non-textual such as images, audio, video, CGI links, Java applets, and ActiveX components; user behaviour - long queries increase recall precision but most queries to search engines are one to two words in length [6]. The information ordering techniques resorted by libraries are difficult to apply and justify to web as there is always a tolerable backlog in the library. Thus web and search engines arrived at a mechanism to auto-index sources based on terms present in the source. At its most basic level, for every word, a search engine maintains a list of all known web pages containing that word [5]. As a result, for any search made on web, the user gets all related pages dealing with some aspect of the search term. Some of these search results are totally useless, but some links are quite useful validating the time and effort spent in such searches. While a system of quality ratings for Internet sites is too much to hope for, it is reasonable to ask for comprehensive depositories, electronic libraries where a record of significant communications would be preserved for reference and study [10]. The augmented presence of electronic information on the networks has in any way bypassed the user from the library or the intricacies of our understanding of user needs lead to a lack of library use are to be studied from various angles.

17.7. USER AVOIDANCE/BYPASSING

The same proportions of scientists still browse to identify scholarly articles to read, but more are using online searches and the proportion of readings identified through online searches appears to be increasing, while use of the remaining means — except for browsing — has been decreasing [13]. Library acquisitions suffered a serious setback in recent years unable to withstand the price rice and budgetary constraints forcing users to look beyond the library for their varied information requirements. My contention is that librarians are not yet acting as true consumers and until we do that, we cannot blame predatory publishers for taking advantage of the situation [12]. Another issue involves the very large, and rapidly increasing, number of articles obtained through photocopying, interlibrary loan, document delivery, preprints, and reprints [13]. The right step in assessing whether there is a depleting user interest in libraries is to study the use patterns over the years and are we serious enough to conduct an objective assessment is the key issue. In a country like India, where the population growth has not yet stabilised, going by numbers will not attribute for any of the qualitative aspects. This author has not seen any reduction in book issues in an academic library, but all the new acquisitions are being used to the same extent or crossed a threshold is doubtful. But what is seen is the fall in library attendance, this is a plain statement as of now, as supporting statistics is yet to be compiled, fewer users actually visit the library, and very few still spend much time, a lot others use library through photocopies, networks, accesses etc. It is difficult as such to quantify use as the library has statistics only about explicit use, but there are also implicit use through browsing, consulting etc., which are arduous to be quantified. There are also vital questions about mere issuing a book or taking a photocopy of a journal article attribute to use and here comes the qualitative assessment of use. How many libraries have assessed the journal use by quantifying the use of individual articles from individual issues? Perhaps as professionals we are afraid to look at these issues as the results of such assessment may force the authorities to look at the investments on a service institution like library. Like Reenen's comment [12] about false consumers, it seems that librarians are also poor managers, as if to afraid a self-assessment of library use or to undergo performance audits. If we go by citations to articles, libraries have to seriously admit the fact the users are seriously getting addicted to web resources. In the Proceedings volume of CALIBER 2001, the annual conference of INFLIBNET Centre, there are 39 papers published in full contained a total of 346 references, out of which 157 pertained to electronic information on web sites. The major problem areas for citations in the digital realm are both philosophical and physical, the philosophical problem is in defining the unit carrying scientific contributions: what should be cited, what should be pointed to, the physical problems are those of longevity and authenticity [8]. It seems that as readers of journals, scientists are very progressive and supportive of free electronic journals, but as authors of articles they are very conservative in their choice of where to submit their manuscripts [4]. Though users are not receptive, they will be forced to scan in many cases long SDI and CAS printouts prompted by the inherent difficulties discussed earlier of expressing concretely the information requirements and the problems of information processing and retrieval. The library professionals do matching of all the terms suggested by the user and their relationships, and as a result sometimes discard some relevant information on the one hand and add some noise on the other. The users are also not patient enough to constantly interact with the library staff to modify their profiles to improve the relevance of information services, may be due to the time constraints on their part. Again by a rough assessment, it is doubted that less than 10% of the users usually respond to SDI results sent and the remaining are either using it as it is or rejecting it straightaway. Out of those responds, only a few show their willingness to constantly give feedback to modify their information requirements or keywords and to improve the utility of such services.

17.8. PRESENT LIBRARY

The fixed roles suggested by Levy [7] for researchers, publishers, and libraries are either overlapping or changing in the electronic scene. There are cases where an author or a library is acting as electronic publisher, and there are publishers providing a wide variety of information packages than sheer contents of printed journals. The different electronic information services formulated as a result of the arrival of various electronic products are Online Public Access Catalogue (OPAC) search services, database search services, digital and virtual library reference and access services. With the availability of affordable feature-rich software for automating house-keeping operations in the library like identifying, consolidating, procuring and processing books as well as to handle their issue, return, renewal and reservation, and serials control, most of the operations handled manually would be performed now in an efficient manner in less time. Also the system must be able to answer queries about the status of an operation such as when a book was approved, when it was ordered and when it has been received etc. The remarkable advantages have been in assigning more relevant keywords, easy to cross-refer related entries, and in hosting OPAC that can search on all the bibliographic fields like author, title, publisher, keywords, class no, etc. All the collaborating libraries in a network or consortium can adopt one automation system on a specific platform so that the different individual OPACs can be combined to generate union databases so that the utility of search services must be further enhanced. The bibliographic search services may be used in relation to OPAC search to identify the different articles in journal holdings of the library. If there are full text databases, this will work one step further to get an electronic version of the original article. Most of the printed reference sources get outdated immediately after its printing, and to refresh the holdings with every new edition of a particular source is a difficult overture for our libraries due to budget and space constraints. Internet enabled reference service has come as a boon to the libraries as a considerable number of reference questions can be answered by web surfing alone. The full text resources populated on the web from various institutions as digital and virtual libraries also should supplement the literature collection activities of researchers. A large number of journal publishers now offer free access till abstracts of articles published in their journals and for subscribers to even access the full text version of articles in HTML/PDF. Nowadays, a lot of books come with some electronic attachments in floppies or CD-ROMs or permits to access some materials from the publisher site. Thus libraries have a considerable chunk of resources in electronic form which can be accessed from either the Internet or can be hosted on the Intranet. And the library is undergoing a smooth transition from an information supply/leasing centre to an information access centre.

The real issue is has the library really lost its ground in the emerging information scene. Even the critics will not say so or doubt librarianship as a mere clerical and manual operation with out any professional virtues. The concerns expressed are only to vitalise the professional skills and rejuvenate the style of working and reorient our rightful place in the positive dissemination of information. May be our feeling that library as a central place in the Institution where everyday large number of users visit like a cinema hall or public utility has lost some ground in the electronic scene. The scholarly journals are read over a long period of time following publication very much like a nuclear decay curve, and older articles may not be available electronically [13] and it is the duty of libraries to provide access to such print only materials. Apart from continuing information services provided erstwhile for print sources, the electronic dominance has reassured the library more as an information service centre than as an information storehouse. It is imperative on institution heads and information managers to trace, identify and host electronic information such as book floppies, CD-ROMS, and electronic databases on the library LAN or Institution's Intranet and requires bargaining with publishers for local or web access of subscribed journals. Facility for Internet access also may be arranged in the library if such facility does not exist in other departments of the Institution so that patrons may be able to browse beyond the library collection for their information support. As far as possible, especially for reference and information services, looking at web also must be instilled on the reference staff so that dated sources may be circumvented in rendering such services.

17.9. CONCLUSION

Like building collection, and providing services, improving access to information should be the guiding criteria for libraries in the electronic era. We have to design new set of parameters to judge up on operational efficiency and performance effectiveness of libraries. The traditional libraries boasted that they attracted a lot of users to stay inside their premises for comparatively longer times whereas a modern librarian will be concerned more about carrying information to users' desktops. No library how rich its budget allocation and collection may be is in a position to satisfy all users demands. As a person well versed in the intricacies of the emerging information market, he is frank enough to admit that information needs of all users are not to be met by the library alone. Collaboration with other libraries through consortia or networks increases the quantum of resources available for users, and will be regarded as indications of mature thinking than as weakness. Most of our libraries spent a lot of public money for information needs of a small percentage of the population and optimizing that spending for the benefit of a large number of users is the need of the hour. Whether users has lost interest in our services or are they bypassing us are crucial questions to be studied from library and user perspectives and to be deliberated in professional forums and user-library meets. May be we are going through a passing phase and this is the right time to have a close introspection and critical look at our collections and services in the light of complex user needs, hazy use patterns, and ever increasing spread of internet and electronic information.

REFERENCES

1. Bartschi, Martin et al., An Overview of Information Retrieval Subjects, IEEE Computer, May 1985, pp. 67-84.
2. Batty, David, WWW — Wealth, Weariness or Waste: Controlled vocabulary and thesauri in support of online information access, http://www.dlib.org/dlib/november98/ 11batty.html
3. Bishop, Ann Peterson. Logins and Bailouts: Measuring Access, Use, and Success in Digital Libraries, The Journal of Electronic Publishing, 4(2), December 1998, http://www.press.umich.edu/jep/ 04-02/bishop.html
4. Björk, Bo-Christer, Turk, Ziga. How Scientists Retrieve Publications: An Empirical Study of How the Internet is Overtaking Paper Media, The Journal of Electronic Publishing, 6 (2), December 2000, http://www.press.umich.edu/jep/06-02/bjork.html

5. Clever, Hypersearching on the Web, Members of the Clever Project, Scientific American, June 1999, pp. 44-52.
6. Lagoze, Carl, From Static to Dynamic Surrogates: Resource Discovery in the Digital Age, http://www.dlib.org/dlib/june97/06lagoze.html
7. Levy, David M., Digital Libraries and the Problem of Purpose, http://www.dlib.org/dlib/ january00/ 01levy.html
8. Lindquist, Mats G. Not Your Father's References: Citations in the Digital Space, The Journal of Electronic Publishing, 4(3), March 1999, http://www.press.umich.edu/jep/04-03/lindquist.html
9. Line, Maurice B., Draft Definitions: Information and Library needs, wants, demands, and uses, Aslib Proceedings, 26 (2), Feb 1974.
10. Orlans, Harold. A, Home Scholar's Electronic Woes, The Journal of Electronic Publishing, 3(3), March 1998, http://www.press.umich.edu/jep/03-03/orlans.html
11. Paisley, W J, Information needs and users, ARIST, 3, 1968, pp. 1-30.
12. Reenen, Johann Van, Library Consumerism in the Digital Age, The Journal of Electronic Publishing, 3(3), March 1998, http://www.press.umich.edu/jep/03-03/ vanreenen.html
13. Tenopir, Carol, King, Donald W., Designing Electronic Journals With 30 Years of Lessons from Print, The Journal of Electronic Publishing, 4(2), December 1998, http://www.press.umich.edu/jep/04-02/king.html

PART 5: COMPUTER APPLICATIONS

18
Database Management Systems

18.0. INTRODUCTION

It is worthwhile to define the terms of data, database, management, and system at the outset. The Oxford English Dictionary describes data as the quantities, characters, or symbols on which operations are performed by computers and other automatic equipment that may be stored or transmitted [1]. Data is any representation such as characters to which meaning might be assigned [2] like details of a book represented in a catalogue card such as its title, or author name, or call number. It can be defined also as information in its rudimentary form and data elements may be letters, numbers, facts or symbols [3]. A structured collection of data held in computer storage that also incorporates software to make it accessible in a variety of ways forms a database [4]. A collection of data fundamental to an operation organised by some predefined structure is termed a database [2]. A database, also referred as databank or information bank, is an organized and often-interrelated collection of computer based data [3]. Database management is concerned with organisation and manipulation of data in a database and a software package that facilitates all the functions required for database management is regarded as a database management system (DBMS) [4]. A DBMS is nothing but an application software (computer program/s facilitating a predetermined application) used to efficiently extract and manipulate the information contained in the database [2]. It stands as a generic name for the software system that facilitates the tasks of creating, maintaining, and accessing a database [3]. The term system comes in the term DBMS to designate the integrated set of programs which works in unison to offer requisite functionalities for efficient and effective handling of data accumulated in the database.

18.1. CONTRAST WITH EARLY SYSTEMS

Before the advent of DBMSs, data manipulation was achieved with the help of file-processing systems that offered primitive features when you compare them with today's versatile database systems. These file-processing systems supported by a conventional operating system stored permanent records in various files and different application programs are written to add/delete/extract data. New programs are written and new files are created when there is any need for doing so, which leads to certain limitations that victimise their performance. Some of these limitations fall into the heads of:

* **Data redundancy**: Since the files and programs are created at various intervals which sometimes are developed in different formats or programming languages, forcing the same information/data to be replicated in several files. For example, the title and edition of the book may be entered in different formats (Main title, Subtitle or Main title: Subtitle, only main title, all in bold, or small or title cases for title, or 3rd. edition, III edition, 3 ed., Third edition, etc., for edition) and repeated in the Holdings file and Circulation file. This repetition of the same data must also lead to more memory consumption, which is not a constraint as such due to advances in cheaper memory technology. But still redundancy is to be curtailed to arrest the huge access time incurred as a result of duplication of data.
* **Data Inconsistency**: It is a byproduct of redundancy. If

you are modifying data in one file, the duplicated data in other files will not be automatically modified resulting in different versions of the same data in different files. The edition information modified for a book in the Holdings file would not be reflected in the information for that book in the Circulation file.

* **Integrity Problems**: The data values stored in the database must enforce certain types of consistency constraints like the entitlement of books to be issued for a certain category of users. For example, a particular library would like to issue a maximum of 4, 6, 8, and 10 books respectively to undergraduate, postgraduate and research students and teachers. No issue system is supposed to issue more than the specified entitlement. In a railway reservation system, think how much chaotic the system would be if two people enter one compartment with the same berth number, or more than 72 passengers are given berths in a sleeper coach. Since file handling systems incorporate these constraints by adding appropriate lines of code in the application programs, they would be difficult to enforce when new constraints are added and the problem gets compounded when different data sets and files are to be accessed simultaneously.

* **Data Access Problems**: Think of a situation that you have got a program to list out all the books issued on a specific date. Now if you want to know all the books issued by one member during different days, you have no other option but to generate separate lists for all days and then separate out manually the details for the member you are interested in. Alternatively, you have to write another program for listing issues member-wise. But tomorrow if you are interested in the issues of books in a particular discipline, again either manual tabulation from the day wise list or development of another program is required.

* **Atomicity Problems**: If you are renewing a book or issuing one against reservation, the system is supposed to engage

in a certain set of tasks. In the case of renewal, first of all it has to check whether any member has reserved the said book and if not, then it has to advance the return dates, and mark accordingly the respective tags in the circulation file that the transaction is a renewal. In the case of reservation, on issuing the book, the system should cancel the said member from the priority queue. If midway during such transactions, there is a system failure or power failure, the system should be alert enough to maintain the transactions to be atomic. Such transactions should occur in its entirety or not at all, which is difficult to maintain with file handling systems.

* **Security Problems**: Access to the database system must be secure enough to prevent illegitimate access. Think of a situation that a library database system gives unrestricted access to its clients leading to cancellation of books issued by the patrons, forcing the library difficult to enforce even the fundamental laws of library science. The patrons should be given permission to access only the catalogue information. Further different priorities and access rights can be enforced for library staff. A person working in the Acquisition section has no use of journal or circulation information. Priorities are to be earmarked for personnel in different sections, and even for people working in the same section in different wings and grades. The ideal situation would be like the Acquisition-Incharge holding access rights for all modules related to that task whereas a Professional Assistant dealing with book ordering gets access to that part of the database system dealing with book requests, sanction, orders and vendors, but not the fund/payment management part.

* **Synchronization**: It is quite natural that more than one user will be accessing the system, and that too may so happen that two persons must access the same data item. On the reservation desk, two counter clerks accessing the book and circulation files to reserve a title "Principles

of Database Management" by James Martin demanded by two users almost at the same time. Suppose the library holds only one copy of the book, both of them will be accessing the same data to make the required reservation. Since no single processor computer data handling system can provide simultaneous access to the same data set, the transactions are queued up, and because computer works faster and gives us time quickly, human beings are not able to identify the time lag. Out of the two people tried to make the reservation, one will get first chance to mark priority number, say 6, then the next one will get chance after that transaction to assign the priority 7.

* **Management Control**: Difficult to enforce uniform policies in a library as data gets scattered in different files often with difficulties in declaring relations. If a library wanted to issue journal volumes overnight only for those members with a proven track record in book issues, the file handling system has to update the status of each member from the book circulation module or it has to replicate the whole files from that module.

18.2. FEATURES

In contrast to a traditional file handling system, a good DBMS must be free from all the constraints and problems discussed above. Moreover the traditional systems are design driven as they require design changes each time one wants to handle new types of data in contrast to the data driven style of functioning of today's DBMS which guarantees data changes over time without any design changes. Also such a vital resource like data has to be shared by different applications that are not only existing but also which may be thought of in the future. The system should be built to accommodate the changing needs of the library.

Data Independence enables one to modify the physical and logical schema (see the different data views in next section) without modifying the application programs. Application programs must focus on data, their organisation and retrieval rather than on the intricacies of data representation, where they are located and how they are accessed.

The database system should assure fast access to requisite information. The development cost must be commensurate with the information returned by the system. Management controls or specific roles to control access to the system should be strictly ensured for add, modify or delete data. It should also address certain anomalies such as:

* **Updation Anomaly**: This has come as a result of data redundancy, forcing duplicated data to be updated only at one place leaving it unchanged in other places.
* **Insertion Anomaly**: Hindrances in data entry due to constraints that has crept into the system as a result of weak and shortsighted design. For example, you can not register for a member unless s/he has issued at least one book.
* **Deletion Anomaly**: This is the opposite of insertion anomaly mentioned above. If a member has returned all the issued books, inadvertently all details about the user will be deleted as a result of this.

18.3. DATA VIEWS

Since intended as a group of interrelated files to systematically manage data, a DBMS will hide certain details of how the data are stored and organised in the system. It should offer certain views of the data at physical, logical, and view levels as shown in figure 18.1. It is not expected of all users of a DBMS to be computer proficient and hence data abstraction at these levels would facilitate them to use and interact with the system free from inherent intricacies and complexities.

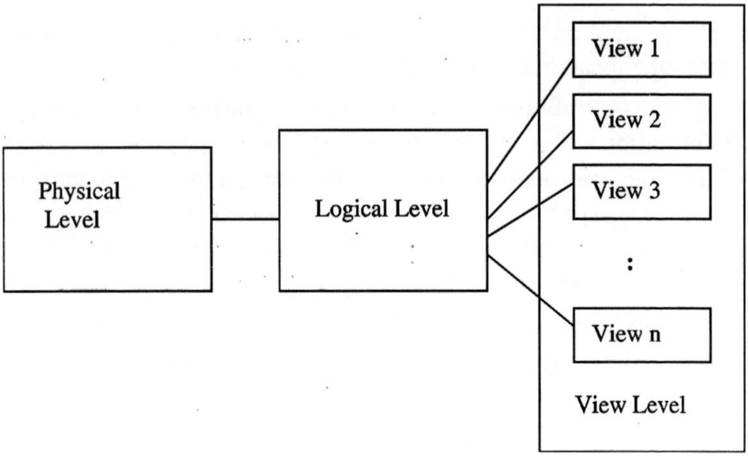

Figure 18.1: Levels of Data Abstraction

Physical level deals with how data are actually stored in the computer storage. This can be viewed at different levels of abstraction like that of files and records or bits and physical addresses on storage devices. A library database at this level is a mere accumulation of certain database files or few bytes of memory.

Logical/ conceptual level represents data and relationships among them. The motivation here is to map the complex physical structures into simple logical structures. Often regarded as the Database Administrator view, who must identify what are all the data to be kept in which database files. Consider the situation of user details in the user file, book details in the book file, and circulation details about what books are issued to which members in the circulation file with the relation connecting these files as the operation of loaning out collection for use outside the library premises.

A **View level** may be the same or more abstract (or less concrete) than the conceptual level whereas physical level is the most concrete among all three. Most of the users are concerned with using the DBMS for some limited specific tasks even though the system is intended as a large repository of data to handle different sophisticated tasks. A person working in the journal section has no interest to browse the book related tasks of acquisition, processing or circulation. If s/he is working to generate a consolidated list of journals for renewal, though information about budgeting may be required, but no information about accounting and payment operations are necessary. One of the virtues of a good DBMS is that it hides a lot of unwanted or alien and penumbral data from users, which otherwise would have been forcefully scanned by them in the manual or file handling systems.

18.4. INSTANCES AND SCHEMAS/SUBSCHEMAS

The contents of the database change over time as and when new information is added or old information is either modified or deleted. The collection of information stored at a particular instant in the database is called an instance (also denoted as extension or database state) of the database. When the database is designed, we concentrate on the overall structure of entities and their relations and the mechanisms by which they are mapped from one level of data abstraction to the more concrete level, which is termed as the plan or schema or intension. Thus we have the physical schema at the physical level, logical schema at the logical level and subschema at the view level. In other words a database system has many views and accordingly many subschemas, whereas only one logical and one physical schema.

18.5. DATA MODELS

The basic structure of a database is the data model that describes data and their relationships, and inherent constraints. Three types of data models have been proposed so far, viz., record based logical model, object based logical model, and physical model, of which physical data models are beyond the scope of this discussion.

18.5.1. Record based Logical Model

This model represents data at the logical level and view level. Here database is structured in records where each record is composed of fixed number of fixed length fields (information about a book in the catalogue card can be taken as a record in the database and title, author, etc. as fields). The fixed-length records are widely used, as they are simpler for implementation at the physical level. There are three types of record-based logical models, namely relational model, network model and hierarchical model, of which the relational model is the most popular.

18.5.2. Relational Model

In the relational model, the database is organised as a collection of tables where each column of the table is a field and each row as a record. The tables are related with the help of common fields. For example, for a library database, the book table (Table 18.1) may contain the fields of acc_no, author, title, publisher, and call_no; the user table (Table 18.2) contains user_code, name, address, and category; and the issue table (Table 18.3) with user_code, acc_no, and issue_date. Say for example, in the book table (Table 18.1), if we take one entire row, it will contain the details of one book, which is taken as a record, and the accession number of that book will be entered in the acc_no field.

Table 18.1: Book Table

Acc_No	*Author*	*Title*	*Pub-lisher*	*Call_No*
171096	Ranganathan, S R	Five laws of library science	UBS	020.1 RAN/F N88
172022	Flynn, Roger R	An introduction to information science	Marcel Dekker	020 FLY/A N87
172009	Lancaster, F W	Indexing and abstracting in theory and practice	Library Asso-ciation	025.3 LAN/ I N98
168374	Kumar, Krishan	Research methods in library and information science	Vikas	020.723 KUM/R N92
105738	Parker, C C	Information Sources in Science & Technology	Butter worths	020 PAR/I N75

Table 18.2: User Table

User_Code	Name	Dept	Category
20102	Abhishek Kumar	Library Sc.	U G
19361	Manish Gupta	Physics	Gr. B
18315	Sunil Kumar	Central Lib.	Gr. A
26051	Nachiketa	Library Sc.	P G
27403	Vijay Singh	Metallurgy	Gr. B

Table 18.3: Issue Table

user_code	acc_no	issue_date
26051	105738	12-01-00
18315	168374	15-02-00
26051	172022	15-02-00
27403	168374	18-05-00
20102	172009	23-07-00

There may be three types of relations in these tables: one-to-one, one-to-many or many-to-one and many-to-many depending on the number of elements in the relationship set. For example, a particular book can be issued only to one user at a time, so the issue relation between book and user here is one-to-one, but different books can be issued at one time to one or more users, giving the issue relation one-to-many characteristic also.

18.3.3. Network Model

Network Model restricts all relations to be many-to-one and is represented by a collection of data and relationships are represented by links/directed graphs as in figure 18.2.

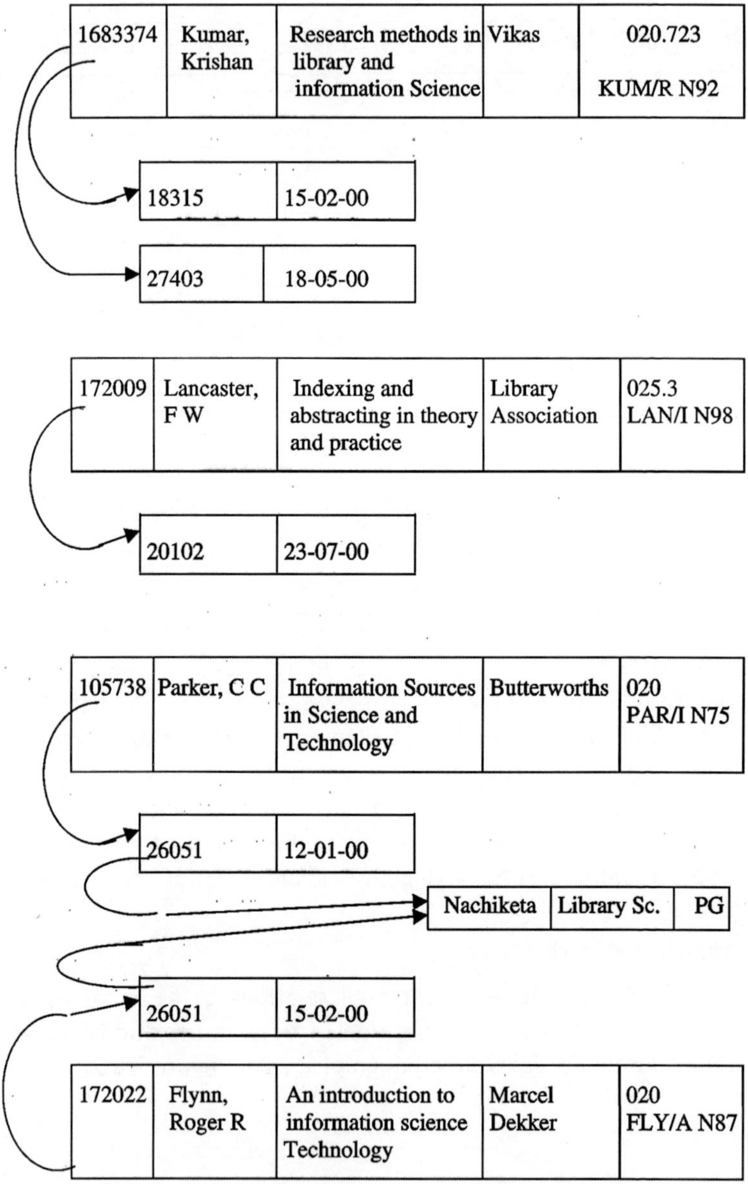

Fig. 18.2: Illustration of Network Data Model

18.3.4. Hierarchical Model

A hierarchy is similar to a network model in which all links point from child to parent. In Hierarchical model, records are organised as a collection of trees in contrast to arbitrary graphs as in figure 18.3.

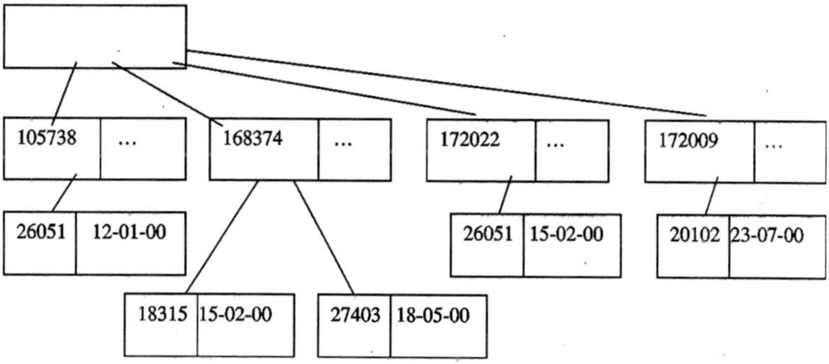

Fig. 18.3: Illustration of Hierarchical Data Model

18.6. OBJECT BASED LOGICAL MODEL

Object based logical models offer flexible structures to specify data constraints, and the more prevalent ones are Entity-Relationship Model and the Object-Oriented Model.

18.6.1. Entity Relationship Model

In the entity-relationship (E-R) model, the whole database can be modeled as a set of entities and relationships among them. Any distinguishable object that exists in the real world is treated as an entity. In the library perspective, books, users, vendors, binders, etc., are entities. There are certain attributes that describe the entity in the database, for an entity like book, some of the attributes are author, title, edition, call_no, accn_no etc. A relationship is an association among entities like the 'supplied by' relation between vendor and book. E-R model is famous as the graphical representation (also called as E-R Diagram) helps us to structure entities, their attributes and relationships in the database design stage. In the E-R diagram, rectangles denote entities, ellipses represent attributes, diamonds stand for relations, and lines (plus arrows indicate one in relations such as one-to-one and many-to-one) link attributes to entities and relationships to entities. For clarity in understanding, each symbol is labeled with the entity or relationship it represents. A typical E-R diagram from the library context involving book and user is shown in figure 18.4.

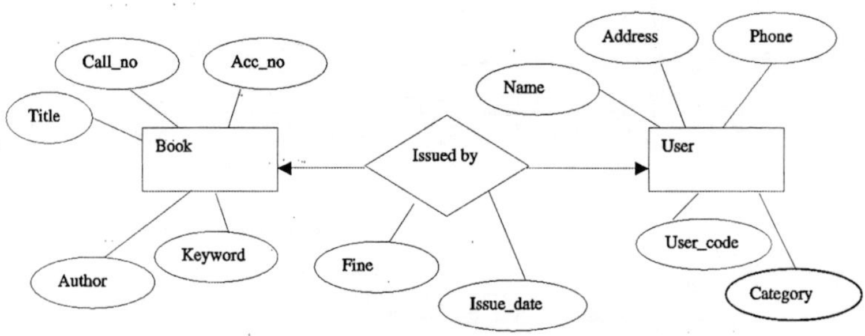

Fig. 18.4: E-R Diagram for the Book Issue Relation

18.6.2. Object-Oriented Model

This model is based on the principles of Object Oriented Programming like C++ where objects form the building block of databases. An object contains both data (called as instance variables) as well as code (called as methods) that operate on the data. Objects with same type of values and same methods form classes. So a particular book is an object whereas the book with instance variables title, author, acc_no, call_no etc., is a class. When we supply these variables with values of one particular book: Principles of Database Systems, Jeffrey D. Ullman, TB30554, 005.74 ULL/P N84, it becomes an object of the class book. The present day relational database systems like Oracle also uses the concepts of object models to improve data handling and retrieval features, and therefore it becomes difficult to stick to tight classification of data models on these lines.

18.7. NORMAL FORMS

Let us examine one Unnormalised relation in Table 18.4. This structure is not at all feasible for storing as a file in computer as the Book contains a lot of attributes on one hand and transactions contains different number of entries.

Table 18.4: Unnormalised Book-Transaction Relation

Book				**Transactions**	
Acc No	Title	Publisher	User_Code	Issue_date	Reservation _date (#)
156231	DBMS		MGH	24302	21-Mar-2000
			25123		04-Apr-2000 (7)
			18476	12-Aug-2000	
Acc No	Title	Publisher	User_Code	Issue_date	Reservation _date
173872	System Anal.	PHI	12147		09-Mar-2000 (12)
			23467	21-May-2000	
Acc No	Title	Publisher	User_Code	Issue_date	Reservation _date
142564	Algo-rithms	AWS	18199	12-Jun-2000	

Relations are to be normalized to avoid inconsistencies and to prevent any imminent data loss when existing relations are altered for insertion, deletion, or updation. Inserting new data to a relation should be possible without leaving blank fields for some attributes. Similarly deletion of a row of relation/ table (tuple) should be without losing any vital information and updating the value of an attribute in a tuple without exhaustively searching all tuples in a relation. The unnormalized relation in Table 18.4 can be normalized into First Normal Form (1NF) by converting each composite attribute into individual attributes as in Table 18.5.

Table 18.5: 1NF

Acc No	*Title*	*Publisher*	*User_Code*	*Issue_date*	*Reservation_date*	*Prio_#*
156231	DBMS	MGH	24302	21-Mar-2000		
156231	DBMS	MGH	25123		04-Apr-2000	7
156231	DBMS	MGH	18476	12-Aug-2000		
173872	System Anal.	PHI	12147		09-Mar-2000	12
173872	System Anal.	PHI	23467	21-May-2000		
142564	Algorithms	AWS	18199	12-Jun-2000		

But the 1NF relation mentioned composed of attributes relating to book, issue and reservation, which can be easily separated into Second Normal Form (2NF) relations as in Table 18.6. The attribute Acc_No in the Book relation uniquely identifies other attributes like Title or Publisher hence it is called a key of the relation, and other attributes are called as non-key attributes. Similarly Acc_No and User_code is the composite key for the Issues relation and the Reservations relation. Thus a relation is in 2NF if it is in 1NF and all non-key attributes are functionally dependent (given the key attribute, one can correctly identify the non-key ones) on the key attribute(s).

Table 18.6: 2NF Relations

Acc No	*Title*	*Publisher*	*Acc No*	*User_Code*	*Issue_date*
156231	DBMS	MGH	156231	24302	21-3-2000
173872	System Anal.	PHI	156231	18476	12-8-2000
142564	Algorithms	AWS	173872	23467	21-5-2000
			142564	18199	12-6-2000
	Books			**Issues**	

Acc No	*User_Code*	*Reservation_date*	*Prio_#*
156231	25123	04-Apr-2000	7
173872	12147	09-Mar-2000	12

Reservations

In a library, if the entitlement of books to be issued is dependent on the course of study, we can see a dependency on the non-key attributes of category and entitlement as shown in Table 18.7.

Table 18.7: Dependency on Non-key Attributes

User_ Code	*Name*	*Address*	*Category*	*Entitle-ment*	*Issue_ date*
24302	Mukesh Kumar	203, R K	P G	6	21-Mar-2000
18476	Rakesh Singh	113, V S	U G	4	12-Aug-2000
23467	Manas Verma	201, RK	P G	6	21-May-2000
18199	Mayank Chatterjee	141, VS	U G	4	12-Jun-2000
24318	Sangeeth Kumar	108, RK	P G	6	21-Jun-2000

Repetition of Category and entitlement in table 18.7 can be avoided by separating them into another table and we get the relation converted to Third Normal Form (3NF) as in Table 18.8. A relation is said to be in 3NF if it is in 2NF and no non-key attribute is functionally dependent on any other non-key attribute.

Table 18.8: 3NF

User_Code	*Name*	*Address*	*Category*	*Issue_date*
24302	Mukesh Kumar	203, R K	P G	21-Mar-2000
18476	Rakesh Singh	113, V S	U G	12-Aug-2000
23467	Manas Verma	201, RK	P G	21-May-2000
18199	Mayank Chatterjee	141, VS	U G	12-Jun-2000
24318	Sangeeth Kumar	108, RK	P G	21-Jun-2000

Category	*Entitlement*
P G	6
U G	4

For a relation that has more than one key, and when an attribute of a composite key is dependent on an attribute of the other composite key, convertion to Boyce-Codd Normal Form (BCNF) is required. In the relation shown in Table 18.9, the composite keys are course_no and Professor and course_no and textbook. If Professors based on area of specialization are teaching courses and they are favouring book written by a particular author, the duplications are avoided by going in for another relation with Professor and Textbook, and by avoiding the Textbook from the original relation as in Table 18.10.

Table 18.9: Composite Keys

Course_no	***Course_name***	***Professor***	***Textbook***	***Credits***
216	Cataloguing Theory	Singh	Fundamentals of Library Cataloguing	4
218	Classification Theory	Tewari	On Classifying Books	4
220	Information Systems	Kumar	Essentials of System Design	5
115	Advanced Classification	Tewari	On Classifying Books	4
117	Advanced Cataloguing	Singh	Fundamentals of Library Cataloguing	4

Table 18.10: BCNF Relations

Course_no	***Course_name***	***Professor***	***Credits***
216	Cataloguing Theory	Singh	4
218	Classification Theory	Tewari	4
220	Information Systems	Kumar	5
115	Advanced Classification	Tewari	4
117	Advanced Cataloguing	Singh	4

Professor	Textbook
Singh	Fundamentals of Library Cataloguing
Tewari	On Classifying Books
Kumar	Essentials of System Design

To illustrate multivalued dependencies among entities normal forms like 4NF and 5NF are required.

7.8. DATA FLOW DIAGRAMS

A data flow diagram (DFD) is a graphical representation of a system in terms of the input data to the system, different processing carried out on the data, and the output generated. It uses very limited number of simple symbols like rectangle to denote external entity, circle for processes, parallel lines to represent data store, rectangle with one edge modified as a side (pentagon) to represent output, and arrow lines to indicate data flow. A DFD for current journal module of a library system is shown in figure 18.5.

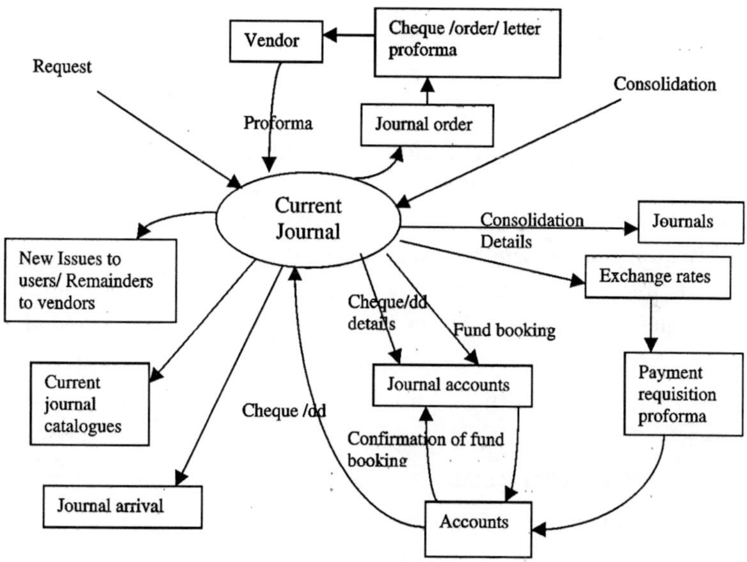

Fig. 18.5: DFD for Current Journal Module

7.9. QUERY LANGUAGES

The language interfaces provided by database systems that facilitate to systematically query and interact with the system are called as query languages. One of the most prominent example of a query language is the Structured Query

Language (SQL) used by database systems like Oracle. SQL also include features for identifying data structure, modifying data, and for specifying the various security constraints. A typical SQL query would be like:

select <attribute(s)>

from <table(s)>

where <condition>;

For example, take a simple SQL query like:

select user_code, issue_date

from issue

where acc_no = "168374";

will return the results

18315, 15-02-00

27403, 18-05-00

This query implies to select the fields user_code and issue data from the table issue for which the accession number field contains the value 168374. Since two users issued that book, the concerned results are returned by the system as answer to this query. If no where clause is mentioned, all user_codes and issue_dates in the issue file are displayed. If we use select * in the query, then all fields in the issue table will be returned.

If we have a reservation file and the user 27403 has also reserved a book with acc_no 172022 on 21-09-00, then a query like,

select user_code

from issue, reservation

where issue.user_code = reservation.user_code;

will yield the value 27403

Just like 'select' command searches out data entered into a table, insert command will insert new data into one. For example, the following command will issue book with accession number 172022 to user having code 27403 on 30th Sept 2000.

insert into issue

values ('27403', '172022', '30-09-00');

To create a new table for reservation with title, call_no, user_code, reserv_date, and priority_no, we have to use the following command,

```
create table reservation
(title          varchar(100),
call_no         varchar(25),
user_code       varchar(50),
reserv_date     date,
priority_no     integer);
```

This command will create a table with the title, call_no and user_code as an alphanumeric characters with a maximum of 100, 25, and 50 characters respectively, whereas the date is entered in date format 'dd-mmm-yyyy', and priority number as integer.

SQL also offers options to frame complex queries with the help of nesting commands and using set operations like union, intersection, and so on.

18.10. COMPONENTS

The basic components of a DBMS include:

* Data Definition Language (DDL) to translate the schema for creating a logical and physical layout for the database. Data Definition Language (DDL) is the specialized language in which the description of the database schema is written. When DDL is compiled, a set of tables or instructions that specify the implementation details of the database is generated which are stored in the data dictionary (file containing metadata or data about data) or data directory.

* Procedures to add new data or to modify existing data. To enable efficient human interaction with the database system, and to facilitate search, insert, modify or delete data, Data Manipulation Language (DML) is supplied with the system. Procedural DMLs stipulate the user to

specify how to get what data whereas Nonprocedural DMLs require from the user only input about what data are required. The commands of DML that deal with retrieving data from the system are regarded as query language.

* Query Translator to translate queries into a sequence of procedure calls to retrieve data from the database
* System Software modules to handle system tasks such as file/buffer management, security, reliability, concurrency control, etc.

18.11. FUNCTIONS

18.11.1. Transaction Management

A transaction is a set of operations that are to be performed together to achieve a single logical function in the database application. It should satisfy the atomicity and consistency requirements discussed earlier. For example, a circulation transaction has to check the following:

* Whether the book brought for issue is the one meant for doing so. It does not belong to specialized collections like reference, journal etc.
* The member in question is a valid borrower, and if so, s/he has not exceeded the entitlement of the category in question.
* If it is a renewal operation, verify whether any fine is incurred, and if so take appropriate measures to collect the requisite amount. Also verify that nobody has reserved for the same before reissue.
* If the issue arose out of a reservation operation, it should change the priorities in the reservation list.
* In the event of a power failure or any data loss during the transaction, the system should take effective security steps to either modify all required data files or negate the whole transaction without modifying any files by issuing satisfactory abort/error messages.

18.11.2. Concurrency Control

A database programmer has to define properly the various transactions such that the database consistency is maintained. The transaction management component must ensure the atomicity properties by assuring that a failed transaction has no effect on the state of the database. When different transactions concurrently update the database (the Acquisition section is adding a duplicate title, a similar title is processed in the Processing section, a user is issuing the book, and another user reserving the same book immediately after, etc.) the concurrency control manager has to control the interaction among the concurrent transactions.

18.11.3. Storage Management

A storage manager program module works as an interface between the physical data stored in the system and the application programs and queries submitted. The storage manager translates DML statements into system commands for file operations and is responsible for storing, retrieving, and updating of data in the database.

18.12. FILE ORGANIZATION

At the physical level, a database has data files that store the database. Data dictionary holds metadata about the structure of the database. Indexes offer fast access to data with specific values. Statistical data about the data in the database is also maintained for efficient query execution.

The crucial point in file organization is how to represent logical data models in physical files as a sequence of records. Some of the predominant file organization methods are:

Heap file: Any record can be placed in any vacant place in the file without any ordering. There may be different files for different relations.

Sequential File: Records are organized sequentially, as the name implies based on the value of search key. The pointer in each record points to the next record in search-key order and to minimise access time as far as possible, records are stored physically in search-key order. Since maintaining physical sequential order is difficult as records are inserted and deleted, the following procedure is followed: Locate the record in the file that comes before the record to be inserted as per search key order. If there is space left after a previous deletion within the same block, insert the new record there, else insert the new record in an overflow block. In either case, adjust the pointers so as records are chained in search-key order as shown in figure 18.6. The drawback with this arrangement will be felt after a large number of records were kept in the overflow block, forcing the file to be again reorganized physically often with much system load. There are also variants of this sort of file organization like the Indexed-Sequential file.

Hashed file: A hash function is computed based on some attribute of each record, and this function implies the block number of the file where the record will be placed.

Clustering file: Related records of different relations are stored on the same block of the file for its easy fetching by one read/write operation.

18.13. INDEXING

Indexing enables us to quickly and efficiently retrieve data stored in the database. Database files can be indexed in two ways, either to index all fields and all terms (dense) or do it selectively (sparse). In dense index, an index record appears for every search-key value with a pointer to the first data record with that value, as in figure 18.7. In sparse index, not all records/ search keys are indexed, as in figure 18.8 and hence to find a record, we look for the index entry with the largest search-key value that is less than or equal to, and follow the pointers to find the desired record. There are other methods like tree structure (B-tree and B+-tree) to index data that facilitates faster retrieval.

18.14. SECURITY

System security is a crucial issue for the DBMS as we are going towards a more and more wired world where a large number of database servers are kept on the network, making your system often within the reach of hackers. Security policies are to be properly framed and effectively enforced to deal with illegal/alien access to the system. On the first hand, database systems are discouraged from putting on the public network. If needed and no other alternative exists, do so only through network security options like firewalls, which will make the database server to be accessed only on the private network and only to select users on the public network. Apart from this all access to the database server will be done through login and password. These passwords are also changed periodically to prevent any guessing from others. Different permissions/roles as mentioned earlier for different category of users depending on expected requirements and work would be further framed to follow foolproof multi-user access to the system.

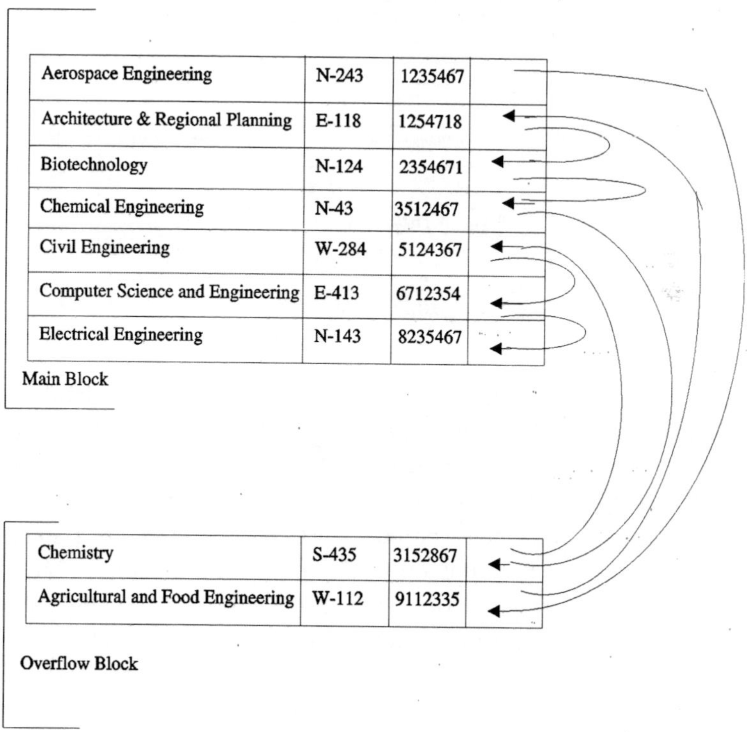

Fig. 18.6: Sequential File Organization

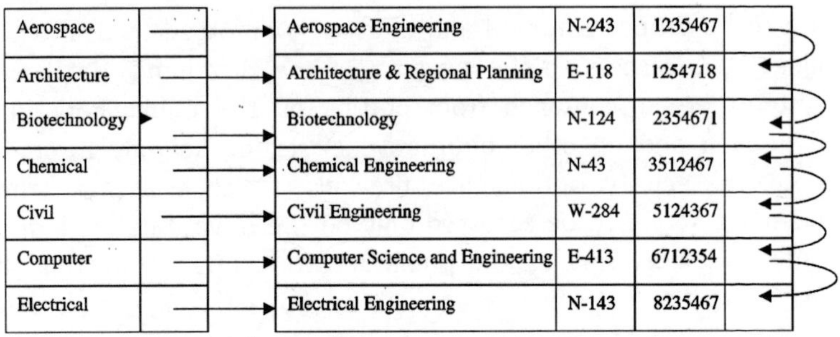

Fig. 18.7: Dense Index

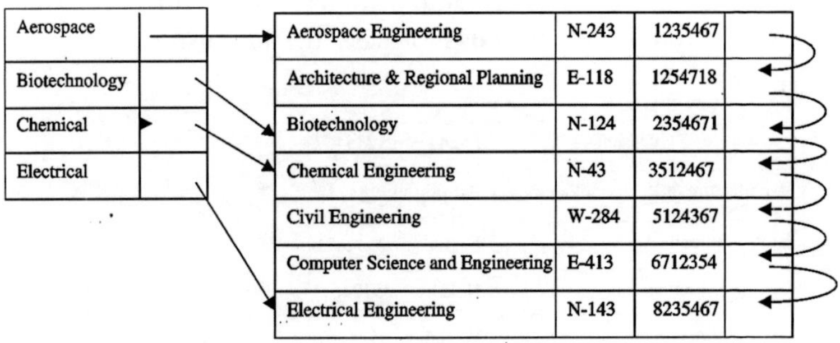

Fig. 18.8: Sparse Index

18.15. ARCHITECTURES

There may be different viable architectures for a database system and the decision to prefer a particular architecture will solely depend on the activities of the Organization, and its database applications. In the centralized architecture, database system is run on a single computer. If it is a PC, then it is a single user system, and if it runs on a server with multi user operating system, then it will function as a multi user system. The multi user systems are normally accessed through dumb terminals. The affordability of powerful personal computers (PCs), brought in better processing power at the terminal side permitting client-server sort of access to the database system. Parallel and distributed systems use the fruits of latest research in parallel and distributed computing for database applications. Parallel systems improve processing and search speeds with the help of multiple CPUs and Disks working in parallel performing multiple operations simultaneously. In the case of extremely large database applications such as the operations of a multinational company, they have to work with huge databases and/or with a number of transactions at one point of time, and parallel database systems work in parallel to increase the number of processes handled at one instant and to answer queries and support accesses quickly. For a distributed database, the database is stored on several computers interacting with one another through various communication media. If all IITs decide to have their library database to be shared, they can work out a distributed database system permitting local transactions for user issues, as well as global transactions for resource sharing and Inter Library Loan.

18.16. PRODUCTS

Several products are available on different operating system platforms to handle database applications. Some of the packages on PC version are dBase, Microsoft Access, and Personal edition of Oracle. Sophisticated packages like Oracle and Sybase on server versions are available to support wider data management applications of bigger institutions. It is beyond the scope of this brief write-up to go into the features of any of these products. Perhaps library courses should include hands-on experience on at least one DBMS package to begin with. If one is proficient with one system, nuances of others can be easily learned after some trials by browsing online manuals.

18.17. STEPS IN DBMS DEVELOPMENT

Step 1: Requirements are to be collected and analyzed. Identify the different entities, attributes, and relationships, modules and other such elements required.

Step 2: Normalize the relations into 3NF and higher.

Step 3: Draw ER Diagrams to properly identify, structure and represent the entities, attributes and relations.

Step 4: Draw Data Flow Diagrams (DFDs) to represent the data flows into, inside and from the system.

Step5: Decide upon the table structure to handle the different tasks and data storage.

Step 6: Critically evaluate and modify the design.

Step 7: Implementation using proper database software, procured after thorough cost-benefit analysis. (If no commercial software is under consideration, do own development using data files and massive programming to link up these files and to achieve the sophisticated database operations.)

Step 8: Testing of individual modules and then integration testing of all modules.

Step 9: Decide up on user permissions and system security.

Step 10: Preparation of user manuals and training modules.

Step 11: Final release.

18.18. IMPLICATIONS FOR LIBRARIES

Being widely concerned with organizing and providing selective access to information, database systems are of vital importance to the library and information science discipline. Most of the manual tools used in the library like catalogues, indexes, etc., are given way to their computerised variants after the spread, affordability and advancement of computer and other IT gadgets in the country. A significant number of libraries attached to research and academic institutions have started some initiatives to convert manual catalogues and start user issue services and other repetitive house keeping tasks with the help of library automation systems. Some such packages [5] are available from commercial vendors at a price and some in-house developments also have come up from government funded institutions.

Another type of databases that has become more important in recent times is the availability of printed abstracting and indexing tools in the form of electronic databases on CD-ROM as well as for online access through web sites. Some of these databases contain mere bibliographic data whereas few others contain full text of articles from journals and other sources along with powerful search engines to selectively search and scan the information. Numeric databases contain numeric information like physical and chemical properties of elements. Similarly factual databases report political, entertainment or sport events giving more importance to factual data.

Availability of large repositories of information in electronic form has enhanced the importance of database systems. Just like bibliographic sources, we are witnessing the availability of a number of refereed journals and reference sources on the web and in other electronic forms. Most of such systems had a powerful database system in the background to hold and significantly support a massive repository of information. Thus the study and use of database systems has become very important and all the more beneficial in many ways for the library community.

REFERENCES

1. The Oxford English Dictionary, Oxford: Clarendon, 1989, Second Edition, vol. 4, p. 264.
2. Penrod, James I., Douglas, Judith V., Information Technology Literacy, Encyclopaedia of Library & Information Science, New York: Marcel Dekker, 1986, vol. 40, p. 84.
3. Bose, Anindya, Information Resources Management: A Glossary of Terms, Encyclopaedia of Library & Information Science, New York: Marcel Dekker, 1986, vol. 41, p. 108.
4. Op. cit. 1, p. 261.
5. Chaudhury, G G and Chaudhury, Sudatta Text Retrieval and Library Management Software in India, Program, 28(3), July 1994, pp. 253-261.

The following books on databases are widely consulted for the preparation of this write-up:

1. Silberschatz, Abraham, Korth, Henry F., Sudarshan, S, Database System Concepts, New York, McGraw Hill, 3rd edition, 1997, xxii, 821 p.
2. Rajaraman, V, Analysis and Design of Information Systems, New Delhi: Prentice Hall, 1998, xi, 359 p.
3. Ullman, Jeffrey D., Principles of Database Systems, 2nd edition, New Delhi: Galgotia, 1996, vii, 484 p.
4. Majumdar, Arun K, Bhattacharya, Pritimoy, Database Management Systems, New Delhi: Tata McGraw Hill, 1996, x, 475 p.
5. Elmasri, Ramez, Navathe, Shamkant B., Fundamentals of Database Systems, 3rd Edition, Addison Wesley, 2000, xxvii, 955 p.

19
Databanks

19.0. INTRODUCTION

Any 'well defined piece of information containing its whole meaning within itself, i.e. intelligible without the need of explanations or a context, referring to well defined subjects and capable of being expressed by compact signs such as a number, a mark in a box, a name, a diagram or a photograph' could be termed as data [7]. A collection of such data with proper inventory mechanisms as in a bank where money belonging to different people are separately identified, arranged and returned, though they are kept together, is regarded as a databank. The terms 'databank' and 'data bank' are prevalent and are used more or less interchangeably, however in this write-up we stick to the first one. There are as many definitions to databanks as many authors, as each author wanted to describe it in a particular way. Lufkin denotes it as 'a file of data derived from a variety of sources and stored in a manner suitable for access by a number of users' [1]. He mentioned that the term first originated in the late 1960s for a data system that combined school, tax, utility, welfare, health, police and other files for use by a municipal government. The different departments could depend on this bank for essential data to take strategic, tactical and operational decisions. Perhaps the term has not gained much usage due to the widespread protests generated against these early systems, as they encroached on the privacy of individuals forcing law makers to arrive at a code of ethics that struck a balance between the data needs for able governance and a person's fundamental right to maintain sufficient privacy.

There are other definitions of databank, as Bose deems it as 'an organized collection of computer-based data that are ready for transfer and access' and argues that the terms 'data bank, info bank, database are somewhat interchangeable' [2]. A databank may also be called as a repository of data, usually covering some specific topic [3]. Logley and Shain suggest databank as synonymous with database which they define as 'a collection of interrelated data stored so that it may be accessed by authorized users with simple user-friendly dialogs. The database structure is independent of the programs that use the data and a common controlled approach is employed in adding, deleting or modifying the data' [4]. Burton identifies 'a comprehensive collection of libraries of data', such as 'one line of an invoice may form an item, a complete invoice may form a record, a complete set of such records may form a file, the collection of inventory control files may form a library, and the libraries used by an organization are known as its databank' [5]. Though a databank is 'usually used as an alternate term for database', it is 'sometimes used to refer exclusively to a collection of factual or numeric data as distinct from a bibliographic database, which gives references to documents' [6]. A subject-specific, knowledge-based dataset that can be universally displayed on any computer system is called a databank; it may or may not contain internal references or external links to other databanks or to image, audio, and/or video files [36]. Cronin quotes Cuadra's two-tier typology for databases into Reference (comprise of bibliographic and referral) and Source (numeric & statistical, fact-answer oriented, chemical & physical properties, and full text) as 'acceptable and convenient, though by no means perfect' [8]. A referral database may hold information about 'a list of educational establishments and their distinguishing characteristics, or a list of all individuals engaged in funded research in a particular area' [10]. Source database (or databank) comprises of 'databank, fact bank, data file, non-bibliographic database, numeric database or information bank' [10]. The problem with reference databases are that they only act as pointers to information whereas source databases hold (stand-alone) information. Some of the vital sectors 'with specific requirements' of databanks are 'Science & Technology (e.g. environmental data, thermodynamic properties, biomedical data, subatomic physics), the Social Science & the Humanities (e.g. education, demographic data, public policy), Economic & Finance (e.g. trade figures, business information, macro-economic time series) and Legal (e.g. case law, regulatory information, patents)' [10]. Labin estimated the minimum number of databanks required to cater to the entire spectrum of exact sciences and resulting technologies as 1500 (by assessing 25 banks per field for the 60 approximate diverse fields existed then) and another 1500 to feed economics and social sciences [19].

Thus, before proceeding further, we should attempt at some classification on databanks, in the light of the above discussion and the standard terminology being followed in Library Science, Information Science and Computer Science:

* There is not much distinction between the terms, databank and database, though the latter one has gained more currency and usage. However by the term database, the predominant genre that will come to one's mind is the wide array of bibliographic databases.
* Databank may be an apt term to denote other versions of databases like numeric, factual, structure, full text etc. Since the term 'databank' is slowly going into oblivion, there are indications to regard all these types as databases, with qualifiers to precede it like bibliographic databases, numeric databases, full text databases etc.
* Databanks are generally produced by sophisticated data centres which collect, refine, process, organise, and disseminate large chunk of data on a particular specialization. It is not the data as such, but the value

addition done at the data centre during these various sages makes the databank appropriate and amenable for use.

* There is enough scope for library professionals to cope with identifying and motivating clients to use various databanks. They can also devise mechanisms to enhance the visibility of local data by creating in-house databank prototypes through data documentation work.

19.1. DATA DOCUMENTATION

The normal documentation process undertaken in a library is concerned with literature (of formal/informal and published/unpublished sources to a large extent) and hence regarded as literature documentation in contrast to the data documentation process undertaken to develop databanks. Also libraries, information and documentation centres collect and disseminate bibliographical information, as an outcome of literature documentation. In the case of data databank development, data from diverse sources are to be documented. In the case of literature documentation, Labin laments on the '50% noise and 50% miss' in information retrieved from bibliographic databases as indexing is done on concepts where the indexer 'did not know what to look for in them' and user 'requiring them did not know what to ask for' [7, 24]. In contrast to the aspirants of literature documentation which are largely researchers, the data documentation produced databanks are widely consumed by a varied clientele, ranging from researchers 'who need data two out of three times' to a 'vast group of people who need data nine out of ten times' as they answer 'who makes what, who said what, who took part in what' [25]. The miss and noise in data retrieval is widely curtailed in data documentation due to the fact that, most of the time, the approach for data is only for 'known' items whereas a person may seek both 'known' and 'unknown' documents (documents with attributes other than subject not known) in bibliographic databases. When a person is querying a physical property databank about the boiling point of water, s/he is only interested in 100^0 C, and not its freezing point is 0^0 C or its chemical formula is H_2O. Just compare this query with the case of a person looking for studies conducted to correctly assess the boiling point of water in a bibliographic database. This query will retrieve the bibliographic details of different research work conducted on this problem documented in the database. In short, answers to searches from databanks, are obviously conducted in a different perspective from bibliographic databases, and in most of the cases retrieve more crisp and factual results. One of the most appealing aspects of a bibliographic record is its structural clarity as all entries contain common fields like author, title, publisher, keyword etc., whereas this is not true of constituent elements in a databank which stipulates the need for 'data labelling' [18]. This is achieved through 'descriptors as markers to identify elements or clusters (and relationships between sets of data) and to make explicit additional values of the data presented' [18]. Data documentation is emphasised to decipher the codes, parameters and other characteristics pertaining to the data stored. Theoretically a 1:1 relationship between recall and precision is expected from databanks, as data are self-sufficient [18].

19.2. STEPS IN DATABANK DEVELOPMENT

Since data documentation is a more involved task and the process can invigorate the data thus collected through certain value addition procedures, it does involve certain steps right from data identification, collection, cleaning, storage, and dissemination.

a) Data Identification: Most of the databanks are topical and the sources or channels which produce data relevant to the field are to be identified.

b) Data Owning: This involves mechanisms/ arrangements to procure on lease or rent or through other copyright paid/copyright free data. In cases like factual or directory data, the ownership rights may not rest with anybody, and the data centre may be free to collect and build them.

c) Data Collection and Compilation: The data must be

collected in some predefined format with enough details so that the databank may be able to service satisfactorily the different data requirements expected of it. For e.g., in the preparation of a numeric databank covering the educational statistics of the country, it is apt to include not only the Universities, but also the wide variety of colleges spread over the length and breadth of the nation. If it was decided first to collect only the PG level, then do so for all MA, MSc, MCom, MTech, and other post graduate degrees or if it was decided to collect only discipline wise, do so accordingly. There must be a standard and well laid out action plan to collect and compile the data that must come under the purview of databank intended and discipline concerned.

d) Data Validation and Cleaning: The usage of the databank depends not only on its coverage but also on the validity of data stored. Tough measures are to be framed to validate the data collected before incorporating them into the databank. If they can be verified through observation/ experiment like scientific data, do so accordingly, where as the validity and authenticity of the originals are to be cross-examined for data concerning social science, or humanities. To tide over the problem of entering into any legal hassles from users for the authenticity and reliability of data supplied, some of the databanks resort to the lazy way of throwing the responsibility to the sources from where they took the data, as validation is an extremely heavy task requiring 75-80 % of the work load [12]. To have control of the terms used in the databank and to standardise the same, data dictionary compilation must also be attempted.

e) Data Conversion and formatting: Some of the data may be computerised, some may be in printed/handwritten form. The data from diverse forms are to be keyed into the computer, and these are to be formatted with suitable standardization to facilitate systematic access at the retrieval stage. All aspects of database design and development for storage, organisation and implementation of databank files on a computer are also to be considered.

f) Inverted/Index file generation: Most of the queries to the databanks may not be simple and straight forward like the boiling point of water, but for all substances having a higher boiling point than water. 'To do this and above all to do it in a conversational mode, it is obviously necessary to prepare an inverted file' [26]. Moreover in the computerised environment, where significant technological advances making computers more affordable and affable, one can index the diverse attributes of the data stored to ease retrieval from all these access points.

g) User Interface Design: The formatted data and the inverted files will help easy access to data, only for the developers. The bibliographic and other library databases vouch for the assistance of a trained professional intermediary, as they demand expertise on the search process rather than on the subject field covered. However, databanks 'offer computational facilities' and hence are 'often used not by trained intermediaries, but by end-users' as efficient use of the system require a knowledge of complicated 'system protocols, statistical analysis packages and programming ability' [14]. Also, the 'end-user has specific subject or technical skills which enable him to do with the data what he wants at the moment of retrieval, a fact which makes the intervention of the information specialist superfluous' [14]. This implies that databanks are widely used by the end-users and hence it is imposing to have a functional as well as interactive user interface to ensure proper dialogue, consistent interaction and data retrieval by them.

h) System Integration: The separately created data files, inverted files and the user interface have to work in unison to achieve adequate data search and retrieval from the databank. The computer hardware and other ancillaries required in ensuring smooth and speedy access to the system must also be selected and procured at this stage. The different modes of access to the system will be explored in a later part of this discussion. Enough security controls for accessing the system must be devised and incorporated, to realise the amount of money and resources spent for fabricating the databank, and to keep the confidential data away from mischief. The obvious measure for security option at the user level is to frame user passwords and stressing to change them periodically. The security measures at the system level are to keep it blocked from private data networks with the help of firewalls. Security violation is more a syndrome in the hands of hackers that one should tackle it only with consistent measures for prevention of invalid access, and keeping constant vigil on any and all interactions with the system as well as continuous observation of the data access trends.

19.3. ACCESS MODES

Once the databank is developed, it should be put for access by clients only with the help of some communication medium or by taking copies on archival discs for distribution. There are merits and defects for each of these approaches, and the routes followed are mostly decided on a case to case basis by the developer, or the user. Labin mentions about the 'colossal cost of the telecommunications' to permit data retrieval through telephone and deem the 'total "phone-in" data network' as 'Utopian objective' [27]. The possible options for access to databanks include:

i) **Through Public Telecommunication Networks**: If other options are not present or are not viable, it is not altogether a bad idea to utilise the public communication carrier due to its wide reach and continuous availability. For e.g. INFLIBNET at its infancy explored to facilitate access to their databases through I-Net of Dept of Telecommunications (now BSNL). The justification for using phone networks are also advantaged by the fact that the user has to 'conduct a much briefer dialog' than a person 'looking for references' from a bibliographical database [27].

ii) **Through Online hosts**: Some of the databanks available only through online data hosts have to be accessed by paying subscription or access fee apart from phone charges. As such, this route is relatively less used in the country as a result of the exorbitant costs involved plus the existence of cheap alternatives.

iii) **Through Library Networks**: Huber discusses at length the different databanks made accessible through the Euronet [9]. The library networks in our country such as INFLIBNET, DELNET, and other city-based networks have already made a beginning to facilitate access to bibliographic databases (either through modem attached telephones or via web sites). They have not ventured into databank field only due to want of popular databanks from Indian data centres. Once they are available, the same route followed for bibliographic data access could be explored for databanks too.

iv) **Through data networks**: Another option to access databanks is through data networks like ERNET (Education and Research Network of Dept of Electronics), NICNET (National Informatics Centre Network) or through Internet Service providers (ISPs) like VSNL (Videsh Sanchar Nigam Ltd.), Satyam Infoway etc.

v) **Through Internet/Web**: The predominant mode of access to databanks in recent years, especially for educational and research purposes is through protocols over Internet (World Wide Web to a large extent). The data centre or vendor can provide access to databanks through their web site, with options for restricting exclusive access to clients. Some of the databanks available over Internet will be elaborated in a later part of this paper. Access on this mode will also depend to a large extent on communication channels rented through phone/&ISPs.

vi) **Through electronic distribution media**: Diskettes or Compact Discs of the databanks could be made for circulating among users. The drawbacks of this approach are poor control over data access from invalid users, and currency of data circulated (not so significant like bibliographic databases when new data is not a mere update of the existing one). The Indian Standards distributed on CD-ROM by Book Supply Bureau, is an example. Why this cheap option is not widely followed by databank developers is a crucial issue to be considered, as reasons are many; as they want exclusive rights over data, due to the less number of clients, and in many cases for profit motivations from selective access.

19.4. FEATURES

Some of the basic features of databanks that distinguish them from bibliographic databases are as follows:

a) Data Holding Capacity: Bibliographic database acts as a mere surrogate to the document, and they either give information about or access points to the original. Indicative abstracts can at best summarise the major findings of the document concerned, but for a person interested to know the details has to consult the original. However, databanks are data repositories and on accessing will flash the relevant data available, and the user has to go nowhere else to grab the details. In short, this data holding capacity enriches them to be treated as good as the original.

b) Restrictiveness: Cronin argues that 'bibliographic databases provide information about publicly available materials, but non-bibliographic databases offer information as a commodity' and hence 'a substantial number of databanks are available only to closed user groups' [10]. In contrast to public domain materials consumed by bibliographic databases, the databanks used to accumulate data from restricted sources also specifically meant for the consumption of chosen few, and hence impose certain restrictions on 'who should access how much data' from the bank.

c) Acute Specialization: When we deal with bibliographic databases, the specialization may come down to the subject level like Physics Abstracts for Physics, or a stream like Engineering Index for all branches of engineering. In the case of databanks, may be the gene structure of one living organism can be framed as a databank, and to get the same for another organism, a person has to consult another bank.

d) Data Features: The data in databanks differ from the unilateral features of the same in bibliographic databases (functionally and operationally heterogeneous), and are variable in character; quantitative, semi-quantitative or qualitative; presented numerically, alphabetically, alphanumerically, graphically or symbolically; time-dependent or time-independent; location dependent or location independent; primary, derived or theoretical; deterministic or stochastic [11]. Labin characterises data into long-term data (conventional properties of substances or installations which remain valid for a long time and which are inquired about for their own sake) and short-term data (like temperature and pressure at a particular place during a specific time, which are usually used as transitional raw materials for other studies) [12].

e) Access Charges: There may be public domain databanks that can be accessed free of cost. But the norm for accessing databanks is for an 'annual fee, or signing-on charge plus reduced annual subscription', and in 'general no linear time-charge relationship' as applicable to bibliographic databases [13]. Some systems also charge for the sophisticated data analysis facilitated after data extraction [13].

f) Update Exercise: Updating of bibliographic databases implies 'leisurely incremental increase' [14]. This is not the case with databanks as 'discovery of new measuring techniques or materials' may sometimes lead to formatting changes or 'major structural overhaul for the databank' [14].

g) Update Frequency: The importance of data on decision making stipulates faster update procedures and frequent updates. 'Timeliness for bibliographic database may be measured in terms of months or weeks, may have to be calculated in terms of hours or minutes' for databanks dealing with 'fast changing fields' [14]

h) Search Time: Databanks consume obviously less search time since the questions concerning data needs are more evident, as explained earlier. Huber suggested that 'the time needed for answering a query with a bibliographic file via a network tends to be 20-30 minutes, a databank usually needs only 8-15 minutes' [15].

i) Answer diverse data needs: Data may or may not

require manipulation to answer the users' queries satisfactorily. A chemistry databank should be made functional enough to answer material based or property specific queries. The same is the case with a social science database which has to give a data estimate based on the historical aspect, sociological aspect, and so on. This warrants the data elements to be widely indexed on the different attributes that qualify the data to answer wide-ranging queries.

19.5. TYPES AND EXAMPLES

Databanks may be broadly classified based on the style of presentation of data content and the discipline it belongs to. It is very difficult to give an exhaustive list of the databanks available, as the number crossed many thousands, and a lot of them are poorly advertised. An attempt is made here to give an indicative list of some of the databanks available in different types and various fields:

* **Numeric and Statistic**

International Atomic Energy Agency (IAEA), known to library professionals as the producer of INIS (International Nuclear Information System), brought out two databases (with numerical and bibliographic data combined) Nuclear Data Information System (NDIS) and Atomic and Molecular Data Information System (AMDIS).

* **Factual**

IAEA has a factual database called Power Reactor Information System (PRIS) on power reactors in operation, under construction, planned or shut down, and data on operating experience with nuclear power plants.

* **Directory**

Gale Research Inc. offers their printed directories on CD-ROM and through GaleNet, a web based service [31]. INSDOC (now NISCAIR) brought out in floppy form its 'Directory of Scientific Research Institutions in India'.

* **Full text/image**

There is no dearth of full text/image (instead of keying

in, image databases use scanned pages of printed text) databases in the post web era, as almost all the standard publishers offer electronic versions of their journals and other sources through their web sites. Some of these can be accessed with out paying any additional fee for the printed subscription. IEEE/IEE offers their journals, conferences, and standards as IEL (IEEE/IEE Electronic Library).

* **Scientific & Technological (Properties, Structures, Data tables, etc.)**

Asia Health, Environmental, and Allied Databases (AHEAD) is a major databank effort of few Asian countries including India (NISCOM of CSIR is the nodal agency in India) sponsored and supported by International Development Research Centre (IDRC), Canada. The CD-ROMs allow full text searching and display of text, illustrations and tables on environmental and resource management, traditional medicines and natural products, occupational health and safety, natural toxins and tropical diseases.

Kirk-Othmer Encyclopedia of Chemical Technology provides on CD-ROM, the full text, including images of the comprehensive reference work on applied chemical science and industrial technology (available from vendors like Dialog). Dialog OnDisc Polymer encyclopedia contains the complete text of the 19 volume 2nd edition of Encyclopedia of Polymer Science and Technology, covering natural and synthetic polymeric materials; their molecular, physical, mechanical and biological properties with special emphasis on process and product oriented data. Royal Society of Chemistry provides databanks like, Chemical Business NewsBase (CBNB)- current facts and figures on chemical companies, new products, markets, legislation, environmental aspects, new technologies etc.; Pesticide Fact File with full name, structure, physical and chemical properties, manufacturing companies, uses, product and residue analysis of over 700 pesticides; through different online hosts such as Data-Star, Dialog and STN.

The National Nuclear Data Center (NNDC) at

Brookhaven National Laboratory of USA offers the following databanks: Evaluated Nuclear Structure Data File (ENSDF) [29] containing evaluated experimental data on nuclear level properties, radiations, radioactive decay and reaction data, Nuclear Data (NUDAT) having evaluated numeric data extracted or derived from ENSDF, Cross Section Information Storage and Retrieval System (CSISRS) with experimental data on neutron, photon, and charged particle reactions, and Evaluated Nuclear Data File (ENDF) on evaluated nuclear reaction and decay data.

A representative list of databases such as ENZYME, GenBank, PROSITE and their contents of interest to biotechnology is listed by Chandran [32]. Most of the databases developed in the filed of Indian biology (thanks to the effort of Bioinformatics Centres of the Dept of Biotechnology, Govt. of India) are bibliographic, but a few of them contains information other than bibliographic like directory type [33]. The Mammalian Comparative Mapping Database documents the existence of homologous genes and their chromosomal location among mammalian species [34]. The Cambridge Structural Database (CSD) and the Brookhaven Protein Data Bank (PDB) are primary resources for a variety of specialities like molecular biology, medicinal chemistry, pharmacology, crystallography, structural chemistry etc. The CSD contains precise, accurate, and elaborate information on the molecular structures of around 45000 organic compounds. The PDB holds the atomic coordinates of hundreds of protein structures determined by X-ray crystallography [35]. The Protein Data Bank (PDB), the single international repository for the processing and distribution of 3-D macromolecular structure data primarily determined experimentally, is operated by the Research Collaboratory for Structural Bioinformatics (RCSB) and is supported by the U.S. National Science Foundation, the Department of Energy, the National Institute of General Medical Sciences and the National Library of Medicine [37]. Baylor College of Medicine offers a collection of links to various databanks related to the field of molecular biology, biotechnology and bioinformatics such as, EMBL simple sequence retrieval, SRS sequence retrieval system, SWISS-PROT full text search, Gene Map of the Human Genome, Genome Sequence Database, TBASE - Transgenic/targeted mutation database, etc. [38]. Pasteur Institute provides an imposing collection of links to various bioscience databanks accessible over the WWW like DNA databanks, Protein databanks, Structure databanks, and Genomic databanks [39].

* **Social Science & Humanities**

(Historic, Economic, Political, Social, Linguistic, or Literary treatment)

LEXIS-NEXIS, owned by Mead Data Central earlier, and now by Reed Elsevier are two major full text databases. LEXIS offers full-text searching of legal materials and NEXIS provides full-text searching of newspapers, newswires, and magazines [30]. Chadwyck-Healey (www.chadwyck.com) through LION (Literature Online) provides web access of arts and humanities databases such as full text of English and American Poetry, prose and drama from 600 AD to the present [31]. Smart-text Solutions Inc. (SSI), a Canadian company is offering on-web access of databanks on airports, city government, emergency management, fire safety, hospitals, human resources, and law enforcement [36]. 'Kompass India' of Teledirect Informatics, New Delhi contains information on about 50000 Indian companies. 'Impex Databank' is a computerised databank on India's exports and imports, sourced from Customs daily list by the Maharashtra Industrial and Technology Consultancy Organisation Ltd. (MITCON), Pune. A databank on various aspects of northeastern states of India is available on the web, to serve as a single-window information dissemination platform on various socioeconomic development projects in the region [40].

19.6. CONSTRAINTS AND PROBLEMS

The key impediments that curtail the requisite use of databanks may be viewed from the following perspectives necessitated by technical, social and economical compulsions.

i) **Data Validation**: The prime difficulty lies with 'validating the data' and 'in establishing how reliable they are' as 'the available sources in literature, reports, or collections are much less reliable than thought and require extensive checking' [12].

ii) **Unwieldy Inverted Files**: To facilitate retrieval from different access parameters and as data exclusivity is only maintained by storing 'similar data belonging to the same field for each subject in all its circumstances', the inverted files grow huge forcing it difficult to handle, further delaying the search procedure that discourage users.

iii) **Terminological Headaches:** Labin emphasizes that 'majority of subjects are given different names by different authors', dealers assign different names to the same materials or instruments for 'commercial exclusiveness' and there are different languages to consider [19]. This problem can be eliminated by compiling exhaustive data dictionaries to work with the databanks at the preparation and use stage.

iv) **Secrecy**: There is a 'secrecy surrounding data' [19] that some databanks have to live with it. Difficult to either compile such databanks or service them to all users, as specific data can be disseminated only to authentic users.

v) **Copyright Problems**: Most of the data published in formal sources are under the purview of copyright restrictions, and difficult to extract such data by others for incorporation in databanks.

vi) **Data Explosion and Data Shift**: Research and Development activities in different disciplines are always on the rise, often in fresh areas, and even entertainment tastes are changing forcing the consumption pattern of data for various needs always variable. It is not only the quantity, but also types and features of data used keeps on changing, so this aftermath of data explosion and data shift assigning considerable difficulty for databank developers to decide 'what sort of data to hold and which ones to reject'.

vii) **Poor Vendor Cooperation**: Most of the databanks are

operated by data centres or the developers. In the case of bibliographic databases, the same vendor or host may supply multiple databases facilitating more data access in a cost-effective manner. Brigish opines that 'non-bibliographic systems host a limited number of databases (1-5) with the result that specific functional needs of end-users cannot always be met with a single vendor' [16]. Since the data centres are working in a different environment than bibliographic hosts, such cooperations are unlikely demanding separate consultation of different databanks of interest.

viii) **Inefficient Marketing**: Databanks are suffered from poor marketing (often only for primary user community) and minimal advertising [10]. This lacunae is further augmented by 'the lack of adequate secondary service coverage' [10].

ix) **Absence of Standardization**: Data for different disciplines follow different formats, as the parameters required for each data application may be different. One record from a structure databank is totally alien to that from a demographic databank. Thus it would be difficult to arrive at an across-the-board standardization for databanks. Since in many fields, 'international standard classification is a dream' and thus the databank producers must indicate the national variations, 'unless already ironed out at the data capture stage' [18].

x) **Labour and Time Intensive**: The databank preparation involves 'labour and time intensive tasks of data tagging and flagging at the pre-input stage' [13].

xi) **User Interface Problems**: Though appreciable growth potentials are predicted for databanks, the expected targets are not achieved also due to the large scale absence of 'user-friendly and easily assimilable command languages' [13].

xii) **Costly**: Databanks are generally less cost-effective as one bibliographic database may satisfy a bunch of disciplines whereas a single subject like chemistry may require multiple databanks. The fund-starved libraries often find it increasingly difficult to procure databanks as a result of the resource crunch and inflation.

xiii) **Commercially Not Viable:** As most of the databanks deal with acute specialization, and hence of interest to a lesser number of patrons, making the running of such systems for a longer period not so viable in terms of market forces.

19.7. SERVICES FROM DATABANKS

The ideal service that can be thought of from databanks by libraries and information access centres is to subscribe them through any of the access modes described earlier, and make them available for clients to use. The merits of end-user searching on databanks were also highlighted before. Information professionals can incorporate databanks also as another type of source to conduct reference and other information services like, search services on request, Current Awareness Service (CAS) on new updates or latest data items, Selective Dissemination of Information Service (SDI) with the help of a carefully framed user profiles etc. Cumulations of Experts, directories could also be framed from data selected and prioritised from the databanks at the individual institution level.

19.8. EVALUATION

Cronin advocates that evaluation of databanks would cover the areas of; content such as coverage (depth, scope, time), parameter count, data documentation, formatting (layout, compression), currency, accuracy; accessibility/usability like availability of user-selectable search parameters, conversationality of the command language, usability of interfacing software; cost in terms of subscription/down payments, access charges, computational charges; meta features of statistical/forecasting software, graphical display capability, interfacing/linking features, data extraction & merging features; and reliability (data integrity/validation) [20]. Another set of medium specific parameters concerned with evaluation of web resources can be added as some of the databanks are increasingly being made accessible over web. Apart from the five traditionally used criteria to evaluate print resources, viz. accuracy, authority, objectivity, currency and coverage, there are problems of marketing oriented web pages; pages blending entertainment, information and advertising; hypertext links; software requirements; search engine retrieval; instability of web sites; susceptibility to alteration as vital impediments for web resources [17]. Nicholls and Ridley proposed a general evaluation framework of electronic resources to fall under the layers of content, indexing, search engine, user interface, and system for satisfying the functions of basic value, subject analysis, search power, ease of use, and platform respectively [28].

Lancaster included number of sources, type of source, number of items, time span, completeness in relation to user needs, uniqueness and overlap in coverage factors; time lag and frequency of update in time factors; and degree of vocabulary control, specificity of the vocabulary, searching aids provided, semantic and syntactic ambiguity, exhaustivity (number and variety of access points), accuracy and consistency in indexing/vocabulary factors [21]. He also identified that users evaluate an information service in terms of its cost (direct and indirect), response time, qualitative considerations (coverage/completeness, recall, precision, novelty, accuracy), and cost-effectiveness [22]. The database characteristics affecting the performance of an information retrieval system comprise of subject coverage (or appropriateness for a particular audience such as level of treatment), indexing (number of access points or exhaustivity, quality and consistency), vocabulary (specificity, semantic & syntactic ambiguity, extent and quality of vocabulary "structure"), and indicativity of record (ability to determine relevance of item from the data provided) [23].

An ideal evaluation framework for databanks has to address the following criteria to assess the data, system, medium and user specific attributes:

* **Data Specific**

All attributes related to the content and context of data stored must be explored in this evaluation stage.

Coverage: Extent of items in terms of type of sources, languages, duration in time period; and style of presentation. Completeness of data in relation to user needs.

Entitlement: Meant for what sort of use by which type of audience.

Style: What type of formatting is used to present the data on computer screen and print.

Exhaustivity: Whether all the required parameters relevant to the data are incorporated.

Indexing: How well indexed is the data to retrieve from different access points and search contexts. What are the searching aids provided.

Vocabulary: Degree of vocabulary control, specificity of the vocabulary, semantic and syntactic ambiguity, and the steps to improve the data dictionary.

Data documentation: How efficient and effective is the data inventory attempted.

Currency: How current are the data items. How frequent are new data added. In the case of retrospective items, whether they stood the test of time to effectively archive the data then existed.

Accuracy: How accurate and reliable are the data stored. Are there enough safeguards to validate the data included in the databank.

Authority: The credentials of the producer. If the databank is produced by a research centre with enough safeguards and checks to clean the data merged, there would not be any doubts on the part of users.

Objectivity: Is the data presented is neutral without taking any sides, if the field happens to be so controversial with diverse schools of thought.

* **System Specific**

Hardware dependence: Often system resources required at the databank side are not a compulsion as they are required only at one or a handful of places. But if the databank insists for sophisticated system resources at the client side, it will be a major hindrance. The databank should permit access through a wide range of options, right from VT100 terminals or low end PCs to sophisticated computers.

Software features: How usable and functional is the search software supplied to search the databank in an interactive mode. Which are the display and formatting options provided. Provisions for manipulating extracted data. Apart from search software, any other software like browsers for web-enabled access is required. Any restrictions on operating system or networking software.

* **User Specific**

Accessibility/usability: Of the user interface, search software and data items.

Customization: Provision for user-selectable search parameters, search process etc.

Cost: Modus operandi for provision to clients, through subscription/down payments, any other extra communication, access or computational charges. Cost effectiveness, satisfaction, and relevance of data retrieved against a query.

* **Medium Specific**

Constraints suffered on account of the media in which the data is disseminated or databank is accessed through.

Telephone: Reliability, capacity, reach, and charges of the phone network.

Online hosts: Spectrum of databanks available from the host.

CD-ROM: Does the data on CD conform to the one available on network. How frequent are the discs updated. Any special features offered by the search software. Hardware, software options supported.

Web enabled: Is the site suffered from too many advertisements. How efficient are the hypertext links and how far stable is the site. Steps taken to continuously refresh and avoid missing links, if any. Options for user access and precautionary mechanisms for preventing unauthorised access.

19.9. SCOPE FOR PROFESSIONAL ENRICHMENT

The different types of services that may be formulated from databanks are already explored in section 8. To fine tune and take each of these services to the highest level of user satisfaction requires strong professional commitment on the part of library professionals. However, the library and information professionals would be able to venture into two further options for professionally enriching databank use and development.

Databank Documentation: If databanks are considered just like any other source of information, they could also be documented as being done for other sources. If the databanks are documented in such a fashion about their general coverage and what are all the subject fields discussed, a user interested in data pertaining to a topic can first consult this documentation (a database of databank from a bibliographic/inventory control viewpoint) before consulting the relevant databanks. This will lead to significant reduction in time, money (if different banks are accessed through networks) and effort. Indirectly this may boost more data use as 'the right user can find more time to consult the right databank'. Since the databanks are very poorly documented in secondary sources, only an alert professional may be able to resort to various means of contacting data centres and other libraries, searching internet etc. to assess the availability of databanks in different fields. Such exercises may also lead to the compilation of a union catalogue/database of databanks.

Databank Development: Most of our research centres and institutes generate substantial extent of data as a result of their in-house activities. Generally some portion of this data only may get reflected in formal sources like research articles or conference proceedings. In the case of some institutions like official statistical units whose sole job is to collect and compile data. The library and information units can contribute extensively to these initiatives in compiling and keeping inventory of data thus amassed as local databanks.

19.10. CONCLUSION

Bibliographic databases are as such important for libraries as they contribute in furthering the control and use of large quantum of primary sources procured and kept for service in a library. But users, most of the time, are not in need of just bibliographic information, or the primary sources, and they need hard core data that will help them in performing various research, academic and social activities. Thus, though the term databank is of less currency than database, there has been a mammoth jump in the spread of non-bibliographic databases (databanks) like numeric, factual and full text databases. The original data content in databanks offer one-step information resource to the clients and are very important sources to be considered for subscription/access/procuring in a library. The veining interest in databanks is only due to the different constraints illustrated and can be overcome only by alert professionals engaged in proactive information services. But the diverse access modes attainable in the present scene and the large number of databanks available made it feasible for libraries and their clients to explore the multifarious options available and challenges ahead to assimilate databanks for diverse data needs.

REFERENCES:

1. Lufkin, D. H., Data bank, in Encyclopaedia of Computers (ed. Rolston, Anthony), 1976, pp. 388-389.
2. Bose, Anindya, Information Resources Management: A Glossary of Terms, Encyclopaedia of Library & Information Science, New York: Marcel Dekker, vol. 41, p. 108.
3. Dictionary of Computing, Oxford: Oxford University Press, 1983, p. 897.
4. Logley, Dennis and Shain, Michael, Dictionary of

Information Technology, New York: John Wiley, 1982, p. 83.

5. Burton, Philip E., A Dictionary of Minicomputing and Microcomputing, New York: John Wiley, 1982, p. 64.
6. Meadows, A. J., et al, Dictionary of Computing and IT, 3rd ed., London: Kogan Page, 1987, p. 62.
7. Labin, Edouard, Information Analysis and Databanks, Proceedings of 2nd European Congress on Information Systems and Networks, Luxembourg, 27-30 May 1975, Munchen: Verlag Dokumentation, 1976, p. 125.
8. Cronin, Blaise, Databanks, Aslib Proceedings, 33(6), June 1981, p. 243.
9. Huber, Wolfgang, Databanks and Euronet in Proceedings of the 5th biennial CODATA Conference, Oxford: Pergamon, 1977, pp. 199-201.
10. Op. cit. 8, p. 244.
11. Luedke, J A et al, Numeric databases and systems, in ARIST 12, 1977, pp. 119-181 (quoted by Cronin)
12. Op. cit. 7, p. 132.
13. Op. cit. 8, p. 245.
14. Op. cit. 8, p. 246.
15. Op. cit. 9, p. 199.
16. Brigish A, The databank switch: the trend towards specialization, The Information Manager, Spring 1980, pp. 19-20 (quoted by Cronin)
17. Tate, Marsha and Alexander, Jan, Teaching Critical Evaluation Skills for World Wide Web Resources, Computers in Libraries, 16(10), November/December 1996, pp. 50-54.
18. Op. cit. 8, p. 247.
19. Op. cit. 7, p. 134.
20. Op. cit. 8, p. 248.
21. Lancaster, F. W., The evaluation of machine readable databases and of information services derived from these

databases, in Evaluation and scientific management of libraries and information centres, Leyden: Noordhoff, 1977, p. 82.

22. Op. cit. 21, p. 88.
23. Op. cit. 21, p. 97.
24. Op. cit. 7, p. 127.
25. Op. cit. 7, p. 128.
26. Op. cit. 7, p. 133.
27. Op. cit. 7, p. 135.
28. Nicholls, Paul and Ridley, Jacquline, A Context for Evaluating Multimedia, Computers in Libraries, 16(4), April 1996, p. 38.
29. Tuli, J. K., Evaluated nuclear structure data file, Nuclear Structure and Methods in Physics Research, A 369, 1996, pp. 506-510.
30. Tenopir, Carol, and Barry, Jeff, The Data Dealers, Library Journal, May 15, 1997, pp. 33-34.
31. Op. cit. 30, p. 31.
32. Chandran, Suresh, Does biotechnology need a new database treaty?, Current Science, 73(8), 25 October 1997, p. 655.
33. Chavan, Vishwas and Chandramohan, D, Databases in Indian biology: The state of the art and prospects, Current Science, 68(3), 10 February 1995, pp. 275-278.
34. Nadeau, Joseph H. et al, A Rosetta Stone of mammalian genetics, Nature, 373, 26 January 1995, pp. 363-365.
35. Duax, William, Crystallographic Databases and Molecular Biophysics, Physics Today, January 1986, pp. S-24-S-25.
36. www.smart-text.com/topical.html (accessed on May 2, 2001)
37. Berman, H. M. et al, The Protein Data Bank. Nucleic Acids Research, 2000, pp.235-242.

38. Baylor College of Medicine, http://mbcr.bcm.tmc.edu/databases.html (last updated on May 26, 1999, accessed on April 15, 2001)

39. http://bioweb.pasteur.fr (accessed on April 26, 2001)

40. http://nerdatabank.nic.in (accessed on May 2, 2001)

20
Stores Monitoring System

20.0. INTRODUCTION

Stores Demand Note, SDN is a proforma designed by Central Stores (CS) made available to the departments of Indian Institute of Science (I.I.Sc.) to request for materials they want to indent from the centralized acquisition system. Different coloured forms are available for different types of items like Stationery, Hardware & Miscellaneous, Electronic, Electrical and Chemical of which NCSI is availing only the first four. SDNs are to be sent in triplicate of which one is sent back along with the item to the concerned department, one forwarded to finance section while another is kept at CS. Since CS has computerized the purchase and distribution operation, they have given unique code Number (CODENO) with one Roman capital followed by four digit number (two digit additions after a /, in some cases). SDNNO (SDN Number) for stationery items starts with AB followed by numerals while CODENO starts with S and the SDN is pink in color. In the case of HW & Misc, SDN is green in colour, SDNNO beginning with B and CODENO having H as first character. D and L were the respective characters for electronic items and the SDN is coloured blue. The format is the same for different types of SDN which generally includes department, date, debit head, description of materials, quantity both indented as well as issued, codeno, stock balance, unit rate, total value (cost of each item) remarks, total (of the total value of individual items), centage, grand total (total to which the centage, if any is added) along with signature of the Store's Supervisor/Store Keeper and the receiver and issue date. Upto six items of a particular type can be indented by one SDN. SDNs forwarded by the department head, were sent to the CS in triplicate and they return the department copy with the items indented available in the stocks with the blank columns in the SDN like quantity issued, unit rate, total value filled in. It is the duty of the office incharge to notify any inconsistency in quantity issued or other details, to the CS immediately. A catalogue depicting the stock of CS is supplied to the departments for their consultation and guidance. The details provided in the catalogue include item code (codeno), description of material, accounting unit, minimum to indent.

20.1. SD-NOMS

The present package Stores Demand Notes Monitoring System (SD-NoMS) provides for data entry as and when needed; as well as the generation of monthly and annual reports. It also enables to search databases and for data modification at any stage. Since we are able to request upto six items by one SDN and each item so indented is a record in the database, to avoid repeating the same information, the different details in the SDN are separated into two tables (databases). The stores database SDNSTO will generally contain the repeatable fields, or common details which would otherwise have been repeated upto a maximum of six times with each item indented under one SDN, like date sent and processed (issued), debit head, SDNNO, type etc. These are the elements from the SDN point of view. The request database SDNREQ generally holds the details of each item indented like material, quantity, codeno, total value etc, or these are the elements from the material or item point of view. SDNNO is the common field, which links the two databases. The detailed structure of these two databases are given in tables 20.1 and 20.2, and the hierarchy of different menus operating in SD-NoMS is given in figure 20.1.

Table 20.1: Structure of Stores Database, SDNSTO

Field	Field Name	Type	Width	Dec	Index
1	DEBITHEAD	Character	20		N
2	SDNNO	Character	6		Y
3	DATESENT	Date	8		N
4	TYPE	Character	10		N
5	DATEPROC	Date	8		N
		Total	53		

Table 20.2: Structure of Request Database, SDNREQ

Field	Field Name	Type	Width	Dec	Index
1	SDNNO	Character	6		Y
2	MATERIAL	Character	25		N
3	QTYIND	Character	4		N
4	QTYISU	Character	4		N
5	STOCKBAL	Character	5		N
6	CODENO	Character	10		Y
7	UNITRT	Numeric	10	2	N
8	TOTVAL	Numeric	10	2	Y
9	CENTAGE	Numeric	10	2	N
10	REMARKS	Character	20		N
		Total	105		

As mentioned earlier, data entry and report generation are the routines controlled by this package. The only data validation employed is the updation of SDNREQ only with an SDNNO present in SDNSTO. Options are provided in the main menu to have data entry, report generation, or exit. Data entry is further sliced as data entry in SDNSTO, SDNREQ, or exit to main menu. The user is free to go for data entry as a two step process both before and after going to CS or just in one step, after the receipt of department copy of SDN and materials from the CS. All the columns of SDN, which in turn, form the fields of the databases were filled up only by the time of receipt of office copy from CS. The report menu is provided with submenus in two hierarchies; first by time and then by type as well as item. Reports can either be viewed on screen or be printed. Report menu is first subdivided as monthly or annual report or we can go back to the main menu. In the second step, monthly report can be summarised either by type or item which should be viewed on screen or printed, or we shall trail back to the report menu. Similar options were made operational with annual reports too.

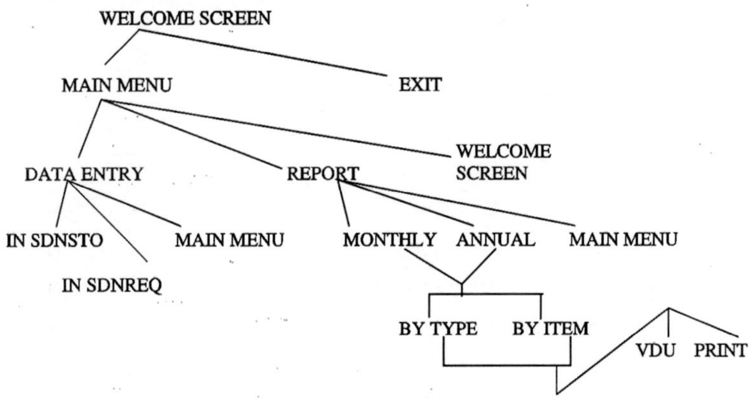

Fig. 20.1: Menu Hierarchy of SD-NoMS VDU PRINT

20.2. INSTALLATION AND MENUS

To facilitate ease of access of the package to users, it was installed in the following manner. It is ensures that both data bases SDNSTO and SDNREQ as well as all the programs shown in the hierarchy along with index files (SDNNDX.NDX, SDNSTO.NDX, SDNREQ.NDX, SDKID.NDX and others, if any), are located in the drive containing dBASE executable files. A batch file called SDN.BAT is installed, at the main drive where path is provided for accessing important files from any other hard disc drive. Thus user will get the welcome screen and thereafter can go to any module of the package by choosing option of interest, from any drive, by typing SDN at drive prompt. The exit to DOS option has been provided only at the welcome screen. This is one special feature adopted throughout the package where default is to the menu earlier in the hierarchy. Thus smooth toggling from different menus to the first screen is ensured.

20.2.1. SDN.BAT file

Echo off

cls

drive where dBASE is installed

cd \dBASE

name of dBASE executable file space SDWEL

redirection to the main drive

(SDWEL is the program to generate the welcome screen)

20.2.2. Main Menu

The main menu prompts the user to any of the three options, viz. data entry, report generation as well as exit to welcome screen. The case loop is followed to redirect control to programs dealing with the respective functions of data entry or report generation, and program exit to welcome screen by default. The use of case for loop control is followed throughout the package to satisfy multiple menu options, as it is found handy.

20.2.3. Data Entry Module

The user advocating for choice 1 in the main menu is lodged to this menu. The user is prompted to select the option for either data entry in SDNSTO or SDNREQ, or for exit to main menu. The dBASE program uses case looping to implement it. This method of loop control is followed throughout the package to satisfy multiple menu options, as it is found handy.

20.2.3.1. Data Entry in SDNSTO.DBF

The choice of 1 in data entry menu passes control to SDNSTO. The user is free to edit the existing data, append new records, and browse in SDNSTO or to go back to data entry module. A usual screen of the menu is added in figure 20.2. Similar options are available for modification of data in the SDNREQ database while picking option 2 from the data entry menu. The user is first asked to enter an SDNNO and data manipulation in SDNREQ is permitted only if the SDNNO entered is present in SDNSTO, else an error message for retry is flashed.

```
DATA ENTRY IN SDNSTO
---- ----- -- ------
  1.EDIT
  2.APPEND
  3.BROWSE
  4.EXIT TO DATA ENTRY MENU

  Enter Choice:
```

Fig. 20.2: Data Entry Menu for SDNSTO.DBF

20.2.4. Report Module

Report menu is accessible to user, when choice 2 selected from the main menu. The report option is subdivided in two hierarchies; first by time (month or year) and then by item (each of the individual items indented) or by type (the broad classification of items into stationery, hard ware, electronic etc.). The program implementation is with the case control construct of dBASE.

20.2.4.1. Monthly Report Menu

The user gets this menu by choice 1 made in the report menu. User can see either total money spent for a particular type or a particular type as well as item, during the month on the screen, or can get a printed copy. Accordingly four options were provided to the user as in figure 20.3. Separate programs were made to direct the report to monitor or printer, for convenience.

```
MONTHLY REPORT MENU
------- ------ ----

1.MONTHLY REPORT BY TYPE ON SCREEN
2.MONTHLY REPORT BY TYPE ON PRINT
3.MONTHLY REPORT BY ITEM ON SCREEN
4.MONTHLY REPORT BY ITEM ON PRINT
5.EXIT TO REPORT MENU

Enter Choice:
```

Fig. 20.3: Monthly Report Menu

In the case of monthly report by type, only categorisation up to SDN level is required and the program first asks for a month and year. It then adds cost for each of the items falling under a particular type to a temporary variable and provides a display of cost incurred for each of the types on the termination of the task. For monthly report by item, the identification of each of the items indented is needed, i.e., one has to go further from the SDN level to the item level. Like the earlier report, the user is prompted to enter a month and year of interest. The program first looks in SDNSTO and identify SDNNO for all the items indented during that month using the DATESENT field. It then copies TYPE of all such records as TTYPE to a temporary database SDKID.DBF. With these SDNNO, it then appends fields MATERIAL as MAT, TOTVAL as VALUE and CODENO as NUMBER from SDNREQ to relevant records. The fields of special interest to the program are DATESENT and TYPE in the first and CODENO, MATERIAL and TOTVAL from the second as well as the common field SDNNO. First it accumulates items falling in a particular type. For a particular CODENO, it sums up the TOTVAL for all the repeated occurrences and also counts such occurrences and puts it in the COUNT field. The field STAT is to signal the skipping of same record at the second instance. This is repeated for all records. The structure of the temporary database is shown in table-20.3. The program can be split into subprograms like the first part which will get the month and year of interest to the user. The second part of the program will signal an error message if no transactions were done during that period. The third part adds the TOTVAL if the item codes are repeated, whereas the last part will display the data.

Table 20.3: Structure of the Temporary Database, SDKID.DBF

Field	Field Name	Type	Width	Dec	Index
1	NUMBER	Character	10		N
2	MAT	Character	30		N
3	VALUE	Numeric	10	2	N
4	COUNT	Numeric	3		N
5	STAT	Character	1		N
6	TTYPE	Character	10		N
		Total	65		

20.2.4.2. Annual Report Menu

The user can utilise this menu when option 2 is chosen from report menu. Similar menus and provisions that have been provided for monthly report are available for annual reporting too. The only difference is that the user is prompted for only year of concern, and the data displayed is more, as they accumulate a whole year's transaction. Accordingly time consumed to generate such reports is more. The choices made available to the user are the same as those for monthly reports as in figure 20.3; the format and content of reports is exactly the same as that for similar monthly reports. To have a feel of the programs used, the program for printing annual report by item is attached in the Appendix 20.1. Other programs may be collected for reference from the author.

20.3. CONCLUSION

The package is tested using stores transaction data of NCSI for the years 1992 and 1993 and found working satisfactorily. The user can easily access the package and it is quite user friendly. The data entry operation monitored by it is quite smooth and all statistics regarding acquisition from Stores can be generated in an appealing format. The menu displays threw open avenues for the user to exploit the resources of the package. Since data validation checks of a higher order were not done, the package works well even if some of the fields of either or both the databases are empty. The only data validation check attempted at present is the search for SDN number, SDNNO in the stores database, SDNSTO for updation in the request database, SDNREQ. The reports generated by SD-NoMS contain all the necessary details and the format as well as layout can be easily modified. Deletion of some of the fields, like DATEPROC(essed) in SDNSTO and quite large number of them like UNITRATE, CENTAGE,REMARKS etc, in SDNREQ will make the package more compact and increase its speed of operation, which is a matter of concern especially while generating annual reports. There exists a strong need to impose strict data validation checks for better accountability of the package. Since the material field is very descriptive, it is better to design short standard abbreviations for the often-indented items and can better do away with the details.

Though the package is designed only for stores monitoring of NCSI, it will be appealing to view it as a module of a larger Office Automation System (OAS) of a Library or Information Centre. It is not out of place to modify the package with appropriate minor changes in the fields for a vendor system of acquisition of books or periodicals in a library or other similar applications, apart from the one for which it is pursued.

REFERENCES

1. Kent, Eben.L. : dBASE in "Encyclopaedia of Microcomputers",V.4, PP.389-405, New York: Marcel Dekker,1990.
2. Simpson, Alan: Understanding dBASE III+, New Delhi: BPB, 1st ed., 1986.
3. Dinerstein, Nelson T.: dBASE III+ for the programmer, New Delhi: Galgotia, 1988.
4. Beiser, Karl: dBASE IV, Westport: Meckler, 1990.

5. Jeevan, VK J: Stores Demand Notes Monitoring System for NCSI, Minor Project Report of 'Training Course on Information Technology Applications to Libraries & Information Centres', 1993-94, NCSI, I.I.Sc, Bangalore.

APPENDIX 20.1

dBASE PROGRAM FOR PRINTING ITEM-WISE ANNUAL REPORT

```
set talk off
set status off
set bell off
set proc to ARPT4
clea
   @1,1 to 23,79 doub
   @2,2 to 4,78
do action
procedure action
use sdkid
go top
do while .NOT. EOF()
   dele
   skip
   loop
enddo
pack
mmonth=0
r=0
myear=0
```

```
select a
use sdnreq index sdnreq
select b
use sdnsto index sdnsto
@3,25 say "YEARLY REPORT"
@10,10 say "Enter the year"
@10,50 get myear pict "9999"
read
go top
*This part of the program prompts for year
returnflag=0
go top
do while .not. EOF()
   if(year(b->datesent)=myear)
   returnflag=1
   exit
   endif
   skip
   loop
enddo
*This part checks whether any valid records exist for that year
if returnflag=0
   @20,10 say "No transaction for this year"
   wait
else
clea
r=6
@1,20 say "NATIONAL CENTRE FOR SCIENCE
INFORMATION"
@4,1 say "CODE NO."
@4,12 say "MATERIAL"
```

```
@4,63 say "OCCURS"
@4,74 say "AMOUNT"
@3,1 SAY REPL("-",79)
@5,1 SAY REPL("-",79)
@2,15 say "REPORT OF SDN TO CENTRAL STORES FOR THE
YEAR"
@2,62 say year(b->datesent)
   do genrpt
endif
proc genrpt
r=6
mvar=space(10)
mtype=space(10)
select 1
use sdnreq index sdnreq
select 2
use sdnsto index sdnsto
select 3
use sdkid
sele 2
msdnno=space(10)
msdnno=0
oldsdnno=space(10)
r=6
flag="Y"
do while .NOT. EOF()
   if year(datesent)=myear
   if sdnno = oldsdnno
   skip
   loop
   else
```

```
   store sdnno to msdnno
   store sdnno to oldsdnno
   store type to mtype
   endif
   else
   skip
   loop
   endif
   sele 1
   go top
   do while .NOT. EOF()
   if  sdnno=msdnno
   sele 3
   appe  blank
   replace  sdkid->ttype  with  mtype
   replace  sdkid->number  with  sdnreq->codeno,;
   sdkid->value  with  sdnreq->totval,;
   sdkid->mat  with  sdnreq->material
   sele 1
   r=r+1
   endif
   skip
   loop
   enddo
   sele 2
   skip
   loop
enddo
sele 3
go top
```

```
mnumber=space(10)
cnt=1
tot=0
mmat=space(30)
oldreccount=0
test=0
    do while .NOT. EOF()
    if stat = "P"
    skip
    loop
    endif
    store recno() to oldreccount
    store sdkid->number to mnumber
    store sdkid->value to tot
    store sdkid->mat to mmat
    store sdkid->ttype to mtype
    go top
    do while .NOT. EOF()
    if recno()=oldreccount .or. stat = "P"
    skip
    loop
    endif
    if     sdkid->number=mnumber
    cnt=cnt+1
    tot=tot+value
    endif
    skip
    loop
    enddo
    appe blank
    replace sdkid->ttype with mtype
```

```
    replace sdkid->count with cnt,;
    sdkid->value with tot,;
    sdkid->stat with "P",;
    sdkid->number with mnumber,;
    sdkid->mat with mmat
    go oldreccount
    cnt=1
    skip
    loop
    enddo
    sele 3
    go top
    do while .NOT. EOF()
    if sdkid->stat # "P"
    dele
    pack
    endif
    skip
    loop
    enddo
pack
sele 3
go top
oldreccount=0
do while .NOT. EOF()
   store recno() to oldreccount
   store sdkid->number to mnumber
   go oldreccount
   skip
   do while .NOT. EOF()
```

```
    if mnumber = sdkid->number
    dele
    endif
    skip
    loop
    enddo
    pack
    go oldreccount
    skip
    loop
enddo
sele 3
go top
do while .NOT. EOF()
    if count=0
    replace count with 1
    endif
    skip
    loop
enddo
*The above part sum totval for same codes
set device to print
@LC,15 say "ITEM-WISE REPORT OF SDN TO CENTRAL
STORES FOR THE YEAR "
@LC,70 say myear
LC=LC+1
@LC,1 say "———————————————————————"
LC=LC+1
@LC,1 say "CODE NO."
@LC,12 say "MATERIAL"
@LC,65 say "OCCURS"
```

```
@LC,72  say  "AMOUNT"
LC=LC+1
@LC,1   say  "——————————————————————————"
LC=8
flag=0
sele 3
go top
set filt to ttype="ST"
go top
do  printing
go top
set filt to ttype="HW"
go top
flag=0
do  printing
go top
set filt to ttype="EL"
go top
flag=0
do  printing
use  sdkid
go top
do while .NOT. EOF()
   dele
   skip
   loop
enddo
pack
close  all
set device to screen
wait
```

```
proc printing
do while .not. EOF()
   if flag=0
   @LC,2 say sdkid->ttype
   LC=LC+1
   @LC,2 say "——————"
   flag=01
   LC=LC+1
   endif
   @LC,1 say sdkid->number
   @LC,12 say sdkid->mat
   @LC,65 say sdkid->count
   @LC,69 say sdkid->value
   LC=LC+1
   skip
   loop
enddo
LC = LC+1
@LC,1 say " "
return
```

21
Web Mails

21.0. INTRODUCTION

Internet has grown from 15 nodes and 21 hosts in 1971 (2 years after its birth) to 4 million hosts in 1995. CERN released World Wide Web (WWW) in 1992 and since then the proliferation of web is manifold, from 130 WWW servers in 1993 to 1 million in 1997. This population is estimated to be doubling every six months. Web has become the dominant protocol over Internet. We can even access telnet, ftp, gopher etc. through web. Today's web is a less than useful browser because animation or dynamic content require a flood of proprietary plug-ins or java. The existing search engines look for any possible match, resulting in irrelevant retrieval (a search for computer chips may also flash potato chips and the mention of the word chip in other contexts). With current HTML, if URL is changed, the name has to be changed manually on each link. Also updation of different forms of publishing like paper, web and CD-ROM needs exporting and reformatting for each type of media. But a shift is on the doorstep and a new web is evolving with Dynamic HTML (DHTML) and Extensible Markup Language (XML) which moves more of the processing for animation and dynamic content to the browser. XML documents contain even user-defined tags and enable to put contexts which forbids false retrieval. With XML, a centralised link management can update all instances of a URL and all forms of publishing can be done from one master document. There are three important offshoots of web technology: web databases, web commerce & web mails. Some of the Service Providers offering web mails are :

Hotmail	http://www.hotmail.com
Yahoo	http://www.yahoo.com
Google mail	http://www.gmail.com
Rediffmail	http://www.rediffmail.com
Mailcity	http://www.mailcity.com
Mailexcite	http://www.mailexcite.com

....

21.1. FEATURES

* Free Facility. Surviving through advertisements
* No special client software needed. only a browser plus access to the web
* E-mails can be viewed anywhere on the globe. Not localised
* POP (Post Office Protocol) - Internet standard to retrieve mail from any mail server. Download web mail to our PC using an e-mail clients like Netscape Mail
* Support attachments- Zipped files, Sound & Images. Copied to local computer for viewing (precautions about virus needed)
* Possibility to download messages to local computer - through POP / cut & paste to offline programs like MSWord
* Can be printed using print function of browser
* Does not support text based browsers

21.2. LIMITATIONS

There is a catch to a free facility like web mails and will be bombarded with too much advertisements and cookies. Also the time to access our mail and their delivery all depend on the infrastructure and network traffic, testing our patience in the present context in our country.

21.3. HOW WEB MAILS REACH US?

Done through the Mail Server (located on the Server managed by ISPs engaged in transmitting and receiving messages), Mail Access Protocol (Communicate between server and client, it is a Network Protocol but actual sending of mail by SMTP or Simple Mail Transfer Protocol) and Mail Client (which process our e-mail: read, file, send etc. manage address books, thesaurus, spell checks e.g.: Pine, Eudora ProMail/Light)

21.4. MODES OF ACCESS

There are three modes: Offline where Mail is downloaded from the server to our computer and once downloaded, deleted from the server; Online in which all e-mail including inbox reside on the server, a temporary copy will be made on our computer, which is erased on termination of session; Disconnected/Resynchronisation mode is a combination of offline and online such that original message on server, copy retained on our computer.

21.5. CASE STUDY: HOTMAIL (HTTP://WWW.HOTMAIL.COM)

A Microsoft Subsidiary with over 8 Million user ids and 2MB space is provided on registration for each user. If you want to cancel your account, don't use for 120 days. It also provides News Services- MSNBC News, Sports, NetGuide etc. and calssifieds. To register a new account, click the sign up link and fill up the form. Once registered, you can give your login and password to check e-mails. The mails arrived will be In-Box and will be listed with details like from, date, subject, and size. Click on the hyperlink (sender) to read the message. After reading the message can be deleted or moved on to a folder. Pick the compose option to type a message and sending. Address books and aliases can be made using Addresses option. Folders (standard as well as user created) can be accessed and made using that option. Online help messages available to use the facility comfortably.

REFERENCES

1. Parthasarathy, Anand, 'You have Mail' - and more, The Hindu Science & Technology Supplement, Thu, June 4, 1998, Page 23
2. Palme, Jacob, Electronic Mail, Boston: Artech House, 1995
3. http://www. hotmail.com, online help manual
4. Baran, Nicholas, The greatest show on earth, Byte, July 1995, pp. 69-86.
5. Mace, Scott et al., Weaving a better Web, Byte, March 1998, pp. 58-68.

PART 6: DIGITAL LIBRARIES

22
Building Digital Libraries

22.0. COMPUTING IN LIBRARY

A library is a place where information is disseminated to needy clients in a user-friendly environment professionally. The application of computers for the various tasks by which information is collected, processed, organised and showcased was a significant development in the latter part of this century. The computerised processes gave way to dynamic as well as interactive products like the inventory/database of the collection which can be searched and accessed electronically widely designated as the Online Public Access Catalogue (OPAC), in contrast to the comparatively static card catalogue. Most of the libraries attempted at automation made it a point to computerise their catalogues even retrospectively to claim some amount of in-house computerisation, and to justify the money and labour put into it. More over this offers considerable help to the users who largely depend on the collection for their varied information requirements. The OPAC helped in retrieving most relevant information that match a particular query and other automated routine operations like circulation rivalled equivalent manual counterparts. No library collection is fit enough to satisfy the information needs of the ongoing process of mission oriented, target fixed, result imperative, present day research, which require information from different specialised journals, conference proceedings, research reports, patents, standards, etc. The printed abstracting sources were found to be so weak to help in this vexed situation where time is the significant player which resulted in the evolution of electronic equivalents for online access or in CD-ROM/floppy form. The popularity of bibliographic databases also saw the emergence of fulltext databases like IEEE/IEE publications on CD. The recent years witness the large scale boom of Internet/ Web the world over leading to the acceptance of web as an alternate delivery mode of information products. You never see a renowned publisher with out a web site now, and most of the international journals offer some provision to access the abstracts/full text of paper through web along with the print subscription. So the information work place is swiftly undergoing a smooth transition from the 'owned-paper-dominated-manual' environment to that of 'shared-access-oriented-electronic' environment.

Like we categorise the computer generations as per the existing technology then prevalent, the penetration of computing and IT infrastructure in libraries can be assessed by a similar classification.

(Traditional) Library ⇒ Computerised Library ⇒ (Computerised Library + Electronic Databases) ⇒ Digital Library ⇒ ?

A large number of libraries, especially public and academic libraries still continue in the pre computer era as first generation in our country. The real fruits of automated library practice can be revealed to the public only by evolving some measures to computerise the large number of public and academic libraries. The special libraries attached to research and higher education were lucky enough to gather resources to attempt at automating their inhouse routine operations and in hosting OPAC (to mature to second generation libraries), some of them also set up facilities to service electronic databases (a satisfactory growth to third generation), a few of them evolved desired infra(info)structure to perform in the post internet era permitting internet surfing, hosting of full text database access, and vision, dreams and programs to become digital libraries in the least possible time (fourth generation libraries). The number of libraries goes down in the higher generations, due to lack of resources or other priorities of the affiliating institution. The major advantage of the progress to the higher generations is the considerable increase in the quantum of information available online. While conducting a journey through these generations, one can see that in the first generation all the information sources and surrogates exist offline whereas the surrogates of collection at least may be online in the second generation. The surrogates of not only collection but also outside information can be accessed online for third generation; apart from the surrogates, some contents also can be accessed online in the fourth generation libraries (online access to all contents will continue to be a long cherished dream of librarians). The goal of fourth generation libraries in the specialised research and academic centres in our country should be to groom their information facilities to fully functional digital libraries, comparable with similar facilities in the developed countries, in the new millenium.

22.1. DIGITAL LIBRARIES

Digital Libraries appear different things to different people [1-4]. The Information Infrastructure Technology and Applications, IITA Working Group consider 'digital libraries as systems providing users with coherent access to a very large, organised repository of information and knowledge'. Ray R. Larson defined it as 'a global virtual library - 'The Library' of thousands of networked electronic libraries'. Association of Research Libraries treat them as "not a single entity, requires technology to link the resources of many, linkages transparent to the user, permits universal access, not limited to document surrogates but extended to digital artifacts". There are other negation definitions like 'library without walls' or 'library without books' and synonyms or related terms such as 'electronic library' or ' virtual library'. Digital Libraries may be treated as repositories of high quality information content in digital form on diverse formats permitting access over different electronic networks.

Some of the purposes of digital library identified by the different ongoing projects (listed in the next section) are: to collect, store and organise information and knowledge in digital form; to promote economic and efficient delivery of information; to leverage the considerable investment made in computing/communications infrastructure; to strengthen communication and collaboration between research, business, government and educational communities; and to contribute for lifelong learning opportunities.

22.1.1. Digital Library Projects

1. **Networked Computer Science Technical Reports Library (NCSTRL), http://www. ncstrl.org/** , to distribute globally technical reports on Computer Science at Cornell University, USA.

2. **Sun Sites, http://www.sun.com** , at renowned educational and research institutions around the world, to promote the growth and reach of the Internet

3. **Centre for Experimental and Constructive Mathematics (CECM), http://www.cecm.sfu.ca/** , a specialised Digital Library on Mathematics at Department of Mathematics & Statistics, Simon Fraser University, Canada

4. **IBM** Digital Library, **http://www.ibm.com/Features/library** , a hub of commercial hardware solutions for Digital Libraries

5. **six NSF/ARPA/NASA funded projects at** :

5.1. **Informedia digital video library, http://fuzine.mt.cs.cmu.edu/im/** , Carnegie Mellon University for full-content search and retrieval from digital video libraries

5.2. **Illinois digital library project, http://www.grainger/uiuc.edu/dli/** , University of Illinois, Urbana Champaign to search and display articles (text & figures) of scientific journals, in SGML format from the publishers

5.3. **Alexandria digital library project, http://alexandria.sdc.ucsb.edu/** , University of California,

Santa Barbara to access digitised maps, images, air photos, etc.

5.4. **University of Michigan digital library project (UMDL), http://sils.umich.edu/ MDL/ Homepage.html** , on earth and space sciences

5.5. **University of Berkeley digital library project, http:// elib.cs.berkeley.edu/ ~wilensky** , for intelligent access to multi-media documents

5.6. **Stanford digital library project, http://www-diglib.stanford.edu/diglib,** on technologies for a single, integrated and "universal" library

6. **US Library of Congress, http://lcweb.loc.gov/loc/ndlf/ digital.html** , has three digital library collections: "American Memory " for history; "THOMAS" for law; 'Library Periodic Report' of the National Digital Library Programme (to digitize materials related to U. S. Heritage and Culture)

7. **British Library's Initiative for Access, http:// www.bl.uk/** , has two projects-The Patent Express Jukebox to provide access to over one million of European and American patents; and Portico, their WWW server

8. **Los Almos National Lab e-print Archive, http:// xxx.lanl.gov/blurb/ pg96unesco. html** , to distribute p/reprints on Nuclear Physics

9. **The University Licensing Program, (TULIP) http:// www.elsevier.com/** , between Elsevier Science and 9 US Universities for networked distribution of journals

10. **Visible Human Project, US National Library of Medicine (NLM), http:// www.nlm.nih.gov/research/visible/ visible_human.html** , anatomically detailed, 3D representations of human body knowledge structures to link visual knowledge and names of body parts

11. **Red Sage Digital Journal Library Project, http:// www.cnri.reston.va.us/home/ dlib/** , UCSF, health sciences, collaboration with AT&T Bell Labs and publishers to explore technical and behavioural issues of electronic delivery

It is difficult to discuss all these projects at length in this short paper, but some details on two interesting projects of NCSTRL and SunSITE is provided in the following sections.

22.2. NETWORKED COMPUTER SCIENCE TECHNICAL REPORTS LIBRARY (NCSTRL)

The Networked Computer Science Technical Reports Library (NCSTRL, pronounced "ancestral") is an open-architecture, network-based system, made available for non-commercial use from a number of participating institutions and archives. The project is a collaborative effort by universities to publish their computer science technical reports and other relevant materials electronically. It is the outcome of two earlier projects, the ARPA sponsored Computer Science Technical Reports (CSTR) project and the NSF supported WATERS effort, as both of them caused a substantial amount of digitized material on the Internet. The CSTR project created a protocol Dienst for implementing distributed digital library servers and the WATERS effort evolved a system to link distributed FTP repositories via a centralized index. An open architecture framework for linking heterogeneous digital libraries has been developed along with tools for accessing and managing collections of network-based information. NCSTRL is built upon this framework as a testbed for experimentation with digital library technology, in a modular fashion favouring introduction of new components and technologies, as and when required. Anyone can access NCSTRL through a Web browser and the collection also has an open interface to access by software agents. The system uses distributed storage and retrieval system, Dienst server (also called NCSTRL-standard site) which is a mid-range Unix workstation plus WWW server with Perl supporting documents in multiple formats. A reduced scale version, NCSTRL-lite site is a computer linked to Internet with an ftp server allowing anonymous access. So NCSTRL can be represented as:

NCSTRL⇒ standard sites + lite sites + central Dienst indexer for the lite sites

A group of sites sharing the Dienst protocol form a single distributed collection, where each site will typically run repository, index, user interface and services for documents of that site, one of the sites run a meta service defining the set of sites. The objects in the collection are identified by "handles" (a location independent handle uniquely specifies a document) registered in the system developed by the Corporation for National Research Initiatives (CNRI). For exchanging bibliographic information, the participating sites uses RFC 1807 standard developed by ISI and Stanford.

NCSTRL Lite sites maintain their bibliographic records in refer citation database file bibs.refer to access via FTP or HTTP. For NCSTRL-Lite, there are seven required fields and three optional fields (Table 1). Each field in refer starts on a new line with '%' followed by a letter denoting the name of the field, one or more spaces and then the value for that field and a bibliographic citation must be terminated by a blank line (see a sample bibliographic entry in fig 1). A forms-based facility called Techrep was written to maintain the necessary information of an organization to participate as a "Lite" site, which composed of the bibliographic management software, and the forms-based user interface. The bibliographic management portion of techrep is a command line program to manage the bibliographic files in a directory for ftp/http access whereas the web interface handles all interactions with users who wish to POST, UPDATE, or DELETE a technical report.

Table 1: NCSTRL Database Fields

Tag	Explanation	Status
%A	name of the author (last name, first name MI) multiple authors listed using separate %A fields	Required
%T	Title of the report	Required
%D	Date the report was issued "mmmmm dd, yyyy"e.g. July 4, 1994	Required
% Z	Date & time the bibliographic record was last modified (not the report) e.g. Mon, 28 Aug 95 18:04:22 GMT.	Required
%R	report number e.g. CS-95-33	Required
%I	report issuer, e.g. Department of Computer Sc., Univ. of Virginia	Required
% U	URL for the report	Optional
% X	abstract	Encouraged
%K	Keywords	Optional
%Y	categories	Optional

%A Son, Sang H. ⟶ *Author*
%A Agarwal, Nipun ⟶ *Author*
%T Synchronization of Temporal Constructs in Distributed Multimedia Systems with Controlled Accuracy ⟶ *Title*
%R CS-93-57 ⟶ *report number*
%D October 28, 1993 ⟶ *date of issue of report*
%Z Tue, 29 Aug 1995 20:09:55 GMT ⟶ *date of bibliographic record*
%K Multimedia, Synchronization, ATM, Temporal Constructs ⟶ *keywords*
%Y H.5.1 Multimedia Information Systems ⟶ *category*
B.4.1 Data Communications Devices
%X With the inception of technology in communication networks ⟶ *abstract*
such as ATM it will be possible to run multimedia applications on future integrated networks. ...possible temporal relations.
%U ftp://ftp.cs.virginia.edu/pub/techreports/CS-93-57.ps.Z ⟶ *URL*
%I Department of Computer Science, University of Virginia ⟶ *Issuer*
**** this is a blank line ****

Fig. 22.1: A sample bibliographic entry from NCSTRL

The servers of NCSTRL inter-operate using an open protocol supporting three services of repository : store and provide access; index: searches over bibliographic records; and user interface: human front-end. The searching works in the sequence: first a web browser opens a connection to user interface gateway; the gateway then returns a form for searching; once the form is filled up and submitted, the gateway processes the search and flash a hit list. Each of these hits can be accessed in full text by following appropriate links. One can search the entire NCSTRL collection for a document with either a simple search or a fielded search. Simple search consists of a single text entry box to accept keywords to search the author, title, and abstract fields. The fielded search form allows to search on several fields of the bibliographic data, and/or to limit the search to specific institutions. The searches can be conducted year wise for a single year, a range of years or all years; author wise with a single letter, range of letters or all authors; or for one or more institution. There is also provision to sort the results of search, which are displayed in the format title, author(s), document id., and institution.

22.3. SUNSITE INDIA, HTTP://SUNSITE.IISC.ERNET.IN

Sun SITE (Software Information and Technology Exchange) is sponsored by Sun at renowned educational and research institutions around the world. These sites were created to promote the growth and reach of the Internet by developing internet access tools, archiving information of general interest, providing content based on geography and as a large public domain software repository. As on December 1999, there are 56 such sites out of which 8 are in North America like the Sun SITE Digital Library at University of California at Berkeley and Sun SITE UTK at University of Tennessee, Knoxville (featuring Java SITE). Among other sites, 2 are located in Central America, 4 are in South America, 1 in Africa (Sun SITE South Africa at University of the Witwatersrand, Johannesburg), 2 in Australia, 29 sites in Europe, and 2 in the Middle East. The 8 Asian sites are: SunSITE India at Indian Institute of Science, Bangalore (http://sunsite.iisc.ernet.in); Sun SITE Hong Kong at University of Science and Technology, Hong Kong; Sun SITE Japan at Science University, Tokyo; Sun SITE Korea at Seoul National University, Seoul; Sun SITE People's Republic of China at Tsinghua University, Beijing; Sun SITE Taiwan at National

Chung Cheng University, Taiwan; Sun SITE Thailand at Assumption University, Bangkok; and Sun SITE Philippines at Ateneo de Manila University, Manila.

The SunSITE India is a joint initiative of the Indian Institute of Science and Sun Microsystems as a large public software archive, maintained on SunSITE India server, a SUN Ultra 150 Enterprise server with 18GB of hard disk storage, donated by Sun MicroSystems. The project is managed by the Supercomputer Education and Research Centre (SERC) of the Institute. The collection is comprised of:

* materials about the 1998 Nobel Prize
* a set of downloadable System Administration Manuals in PDF format for Sun Solaris and SGI IRIX (manual for Unix to appear soon)
* SunSITE India Virtual Library- a growing collection of on-line electronic books and tutorials on various computer and programming-related topics such as, Intranets, CORBA, Java, JavaScript, Linux etc.
* Netscape Mirror- all latest binaries of Netscape Software from the official Netscape Mirror Site maintained by CSA, IISc
* a collection of precompiled binaries of various packages for Sparc Solaris
* the Bengali Writer- a complete font setting package, developed in the Indian Institute of Science, that can convert Roman text into Bengali fonts
* the GNU-Win32 tools are ports of the popular GNU development tools for Windows NTand 95
* Java Stuff - Java-related materials; mpiJava, an object-oriented Java interface to the standard Message Passing Interface (MPI) developed under the HPJava Project at Syracuse University
* goodies for Web Developers- collection of GIF/JPG images — icons, buttons, rockets, animated gifs etc.
* and the Current Science On-Line – electronic access

through a web browser of all articles published in the journal from the issue 75 (4) of 1998 August 25 to the latest.

Current Science, founded in 1932 published by the Current Science Association in collaboration with the Indian Academy of Sciences, is "intended as a medium for communication and discussion of important issues that concern science and scientific activity". This resource is very vital for information professionals as it not only gives online access to a reputed Indian scientific journal but also shows how intellectual information available locally can be disseminated online using IT gadgets. With this discussion on two important projects, let us discuss the technology implications of a digital library.

22.4. DIGITAL LIBRARY SYSTEM (DLS)

The digital library technology projects of NASA and Stanford University gives a feeling of the system and communication resources involved in fully functional digital library development. The Digital Studio (DS) of NASA at Dr. Robert H. Goddard Space Flight Center (GSFC) (http://dlt.gsfc.nasa.gov), is a multi-platform multi-operating system network concentrating on the research and development of information technologies. The presence of different platforms allows the DS to support software developed for various architectures. The network hardware will permit the future inclusion of emerging networking technologies, such as fast ethernet and ATM. Presently DS is build up on hardware from companies Sun, Hewlett-Packard, Apple, and Silicon Graphics with a variety of software on each platform. The main components of DS are in box 22.1. Future expansion of the DS network will include the use of ATM technology, by adding ATM switches and cards to the network to act as a testbed for future development.

The Stanford Digital Library Technologies Project (SDLT) (http://diglib.stanford.edu) is a part of the federally funded Digital Library Initiative Phase 2 (DLI2), started in 1999 with assistance from NSF, DARPA and some other National Agencies of the US Govt. The sole aim of the project is 'to design and implement the infrastructure and services needed for collaboratively creating, disseminating, sharing and managing information in a digital library context'. Another goal is to demonstrate technologies on the emerging California Digital Library (CDL) and to implement and evaluate them on a testbed system to be built with the collaboration of the San Diego Supercomputer Center (SDSC). SDLT is a part of three coordinated proposals from the University of California at

Paper.gsfc.nasa.gov (128.183.113.145) — a Sun Microsystems SPARCStation20 Workstation, running Solaris 2.3, with 64 MB RAM, 2 GB of disk space, a 20" color monitor, an external CD-ROM drive, and a SunVideo Camera (currently supports an ethernet interface, with plans to support ATM also).

Monkey.gsfc.nasa.gov (128.183.113.144) — an Apple Power Macintosh 8100/80 workstation, running System 7.1.2, with 32 MB RAM, 115 MB of disk space, a 17" color monitor and an internal CD-ROM drive (currently supports an ethernet interface).

Rock.gsfc.nasa.gov (128.183.113.144)—a Silicon Graphics Indigo2 Workstation, running IRIX 5.3, with 64 MB RAM, 2 GB of disk space, a 20" color monitor and an internal Dual Speed CD-ROM drive (currently supports an ethernet interface).

Wrench.gsfc.nasa.gov (128.183.113.144) — an Apple Power Macintosh 8100/80 Workstation, running System 7.1.2, with 32 MB RAM, 115 MB of disk space, a 20" color monitor and an internal CD-ROM drive (currently supports an ethernet interface).

Scissors.gsfc.nasa.gov (128.183.113.146) — a Hewlett Packard Model 755 Workstation, running HP-UX 9.05, with 128 MB RAM, 4 GB of disk space, a 19" color monitor, a 4mm DDS tape drive and an internal CD-ROM (currently supports an ethernet interface).

Termite.gsfc.nasa.gov (128.183.113.146) is a Hewlett Packard LaserJet 4Si MX printer.

These digital library machines are connected to a Cabletron SEHI-24 Hub to the **Rtr-dl.gsfc.nasa.gov** (128.183.10.50), a Cisco 7000 multiprotocol router with capability to serve multiple interfaces, including four ethernet and one ATM.

Box 22.1: Configuration of Digital Studio of NASA

Berkeley UCB, the University of California at Santa Barbara UCSB, and the Stanford University, which "together yield a synergistic and comprehensive digital libraries project". The Stanford component will develop the base technologies required to overcome the most critical barriers to effective digital libraries, like the heterogeneity of information and services; the lack of powerful filtering mechanisms; unavailability of library interfaces and tools effectively operate on portable devices; and lack of a solid economic infrastructure. The collection in the first phase, DLI1 was primarily computing literature with a strong focus on networked information sources, found on the World Wide Web. The "InfoBus" protocol, implemented on top of a CORBA-based architecture using Inprise's Visibroker and Xerox's ILU, provides a uniform way to access a variety of services and information sources through "proxies" acting as interpreters between the InfoBus and native protocols. A second area of focus for the Stanford Digital Library Project is the legal and economic issues of a networked environment. The on going developments are focussed on:

* InterServ, a suite of protocols and models for the interoperation of heterogeneous collections and services, build on the current Stanford InfoBus, to handle services and dynamic information artifacts such as applets and plug-ins.
* Value filtering mechanisms to find information based on its value, in contrast to simple its textual similarity on query
* Services/tools for continuous access to information through mobile, handheld devices.
* Design and implementation of a scalable economic infrastructure for integrating different payment mechanisms and for protecting intellectual property, across services/platforms.

Marcus Herzog (http://www.dbai/tuwein.ac.at/staff/herzog/DL/technology.html) listed out software tools for digital library like agent software for Internet searching from California

Software Incorporated (http://www.calsoft.com), software for gathering and organizing Internet-based information by Harvest Information Discovery and Access System (http://harvest.cs.colarado.edu), software agents capable of searching, analysing, and monitoring data from Verity (http://www.thunderstone.com), software for content providers to index and publish large databases on the Web from WAIS Inc (http://www.wais.com) and the Agents resources at the Computer Science department of the University of Maryland Baltimore County (http://www.cs.umbc.edu/agents).

The basic functions involved in setting up a digital library are identification and collection of contents to be digitised; classification and digitisation of these contents; editing, formatting and storage of the contents; designing search engines to selectively search and access the contents; and publishing contents digitally for end-user access. Each of these functions involve certain subtasks like transforming print-on-paper information into digital form; storage, retrieval and handling of "easy-to-use" electronic information; converting data from diverse media or formats into digital format; the necessary classification techniques for improving retrieval efficiency; managing devices for large massive storage, with multilevel hierarchical storage structures, supporting differing speed storage devices and varied capacity processors; editing and formatting of contents in HTML, VRML, PDF, JPEG, MPEG etc.; browsing and querying facilities for content based retrieval; options to promptly distribute as well as safely access information via standard communication and computing infrastructure; security of delivered contents by different cryptographic/encryption methods and appropriate firewall mechanisms. The technical requirements at each of the stages of DLS development may be roughly as shown in Box 22.2. To think about such systems for library work in our country now is a matter of distant possibility, but there are indications of some changes in institutions like the national academic and R & D centres.

Capturing

Data capturing equipments such as high resolution scanners, VCP and compatible capture cards to handle audio, video, images and text.

Storage

Server with multiple CPUs, with RAM in GB range and HDD of few 100 GB to TB.

Few workstations of decent configuration with enhanced processor speed and storage.

Few CD-Recorder/Writers, Jukebox, etc.

Search Engines / Retrieval

Software for database management, webservers, content authoring/ editing etc.

Developmental software (Visual Studio, C++ , Java & Internet Tools etc.,)

Few multimedia PCs

Dissemination

ATM/100 mbps Card and high speed routers

Large display terminals for servers and workstations

LCD displays for projection

High/low resolution printers

Box 22.2: Technical Requirements of DLS

22.5. NEED FOR DIGITAL LIBRARIES

There is no doubt about the utility of digital libraries as they facilitate live and interactive access to a wide variety of contents online. We all experience the benefits of good websites as they answer a wide range of information requirements, which are not thought of in the pre web era, where such information was collected after much personal persuasion. The internet facilities existing in the premier education and research institutions can be tapped for building digital kiosks as a storehouse as well as service centre for all online information available at that site. The digital library development needs a two pronged strategy to digitise local contents as well as to devise options for accessing external resources. Generally there is a feeling that most of the information sources available in our libraries are copyrighted by international publishers, and we are not in a position to provide online access to those contents. They are comfortably forgetting the large quantum of local contents produced by most of our research institutions, viz., conference proceedings, research reports, theses, manuscripts/preprints of research findings, which can be digitised for access like the web access of Current Science through SunSite India.

The problems for digital library development are manifold in India. The lack of interest on the part of parent institutions and the absence of action plans or priorities to that extent is the major hindrance. Though computer and communication infrastructure is improving considerably in the country, their availability for information work is not that much appreciated by the bigwigs in organisations. Even in places where infrastructure is available, there is acute shortage of competent manpower to take up the task of digitising local contents and evolving digital information repositories. The students, faculty, curriculum and training methodology at the disposal of our library schools have to be visibly improved to meet this challenge. Coupled with this is the steps to be taken for continuing education for retraining the exisiting staff.

The increasing interest in library website development and migration of information sources and services to the web should be treated as stepping stones in digital library development. The publishers and other information brokers treat digital information as explosive due to easy means of manipulation and put a plethora of restrictions and barriers on their access. It is imperative up on libraries to judiciously utilise enhanced information access options like web access of subscribed journals. The digital resources thus accessed will contribute a lot to the research activities in the country by reducing some of the existing barriers of present information communication channels like time and space. The software boom engulfing the country, as a result of the big leap in computer penetration, sudden rise in proficient manpower, and sizable improvement in communication infrastructure should also be channelised by authorities and information professionals to create and maintain digital information facilities to usher in the new information age.

REFERENCES

1. Communications of the ACM, April 1995.
2. Communications of the ACM, August 1995.
3. Communications of the ACM, April 1998.
4. IEEE Computer, May 1996.

23
Contents for Digital Libraries

23.0. INTRODUCTION

A library is a place where information is disseminated professionally to needy clients in a user-friendly environment. The application of computers for the various tasks by which information is collected, processed, organized and showcased was a significant development in the latter part of the last century. The computerized processes gave rise to dynamic as well as interactive products like the inventory/database of the collection which can be searched and accessed electronically, e.g., the Online Public Access Catalogue (OPAC), in contrast to the comparatively static card catalogue. The single most development that has brought about sweeping changes in the library and information discipline currently in the developed world is that of digital libraries. Though the professionals and libraries in developing countries are also experiencing the virtues of Internet, and electronic information highways, many of these libraries have not gone much farther than the computerization of in-house operations, availing databases in electronic media such as CD-ROMs, and web access of subscribed journals and various free resources. Some of these libraries created web sites basically to project the services and strengths of the library and to serve more as an advertising or public relations medium rather as a digital information gateway. The digital library development should be taken up as an additional task to populate the web sites with valuable in-house contents like the research reports, publications of in-house researchers, and so on. In a country like India so rich in contents of indigenous research and development in disciplines varied from science and technology to social science, humanities and spirituality, there is tremendous might for hosting full fledged digital libraries by appropriately tagging these contents with affordable information technology. The recent years witnessed the boom of Internet the world over leading to the acceptance of Web as an alternate delivery mode of information products. You never see a renowned publisher without a Web site now, and most of the international journals offer some provisions to access the abstracts/full-text of paper through Web along with the print subscription. So the information centre is undergoing a transition from the paper-dominated manual environment to the shared access-oriented electronic environment.

23.1. DIGITAL LIBRARY

As a fresh, lively and dynamic area with a lot of enthusiasm and activity by researchers from different disciplines, institutions and countries, digital libraries are viewed in different perspectives [1-4]. The Information Infrastructure Technology and Applications (IITA) Working Group consider 'digital libraries as systems providing users with coherent access to a very large, organized repository of information and knowledge' [13]. Association of Research Libraries (ARL) regarded them as "not a single entity, requires technology to link the resources of many, linkages transparent to the user, permits universal access, not limited to document surrogates but extended to digital artifacts" [14]. Noerr suggested two possibilities for a digital library, either a 'library that contains material in digitized form'; or a 'library that contains digital material' [15]. There were other negation definitions like 'library without walls' or 'library without books' and synonyms or related terms such as 'electronic library' or 'virtual library'.

Digital Libraries may be treated as repositories of massive amount of high quality information content in digital form in multiple servers on diverse formats permitting access over different electronic networks in a distributed environment.

Some of the purposes of digital library identified by the different ongoing projects were to [5]:

* collect, store and organize information and knowledge in digital form
* promote economic and efficient delivery of information
* leverage the considerable investments in computing/ communications infrastructure
* strengthen communication and collaboration between research, business, government and educational communities
* contribute for lifelong learning opportunities

The basic functions involved in setting up a digital library are:

* identification and collection of contents to be digitized
* classification and digitization of these contents
* editing, formatting and storage of the contents
* designing search engines to selectively search and access the contents
* publishing contents digitally for end-user access

Each of these functions involves certain subtasks like:

* transforming printed information into digital form
* storage, retrieval and handling of "easy-to-use" electronic information
* converting data from diverse media or formats into digital format
* classification techniques for improving retrieval efficiency
* managing devices for large massive storage, with multilevel hierarchical storage structures, supporting

differing speed storage devices and varied capacity processors

* editing and formatting of contents in formats like, HTML, VRML, PDF, JPEG, MPEG, etc.
* browsing and querying facilities for content based retrieval
* options to promptly distribute and safely access information via standard communication and computing infrastructure
* security of delivered contents by different cryptographic/ encryption methods and appropriate firewall mechanisms

What is lacking, especially in developing countries, is a coordinated collaborative approach to bring in institutions and identifying contents valuable for digitization with sufficient monetary and infrastructure support.

23.1.1. Need and Purpose

Digital libraries aim at unhindered access to contents over computer and communication networks, which justify the need for resorting to such a setup for useful information resources. Digitization may also be taken as a visible proposition to enhance their life by preservation apart from the virtue of increased and easy access, thereby furthering usage. In the digital form, since users can make any number of copies and only these copies of the material are being used, at one point of time, there exist fair chances of at least one electronic copy to be available on the network for use by posterity. Many of printed materials do not have any index, and indeed when available they are visibly archaic, these materials in digital form laced with functional and exhaustive search engines will go a long way in effective access and efficient bibliographic control of the country's output.

The aspects of everlasting preservation and enhanced access must be ensured vigorously now by the applications of new technology for digitizing and electronic access of invaluable contents. Advancements in computer and information technology with breakthroughs in memory technology has not only reduced the cost of infrastructure required for hosting digital libraries, but the demonstrated success of a wide variety of projects in USA and Europe also endorsed the chances of their survival even in a developing country. Since digitization and digital library development are stupendous tasks involving computer and communications infrastructure, and considerable specialized human skill, a digital storage and selective search and access facility can be set up by formulating a collaboration of few institutions active in computerized information handling.

23.1.2. Why to digitize?

The real question of "to be or not to be" for digitizing resources would find justifications in:

i) It is not only the availability of digital technology that is important but the point to be stressed is its affordability with each significant improvement in the technology driven by market forces.

ii) Digitized materials can be easily searched and retrieved that will definitely augment their use.

iii) Resources digitized could be easily shared among members of the library network or consortia. If each library does its bit to digitize even a part of the collection, the ultimate result will be considerable for sharing among different members.

iv) If not the full text available outside Intranet or members of the consortium, mere search and inventory facilities over the Internet itself will significantly enhance the image of the library and its better visibility among other similar facilities.

v) Less likely to be damaged than print counterparts, as they have no physical form to yellow and decay with age, and loaning out a copy does not relinquish the original [21].

vi) Require less space for storage and hence reduction in the building space required.

23.1.3. What to digitize?

Chapman and Kenney suggested that the source documents themselves as the focal point for conversion decisions and not current users' needs, current service objectives, current technical capabilities, or current visions of what the future may hold [22]. The US Task Force on Archiving of Digital Information, established by the Commission on Preservation and Access and the Research Library Group [23], found that many of the criteria librarians have used to archive print content apply equally well to digital information:

* appraisal of the subject and discipline in relationship to the institution's collection goals
* the quality and uniqueness of the content
* its value now and for the future.

Any library must identify two types of sources for digitization as per their use characteristics. Sources always in high demand in less number of copies may be the obvious choice. There may be sources less used, as they are difficult to be handled in the present form and could be digitized if that will lead to more use of them. The acute problem while pondering over library digitization is the crucial question of copyright and intellectual protection involved for most of the library materials. Libraries subscribing to a journal or buying a book are entitled for certain rights to put these materials to "fair" use of its clientele. Publishers and other copyright owners may turn a blind eye to photocopying a few pages from them for classroom use or for research work. The so called virtues what we attach to digital technology like ease of use, modification and distribution were treated as threats to their rights by the copyright owner. Whatever security and safeguards ensured to protect the use exclusively for authorized user community can be easily broken by others as technology centric precautions will stand only till a person better in technology than you. More over the publishers don't ease their rights to others as they themselves were engaged in a digitization plan of new publications and in some cases even retrospective materials selectively.

Thus our libraries are left with a choice of digitizing only few materials. But an ingenious action plan will enable us to even find three types of materials as per copyrights involved, viz. a lot of such materials that are copyright free, copyright owned, and copyright transferred or bought. Copyright free materials belong to those in the public domain like government documents or old books for which the copyright is either expired or not enforced. Since these materials are old or easily available, care should be taken to first identify the usage rate of them from statistics generated by library automation package. Digitize only the maximum used ones and does a less used one only when demonstrated that difficulty in handling in the present form is hindering its use. Since our publishing industry is not as streamlined as in developed countries one can see a lot of publishers go into oblivion after publishing a handful of titles. As they may be willing to transfer the rights for local digitization, this is one way of copyright buying by individual libraries or consortia without spending much. Other means of buying the rights will be a very difficult proposition at least for our libraries as funds are always on the decline whereas sources, users' demands and prices are always on the uphill. A detailed discussion on specific contents for digital library development will be attempted later.

23.1.4. How digitization?

Digitization is a task that involves considerable expenditure both in terms of computer systems and proficient human resources, which are difficult to find and nurture in many libraries. As a country with significant developments in the field of digital libraries, even in USA, the notable features that guided some of the successful projects are as follows [7]:

a) no single model or method to follow

b) each project have taken a unique approach determined by its goals, resources, and the extent to which creativity and novelty are encouraged

c) importance of strong organizational commitment, a critical mass of information, and a well defined collaborative approach

The Colorado Digitization Project (CDP at http:// coloradodigital. coalliance.org/) cautions the following [24]:

* Scanning at the highest resolution at an appropriate level of quality to avoid rescanning and re-handling of the originals
* Creating and storing a master image file
* Using system components that are non-proprietary
* Using image file formats and compression techniques that conform to industry standards
* Creating backup copies of all files on a stable medium
* Creating meaningful metadata for image files or collections
* Storing media in an appropriate environment
* Monitoring and recopying data as necessary
* Outlining a migration strategy for transferring data across generations of technology
* Anticipating and planning for future technological developments

Since the different steps in digitization listed below must be identified and a workflow would be carefully designed and executed by each library, it is only possible to highlight the major challenges under each of the steps here. Deciding on appropriate formats for incorporating the contents in to CD or on web will be dependent on the presence of different software required, and the means to support any extra systems needed as well as the size and features of materials to be digitized.

23.1.4.1. Content Identification and Selection

Since contents of wide variety are available at the disposal of digitization effort, the first step is to identify and select what to digitize and what not to. Policies and programmes of the library and on top of that the users' expressed and expected needs should influence this decision. The motivations would be on various counts such as costly and rare materials to prevent their mutilation and damage, frequently and demanding materials to increase their access, difficult to retrieve materials to improve their search and dissemination, under used materials to extend their use, etc.

23.1.4.2. Content Capturing

Let us identify only textual sources in the beginning, and focus on internal contents first. Retrospective data could be digitized either by keying or by scanning. So some data entry terminals (PCs) and scanners are essential. Both of these can be procured from the market for as low as Rs. 30000. Sophisticated contents like images, video and sound (not so important if we consider an academic library where majority of the collection is largely textual) may be converted at a later stage when the digital library development acquires enhanced monetary support by procuring equipments such as high resolution scanners, VCP, multimedia machines (workstations as well as servers) and compatible capture cards to handle audio, video, images.

23.1.4.3. Content Indexing and Metadata

Indexing is required for the digitized contents to search and access contents in a selective way like OPAC for printed contents. Decisions are to be taken regarding what to be indexed (author, subject, keywords, phrases, etc.), usage of stop words, vocabulary control, proximity searches, language and period limiting etc. Indexing strategy comprises not only of what types of fields are to be indexed, but how they are to be treated (exhaustive or sparse). How the content and index files are to be linked and what sort of access points are provided? May be the library is going for a modular fashion; they can prepare hypertext links to provide access to the digitized contents. Once the contents acquired sufficient volume, they can look for a database management system to link the index and contents. Using the Dublin Core framework as the basis, the CDP identified eight optional elements and seven mandatory elements of creator, title, subject, description, identifier, date, and format [24].

23.1.4.4. Formats

The easiest option for electronic access is through Web by converting the electronic full text available in the pre-production stage into html format. Added materials like figures/ tables may be converted in to formats like gif/jpg whichever is convenient for the individual institution. Also electronic provision of full text can be handled more appropriately in Portable Document Format (PDF) using Adobe Acrobat software. The electronic file in PDF handles text and other forms of figures and tables equally well and looks just like a journal page on screen and in print. Only disadvantage is that file sizes are comparatively big, occupies more space on the server (not a troublesome job as the improvements in technology have substantially reduced hard disk costs) and takes more time in downloading. The software to read PDF files Acrobat reader is freely downloadable from many sites (like, http:// www.adobe.com) thus requiring no investment at the client side. Over 95 % of the 600 international journals out of the 800 subscribed at a premier library of India provide the table of contents with abstract as html files and the full text in PDF. The remaining uses different formats of html, PS, etc. When different formats are available, how to prefer and stick to one requires both technical and administrative feasibility studies. Sometimes, the volume of contents to be handled is more, often warranting handling of scanned images and CD archiving.

23.1.4.5. Storage

PCs are marketed now with 20-40 GB HDDs 128-256 MB RAMs for as low as Rs. 35000. So with limited investment, the library may be able to order a better PCs and servers. If money is a problem to get Unix Operating system, they can do with shareware like Linux. During the initial stages, it is also appropriate to work with NT servers. Configure at least one machine with good configuration as a server to hold and service the digital contents. Noerr assumed text, in general, is stored at one byte per character and assumed 2 bytes per character for multi-lingual, with 100% indexing overhead. The storage required for a small collection of 100,000 articles averaging 5 pages (2000 characters per page), all in English stored in full text, and indexed for proximity and structural searching is 3GB [20].

23.1.4.6 Search Engines / Retrieval

The library needs software for database management, Web servers, content authoring/ editing, etc., and developmental software (Visual studio, C++, Java & Internet tools etc.,). As most of these tools are in the public domain, the library does not find it difficult to use at least a few of them for its in-house digitization routines.

23.1.4.7. Dissemination

If the campus is well networked, then without much investment from the library side, the contents may be made accessible on the Intranet. It is easier to host the borrowed external contents also in this mode. However access restrictions are to be put on these contents either with login/password or and IP filtering when access is provided over Internet. The library is always free to host its internal contents on the Internet. The Internet infrastructure required for hosting the digital library depends on different parameters such as the quantum of contents to be hosted, number of simultaneous users expected, over and above the bandwidth constraints on the national level. 1 Mbps bandwidth will play videos in real time and internal LAN technology has already crossed the 1Gbit barrier. Thus institutions with a functional Intranet and leased line connection from VSNL or other Internet Service Providers (ISPs) will not face many hindrances for content delivery.

23.2. INDIAN SCENARIO

Digital library projects and developments in the country are so many, and a large number of them are at an aggressively enthusiastic preliminary stage. Indian Institute of Science (IISc.), Bangalore collaborated with IBM and SUN

Microsystems to host respectively the IBM Digital Library and SUN SITE in their campus. Indian Academy of Science, Bangalore has demonstrated successfully free on-web delivery of their journals through their web site. The Council of Scientific and Industrial Research (CSIR) of India is proceeding with a major project to map the traditional knowledge of the country with the Traditional Knowledge Digital Library (TKDL). The Central University of Hyderabad also has collaboration with SUN to digitize some of its collection. Regional Engineering College, Calicut is involved in a project called Nalanda to create a digital library of books. The Central Library of IIT, Kharagpur has been awarded a project by ARDB for developing a hypermedia digital library on Aerospace science and technology. There is also a strong component of digital library in the Virtual Centre for Technology Enhanced Learning (VCTEL) that focus on the role of technology in knowledge accumulation, storing and dissemination and education in three sectors of university, industry and government. VCTEL is proposed to be set up by the Indian Institute of Technologies (IITs), Indian Institute of Managements (IIMs) and Carnegie Melon University, aimed at providing Distance Education, developing resources for Core Courses, conducting joint Ph.D. Programmes and setting up a digital Library. Training on Greenstone digital library software has been conducted by NCSI of IISc, Bangalore. Inspired by the success of NDLTD, University of Mysore is pursuing a project, Vidyavahini on digitizing theses and dissertations with support from NISSAT. One event that has created a major surge in digital library and digitization initiatives in the country was the holding of the International Conference on Asian Digital Libraries (ICADL) in Bangalore in December 2001. A record number of over 700 participants attended where the average attendance level in professional conferences in the country varies from 150-200. But a large number of the participants were from the Library & Information Science discipline and though the event was held in a place regarded as the "silicon valley" of the country, very few participants from computer and IT related fields showed interest in it. If not full blown digital library initiatives, a lot of institutions and libraries are interfacing a considerable amount of contents on their web sites.

The digital library development in the country needs a two-pronged strategy (i) to digitize local contents, and (ii) to devise options for accessing external resources. Computer and Information Technology tools are being increasingly applied towards improving information organization and services in the country like the industrially advanced countries. Digital library development in the country involves not only cost effective implementation of computer and Information Technology tools, but also contents covering significant areas of knowledge. Most of the traditional information sources such as books or journals are either copyrighted by commercial publishers or are not available in the present access terms for digitization by libraries and information centres. Considering the availability of IT gadgets in the library work place, one can confirm it is not the technology and infrastructure that is hampering the development of fruitful alternatives in digital full text information provision, but to large extent the lack of priorities and absence of formal contents. The present day research and development is not solely dependent on formal sources of information only. Thus digital library initiatives in the country have to explore informal contents or contents owned by our Institutions to arrive at viable alternatives.

23.3. CONTENTS

The spread of higher education, research, and the increased acceptance of science and technology development for solving the ills faced by society in the post World War II period gives rise to a lot of such publications in all areas of human endeavour. Technology growth and perfection as a result of massive applied mission oriented research in emerging areas needed suitable outlets to quickly disseminate the new knowledge generated and this lead to further rise in the number of publications. Contents fall in two groups, external and internal.

23.3.1. External Contents

Generally, there is a feeling that most of the information sources available in our libraries are copyrighted by international publishers, and we are not in a position to provide online access to those contents. There are provisions within the fair use principle to host digital/online information from the local collection, as we have photocopied a part of the collection earlier for clients. Improving or enhancing the use of contents is a matter under the jurisdiction of individual libraries to explore and elaborate. And most of the copyright restrictions have two important exceptions, duplicating or transmitting contents for academic purpose as well as copying without any profit motive were not treated as infringements, at least on the Institution's Intranet. The publishers are also offering electronic options like online access through Web of subscribed journals, CDs and floppies containing supplementary material of printed books. Most of these electronic contents can be provided through library servers or intranet along with local contents. Contents procured from publishers or vendors such as full-text databases, online access of subscribed primary journals. There are also offline electronic media like CDs, floppies etc. Some of the areas the individual libraries should concentrate include:

a) Networking with jukebox/CD tower or high capacity hard disk mirroring of optical media disks to serve bibliographic or full text databases, electronic supplements with printed books, CDs of publications/ reports of internal activity.

b) Web access of journals: Currently subscribed journals could be made accessible from the publisher's Web sites either through login and passwords or by specific IP addresses of the institution, with/out paying extra fee on subscriptions. There are also options to join consortia based electronic access of primary resources through MHRD's INDEST consortium, UGC-INFLIBNET's Infonet, etc.

c) Virtual libraries: Links to free web resources on focus areas of the institution.

d) ebooks: Free/fee books in electronic form.

Prioritization is indeed needed in digitizing contents (especially in terms of type and time) as the quantum of contents often fall in large numbers. Most of the external contents have a ten-year retrospective availability.

23.3.2. Internal (local) Contents

Research or annual reports and other publications issued by the parent institution affiliating the library. In addition, there are also p/reprints of research publications and proceedings of conferences hosted by the institution. Contents generated in-house by not-for-profit institutions may be collected and hosted in a distributed fashion by different institutions to achieve this objective. Instructing internal content generation points to have new updates of reports and other publications in electronic form is a valid step to start with digital library development. A detailed discussion of a countywide digital library development initiative using internal contents will be presented in the later part of this paper. There is no dearth of internal contents as knowledge activity is very strong in the country is very strong which grows in many channels.

23.4. CHANNELS FOR INTERNAL CONTENTS

23.4.1. Journals and Serials for Research

Research publications are so vital for any professional discipline and preserving as well as accessing them is the most crucial task and a considerable extent of such articles is published in journals. Ulrich's International Periodicals Directory (37th edition) lists around 157,173 serials in 973 subject headings [10]. The utility of journals is aptly confirmed by Katz, when said that 10 to 20% of the users read a book in a month while 60 to 80% look at a journal during the same period [11]. Hence it would be imperative upon all concerned to take effective steps needed to tackle this form of literature at par with what is happening in the international scenario. Whatever is subscribed in ones' library can be used but can not be digitized due to the copyright restrictions added by the perennial woes of all pervading electronic information. One has to understand the features of the individual journals identified for digitization and find out means to address the problems of transfer of copyright, and access control for electronic access through web. Since backlog of over 40-50 years are to be handled in certain cases, CD archiving of back volumes by keying in only the contents and abstracts, and scanning the full text may be adopted as an alternative. Another issue worth pondering is the constraints of weak infrastructure, especially in terms of network bandwidth. Due to wide use by publishers, PDF has been emerging as the de facto standard for hosting full text journals on the web and this option is suggested as a uniform format, as other formats available like html or gif will not handle both text and figures comfortably.

The pitfalls of journals published from India are many, and they have to be attended from different perspectives, that of the reader, the author, and the editor/publisher. The reader will stress on value and quality for cost, whereas the author expects a sympathetic approach for his/her ideas from the editor and publishing it faster with maximum visibility. For the editor/publisher, balancing these diverse attitudes of these two groups with further pressures from production and distribution costs is an arduous task. In a study of 200 Asian Library and Information Science journals in general, and 70 South Asian ones in particular (of which 57 are from India), Sharma [6] rightly pointed out the problems, which may be extended to journals in other subjects and to some extents contents in other forms like reports, edited books, etc. :

1. Frequency varied from quarterly, semi-annually, yearly, and irregularly and many journals do not appear on time. Sometimes a few issues, or even a few volumes, are combined.
2. The paper used for printing a majority of journals is of very poor quality. It becomes yellow within a few years and maybe, it is not acid-free.

3. It seems that the editors are desperate to get articles and publish them bereft of peer reviewing or proper editing or good proofreading without looking at their quality. Perhaps these laxities coupled with absence of any marketing attribute for their small circulation.
4. Many editors have started journals without proper planning, finances, and marketing that resulted in the premature death of many journals. A majority of the editors are part-time, without any proper help, which makes it very difficult to run a quality and profitable business.
5. Few publishers never replace lost and damaged copies of their journals free. Often even authors do not receive free copies of journals and/or offprints of their articles.

It is impending up on the professionals to work for arresting these pitfalls to the maximum possible extent and to frame an action plan to further the access of intellectual content published in these journals. The action plan should formulate the essential needs, purpose, and objectives of digitization and options to overcome the constraints that keep coming on the way. The absence of peer reviewing mechanism, or even becoming vindictive sometimes, further erodes the quality of papers. It seems, habitually authors reserve their good papers for international journals for better visibility of their ideas, availability of highly specialized publications, and prestige; subsequently deteriorating the quality of contents of the papers published in national ones.

We have seen that in the present state of affairs, journals in printed form are published in very few copies and are exclusively distributed to subscribers. Most of the time, the institutions never encourage professionals to take personal subscriptions to such journals, and they are out of reach to a large number of professionals. Also a few of them are covered in authorized abstracting and indexing journals further deteriorating the chances of proper retrieval of these articles by a prospective reader. The paper used for publishing these journals is of inferior quality significantly reducing their shelf life. Digitization may also be taken as a visible proposition to enhance their life by preservation apart from the virtue of increased and easy access. In the digital form, since users can make any number of copies and only these copies of the material are being used, at one point of time, there exist fair chances of at least one electronic copy to be available on the network for use by posterity. Many of these journals in printed form do not have any index, and indeed when available they are visibly archaic, these materials in digital form with functional and exhaustive search engines will go a long way in effective access and efficient bibliographic control of the country's output.

Over the years, journals published in India have accumulated a considerable chunk ("critical mass") of papers on different areas of knowledge. Now what is needed is a proper framework for collaborative approach influenced by strong organizational commitments. In the case of a majority of journals, publishers or owners of the contents are not so strong in web and allied technologies, and hence identifying a technically sound partner is very much desired. Since some of the journals are over 4-5 decades old, it is very difficult to provide on web delivery for the whole content. To start with, let us concentrate on latest issues for the last 5-10 years. There is a strong potential for CD-ROM publishing in the country [8], and this channel may be explored for the back issues.

The investments required for a CD publishing venture are comparatively small nowadays due to advancements in memory technology, the availability of sophisticated CD-writers and scanners at affordable rates. If the particular journals back volumes are not available in electronic format, and only the print versions exist, the easy route for their conversion in a non-print form is by scanning these pages and incorporating into CD-ROM. Though scanned images occupy 10 times more space than keyed in ASCII, the cost of keying is about 10 times the cost of scanning [9]. The same search engine used for web access of new issues can be used for retrieving these scanned pages by incorporating connections with the content pages. At this stage, it will be difficult to provide search and access provision in the text portion, as they are scanned images. If the quantum of contents in a particular journal is very small, we can alternately bypass this stage by converting the entire contents into electronic format for on-web access. In the CD version, ceased journals of importance also may be included. All ceased journals when available, depending up on priority based on the quality of contents can be incorporated at a later stage on CD-ROM or web site.

23.4.2. Conference Proceedings

As is the case with journals, there are many conferences held under the support of many government and non-governmental agencies covering various fields of specialization in institutions spread across the country. The proceedings of some of these conferences were disseminated in a book form or as special issues of journals. Both of these outlets are bound by the problems of restricted dissemination, but they are comparatively better than many other conferences were no such publications came out. These conferences generate contents, and in many cases of a high standard, which never get the deserving visibility and often end up with out reaching the target population. A decentralized approach to involve multiple institutions to host these contents in electronic form may lead to more focussed research and development activity in many of these areas.

23.4.3. Theses and Dissertations & Preprints, and Research and Status Reports

Along with journals and conference proceedings, these sources also contribute for the proper dissemination of scholarly literature. Most of these sources in its present print format have very limited reach among those interested to use them. Since the authors and their corporate entities have full ownership on these sources, many of the problems that may come up with regard to rights can be easily alleviated with these sources leading to their inclusion as primary sources for digitization.

23.4.4. Textbooks and learning materials

It is not only the generation and production delays but also the distribution factors that are causing problems with the required availability of textbooks and other learning materials. The linear text in many of these sources with difficulties to provide a hypertext approach, multimedia feeling, to incorporate streaming of diverse media and formats, all suggest the benefits of using technology intrinsic electronic media for learning and teaching. There is also the major danger of lack of interest in the static mode of content presentation in printed sources when one is exposed to the widely appealing features of broadcasting and IT intensive presentation tools. Also exposing to these technologies at a young age will help the students to acquire the requisite IT skills at a very young age.

23.4.5. Government Publications

Publications from Government and allied agencies are very valuable as they touch the daily lives of people and many of them provide authentic data concerning various social and economic parameters of the population. Many such publications are distributed primarily in print form, often printed in limited numbers and distributed through archaic distribution networks. The attempts of the National Informatics Centre (NIC) to host web sites of many Government departments and agencies are worth emulating. We need many such attempts to cover the entire gamut of government and not-for-profit publications.

23.4.6. Spiritual/Heritage Sources

Spiritual and philosophic knowledge base of India is very vast and through efforts of national and foreign scholars, right now a very strong printed repository of such knowledge exists in important 'Oriental' libraries spread across the world. Identifying and converting these materials will no doubt improve their reach among those concerned and may even attract new users for these sources traditionally considered as 'not so modern'.

23.4.7. Tourism Information

As a country with different weather conditions, India is an all season tourist destination. Since the national and state governments pursue an aggressive agenda to improve the tourism infrastructure, steps toward easy availability of information concerning geographic aspects, traffic network, must-see as well as facilities available in each and every place and other information bits of interest to tourist must be made available in electronic form in the cyber cafes and the wide network of STD/ISD booths. Such a value added approach to map the tourism potential of India and tourism information in a tourist-friendly manner along with infrastructure improvement may attract more tourists than the enormous money spend on advertisements often depicting India as a mythical destination.

23.4.8. Traditional Knowledge

National development in an increasingly technology intensive social order requires efficient mechanisms for properly recording and fruitfully preserving the Research and Development of a country. As a nation with centuries of intellectual growth and demonstrated progress like ours with not so ordered forms of knowledge recording and distribution, this has achieved significant concern for national policy makers, social scientists and technocrats. We have seen not one but many encroachments on the traditional knowledge of the country through patenting by multinationals. Though the Post World Trade Organization (WTO) world order expressed increasing concern for preserving the intellectual property rights (IPRs) of the country in a properly documented and preserved format, the main reason for these infringements are largely due to the apathy towards constructive organization of such knowledge and making it available in an easily disseminating format. TKDL from CSIR is one such attempt.

The problems with traditional knowledge are that they are not available in a properly written form or were passed through generations predominantly in vocal form. Another area of concern is that they are not tested and validated scientifically in some cases. There is no dearth of traditional knowledge experts and scientists and technologists or patent attorneys and IPR experts or information and computer professionals, but what is lacking is a targeted collaboration of these experts to achieve a common goal. Thus the creation of a digital library of traditional knowledge requires co-operation from experts, Non Governmental Organizations (NGOs) and service arms of the Government to first identify peers and resources in diverse areas of traditional knowledge like Indian systems of Medicine, Engineering, Agriculture, Fine Arts, Folklore, Philosophy and Spirituality. Academic practitioners in these fields also may be able to offer substantial assistance on this count. The services of information professionals working in specialized institutions must be utilized to trace out proper resources and their authenticity be tested by specialists. Then the services of laboratories attached to research/academic institutions to verify the correctness of this knowledge, when they are of scientific nature. Since the discussion pertains to a traditional knowledge repository that can be framed of this exercise at the national level, it is the duty of libraries of various types in the fold of different Institutions to devise techniques for properly recording this knowledge in a digital form and formulating access control. The services of computer professionals are required in this exercise apart from information professionals to design and implement a distributed digital resource for access by different Institutions spread across the country.

A development that has to go side by side with this is the creation of an expert database of traditional knowledge practitioners so that persons interested in seeking their service can be able to easily identify and contact them. Only when traditional knowledge is properly documented and made available for use with options for peer contact and assistance, NGOs or others in need of solving social problems may be able to utilize them. There is no doubt that solutions based on this 'rich but cheap' knowledge will go a long way in further augmenting the Nation's development.

23.5. PROBLEMS AND PROSPECTS

The problems for digital library development are manifold in India. The attempts mentioned earlier present a feel of what is possible on digital library development with Indian contents. But there are many constraints that have to be overcome to mature services to international standards. The main hurdles in the digital library development in a developing country are:

1) The lack of interest on the part of parent institutions and the absence of action plans or priorities to that extent is the major hindrance.

2) Though computer and communication infrastructure is improving considerably in the country, their availability for information work is not that much appreciated in many organizations. There are also personnel problems as the Librarians fail to command a leadership role in many institutions thereby eclipsing their role in strategic planning.

3) How the copyrights are transferred and handled in the digital environment? Institutions, individuals, or private publishers have rights over contents, and how to motivate this varied category to ease their rights to other entities for electronic access provision (when the former are not inclined to do so) will be the main bottleneck. But these issues can be resolved by entering into collaborations between the owner of copyright and institution holding the onus of digitization.

4) Another aspect to be considered simultaneously is how the access rights are implemented? What mechanisms are used to impose restrictions on access? When hosted as a paid facility, how charges are levied from users? How login and password access is strictly ensured? If provided as a free facility, how funds needed to set up the infrastructure and continue the operations are generated? How far the facility can be subsidized with the help of advertisements and sponsorships? Levying

charges for access is a distant proposition, due to the specific nature of usage and the fact that these contents, such as journals, are not attracting much personal subscription now. Instead, sponsorships from institutions, government bodies, and library suppliers can be explored as a viable means to bring in money for this task.

5) Even when hosted as a free facility, enough security mechanisms like firewalls, filtering routers, encryption-decryption etc. must be put on the server side to prevent any trespassing by hackers. Threat perceptions from the vulnerable areas of Internet layer, routing infrastructure, domain name server, and network management [12] has to be addressed from the technical, administrative and operational angles.

6) The advent of computers, internet and the IT boom engulfing the country has changed the way information is collected, organized, and serviced in the country. As a result sweeping changes are happening in different disciplines, how to rightly select useful contents requires careful review and selection by subject experts. Digitization in entirety will only help to preserve the record, and careful selection of contents is thus required for enhanced and continued access by users.

7) Internet bandwidth, which is the maximum amount of data that can be transmitted in a particular time, in the country, has to be sufficiently augmented for faster access of web contents. Though a lot of institutions have designed contents for hosting on the web, most of the time users have to wait rather impatiently to access them. Agarwal [17] mentioned about efforts of VSNL to create a bandwidth of 155 Mbps in four metros, Bangalore and Pune, another 8 cities will get two 8 Mbps links, a further 31 cities will get one 8 Mbps link and around 504 cities/ towns will get 2 Mbps link. A good rule of thumb is that for every user, at least 8 Kbps, preferably 12 Kbps of guaranteed, sustained bandwidth must be available, end-

to-end. [18]. Internet connections in India have exceeded 1.2 million (20.45 lakhs on sept 30, 2000; a 50% growth rate in 3 months [19]) and it is expected to cross 10-million in the next three years. Hope that initiatives like VSNL's six gateways, Dishnet DSL submarine cable between Singapore and Chennai, landing point of FLAG (Fibre optic Loop Around the Globe) and other international under sea links like, SEA-ME-WE (III) (South East Asia, Middle East and Western Europe) and SAFE (South Africa Far East) optic fibre submarine cable will soon improve the Internet bandwidth in the country.

8) Need of financial support for developing digital library prototypes is very much desirable. Thus funding agencies, research councils, and institutions should offer monetary support, especially for augmenting the existing infrastructure, for content leasing, and for staff/volunteer honorarium. The success and experience gained in these projects must be most important for further digitization projects.

9) Proper documentation, retrieval, and access of indigenous knowledge have gained more prominence in recent days, also to preserve the intellectual property rights (IPRs) in the emerging philosophy of free trade and liberalization.

10) The professional staff members working in many libraries in developing countries are so engrossed in administrative and routine jobs related to library operation and administration. Many Institutions need not demand their professionals to pursue such an aggressive role. There are also problems of lack of ability, lack of incentives, and lack of role model initiatives.

11) Even in places where infrastructure is available, there is acute shortage of competent manpower to take up the task of digitizing local contents and evolving digital information repositories. The students, faculty, curriculum and training methodology at the disposal of

our library schools have to be visibly improved to meet this challenge. Coupled with this, steps are to be taken for continuing education programmes for retraining the existing staff.

The increasing interest in library Web site development and migration of information sources and services to the Web should be treated as stepping stones in digital library development. The Internet facilities existing in the premier education and research institutions can be tapped for building digital kiosks as a storage and service centre for all online information available at that site. The publishers and other information brokers treat digital information as explosive due to easy means of manipulation and put a plethora of restrictions and barriers for access. It is imperative upon libraries to judiciously utilize enhanced information access options like Web access of subscribed journals. The digital resources thus accessed will contribute a lot to the research activities in the country by reducing some of the existing barriers of present information communication channels like time and space. The software boom engulfing the country, as a result of the big leap in computer penetration, sudden rise in proficient manpower, and sizable improvement in communication infrastructure should also be treated as an asset and taken advantage of by authorities and information professionals to create and maintain digital information facilities to usher in the new information age.

23.6. CONCLUSION

Like the enthusiasm received for in-house automation and for web site creation, a third boost required in Indian libraries is that of evolving prototypes of digital library. This can be achieved at the individual level and by entering into collaborations with other libraries. It is not technology that is hampering our libraries to venture into digitization but various factors of infrastructure, manpower, finance, and lack of priorities. These problems have no quick remedies and would be overcome only through programmes and follow up action to address them. Apart from identifying and evolving steps to digitize local contents which are the exclusive intellectual property of the Institution concerned, libraries can also procure commercial products available in the market to host as digital libraries on the intranet for better information use of clientele. Some of these tasks can be started by very little investment in terms of a web server and by devoting some staff members, and volunteers. Though "knowledge is power" and there was a feeling earlier that usurping one's knowledge was difficult, but this is not true now with daily improvements in wiring the world. In the emerging networked world, your knowledge is identified as yours and the rights will be attributed to you only when you have properly recorded it and taken enough security mechanisms to improve and maintain it. Resorting to what the developed world does is the right means to give more visibility to the intellectual property of developing nations.

Digital libraries have much significance in preservation and access of contents, and ensuring our supremacy of ideas. The proposed digital library by the contents identified will go a long way in offering the much-needed visibility for these contents and many of these contents find daily usage from different communities for varied requirements. As these contents deeply touch their day-to-day life, this is the right illustration of the right humanizing of technology for improving their social and economic development. Perhaps this is high time to propose an Indian digital library of theses and dissertations, similar initiative for Indian journals as well as out of print books. There is an equal concern for a country so diverse and spread like India to identify national, regional, and local institutions to share the responsibility of digitizing and preserving the country's intellectual output. The emerging information age also calls for proper documentation and conservation of local arts and culture, traditional systems of medicine and engineering, indigenous vocational systems etc. Through pragmatic application of digital technology, we may be able to spread the conserved knowledge to a larger audience not only to improve the living standards of local community but also to claim the country's rightful place in the global village.

REFERENCES

1. Communications of the ACM, April 1995.
2. Communications of the ACM, August 1995.
3. Communications of the ACM, April 1998.
4. IEEE Computer, May 1996.
5. http://sunsite.berkeley.edu/ARL/definition.html (accessed on 06.12.2000)
6. Sharma, R. N., "Development of library and information science periodicals in Asia, with emphasis on South Asia: problems and solutions", 65th IFLA Council and General Conference, Bangkok, Thailand, August 20 - August 28, 1999, (http://www.ifla.org/IV/ ifla65/papers/006-118e.htm, accessed on 02.12.2000)
7. Srinivasan, Padmini, "Digital Library Projects in the United States", DESIDOC Bulletin of Information Technology, 17(6), November1997, pp. 15-21.
8. Chakraborty, Arun Kumar, "Publishing on CD-ROM: Indian Potential", DESIDOC Bulletin of Information Technology, 17(5), September1997, pp. 23-31.
9. Rajashekar, T B, "What's new in Computers? Digital Libraries", Resonance, April 1997, pp. 60-73.
10. Ulrich's International Periodicals Directory, 37th ed., NJ: R.R. Bowker, 1999, p.vii.
11. Katz, William A., "Introduction to Reference Work: Vol 1, Basic Information Sources", New York: McGraw Hill, 1969, p. 98.
12. Atkinson, Randall J., "Towards a More Secure Internet", IEEE Computer, 30(1), January 1997, pp. 57-61.
13. Lynch, Clifford and Garcia-Molina, Hector, Interoperability, Scaling, and the Digital Libraries Research Agenda: A Report on the May 18-19, 1995, IITA Digital Libraries Workshop, August 22, 1995, http:// www.itrd.gov/pubs/iita-dlw/main.html (accessed on 05.12.2000)
14. Association of Research Libraries, Definition and

Purposes of a Digital Library, October 23, 1995, http://sunsite.berkeley.edu/ARL/definition.html, 1/10/96, (accessed on 06.12.2000)

15. Noerr, Peter, The Digital Library Toolkit, March 2000, http://www.sun.com/products -n-solutions/edu/libraries/digitaltoolkit.html, pp. 148-174 (accessed on 04.12.2000).

17. Agarwal, P K, "India's National Internet Backbone", Communications of ACM, 42(6), June 1999, pp. 53-58.

18. Ghosh, Anindo, "Internet Bandwidth: India Needs a Backbone", http://www.ieo.org/ backbone.html (accessed on 10.12.2000)

19. Dikshit, Sandeep, "Growth in Internet Connections Lopsided", The Hindu, Visakhapatnam dated December 10, 2000.

20. Op. Cit. 15, p. 58.

21. Weisser, Christian R. and Walker, Janice R., Electronic Theses and Dissertations: Digitizing Scholarship for Its Own Sake. The Journal of Electronic Publishing, 3(2), December 1997, http://www.press.umich.edu/jep/03-02/etd.html

22. Chapman, Stephen and Kenney, Anne R., Digital Conversion of Research Library Materials: A Case for Full Informational Capture. D-Lib Magazine, October 1996, http://www.dlib.org/dlib/october96/cornell/10chapman.html

23. CPA and RLG, Preserving Digital Information, Report of the Task Force on Archiving of Digital Information, commissioned by The Commission on Preservation and Access and The Research Libraries Group, May 1, 1996, http://www.rlg.org/ArchTF/ tfadi.recommen.htm #practices

24. Bishoff, Liz, Interoperability and Standards in a Museum/Library Collaborative: The Colorado Digitization Project, First Monday, 5(6), June 2000, http://firstmonday.org/issues/issue5_6/bishoff/

24
Digital Archiving

24.0. INTRODUCTION

Digital has become the order of the day due to the significant advances computer and communications technology have brought in the post Internet information age we are living. Libraries are not lagging behind other social service institutions in exploring the new technology available at any point of time to improve information organization and services. This can be amply justified by the use of non-paper media like microforms for decades to archive less/selectively used materials. Compared average times spent on reformatting found that digital conversion needs less time during the conversion stage and more time both in the pre and post conversion stages than for photocopy and microfilming [17]. Managing digital information and archiving them for continued and future use has become a key issue among creators, users and libraries and information facilities consequent to the increased production and consumption of information in electronic form. Most of the advantages perceived with electronic information as far as access and use are concerned have become 'difficult to resolve issues' when one comes to their archiving. The digital technology affords multiple, simultaneous uses from a single original in ways that are simply not possible for materials stored in any other form [1]. Due to its easy to create, host and publish freedom, there are at one time many versions of the same digital document making it difficult for parties and persons concerned to arrive at version control measures to clearly map and record them. There are cases where no one owns the document, the owner is not concerned with maintaining the document, maintenance may not be up to the mark to sustain the use, etc. Owners of intellectual property are unsure about how to price access and worry; given the ease of copying, that the first digital copy of a work they sell may be the only copy they sell [1]. Publishers have also come to realize that digital information is an asset that can generate revenue for decades and are looking after it carefully, but in many digital collections, nobody is responsible for preserving the information beyond its current usefulness and unless somebody pays attention, all digital information will be lost within a few decades [2]. This disinterested worries on the part of various stakeholders is in more than one way delaying the fruitful utilization and application of digital technologies to the advantage of information dissemination and use. Even after more than forty years of growth, the digital world of information technology and communication is still relatively young and immature in relation to the larger information universe, parts of which have been under development for centuries [1]. However there are positive developments as in the case of certain scientific societies and publishers to digitize and archive their publications. The American Physical Society (APS) has recently decided to embark on a systematic program to build complete digital archives of its publications, past and present, and to maintain them into the future [1]. Physical artifacts can lie forgotten for centuries in attics and storerooms, yet still be recovered, however digital information is less forgiving [2]. The motivations for digitization would be on various counts such as costly and rare materials to prevent their mutilation and damage, frequently and demanding materials to increase their access, difficult to retrieve materials to improve their search and dissemination, under used materials to extend their use, etc. Archiving and managing digital information objects therefore are crucial areas of present day library work due to the increasing dependence on electronic publications for education and research.

24.1. DIGITAL ARCHIVES

Archives are different from libraries as they give more emphasis to preservation than use. However with digital documents, this distinction between archives and libraries blurs as digital materials being intangible never get decayed or suffer wear and tear like print materials by mere use. It is the archival function in the system of knowledge creation and use that serves to identify and retain important sources of information and to ensure continuing access to them [1]. Beyond the ubiquitous Web server, there is little consensus about repositories for digital libraries and the field of digital archiving is new [2]. Digital archives are distinct from digital libraries in the sense that digital libraries are repositories that collect and provide access to digital information, but may or may not provide for the long-term storage and access of that information [1]. There are essentially two motivations for creating and maintaining digital archives. First, to ensure that no valued digital information is lost to future generations, and second, certified digital archives will have available to them a critical fail-safe mechanism [1]. In addition to the raw data, digital archiving must preserve ways to interpret the data, to understand its type, its structure, and its formats [2]. Perhaps the most important way that digital libraries can support archiving is through selection regarding what to collect, what to store, what to preserve for the future, and what to discard [2]. The measure of integrity in the preservation process depends on informed and skillful judgments about the definition of the content — the extent to which content depends on its configuration of bits, on the structure and format of its representation, and on the ideas it contains — and for what purposes [1].

24.1.1. Need and Purpose

Digitization may also be taken as a visible proposition to

enhance the shelf life of printed information by preservation apart from the virtue of increased and easy access. In the digital form, since users can make any number of copies and only these copies of the material are being used, at one point of time, there exist fair chances of at least one electronic copy to be available on the network for use by posterity. This may also be viewed as inherent problems and essential challenges in the task of digital archiving and preservation.

'Task Force on Archiving of Digital Information' by Commission on Preservation and Access and Research Libraries Group suggested the following [1]:

* equipment and software required to read and understand information in digital form is changing constantly and may not be available within a decade of its introduction
* cannot save the machines if there are no spare parts available, and cannot save the software if no one is left who knows how to use it
* can lose our heritage in electronic form when the custodian makes no plans for long-term retention in a changing technical environment
* to effectively preserve the rapidly expanding corpus of information in digital form, we need to understand the costs and need to commit ourselves technically, legally, economically and organizationally
* digital media can be fragile and have limited shelf life even under the best storage conditions. Given the rates of technological change, even the most fragile media may well outlive the continued availability of their readers
* Legal and Organizational Issues involve a complex set of interested parties, including the creators and owners of intellectual property, managers of digital archives, representatives of the public interest, and actual and potential users
* digital archives need a high level of systems engineering skill to manage the interlocking requirements of media, data formats, and hardware and software

Beagrie and Greenstein propose the following points [11]:

* Unlike the printed word, digital information cannot be understood without the technical data stored with it, which is normally concealed from the user and needs to be preserved and migrated with the content
* With the current rapid changes and evolution in hardware and software, digital information needs active management from its inception if it is to survive and be kept accessible across different technological regimes.
* The magnetic and optical media on which digital information is stored are impermanent and cannot be relied upon for preservation of their contents for more than a few years or decades.
* Digital data has allowed the development of new types of information: dynamic resources which are constantly changed and updated, highly contingent on their hardware and software environments for the nature of the experience they create
* The provenance and context of digital information is not transparent and easily understood by the user and this needs to be explicitly captured and documented.
* The fixity and authenticity of digital information is an issue due to the ease with which digital information can be copied and amended.
* The rights and terms attached (license) to a digital object when it is created or acquired may fundamentally control how or whether a repository can preserve it or make it accessible to future users.
* The substantial volume and rate of growth of digital information places an increased importance on creating resources which are fit for purpose and cost-effective over their full life cycle.

24.1.2. Attributes to be preserved

Since electronic information is tangible and there are only two clear distinctions of content (subject matter dealt in the document) and file (or document) there is always confusion about what is to be preserved. One can assume that apart from contents and file, we should be cautious about the format in which the file should be stored and the need to store relevant executables or software to read the stored file. In the digital environment, the features that determine information integrity and deserve special attention for archival purposes include the following: content, fixity, reference, provenance, and context [1].

* Content - information and its manifestations
* Fixity - If an object is not fixed, and the content is subject to change or withdrawal without notice, then its integrity may be compromised and its value as a cultural record would be severely diminished
* Provenance - to trace from where it came and must preserve a record of the origin and chain of custody of information objects
* Reference - information objects must have a consistent means of reference. URL may frequently change, especially when migrates from one machine to another and URN supposed to designate an object independently of its particular location at any point in time today exists more in concept than in practice.
* Context - includes a technical dimension, a dimension of linkage to other objects, a communication dimension, and a wider social dimension. The ultimate goal is to preserve not only the bits associated with the original data, but also the context that permits the data to be interpreted [16].

24.1.3. Stakeholders

Seeing the mass of contents and the caution regarding what attributes need to be preserved how, it is so clear that digital archiving can not be conducted by one body, institution or library. Rather it must be a group work over a period of time of the information (document) life cycle by various parties. The following stakeholders have specific interests in the creation, management, dissemination, use or retention of digital information [1]:

* Information creators/providers/owners have initial responsibility for archiving their digital information objects and thereby ensuring the long-term preservation of those objects.
* Certified digital archives have the right and duty to exercise an aggressive rescue function as a fail-safe mechanism to preserve information objects that become endangered.

Another way to look at the different parties who have some say in digital information may be [11]:

* Digital preservation is an essentially distributed process including a range of different (and often differently interested) stakeholders.
* Data creators who attach little or no value to the long-term preservation of the data resources they create are unlikely to adopt standards and practices (are different from or more costly to implement than those which promise the cost-effective development), which will facilitate their preservation.
* Development of appropriate software and tools may play a key role in digital preservation such as key elements of data documentation and metadata can be generated automatically by application software
* Several stakeholders are involved in managing data over the longer term, including data banks, institutional archives, and academic data archives
* No single agency is likely to be able to undertake the role of preserving all digital materials within its purview or the necessary research and development in this field, and co-operative agreements and consortia will be required.

24.1.4. Functions

The archives may or may not be attached with institutions

that generate/consume information. However, both groups of archives have to follow certain functions the pre and post archiving stages to render effective services.

Selection: Archives cannot save all information objects; they must appraise and select for retention the most valuable items as per intellectual judgment about what to include and save and what to exclude [1]. Since there are many sources, types, and generators of content at different intellectual levels and meant for diverse purposes, any archive like the collection development activity in a library needs to be selective. Criteria for such judgments are largely tied to the intrinsic qualities of the material and many of the criteria that have proven useful in the paper world will prove equally effective in the digital environment [1]. Whatever is good in the existing print archives may be borrowed for digital archiving too. Redundancy of information is also important for effective selection [1].

Discovery: Another problem coupled with redundancy is that just because more than one documents, may be at different locations, with different identifiers, the resource discovery tools must be so efficient to provide the required addresses, URLs and metadata. Selectors need to know before accepting an object where a copy of record is stored and if and where additional copies are distributed either as backup or for more efficient retrieval [1].

Processing: Once an information object is identified for inclusion in a digital archives, it needs to be accessioned, that is, prepared for the archives, which involves both describing and cataloging selected objects, including their provenance and context, and securing them for storage and access [1]. This is related to the background operations a library does with respect to classification, cataloguing, indexing, and database updating with respect to new resources added to the collection.

Dissemination: Digital archives have an obligation to maintain the information in a form so that users over the network can find it with appropriate retrieval engines and view, print, listen to or otherwise use it with appropriate output devices [1]. Business records are maintained over long periods of time because a team of people is paid to maintain that specific data and they pay attention to the inter-related issues of security, back-up, and long term availability of data [2]. Dissemination though appears to be simple may be the most crucial step as it involves constant maintenance of the archive for user services.

Standardization: Digital archives must keep abreast of standards developments and make sure that their own technological infrastructure conforms to widely adopted standards [1]. But the problem with standards is that to deal with each and every aspect; we have so many to pick up so that ultimate standardization will be a long way to go.

24.1.5. Techniques

There are different mechanisms to archive digital information for perpetual use. As is obvious the choice to adopt a particular route depends in many cases on the type and nature of materials to be preserved, the infrastructure, resources, and expertise available with the local archive.

24.1.5.1. Refreshing

Refreshing is concerned with preserving the precise sequences of bits like conservation in conventional archiving which looks after individual artifacts [1]. Digital libraries must plan to refresh their collections by periodically copying data onto new media [2]. Refreshing digital information by copying will work only as long as the information is encoded in a format that is independent of the particular hardware and software needed to use it and as long as there exists software to manipulate the format in current use [1]. Since digital information today is produced with dependence on particular hardware and software and it is costly and difficult for vendors to assure "backwardly compatible" or interoperability with competing products, refreshing cannot serve as a general solution for preserving digital information which prompted other kinds of solutions [1].

24.1.5.2. Emulation

Emulation is a chimera since even simple computing environments are much too complex to specify exactly [2]. Emulation is nothing but reading and viewing digital information with the same "look and feel" as the original version by developing "software emulators" as suggested by Jeff Rothenberg [1]. Here emphasis is paid to create and archive emulators of software and operating systems that would allow the contents of digital information to be carried forward and used in its original format [24]

However, neither refreshing nor emulation covers the full range of options for digital preservation, and migration arrived on the scene as a more general solution.

24.1.5.3. Migration

Sooner or later the computer will break down, spare parts will no longer be available, and any program that depends upon the computer will be useless and therefore migration of the content becomes necessary [2]. Migration preserves the content at a semantic level, but not the specific sequences of bits like preservation in conventional archiving which retains the content even if the original artifact decays or is destroyed [1]. The basic principle of migration is that the formats and structure of the data may be changed, but the semantics of the underlying content is preserved [2]. Technically, archiving is more than simply copying bits from one aging storage medium to another; the methods to interpret and manipulate the bits must also be preserved and hence migration of information from one format to another and from one type of computer system to another is likely to be the dominant form of digital archiving [1]. The purpose of migration is to preserve the integrity of digital objects and to retain the ability for clients to retrieve, display, and otherwise use them in the face of constantly changing technology [1]. Although backward compatibility is increasingly common within software product lines, migration paths are not commonly provided between competing software products or for products that fail in the marketplace [1]. Some of the commonly followed migration strategies are change media, change format, incorporate standards, build migration paths, and using specialized processing centres proficient in archiving techniques [1]. The distinction between refreshing and migration was first articulated by the Task Force on Archiving of Digital Information, which recommended a focus on migration as the basic technique of digital archiving [2].

24.1.5.4. Replication

Replication is a basic technique of creating multiple copies due to the vulnerability of single copy such as failing hardware; faulty software; an incompetent or dishonest employee can remove the data; fire, flooding, or other disaster [2]. Effective storage management thus means providing for redundant copies of the archived objects as an insurance against loss [1].

24.1.5.5. Copying to persistent media

Since digital to digital is not as trustworthy and enduring as digital to persistent medium of paper and microforms, this route is suggested as an alternative for maintaining digital information. Creating an archive that contains the definition of formats, metadata standards, protocols and the other building blocks of digital libraries on the most persistent media that is known, e.g., paper or microfilm, and everything should be described in simple text [2]. As long as the preservation community lacks more robust and cost-effective migration strategies, printing to paper or film and preserving flat files will remain the preferred method of storage for many institutions and for certain formats of digital information [1]. Good organizations go one step further and periodically consolidate important records for long term storage on microform, since archival quality microform is exceptionally durable [2].

24.1.6. Costs

Many publishers, librarians and others contemplating the digital future express considerable fear that the digital world of information will not prove less expensive than the traditional paper environment, but in fact more expensive [1]. Developing "processing centers" that specialize in migration and reformatting of obsolete materials may provide a cost-effective method of digital preservation. There are essentially three types of cost [1]:

Storage costs: Components of storage costs include storage device costs, storage media costs, and the costs of operating and maintaining the storage equipment, and of periodically refreshing the media and migrating the data.

Serving Costs: Include providing a document server and software for the server that will support client machines, maintaining the server and access software and of operating the server, and printing on demand a selected portion of volumes used and of delivering those printed copies to the user.

Other costs : for acquisitions, cataloging and reference services

Whatever are the actual costs as per this categorization for a particular archive, 'the Yale model has revealed that the key that unlocks the path to the economies of the digital environment is not technological, but organizational' [1].

24.1.7. Challenges

The problems are beginning to be understood, but, particularly in the field of archiving, the methods are still embryonic and digital archiving is difficult [2]. Since there are many copies which may ultimately lead to many versions or redundant information and how to ensure currency of content is a crucial issue. There are many formats, content management software, search engines, backup mechanisms and how to provide perpetual access – continual access over years irrespective of changes in these multiple and often competing factors and technology.

Technology: There exist as many ills as virtues for technology and computer technology is no different either. How good and effective is technology is also a matter of debate. Not to say that technology is bad, but very new things (especially software) have a habit of not working properly for quite a while

[23]. Even if the media are preserved intact, digital materials become unreadable if the playback devices necessary to retrieve information from the media become obsolete or if the software that translates digital information to human-readable form is no longer available [10]. The database technology is so rapidly changing that each collection must be migrated onto new data management systems, simultaneously with the migration of the individual data objects. Data degradation is a concern, as is the ease with which a document can be changed, either deliberately or by accident, is an issue as well [15]. While some fear that all the work being done to digitize information will be lost with the next major change in technology, software publishers in recent years have been careful to assure that newer versions of software usually accommodate files produced by older versions [20]. In contrast to the source-related concerns only for print archiving, technology related concerns in addition are to be addressed for digital archiving. Access to technology is still limited, limiting the availability of digital information and some may want to include interactive components, CGI-scripting elements that are becoming common on Web sites, elements that are not easily archived because they may change with each "reading" [20].

Storage: Neither disks nor magnetic tape can be relied on for long term storage. The data is encoded on a thin magnetic film deposited on some surface. Sooner or later this film decays. Disks are excellent for current operations, but not for archiving [2]. Digital materials are especially susceptible to loss and destruction because they are stored on fragile magnetic and optical media that deteriorate rapidly and that can fail suddenly from exposure to heat, humidity, airborne contaminants, or faulty reading and writing devices [10].

Natural Threats: There are threats to digital medium as for print medium and there are also concerns about ease of modification, lifetime, technology upgradation and obsolescence. The electronic products are vulnerable to the same enemies that threaten paper, viz. natural threats such as light, moisture, and heat; organic threats such as rodents and insects; and chemical threats such as acid content, air pollution, and plastic, they face new problems like obsolescence [15].

Expenses: Although we can still read manuscripts that are a thousand years old, we cannot read some materials less than 20 years old [15]. (Read the word 'some' as 'electronic' or 'digitized'). Migration to new storage systems is expensive, and there is always concern about the loss of data or problems with the quality when a transfer is made [21].

Evanescence: Printed contents may change only at time periods handled effectively by the library fraternity as they suffer from severe limitations of long and strenuous editorial as well as production routines. Most of these routines cost considerable infrastructure restricting the number of players in the field. But with limited infrastructure (a networked server and few contents), anybody could start an electronic publishing firm (OCLC Researchers estimated about 7 million unique web sites in Oct 2000). A large fraction of contents thus hosted have quick rate of change and in many cases live only for a very short duration. Some of the sudden content changes also lead the users to false links and "404 File Not Found messages". A few of the sites get out of these inconsistencies by keeping older contents having archival value along with fresh versions.

Version control: Another very crucial problem with electronic contents is the quick and faster updates to stay alive in the content race, and how these highly volatile phenomena of different versions in a very short span of time involves tough resource discovery methods for citing and using them. The vital ingredients that hamper these management concerns of information contents are the temporality and volatility issues and how management principles and professional commitment permeate these barriers of time and change becomes a crucial issue as resource discovery and control are key areas of the library profession.

24.2. DOCUMENT MANAGEMENT

In this section, a general discussion on document management in digital form is attempted. This may be applicable both in the case of digital libraries and digital archives as well as libraries interested in optimally managing their digital collection before rendering useful services from such collection.

Some of the purposes of digital library [5] that are of direct concern to document management are:

* collect, store and organize information and knowledge in digital form
* promote economic and efficient delivery of information

24.2.1. Options in a Library

Some of the activities in the library concerned with managing digital documents may include:

a) **CD-ROM Networking:** Networking CD-ROMs with jukebox/CD tower or high capacity hard disk mirroring to serve bibliographic or full text databases, electronic supplements with printed books, CDs cut in-house out of publications/reports of internal activity.

b) **Web access of journals:** Current journals could be made accessible from the publisher's Web sites either through login and passwords or by specific IP addresses of the institution, with/out paying extra fee on subscriptions. There are also options to join consortia based electronic access of primary resources through MHRD's INDEST consortium, UGC Infonet project, etc. Seeing the rapidity by which library automation and CD-ROM technology percolated in the country, there may be many more consortia or at least more and more members of such consortia.

c) **Virtual libraries:** Links to free web resources on focus areas of the institution.

d) **ebooks:** Free/fee books in electronic form.

24.2.2. Type of Documents

In the library perspective, the term content encompasses all types of information sources or documents which will be of interest to clientele, though the term is getting wider usage now to denote electronic information resources and the subject matter covered in them. "Content may be anything, including oral language and natural phenomena, that upon observation appears to have a pattern that can be analyzed for descriptive or inferential purposes" [8]. If we rephrase Yovits et al.'s [12] paradigm "information to be data of value", then we get 'content to be information of value', as the flood of information forces us to be more and more selective and calls for stricter measures to identify, collect, organize, and disseminate vital contents. Document management or content management is nothing but the systematic application of various tools and techniques for the efficient management of information sources in diverse forms (monograph, journal, reports, conference papers, website resources, email/listserv messages, etc.) and media (print, optical, magnetic, electronic, etc.). Here we should also consider the shift undergoing from traditional library management practices and the attempts towards achieving futuristic knowledge management systems. Since the contents comprise, to a large extent from formal printed monographs and serials in paper or microforms, the collection development concerns were thrust upon providing "right resource to the right user at the right time" to satisfy the fundamental laws of library science. Whereas in the aftermath of electronic information products and Internet/Web, the barriers between formal and informal sources are becoming greatly reduced and collection development is leading to access arrangement mechanisms. In the electronic scenario, it is not the document (often regarded as the carrier or physical form of content), but the content is pervasive and more important. This needs new management principles and alertness as well as trained information support staff to trace, track and control electronic resources procured and available free on the web. The availability of local information that institutions would like to share with others and the computer/communication infrastructure emerging also enabled institutions to publish local contents. Well processed and properly connected information that an institution should use to significantly enhance its utility in its sphere of activity becomes knowledge, thus information-intensive industries are putting considerable amount of money, machines and manpower to conserve and do value-addition to this knowledge. Kalseth identified the various strategies to be adopted while implementing knowledge management, such as, document management, improved access to information, use and reuse of information, access to people, learning by participation, networking/ synergies, process orientation, human capital and management culture [3].

Contents fall in two groups, internal and external.

Internal (local): Research or annual reports and other publications issued by the parent institution affiliating the library. In addition, there are also p/reprints of research publications and proceedings of conferences hosted by the institution.

External: Contents procured from publishers or vendors such as full-text databases, online access of subscribed primary journals. There are also offline electronic media like CDs, floppies etc. Contents in this category are sourced from a wide range of options such as web access rights, open access materials like web information resources, contents licensed through consortia, etc.

24.2.3. Steps in Document Management

The basic functions in digital document management are:

* identification and collection of contents to be digitized
* classification and digitization of these contents
* editing, formatting and storage of the contents
* designing search engines to selectively search and access the contents
* publishing contents digitally for end-user access

24.2.3.0. Subtasks

Each of these functions involves certain subtasks like:

* transforming printed information into digital form
* storage, retrieval and handling of "easy-to-use" electronic information
* converting data from diverse media or formats into digital format
* classification techniques for improving retrieval efficiency
* managing devices for large massive storage, with multilevel hierarchical storage structures, supporting differing speed storage devices and varied capacity processors
* editing and formatting of contents in different formats such as, HTML, VRML, XML, PDF, JPEG, MPEG, etc.
* browsing and querying facilities for content based retrieval
* options to promptly distribute and safely access information via standard communication and computing infrastructure
* security of delivered contents by different cryptographic/ encryption methods and appropriate firewall mechanisms and access methods through password/IP authentication of clients

Capturing may involve data capturing equipments such as high-resolution scanners, VCP and compatible capture cards to handle audio, video, images and text. Storage needs servers with multiple CPUs, with RAM in GB range and HDD of few 100 GB to TB and workstations of decent configuration with enhanced processor speed and storage. Search engines/ retrieval software deals with software for database management, Webservers, content authoring/editing, application software, etc. Dissemination requires good network infrastructure with ATM/155 mbps card and high-speed routers, large display terminals for servers and workstations, optical disc reproduction/CD-Writers, LCD displays for projection and high/low resolution printers.

24.2.3.1. Capturing

Let us identify only textual sources in the beginning, and focus on internal contents first. Retrospective data could be digitized either by keying or by scanning. So some data entry terminals (PCs) and scanners are essential and these may be procured from the market for as low as Rs. 30000. Sophisticated contents like images, video and sound (not so important in an academic library where majority of the collection is textual) may be converted later when the digital library development acquires enhanced monetary support by procuring equipments such as high resolution scanners, VCP, multimedia machines (workstations as well as servers) and compatible capture cards to handle audio, video, images.

24.2.3.2. Formatting, encoding and Compression

How data is formatted (written to magnetic media), compressed, and encoded (how internal semantic or syntactic features are represented) will determine its portability across hardware and software platforms and how it may be stored, manipulated, and subsequently enriched [11]. Crucial decisions on these counts are not only required for proper implementation but for efficient use too. Computing formats change continually. File formats of ten years ago may be hard to read [2]. To store digitized files, there are many formats to choose from [13] such as MS Word, LaTeX, Troff, GIF (Graphic Interchange Format), RTF (Rich Text Format), or MIF (Maker Interchange Format), SGML in compliance with their DTDs (Document Type Definitions) [19]. Archive images are saved as TIFF (Tag Image File Format) which is the standard for high quality uncompressed raster images captured by scanners whereas full-sized and thumbnail Web Images are saved as JPEG (Joint Photographic Expert Group), the dominant standard in imaging applications [7]. TIFF is the most prevalent for conversion of paper back-files, HTML/SGML (Standard Generalized Mark-up Language) is used by many large publishers after conversion from proprietary formats, and PDF is the most prevalent format for purely electronic documents [21]. The easiest option for web access is to convert the electronic full text available in the pre-production stage into html format. Added materials like figures/tables may be converted in to formats like gif/jpg whichever is convenient at the individual institution. PDF documents retain all formatting and graphics, permit easy indexing and search by keywords and also allow including links to other sites on the Web or annotations within the article [6]. PDF offers a number of benefits such as read on different platforms; edits can be made at any stage; files much smaller than PostScript files, use less space and transmit more quickly; offers a one-file solution for both print and online; and can view using a free reader [19]. The software to read PDF files Acrobat reader is freely downloadable from many sites (for example, http://www.adobe.com) thus requiring no investment at the client side. Over 95 % of the 600 international journals out of the 800 subscribed at a premier library in the country provide the table of contents with abstract as html files and the full text in PDF. The remaining uses different formats of html, PS, etc. It is important to create the information in formats that are widely adopted today as this increases the chance that conversion programs to new formats will be available as in the case of HTML and PDF so widely used that viewers will surely be available many years from now [2].

Lossless compression removes redundant information in a manner that is completely reversible; the original data can be reconstructed exactly as it was. Lossy compression can not be reversed; approximations are made during the compression that loses some of the information [2]. In the Antique Books conversion, the original page image of over twenty megabytes, but the processed image, both print and background is around 50 kilobytes (400 to 1 compression is achieved by this technique) [9]. Compression techniques may be used not only for saving space at the server side but also to effect fast transfer and retrieval over limited bandwidth.

24.2.3.3. Content Indexing and Metadata

Decisions are to be taken regarding what to be indexed (author, subject, keywords, phrases, etc.), usage of stop words, vocabulary control, proximity searches, language and period limiting etc. Indexing strategy comprises not only of what types of fields are to be indexed, but how they are to be treated (exhaustive or sparse). Implementation of indexes and metadata on the database management systems is also of concern. The popular metadata framework, Dublin Core, contains the following elements [4]: subject and key words, Title, Author or Creator, Publisher, Description (textual description of content); Other agent (the person(s), such as editors and transcribers); Date (of publication); Object type (the genre of the object, such as novel); Form (the data representation of the object, such as postscript file); Identifier (string or number used to uniquely identify the object); Relation (the relationship to other objects); Source (Objects, either print or electronic from which this object is defined); Language, Coverage (spacial locations and temporal duration characteristic); and Rights management. Using the Dublin Core framework as the basis, the CDP identified eight optional elements and seven mandatory elements of creator, title, subject, description, identifier, date, and format [14]. Many project managers acknowledged that the best practice would be to create the metadata at the object-creation stage, or to create the metadata in stages, with the metadata provided at creation augmented by additional elements during the cataloging stage [21].

The information about a data resource's structure, contents, context, provenance, and history influences how a resource is located, managed, and used, and frequently reflects data acquisition decisions and the documentation standards and practices [10]. A database system to keep stock of digitized collection is important, as the task is to provide selective access to the data. Necessary front end to accept search queries and flash matched results would also be developed. Technical processing as is done for other documents will be attempted for digital elements here. On digitizing an item marked in the OPAC, we can also link digital images of contents with associated information in the database.

24.2.3.4. Organization

Indexing required for the digitized contents to search and access them in a selective way like OPAC for printed contents. How the content and index files are linked and what sort of access points is provided is another area of concern. May be the library is going for a modular fashion; they can follow a hypertext link and access to the digitized contents. Once the contents acquire sufficient volume, they can look for a database management system to link the index and contents. A document has different physical parts, links at the file level; they are either stored as independent files or as stored as records in a database at the record level and in most cases identified by a URL/DOI.

24.2.3.5. Storage

PCs are marketed now with 20/40GB HDDs and 128 or 256 MB RAMs for Rs. 35000 and entry level servers for less than a lakh. So with limited investment, the library may be able to order a 100 GB HDD system with 512/1024 MB RAM. If money is a problem to get Unix Operating system, they can do with Linux. During the initial stage, it is also appropriate to work with Windows servers. Configure at least one machine with good configuration as a server to hold and service the digital contents. Noerr assumed text, in general, is stored at one byte per character and assumed 2 bytes per character for multi-lingual, with 100% indexing overhead. The storage required for a small collection of 100,000 articles averaging 5 pages (2000 characters per page), all in English stored in full text, and indexed for proximity and structural searching is 3GB [7].

24.2.3.6. Search Engines /Retrieval

The library needs software for database management, Web servers, content authoring/ editing, etc., and developmental software (Visual studio, C++, Java & Internet tools etc.,). As most of these tools are in the public domain, the library does not find it difficult to use at least a few of these in its in-house digitization and document management routines.

24.2.3.7. Dissemination

If the campus is well networked, then without much investment from the library side, the contents may be made accessible on the Intranet. It is easier to host the borrowed external contents also in this mode. However access restrictions are to be put on these contents either with login/password or and IP filtering when access is provided over Internet. The library is always free to host its internal contents on the Internet. The Internet infrastructure required for hosting the digital library depends upon different parameters such as the quantum of contents to be hosted, number of simultaneous users expected, over and above the bandwidth constraints at the national level. 1 Mbps bandwidth will play videos in real time and internal LAN technology has already crossed the 1Gbit barrier. Thus institutions with a functional Intranet and leased line connection from VSNL or other Internet Service Providers (ISPs) will not face much hindrances for content delivery.

24.2.4. Issues

Formats: When different formats are available, how to prefer and stick to one requires both technical and administrative feasibility studies.

Scanning/Keying Vs Optical/magnetic/semiconductor storage: Sometimes, the volumes and issues to be handled are more, which often warrant handling of scanned images and CD archiving. The investments required for a CD publishing venture are comparatively small nowadays due to advancements in memory technology, the availability of sophisticated technologies for economic duplication and access of optical discs. If the particular journals back volumes are not available in electronic format, and only the print versions exist, the easy route for their conversion in a non-print form is by scanning these pages and incorporating into CD-ROM. Though scanned images occupy 10 times more space than keyed in ASCII, the cost of keying is about 10 times the cost of scanning [22]. The same search engine used for web access of new issues can be used for retrieving these scanned pages by incorporating connections with the content pages. But there may be difficulties to provide search and access provision in the scanned portion. Non-readability of floppies, CD-ROMs, and non-performance of older versions of software are common problems many libraries face in their decade of living with the electronic information.

Lack of Experience: Many libraries are only providing current access to information resources in electronic form and many are not even aware of the difficulties of accessing these materials in future. In some cases like web access of journals, they only own current and not archival access making it impossible to locally archive contents. As is the case with print subscriptions, some publishers are sensitive to the needs of libraries and grant continued access even after the expiry of current subscription to those issues for which they held access rights. However, in this mode access is provided through the publisher's site rather than local archiving at the client site.

Interoperability: Hiding the internal structure and providing all access through a clearly defined interface clearly simplifies interoperability [2]. When a client accesses information in a repository, it needs to know the interface that the repository presents to the outside world, but it does not need to know how it is stored in the repository [2]. If a complete set of standards could be agreed and every organization implemented them in full, then a wonderful level of interoperability might be achieved. In practice, the pace of standardization is slower than the rate of change of technology, and no organization ever completely integrates all the standards into its systems before it begins to change those systems to take advantage of new opportunities or to avoid new difficulties [2].

Copyright: Libraries subscribing to a journal or buying a book are entitled for certain rights to put these materials to "fair" use of their clientele. Publishers and other copyright owners may turn a blind eye to photocopying a few pages from them for classroom use or for research work. The so called virtues what we attach to digital technology like ease of use, modification and distribution were treated as threats to their rights by the copyright owner. Whatever security and safeguards ensured to protect the use exclusively for authorized user community can be easily broken by others as technology centric precautions stand only till a person better in technology than you. More over the publishers don't ease their rights to others as they themselves were engaged in a digitization plan of new publications and in some case even retrospective materials selectively.

Lack of contents: Thus our libraries are left with a choice of digitizing only few materials. But an ingenious action plan will enable us to even find three types of materials as per copyrights involved, viz. a lot of such materials that are copyright free, copyright owned, and copyright transferred or bought. Copyright free materials belong to those in the public domain like government documents or old books for which the copyright is either expired or not enforced. Since these materials are old or easily available, care should be taken to first identify the usage rate of them from statistics generated by library automation package. Digitize only the maximum used ones and does a less used one only when demonstrated that difficulty in handling in the present form is hindering its use. Since our publishing industry is not as streamlined as in developed countries, a lot of publishers go into oblivion after publishing a handful of titles. As they may be willing to transfer the rights for local digitization, this is one way of copyright buying by individual libraries or consortia without spending much. Other means of buying the rights will be a very difficult proposition at least for our libraries as funds are always on the decline whereas sources, users' demands and prices are always on the uphill.

Security: Another aspect to be considered simultaneously is how the access rights are implemented? What mechanisms are used to impose restrictions on access? When hosted as a paid facility, how charges are levied from users? How login and password access is strictly ensured? If provided as a free facility, how funds needed to set up the infrastructure and operations are generated? How far the facility can be subsidized with the help of advertisements and sponsorships? Levying charges for access is a distant proposition, as many journals are not attracting many personal subscriptions now. Instead, sponsorships from institutions, government bodies, and library suppliers can be explored as a viable means to reap in money for this task. Even when hosted as a free facility, enough security mechanisms like firewalls, filtering routers, encryption-decryption, etc., must be put on the server side to prevent any trespassing by hackers. Threat perceptions from the vulnerable areas of Internet layer, routing infrastructure, domain name server, and network management [25] has to be addressed from the technical, administrative and operational angles.

Bandwidth: Internet bandwidth, which is the maximum amount of data that can be transmitted in a particular time, in the country, has to be sufficiently augmented for faster access of web contents.

Paper Centric: We are so addicted to the print environment that we see digital information only as a supplement and not as a substitute. There are various typographic conventions employed to assist the reader such as titles, headings, subheadings, typefaces, punctuation and the like along with column width, proportion, density, paragraphing, page breaks and folios unique to printed sources which are generally neglected, impossible to reproduce or inherently invisible in sequential screen viewing [18]. Also digital information is fragile than paper or microfilm, can be more easily corrupted or altered without recognition, the storage media have shorter life spans, and digital information requires access technologies that are changing at an ever-increasing pace [21]. Since reading lengthy works online is still a formidable task unless you have very good eyes, no one is going to sit and read a whole book on line, and it costs money and time to download it and print it [20].

Mindset: There are human resource implications, including the need for more staff to carry out labor-intensive digital work, the demand for staff with new and different skills, the challenges of "upskilling" and retraining, and the need to redefine job descriptions and skill requirements [10]. Even though contents are aplenty in our libraries for digitization, still there are not many concrete projects for library digitization can be attributed only to the mindset. Here comes not only the lack of interest of the professionals, or the ineffective consumption of professional time for routine tasks leaving them very little time to innovate, but the matter of wide concern is the lack of priorities from the Institution side for framing, supporting and implementing viable projects.

24.3. CONCLUSION

Being a late starter, libraries in the country are slowly waking up to the needs of managing digital documents to a large extent for rendering current services, predominantly through the publishers and aggregators facilities. Many libraries are also creating and serving internal information through various modes of scanning and keying. Digital document management unlike print document management has its own advantages and challenges and it is upon the library administration and professionals to frame proper programmes and effective action plans to transform these new media of information resources to the benefit of library and its clientele. Once such information access will become a dominant mode for information seeking and usage, libraries have to make arrangements for digitally archiving information sources in their vicinity. Archiving is different from management as libraries being social service institutions and major links in scholarly information communication, have an important role to ensure the fail-safe mechanism of archival responsibility for any source of importance to each and every client as implied by the first three laws of library science.

REFERENCES

1. Commission on Preservation and Access and Research Libraries Group, Preserving Digital Information: Report of the Task Force on Archiving of Digital Information, May 1, 1996, http://www.rlg.org/ArchTF/tfadi.index.htm

2. Arms, William Y., Digital Libraries, Cambridge, Mass. : MIT Press, x, 287 p., 2000.
3. Kalseth, Karl, Knowledge Management from a Business Strategy Perspective, FID Review, 1(1), 1999, pp. 37-41.
4. Dublin Core Qualifiers, 2000-07-11, http://dublincore.org/documents/dcmes-qualifiers/ (accessed on 5 June 2001)
5. http://sunsite.berkeley.edu/ARL/definition.html (accessed on 06.12.2000)
6. Weisser, Christian R. and Walker, Janice R., Electronic Theses and Dissertations: Digitizing Scholarship for Its Own Sake, The Journal of Electronic Publishing, 3(2), December, 1997, http://www.press.umich.edu/jep/03-02/etd.html
7. Wolf, Connie and Holland, Douglas, Digitizing and Preserving Plant Images: Linking Plant Images and Databases for Public Access, First Monday, 5(6), June 2000, http://firstmonday.org/issues/issue5_6/wolf/
8. Penland, Patrick R., Content Analysis, Encyclopedia of Library & Information Science, New York: Marcel Dekker, 1971, Vol. 5, p. 633.
9. Thibadeau, Robert and Benoit, Evan, Antique Books, D-Lib Magazine, September 1997, http://www.dlib.org/dlib/september97/thibadeau/09thibadeau.html
10. Hedstrom, Margaret and Montgomery, Sheon, Digital Preservation Needs and Requirements in RLG Member Institutions, A study commissioned by the Research Libraries Group, December 1998, http://www.rlg.org/preserv/digpres.html
11. Beagrie, Neil and Greenstein, Daniel, A Strategic Policy Framework for Creating and Preserving Digital Collections, Version 4.0, 14/7/98, Final Draft, Internet Scout Review, 5(2), 8 May 1998, http://www.ukoln.ac.uk/services/papers/bl/framework/framework.html
12. Yovits M C, et al, Information Flow and Analysis: Theory,

Simulation, and Experiments. 1, Basic Theoretical and Conceptual Development, Journal of the American Society of Information Science, May 1981, p. 187.

13. Fleischhauer, Carl, Digital Formats for Content Reproductions, July 13, 1998, http://memory.loc.gov/ammem/formats.html#VIII
14. Bishoff, Liz, Interoperability and Standards in a Museum/ Library Collaborative: The Colorado Digitization Project, First Monday, 5(6), June 2000, http://firstmonday.org/issues/issue5_6/bishoff/
15. Beebe, Linda and Meyers, Barbara, The Unsettled State of Archiving. The Journal of Electronic Publishing, 4(4), June, 1999, http://www.press.umich.edu/jep/04-04/beebe.html
16. Moore, Reagan, et al., Collection-Based Persistent Digital Archives - Part 1. D-Lib Magazine, 6(3), March 2000. http://www.dlib.org/dlib/march00/moore/03moore-pt1.html
17. Chapman, Stephen and Kenney, Anne R., Digital Conversion of Research Library Materials: A Case for Full Informational Capture, D-Lib Magazine, October 1996, http://www.dlib.org/dlib/october96/cornell/10chapman.html
18. Grenquist, Peter, Why I Don't Read Electronic Journals: An Iconoclast Speaks Out. The Journal of Electronic Publishing, 3(1), September 1997, http://www.press.umich.edu/ jep/03-01/Iconoclast.html
19. Beebe, Linda and Meyers, Barbara, Digital Workflow: Managing the Process Electronically, The Journal of Electronic Publishing, 5(4), June 2000, http://www.press.umich.edu/jep/05-04/sheridan.html
20. Weisser, Christian R. and Walker, Janice R., Electronic Theses and Dissertations: Digitizing Scholarship for Its Own Sake, The Journal of Electronic Publishing, 3(2), December, 1997, http://www.press.umich.edu/jep/03-02/etd.html

21. Hodge, Gail M., An Information Life-Cycle Approach: Best Practices for Digital Archiving, The Journal of Electronic Publishing, 5(4), June 2000, http://www.press.umich.edu/jep/05-04/hodge.html

22. Rajashekar, T B., What's new in Computers? Digital Libraries, Resonance, April 1997, pp. 60-73.

23. Noerr, Peter, The Digital Library Toolkit, 2nd ed. March 2000, Palo Alto: Sun Microsystems, http://www.sun.com/products-n-solutions/edu/libraries/digitaltoolkit.html

24. Rothenberg, Jeff, Ensuring the Longevity of Digital Documents, Scientific American, 272, January 1995, pp. 42-47.

25. Atkinson, Randall J., "Towards a More Secure Internet", IEEE Computer, 30(1), January 1997, pp. 57-61.

25
Digital Libraries or Difficult Libraries

25.0. INTRODUCTION

Technology adoption in libraries seep from developed part of the globe to developing regions, and the pace at which this development reaches a particular depends on the awareness and affordability of its people. As is the case with CD-ROM databases, library automation packages and Web site creation, digital library is the in-thing in library and information science discipline today. Internet and its aftermath reduced significantly the spread of technology to different countries of the world. It is not the technology as such and its spread, the major constraints in digital library development in many countries is the abject lack of primary resources and waning enthusiasm on the part of the authorities and professionals concerned. A conference like this is successfully organised continuously in a comparatively poorer region like Asia is a signal about the changes that are coming and the widespread understanding of the virtues of arresting all barriers in the dissemination of information. Let us take an optimistic and pragmatic account of the different issues to be considered by any library that is attempting to venture into digital library development for consideration of the professional community.

25.1. DIGITAL LIBRARY

Though a very hot topic for research and development in IT intrinsic library and information discipline, the term digital library has been suffering from a nomenclature crisis as the same term is used to denote different manifestations of offering full-text library contents in digital form. Lynch and Garcia-Molina viewed digital libraries as "systems providing a community of users with coherent access to a large, organized repository of information and knowledge" and they possess "the ability to integrate materials in digital formats that have not been well-represented, easy to access, or effectively usable in traditional library collections" [2]. Cleveland opined "digital libraries are the digital face of traditional libraries" with key features such as [3]:

* include both digital collections and traditional, fixed media collections. So they encompass both electronic and paper materials.
* include digital materials that exist outside the physical and administrative bounds of any one digital library.
* include all the processes and services (revised and enhanced to accommodate the differences of new digital media) that are the backbone and nervous system of libraries.
* require both the skills of librarians and well as those of computer scientists to be viable.

Seamans and McMilan suggested that the digital library "adds value and saves time while shifting the times of access" and "reduces need for proximity to information resources, but still emphasizes the quality of those resources" [4]. Fox et al., while attempting to define digital library argues that "To some it simply suggests computerization of traditional libraries. To others, who have studied library science, it calls for carrying out of the functions of libraries in a new way, encompassing new types of information resources; new approaches to acquisition (especially with more sharing and subscription services); new methods of storage and preservation; new approaches to classification and cataloging; new modes of interaction for patrons; more reliance on electronic systems and networks; and dramatic shifts in intellectual, organizational, and economic practices" [5]. Some of the features of the digital libraries to achieve the "lofty goals" include [1]:

* provide fast and efficient access, with multiple access modes
* have collections which contain many formats and
* contain objects, not just representations

We will be basing our discussion in the light of these definitions, however, to make the discussion more concrete, we will stick to the following attributes of digital library:

* substantial amount of contents in electronic or digital form and the necessary infrastructure to offer the same through Intranet and/or Internet
* overhauled most of the traditional routines and practices with considerable value addition to assimilate the changing information environment
* either entered into collaborations or networking with other similar libraries to enhance its resource or service base
* made its presence felt on networks like Internet

Only when individual libraries or their parent institutions devise and implement viable options for infrastructure development in Information Technology, the digital library development get the desired boost.

25.2. PLANNING

Barber emphasized that "every library in any kind of organization that begins to move beyond bibliographic citations to providing online content for its patrons has begun to build a digital library" [6]. The 'technological capacity (i.e., memory capacity, chip densities, and network bandwidth) continues to obey Moore's law, essentially doubling every 18 to 24 months' [7]. Thus the investment in Information Technology

(IT) infrastructure development should always be spent judiciously and the purchase decisions would always keep in mind the present requirements, and the fact that 'better systems must be available cheaper tomorrow'. The Information Technology attributes that required in developing and hosting digital libraries involve:

Hardware: When we talk about digital libraries, we are dealing with substantial chunk of digital contents, and not mere surrogates of printed contents as in the case of the erstwhile automated libraries. Thus they require significantly high-end computer systems to amass the wealth of full-text digital contents. The size of the collection to be digitized coupled with other memory overheads for indexing, and chance for future growth etc., must be the sole criteria to influence purchase decisions. The systems to be ordered are for development, service and backup of digital contents, and few workstations/ PCs for building applications. There is also a need for other types of servers for caching, proxy and ancillary equipment such as scanners, printers, etc.

Software: Apart from software for running normal operations by servers, there could be specific software encompassing the different tools and techniques to build digital library repositories with options to efficiently service them. There could also be efficient search engines and attractive user interfaces to enhance the access of stored digital contents.

Netware: Since the dominant mode of access of digital libraries is through off-library/campus networks, there is a demand for viable network infrastructure both on LAN and WAN. Most of these network hardware effectively functions with the help of powerful networking software.

Bandwidth: We doubt about the relative insignificance of Moore's law at least for bandwidth development in developing regions of the globe. There are certain programs either on the planning or implementation stage to bring in high-capacity Internet bandwidth to India. The prominent among them are 155MB bandwidth from FLAG (Fiber optic

Link Around the Globe), 80 GB links from undersea links like SEA-ME-WE (III) (South East Asia, Middle East and Western Europe) and SAFE (South Africa Far East) [8]. The existing rates for Intranet is in the GB range, but whereas to touch such rates for Internet access in the developing nations will be a futuristic target unachievable with the present pace.

25.3. ARCHITECTURE

Arms suggested that the underlying architecture of the digital library should be separate from the content stored with the following key features as users want intellectual works and not digital objects [9]:

* Names and identifiers are the basic building block.
* Digital library objects are more than collections of bits.
* The digital library object that is used is different from the stored object.
* Repositories must look after the information they hold.

Arms et al. proposed the following components [10] as the digital library framework permits many different computer systems to coexist.

Two user interfaces: One for the users of the library, the other for the librarians and system administrators who manage the collections. A standard Internet browser is used for the actual interactions with the user.

Repository: Repositories store and manage digital objects and other information. There will be part/whole, sequence, etc., relationships among digital materials stored in several digital formats where different versions are created continually with different rights and permissions for access.

Handles: A distributed directory service for identifiers (handles) for Internet resources proposed by Coalition for Networked Research Information (CNRI). By having its own handle, an item may be accessed independently.

Search system: There will be many indexes and catalogs that can be searched before retrieving information from a repository. These indexes may be independently managed and support different protocols.

Information Architecture: Based on data types, structural metadata, and meta-objects. A data type describes technical properties of data, such as format, or method of processing. Structural metadata describes the types, versions, relationships and other characteristics of digital materials. A meta-object is an object that provides references to a set of digital objects.

25.4. ACTION PLAN

Arriving at a model for local development could be explored from descriptions about the ongoing digital library projects elsewhere [11, 12]. Some of these projects concentrated on a particular discipline like law in the case of THOMAS from US Library of Congress, a specific type of collection such as technical reports in the case of NCSTRL, or a specific form of collection like video as is the case with Informedia project at Carnegie Mellon University. Some of these projects used in-house solutions, whereas some others used commercial products. As most of the projects are still on the R& D stages or are in the refining faces for better user access and content delivery, there is no dearth of models, but also there is not a single pathfinder to proceed with. It is up to the individual libraries to evolve a workable model in their local context, by carefully utilising what was preached and practiced by the successful projects. There is also a dearth of contents for the developing regions as most of the quality content providers such as publishers, database providers etc., are based in the US, Europe and other developed nations. May be this lacuna has contributed more for the absence of digital library activities in the developing countries, even though Internet use is on the rise. Since we have the libraries of India and other developing countries in mind, what we are suggesting is a middle path. The salient features of this path is not to go for too sophisticated systems, not be so ambitious in identifying more contents than what can be implemented as workable prototypes in the beginning and then by networking and cumulating such individual but small and manageable framework into country based ones in the first phase with options for merging in a region based manner in the later phase. The resources for digitization will be continuously increased based on the availability and demand.

25.5. RESOURCES

The resources come first in any library and all the other background operations, services and staff are for nothing but optimising access to them. Digital library projects has been reduced as more academic exercises due to the lack of high quality intellectual resources under the custody of commercial publishers who put punitive measures for violating their copyrighted contents. Any digital library development could be successful only if sufficient quantity of contents on demand must be available on its servers. As the publishing fraternity has a different opinion about digital libraries in general and the delivery and access of intellectual information in particular, it is for the library community to explore contents outside the periphery of formal publishing or by entering into partnerships with them to loan or lease out contents. Thus the libraries have to follow a multi-pronged strategy to build digital resources:

External Contents:

Online access of all subscribed journals either through local cache servers or through publishers sites. Always insist for access to back-files, normally available for 10-12 years. Who will digitise the still older ones. Does the publisher permit the library to venture into this area? May be the publishers are not so serious with retrospective conversion as they don't know the demand for them and the lack of sufficient returns in comparison with investments.

Electronic Addendum of Printed books: Disciplines like computer science and engineering where always hand-on practice is more regarded as important, mere printed text does not guide the readers to the required expertise. The publishers have extended this limitation of linear text by supplying floppies, or CDs of supplementary material, which the libraries are finding difficult to manage and service. The present practice is to mark the availability of such information in catalogues and to provide some workstations in the library to access the contents. Is it possible for a more organised access to these materials by hosting them on a server. How to bypass the individual search software and diverse formats may be a possible constraint in this exercise. Though publishers are supportive about digital journals, may be due to the large quantity of contents, and too few users, things are not so ripe with books. The portal Amazon.com deals with fastening the process of printed book procurement by automating the operations. Isn't it odd to restrict such an infrastructure to merely monitor an old operation?. When will such sites or publisher's sites be able to offer electronic books to libraries for a fee or other mechanisms of pricing?

Internal Contents: These comprise of the contents generated in-house by the institution to which the library is affiliated. Some of the inputs to consider are the pre-prints of publications generated by its researchers, research reports, annual reports, proceedings of conferences hosted by the institution etc.

25.6. COPYRIGHT

As a responsible social service institution, it is the prerogative of libraries to effectively guard access to its collection and to ensure that no copyrighted content is misused by anyone through its services. It is also equally important that no request for a licensed collection from a client be turned down if s/he is otherwise eligible to receive it. Arms viewed that "libraries often need to restrict access to parts of their collections for various reasons, including restrictions imposed by donors, concerns about privacy or obscenity, licensing arrangements, and other agreements with copyright owners". Apart from payment for use, publishers and other copyright owners wish to manage access is because "there are other reasons, such as preventing the spread of unapproved derivatives" [13]. To ensure the copyright restrictions honoured by the library, the digital collection may be divided into two parts and there should be mechanisms to permit different access modes. It is up to the individual libraries to earmark internal contents as restricted or free for all and devise likewise options for their access. Even when assigned as free, the library can collect the details of the person accessing through web forms, and this may later help to assess the usage rate. However the copyrighted contents may be offered only through Intranet with IP validation. The access of copyrighted contents should be constantly monitored to curtail any loopholes in security, as well as to make purchase decisions influenced by use. Ives pointed out a strategy "think like the enemy, defense in depth and dynamic defense" and a four-tiered (hardware, system, network, user interface) approach to computer network security management [14].

25.7. STORAGE AND PRESERVATION

The contents once digitised are to be stored on the servers for a sufficient duration to stabilise the confidence of clients. Thus storage and preservation of contents are two key issues that have to be closely monitored in the digital library development. We have seen that how the Moore's law is dictating the market trends in digital electronics and hence better computers with faster processors and massive memory at affordable rates will be available any day after your purchase. So one should be guided largely by the present requirements and rigidity of budget only while procuring storage options. "Most organizations that responded to the question about the periodicity of media migration anticipate a three- to five-year cycle" [15].

The basic motivation behind preservation is not only to ensure the permanence of contents, as is the case for printed contents, but also to make them always amenable to the latest software to guarantee persistent use. Preservation is the aspect of archival management that preserves the content as well as the look and feel of the digital object [15]. The data migration dictated by hardware/software upgrades or changes can be avoided by "emulation, which encapsulates the behavior of the hardware/software with the object" [15]. As there is no system in place to provide the extensive documentation and emulation information required, the best practice for the foreseeable future will be migration to new hardware and software platforms [15]. The intricacies of digital preservation were made further complicated due to the presence of different formats and diverse systems to achieve similar tasks, and even the multiplicity of standards. After briefing about the virtues of formats like TIFF, PDF, and markup languages (HTML/SGML), Hodge observed that "the key preservation issue is the format in which the archival version should be stored" [15].

25.8. WEB PUBLISHING

Perhaps Arms rightly stated that "open access materials on the Internet are making many primary materials available at no cost" [9] and may be this is one prevalent reason for the sudden and quick popularity of digital libraries and electronic journals. We should admit that Web has enabled us to accumulate a large quantum of digital contents and demonstrated the viability of paperless systems that can compete with the traditional setup. Web is build up on a large set of public domain software utilities making it increasingly at the reach of peoples from the developing nations. Publishing on the web is a highly visible activity with relatively little investment, as the software is available absolutely free or for a nominal charge, and the main overheads are hardware and personnel costs. Like the case of automation systems to automate the routine tasks and CD-ROM systems as an alternative delivery medium for information, the libraries and institutions of the developed world are striving hard to bridge the digital divide by building Web sites and by providing whatever digital information they want to offer the outside world.

25.9. CONTENT

In the earlier part of this paper, the different types of

contents that could be used for digital library development were highlighted. Decision is to be taken about whether old information of archival value is to be included if the archives are rarely used, there is little reason to digitize them "unless the reason for their non-use is that they are inaccessible in their present form" [16]. Whether internal or external, new or old, the different steps involved in content development are:

Content Identification: The profile of the clients served must be the main focus in identifying contents for a digital library.

Content Procurement: Arrangements with copyright owners to procure or lease the identified contents.

Content Conversion: Scanning or keying or other means of converting the identified contents.

Content Organisation: Indexing and search engine development to selectively search and access the contents.

Content Storage: Computer systems to hold the contents and index files.

Content Hosting: Network infrastructure required in hosting the contents for access by local and remote users.

25.10. LIBRARIAN'S ROLE

"Computer scientists may be responsible for the technical development of digital libraries, with information scientists focusing on the content, organization, users, and retrieval of information" [17]. Thus the librarians and information scientists should confine themselves to areas where their expertise to identify, track, classify, document, arrange and disseminate information could be efficiently utilised. They can play a major role in devising new techniques and tools for content organisation and dissemination, being well versed in such areas. They should also be able to conduct user studies on the actual and projected demand for digital libraries and electronic information systems. Classification and indexing is getting new insights these days due to the difficulty of Web in delivering huge collection of electronic collection to countless number of users. The flood of false hits flashed by automatic search engines could only be controlled by understanding proper means of knowledge organisation practiced by information professionals. They are also better equipped to bring in the community of publishers and users together through mechanisms for leasing and lending contents so that "right content will be provided to the right user at the right time". Librarians and information professionals also should be able to enhance the spread of access to internal contents by evolving action plans to digitise and service them over Intra/ Internet.

25.11. TRAINING AND SUPPORT

Spink and Cool rightly emphasized that "despite the boom in funding for DL research, development, and publications, DL education is behind in funding and practice" [17]. They observed that digital library (DL) courses are offered in Computer Science or Information Science departments at undergraduate, graduate or the doctoral level and found the primary emphasis is on issues involved in system building and digital collection building. Though use of specific tools and techniques in the construction of digital collections is a major concern, less frequent attention is paid to the study of digital library users and usability. They voice for a hybrid curriculum that brings together the complementary strengths from computer science, psychology, policy studies, and library and information studies [17]. Major topic areas covered in the University of California (UC) Berkeley Library *Institute on Digital Library Development* included digital library theory and practice, HyperText Markup Language (HTML), imaging, optical character recognition, access and indexing, selection of materials for digitizing, and effective training techniques [18]. As digital libraries are still confined to research arena, offering full-fledged courses on this topic in formal degrees at least in developed countries is a matter of distant proposition. However the training needs of working professionals may be pruned up with the help of short-term courses and discussing them as tutorials along with conferences etc. Though substantive information about digital libraries is available free on the Web right now, who is putting it to right use is a matter of introspection of professionals.

25.12.CONCLUSION

Arms suggested that due to information overload, creators must compete for the reader's attention, and opines to search for models of digital libraries where the creator or publisher pays instead of the user [19]. He also drew parallels between Internet information and photography, in contrast to printed information that depends on large teams and expensive technology, which encourage large, hierarchical organizations. Levy rightly pointed out that "the current digital library agenda has largely been set by the computer science community, and clearly bears the imprint of this community's interests and vision" [20]. "What we say about digital libraries and how we understand them embodies and signals our attitude toward the place of information in our culture" and "it is potentially of great consequence not only how we construct digital libraries but how we talk about them, and who we include in the conversation" [20]. Information in its diverse manifestations will continue to influence all aspects of human endeavour, and the principle of least effort coupled with the absence of time in a fast paced information age stipulates the need for high quality digital library systems that can offer full text contents at the touch of a button. The role of a librarian in this massive and pious task is undoubted. Are we sincere in our efforts to take the humanity there and how we will be able to visualise this daunting task is a matter of serious introspection.

REFERENCES

1. http://web.simmons.edu/~schwartz/462-defs.html (accessed on 15 July 2001)
2. Lynch, Clifford and Garcia-Molina, Hector. Interoperability, scaling, and the digital libraries research agenda: A report on the May 18-19, 1995 IITA Digital Libraries Workshop, 1995, August, http://

diglib.stanford.edu/diglib/pub/reports/iita-dlw/main.html#2 (accessed on 11 July 2001).

3. Cleveland, Gary, Digital libraries: Definitions, issues and challenges, UDT Occasional Paper #8, 1998, March, http://www.ifla.org/VI/5/op/udtop8/udtop8.htm (accessed on 5 July 2001)
4. Seamans, Nan and McMilan, Gail, Digital library definition for DL12, 1998, June 16, http://scholar.lib.vt.edu/DLI2/defineDL.html (accessed on 10 July 2001)
5. Fox, Edward A., et al., Digital libraries, Communications of the ACM, 38(4), April 1995, pp. 24.
6. Barber, David, Building a digital library: Concepts and issues. Library Technology Reports, 32,1996, pp. 573-617.
7. French, James C. and Viles, Charles L., Personalized Information Environments: An Architecture for Customizable Access to Distributed Digital Libraries, D-Lib Magazine, 5(6), June 1999, http://www.dlib.org/dlib/June99/french/06french.html (accessed on 10 July 2001)
8. The Hindu, Visakhapatnam, reports dated Nov 16 and Dec 6, 2000.
9. Arms, William Y., Key concepts in the architecture of the digital library, D-Lib Magazine, 1995 July, http://www.dlib.org/dlib/July95/07arms.html (accessed on 8 July 2001)
10. Arms, William Y. et al., An Architecture for Information in Digital Libraries, D-Lib Magazine, February 1997, http://www.dlib.org/dlib/february97/cnri/02arms1.html (accessed on 8 July 2001)
11. Digital Library Initiatives, Building Digital Libraries: Digital Library Projects, The University of Texas at Austin Library Online, June 7, 2001, http://www.lib.utexas.edu/dli/digital.html (accessed on 04.08.2001)
12. Noerr, Peter, The Digital Library Toolkit, March 2000, http://www.sun.com/products-n-solutions/edu/

libraries/digitaltoolkit.html, pp. 148-174 (accessed on 04.12.2000).

13. Arms, William Yeo, Implementing Policies for Access Management, D-Lib Magazine, February 1998, http://www.dlib.org/dlib/february98/arms/02arms.html (accessed on 7 July 2001)
14. Ives, David J., Security Management Strategies for Protecting Your Library's Network", Computers in Libraries, 16(2), Feb 1996, pp. 36-42.
15. Hodge, Gail M, An Information Life-Cycle Approach: Best Practices for Digital Archiving, The Journal of Electronic Publishing, 2000 June, 5(4), http://www.press.umich.edu/jep/05-04/hodge.html hodge.html (accessed on 7 July 2001)
16. Op. cit. 12, p. 26.
17. Spink, Amanda and Cool, Colleen, Education for Digital Libraries, D-Lib Magazine, May 1999, 5(5), http://www.dlib.org/dlib/may99/05spink.html (accessed on 7 July 2001)
18. Hastings, Kirk and Tennant, Roy, How to Build a Digital Librarian, D-Lib Magazine, November 1996, http://www.dlib.org/dlib/november96/ucb/11hastings.html (accessed on 17 July 2001)
19. Arms, William Y., Relaxing Assumptions about the Future of Digital Libraries: The Hare and the Tortoise, D-Lib Magazine, April 1997, http://www.dlib.org/dlib/april97/04arms.html (accessed on 9 July 2001)
20. Levy, David M., Digital Libraries and the Problem of Purpose, D-Lib Magazine, 6(1), http://www.dlib.org/dlib/January00/01levy.html (accessed on 12 July 2001)

Bibliography

1. Abels, Eileen et al., Competencies for Information Professionals of the 21st Century, Prepared for the Special Libraries Association Board of Directors by the Special Committee on Competencies for Special Librarians, Revised edition, June 2003, www.sla.org/content/SLA/professional/ meaning/comp2003.cfm
2. Agarwal, P K, "India's National Internet Backbone", Communications of ACM, 42(6), June 1999, pp. 53-58.
3. American Chemical Society, Will Science Publishing Perish? The Paradox of Contemporary Science Journals, Washington, D.C.
4. Anand, A. K. and Kapoor, Shabad, Manpower for the library and information field in India: a report on employment trends in 1981 and 1982, Annals of Library Science and Documentation, 30 (3-4), 1983, pp. 85-97.
5. Arms, William Y. et al., An Architecture for Information in Digital Libraries, D-Lib Magazine, February 1997, http://www.dlib.org/dlib/february97/cnri/02arms1. html
6. Arms, William Y., Digital Libraries, Cambridge, Mass., MIT Press, x, 287 p., 2000.
7. Arms, William Yeo, Implementing Policies for Access Management, D-Lib Magazine, February 1998, http://www.dlib.org/dlib/february98/arms/02arms.html
8. Arms, William Y., Relaxing Assumptions about the Future of Digital Libraries: The Hare and the Tortoise, D-Lib

Magazine, April 1997, http://www.dlib.org/dlib/april97/04arms.html

9. Arms, William Y., Key concepts in the architecture of the digital library, D-Lib Magazine, 1995 July, http://www.dlib.org/dlib/July95/07arms.html

10. Arora, Jagdish, Indian National Digital Library in Engineering Science and Technology (INDEST): A Proposal for Strategic Co-operation for Consortia-based Access to Electronic Resources, International Information & Library Review, 33, pp. 149-165, 2001

11. Arora, Jagdish, and Agrawal, Pawan, Indian Digital Library in Engineering Science and Technology (INDEST) Consortium: Consortia-Based Subscription to Electronic Resources for Technical Education System in India: A Government of India Initiative, International CALIBER 2003, Ahmedabad, 13-15 February 2003, Conference Volume - Mapping Technology on Libraries and People, Ahmedabad: INFLIBNET, 2003, pp. 271-290.

12. Association of Research Libraries, Definition and Purposes of a Digital Library, October 23, 1995, http://sunsite.berkeley.edu/ARL/definition.html, 1/10/96

13. Atkinson, Randall J., "Towards a More Secure Internet", IEEE Computer, 30(1), January 1997, pp. 57-61.

14. Balaji, V et al., The Information Village Experiment in Pondicherry, Information Today & Tomorrow, 19 (4), December 2000, p.3-p.7 & p.10, http://itt.nissat.tripod.com/ itt20004/infovill.htm

15. Baran, Nicholas, The greatest show on earth, Byte, July 1995, pp. 69-86.

16. Barber, David, Building a digital library: Concepts and issues. Library Technology Reports, 32,1996, pp. 573-617.

17. Barron, Tom, Evolving Business Models in eLearning, March 2002, http://www.sric-bi.com/LOD

18. Barry, Jeff, Automated System Marketplace 2001: Closing in on Content, Library Journal, April 1, 2001.

19. Bartschi, Martin et al. An Overview of Information Retrieval Subjects, IEEE Computer, May 1985, pp. 67-84.

20. Batty, David. WWW — Wealth, Weariness or Waste: Controlled vocabulary and thesauri in support of online information access, http://www.dlib.org/dlib/november98/11batty.html

21. Beagrie, Neil and Greenstein, Daniel, A Strategic Policy Framework for Creating and Preserving Digital Collections, Version 4.0, 14/7/98, Final Draft, Internet Scout Review, 5(2), 8 May 1998, http://www.ukoln.ac.uk/services/papers/bl/ framework/framework.html

22. Beebe, Linda and Meyers, Barbara, The Unsettled State of Archiving, The Journal of Electronic Publishing, 4(4), June 1999, http://www.press.umich.edu/jep/04-04/beebe.html

23. Beebe, Linda and Meyers, Barbara, Digital Workflow: Managing the Process Electronically, The Journal of Electronic Publishing, 5(4), June 2000, http://www.press.umich.edu/jep/05-04/sheridan.html

24. Bengal Library Association, West Bengal Library Directory, Calcutta, BLA, 1963.

25. Berman, H. M. et al., The Protein Data Bank. Nucleic Acids Research, 2000, pp.235-242.

26. Bertot, John Carlo et al., The 1997 National Survey of U.S. Public Libraries and the Internet: Final Report, http://www.research.umbc.edu/~bertot/ala97.html

27. Bhattacharjee, R., Public Library Services in India: Systems and Deficiencies, Country Report: India, http://www.ifla.org/VII/s8/annual/cr02-in.htm

28. Binder, Michael B., Licensing Models: Information as a Commodity, The Journal of Electronic Publishing, 3(3), March 1998, http://www.press.umich.edu/jep/03-03/binder.html

29. Bishop, Ann Peterson. Logins and Bailouts: Measuring Access, Use, and Success in Digital Libraries, The Journal

of Electronic Publishing, 4(2), December 1998, http://www.press.umich.edu/jep/04-02/bishop.html

30. Bishoff, Liz, Interoperability and Standards in a Museum/Library Collaborative: The Colorado Digitization Project, First Monday, 5(6), June 2000, http://firstmonday.org/issues/issue5_6/bishoff/

31. Björk, Bo-Christer, Turk, Ziga, How Scientists Retrieve Publications: An Empirical Study of How the Internet is Overtaking Paper Media, The Journal of Electronic Publishing, 6 (2), December 2000, http://www.press.umich.edu/jep/06-02/bjork.html

32. Bonett, Monica, Personalization of Web Services: Opportunities and Challenges, Ariadne, Issue 28, http://www.ariadne.ac.uk /issue28/personalization/intro.html

33. Bose, Anindya, Information Resources Management: A Glossary of Terms, Encyclopaedia of Library & Information Science, New York: Marcel Dekker, 1986, vol. 41, p. 108.

34. Bradley, P. Personalised news services: how personal, how much news?, Information World Review, (152), Nov 1999, pp. 47-8.

35. Brigish A, The databank switch: the trend towards specialization, The Information Manager, Spring 1980, pp. 19-20.

36. Bush. V, As We May Think, Atlantic Monthly, 176(1), 1945, pp. 101-108.

37. Burton, Philip E., A Dictionary of Minicomputing and Microcomputing, New York: John Wiley, 1982, p. 64.

38. Chakraborty, Arun Kumar, "Publishing on CD-ROM: Indian Potential", DESIDOC Bulletin of Information Technology, 17(5), September1997, pp. 23-31.

39. Chandran, Suresh, Does biotechnology need a new database treaty?, Current Science, 73(8), 25 October 1997, p. 655.

40. Chapman, Stephen and Kenney, Anne R., Digital Conversion of Research Library Materials: A Case for Full Informational Capture, D-Lib Magazine, October 1996, http://www.dlib.org/dlib/october96/cornell/10chapman.html

41. Chard, S. M. Data management: the foundation for Web development in the retail and service industries, First Monday, 4 (9) Sep 1999, http://www.firstmonday.dk/issues/issue4—9/chard/index.html

42. Chaudhury, G G and Chaudhury, Sudatta. Text Retrieval and Library Management Software in India, Program, 28(3), July 1994, pp. 253-261.

43. Chavan, Vishwas and Chandramohan, D, Databases in Indian biology: The state of the art and prospects, Current Science, 68(3), 10 February 1995, pp. 275-278.

44. Choo, Chun Wei, Information Management for the Intelligent Organization: Roles and Implications for the Information Professions, Digital Libraries Conference, March 27-28, 1995, Singapore, http://choo.fis.utoronto.ca/FIS/ ResPub/DLC95.html

45. Choudhury, G. Sayeed, et al., Digital Workflow Management: The Lester S. Levy Digitized Collection of Sheet Music. First Monday, 5(6), June 2000, http://www.firstmonday.org/issues/issue5_6/choudhury/

46. Clayton, J. A step-by-step guide to content management, Digital Publishing Strategies, 2 (3) Nov 97, p.9.

47. Cleveland, Gary, Digital libraries: Definitions, issues and challenges, UDT Occasional Paper #8, 1998, March, http://www.ifla.org/VI/5/op/udtop8/ udtop8.htm

48. Clever, Hypersearching on the Web, Members of the Clever Project, Scientific American, June 1999, pp. 44-52.

49. Cogswell, J, The organization of collection management functions in academic research libraries, Journal of Academic Librarianship, 13, 1987, pp. 268-276.

50. Cohen, Suzanne et al., MyLibrary: Personalized Electronic Services in the Cornell University Library, D-Lib Magazine, 6(4), April 2000, http://www.dlib.org/dlib/april00/mistlebauer/04mistlebauer.html

51. Commission on Preservation and Access and Research Libraries Group, Preserving Digital Information: Report of the Task Force on Archiving of Digital Information, May 1, 1996, http://www.rlg.org/ArchTF/tfadi.index.htm, http://www.rlg.org/ArchTF/tfadi.recommen.htm #practices

52. Communications of the ACM, April 1995, August 1995, and April 1998

53. Cook, Colleen and Thompson, Bruce, LibQUAL+: One Instrument in the New Measures Toolbox, http://www.arl.org/newsltr/212/libqual.html

54. Cronin, Blaise, Databanks, Aslib Proceedings, 33(6), June 1981, p. 243.

55. Cuadra, Carlos A. Commercially funded on-line retrieval services-past, present and future, Aslib Proceedings, 30 (1) Jan 78, p. 2-15.

56. Davenport, Thomas H., Some Principles of Knowledge Management, http://www.itmweb.com/essay538.htm

57. Deshpande, K. S., The librarian, the book trade and collection development: random reflections, Library Science with a Slant to Documentation and Information Studies, 36 (4) Dec 1999, pp.249-56.

58. Dewang Mehta, Software Policy: The New Mantra, The Hindu Survey of Indian Industry 1999, Chennai, Kasturi & Sons, January 2000, pp. 321-323.

59. Dictionary of Computing, Oxford: Oxford University Press, 1983.

60. Digital Library Initiatives, Building Digital Libraries: Digital Library Projects, The University of Texas at Austin Library Online, June 7, 2001, http://www.lib.utexas.edu/dli/digital.html

61. Dikshit, Sandeep, "Growth in Internet Connections Lopsided", The Hindu, Visakhapatnam dated December 10, 2000.
62. Dinerstein, Nelson T., dBASE III+ for the programmer, New Delhi: Galgotia, 1988.
63. Beiser, Karl, dBASE IV, Westport: Meckler, 1990.
64. Dasgupta, Kalpana, Libraries and librarians in India on the threshold of the 3rd millennium: challenges and risks, 66th IFLA Council and General Conference, Jerusalem, Israel, 13-18 August, http://www.ifla.org/IV/ifla66/papers/039-120e.htm
65. Duax, William, Crystallographic Databases and Molecular Biophysics, Physics Today, January 1986, pp. S-24-S-25.
66. Elmasri, Ramez, Navathe, Shamkant B., Fundamentals of Database Systems, 3rd Edition, Addison Wesley, 2000, xxvii, 955 p.
67. Employment News, 1998-1999, Publications Division, Ministry of Information and Broadcasting, India.
68. Feigenbaum, Armand V., Total Quality Control. 3rd ed., New York, McGraw Hill, 1983.
69. Gardner, Frank M., The Delhi Public Library: An Evaluation Report, Zurich, UNESCO, 1957, pp. 26-29.
70. Fleischhauer, Carl, Digital Formats for Content Reproductions, July 13, 1998, http://memory.loc.gov/ammem/formats.html#VIII
71. Fox, Edward A., et al., Digital libraries, Communications of the ACM, 38(4), April 1995, pp. 24.
72. French, James C. and Viles, Charles L., Personalized Information Environments: An Architecture for Customizable Access to Distributed Digital Libraries, D-Lib Magazine, 5(6), June 1999, http://www.dlib.org/dlib/June99/french/06french.html
73. Gilliland-Swetland, A., The Digital Portfolio Archives

project, California University at Los Angeles, Department of Library and Information Science, 1997.

74. Ghosh, Anindo, "Internet Bandwidth: India Needs a Backbone", http:// www.ieo.org/backbone.html

75. Gorman, G E and Corbitt, B J, Core competencies in information management education, New Library World, 103(1182/1183), pp. 436-445, 2002, www.decigi.ufpr.br/ t_compete.pdf

76. Grenquist, Peter, Why I Don't Read Electronic Journals: An Iconoclast Speaks Out. The Journal of Electronic Publishing, 3(1), September 1997, http:// www.press.umich.edu/ jep/03-01/Iconoclast.html

77. Hastings, Kirk and Tennant, Roy, How to Build a Digital Librarian, D-Lib Magazine, November 1996, http:// www.dlib.org/dlib/november96/ucb/ 11hastings.html

78. Hawkins, Donald T., Electronic books: a major publishing revolution. Part 1: General considerations and issues, Online, 24 (4) Jul/Aug 2000, p.14-18, 20-22, 24-26, 28.

79. Hedstrom, Margaret and Montgomery, Sheon, Digital Preservation Needs and Requirements in RLG Member Institutions, A study commissioned by the Research Libraries Group, December 1998, http://www.rlg.org/ preserv/digpres. html

80. Helmer, John F., Editorial: Epidemiology of the Consortial Spore, Information Technology and Libraries, 18 (3), Sept 1999.

81. Hennen Jr., Thomas J. Hennen's American Public Library Ratings (HAPLR), www.haplr-index.com/ rating_methods.htm

82. Hirshon, Arnold et al., International Coalition of Library Consortia (ICOLC) Statement of Current Perspective and Preferred Practices for the Selection and Purchase of Electronic Information, http://www.library.yale.edu/ consortia/ statement.html

83. Hodge, Gail M., An Information Life-Cycle Approach:

Best Practices for Digital Archiving, The Journal of Electronic Publishing, 5(4), June 2000, http://www.press.umich.edu/jep/05-04/hodge.html

84. Huber, Wolfgang, Databanks and Euronet in Proceedings of the 5th biennial CODATA Conference, Oxford: Pergamon, 1977, pp. 199-201.

85. IASLIC, Directory of Special and Research Libraries in India, Calcutta, IASLIC, 1962.

86. IEEE Computer, May 1996.

87. India, Ministry of Labour, Director General of Employment and Training, Bulletin of Job Opportunities in India 1997, New Delhi, Dec 1999, p.73.

88. International Coalition Of Library Consortia (ICOLC), Statement of Current Perspective and Preferred Practices for the Selection and Purchase of Electronic Information, Update No. 1, New Developments In E-Journal Licensing, (December 2001 update to March 1998 Statement), http://www.library.yale.edu/consortia/2001currentpractices.htm

89. InterWise, Inc. and Keegan, Morgan, Live eLearning: Taking the First Steps, A Checklist to Choose a Live eLearning Solution That Suits Your Needs, (accessed from http://www.morgankeegan.com)

90. Ives, David J., Security Management Strategies for Protecting Your Library's Network", Computers in Libraries, 16(2), Feb 1996, pp. 36-42.

91. Jeevan, V K J, Distance or Distress Education for Librarianship, Herald of Library Science, 37(3-4), July-Oct 1998, pp. 196-204.

92. Jeevan, V K J, Open and Distance Learning for Library Science Professionals, University News, 40(16), 2002, pp. 3-9.

93. Jeevan, VK J, Stores Demand Notes Monitoring System for NCSI, Minor Project Report of 'Training Course on

Information Technology Applications to Libraries & Information Centres', 1993-94, NCSI, I.I.Sc, Bangalore.

94. Kalseth, Karl, Knowledge Management from a Business Strategy Perspective, FID Review, 1(1), 1999, pp. 37-41.

95. Katz, William A., "Introduction to Reference Work: Vol 1, Basic Information Sources", New York: McGraw Hill, 1969, p. 98.

96. Kaula, P N, Education and Training of Library Personnel: The Indian Programme, Proceedings of ISLIC International Conference on Information Science, Tel Aviv, 29 Aug-3 Sept, 1971, National Centre for Scientific and Technical Information, Tel Aviv, 1972, vol. 2, pp. 491-507.

97. Keeble, John et al., Your Say, The rise and role of the Knowledge Manager, www.kmmagazine.com/xq/asp/sid.0/articleid.8FF1A428-6C4B-4966-ABF6-172DB0B49A3/qx/display.htm

98. Kent, Eben.L., dBASE in "Encyclopaedia of Microcomputers",V.4, PP.389-405, New York: Marcel Dekker,1990.

99. Kramer, Joseph et al., A User-Centered Design Approach to Personalization, Communications of the ACM, August 2000. 43(8), pp. 45-48.

100. Kumar, P S G, Indian Library Chronology, Mumbai: Allied, 2nd ed., 2000, p. 679.

101. Labin, Edouard, Information Analysis and Databanks, Proceedings of 2nd European Congress on Information Systems and Networks, Luxembourg, 27-30 May 1975, Munchen: Verlag Dokumentation, 1976, p. 125.

102. Lagoze, Carl. From Static to Dynamic Surrogates: Resource Discovery in the Digital Age, http://www.dlib.org/dlib/june97/06lagoze.html

103. Lancaster, F. W., The evaluation of machine readable databases and of information services derived from these databases, in Evaluation and scientific management of

libraries and information centres, Leyden: Noordhoff, 1977, p. 82.

104. Landesman, M. and van Reenen, J., Consortia vs. reform: creating congruence, JEP: the Journal of Electronic Publishing, 6(2), Dec 2000, http://www.press.umich.edu/jep/06-02/landesman.html

105. Levy, David M., Digital Libraries and the Problem of Purpose, D-Lib Magazine, 6(1), http://www.dlib.org/dlib/January00/01levy.html

106. Lindquist, Mats G., Not Your Father's References: Citations in the Digital Space, The Journal of Electronic Publishing, 4(3), March 1999, http://www.press.umich.edu/jep/04-03/lindquist.html

107. Line, Maurice B., Draft Definitions: Information and Library needs, wants, demands, and uses, Aslib Proceedings, 26 (2), Feb 1974.

108. Logley, Dennis and Shain, Michael, Dictionary of Information Technology, New York: John Wiley, 1982, p. 83.

109. Luedke, J A et al., Numeric databases and systems, in ARIST 12, 1977, pp. 119-181.

110. Lufkin, D. H., Data bank, in Encyclopaedia of Computers (ed. Rolston, Anthony), 1976, pp. 388-389.

111. Lynch, Clifford. The Battle to Define the Future of the Book in the Digital World, First Monday, 6(6), http://firstmonday.org/issues/issue6_6/lynch/ index.html, June 2001.

112. Lynch, Clifford and Garcia-Molina, Hector. Interoperability, scaling, and the digital libraries research agenda: A report on the May 18-19, 1995 IITA Digital Libraries Workshop, 1995, August, http://diglib.stanford.edu/diglib/pub/ reports/iita-dlw/main.html#2

113. Majumdar, Arun K, Bhattacharya, Pritimoy, Database Management Systems, New Delhi: Tata McGraw Hill,

1996, x, 475 p.

114. Manorama Year Book 1999, Kottayam, Malayala Manorama.

115. McClure, Charles R. et al., Internet Costs and Cost Models for Public Libraries: Final Report, http://istweb.syr.edu/~mcclure/nclis/FinalReport.html

116. Meadows, A. J., et al., Dictionary of Computing and IT, 3rd ed., London: Kogan Page, 1987, p. 62.

117. Moore, Reagan, et al., Collection-Based Persistent Digital Archives - Part 1. D-Lib Magazine, 6(3), March 2000. http://www.dlib.org/dlib/march00/moore/03moore-pt1.html

118. Mukhopadhyay, Ananda Deb, Integrated Rural Development (IRD) and Information Support System (ISS), IASLIC Bulletin, 48(3), September 2003, pp. 131-140.

119. Nadeau, Joseph H. et al, A Rosetta Stone of mammalian genetics, Nature, 373, 26 January 1995, pp. 363-365.

120. Nayar, B K et al, Demand for Information Scientists in India (An analysis of Advertised Vacancies), Handbook of Libraries, Archives and Information Centres in India, Information Industry Publications, New Delhi, 1984-85, pp. 331-357.

121. Nicholls, Paul and Ridley, Jacquline, A Context for Evaluating Multimedia, Computers in Libraries, 16(4), April 1996, p. 38.

122. Noerr, Peter, The Digital Library Toolkit, 2nd ed. March 2000, Palo Alto: Sun Microsystems, http://www.sun.com/products-n-solutions/edu/libraries/digitaltoolkit.html

123. Orlans, Harold. A., Home Scholar's Electronic Woes, The Journal of Electronic Publishing, 3(3), March 1998, http://www.press.umich.edu/jep/03-03/orlans.html

124. Oxford English Dictionary, The, Oxford: Clarendon, 1989, Second Edition.

125. Padmanabhan, Mohan, Awareness campaign launched to tackle book piracy, plagiarism,

126. Samuel T., Booking the book importers, Herald of Library Science, 30 (3-4) Jul-Oct 91, pp. 232-4.

127. Paisley, W J. Information needs and users, ARIST, 3, 1968, pp. 1-30.

128. Palme, Jacob Electronic Mail, Boston: Artech House, 1995

129. Parasuraman, A., et al., Alternative Scales for Measuring Service Quality: A Comparative Assessment Based on Psychometric and Diagnostic Criteria, Journal of Retailing, 70 (Fall 1994): 201-230.

130. Parthasarathy, Anand, 'You have Mail' - and more, The Hindu Science & Technology Supplement, Thu, June 4, 1998, Page 23

131. Penland, Patrick R., Content Analysis, Encyclopedia of Library & Information Science, New York: Marcel Dekker, 1971, Vol. 5, p. 633.

132. Penrod, James I., Douglas, Judith V., Information Technology Literacy, Encyclopaedia of Library & Information Science, New York: Marcel Dekker, 1986, vol. 40, p. 84.

133. Rajashekar, T B, What's new in Computers? Digital Libraries, Resonance, April 1997, pp. 60-73.

134. Rajaraman, V., Analysis and Design of Information Systems, New Delhi: Prentice Hall, 1998, xi, 359 p.

135. Rajora, Rajesh, Bridging the digital divide Gyandoot: The model for community networks, Tata McGraw-Hill, New Delhi, 2002, XXV, 319 p.

136. Ranganathan S R, Integrated Public Library System, pp. 208-212, in Public Library System, ed. by S R Ranganathan and A Neelameghan.

137. Ranganthan, S R, Prolegomena to Library Classification, vol. 1, 3rd ed., Bangalore: Sarada Ranganathan Endowment for Library Science, Reprint 1994.

138. Rao, Madanmohan, Eight C's of KM Success: Learn from the information technology sector's best knowledge enterprises, 2003, http://www.destinationkm.com/articles/default.asp?ArticleID=1085

139. Reenen, Johann Van, Library Consumerism in the Digital Age, The Journal of Electronic Publishing, 3(3), March 1998, http://www.press.umich.edu/ jep/03-03/vanreenen.html

140. S & T (Science & Technology) Pocket Data Book, Govt. of India, DSIR, New Delhi, 1992, pp. 114-115.

141. Robertson, N, A personalized Web, Internet World, 8 (4) Apr 97, p. 32, 34.

142. Rosander, A C, Applications of Quality Control in the Service Industries, New York: Marcel Dekker, 1985, pp. 3-4.

143. Rothenberg, Jeff, Ensuring the Longevity of Digital Documents, Scientific American, 272, January 1995, pp. 42-47.

144. Rowley, Jennifer, Managing quality in information services, Information Today and Tomorrow, 16(1), January-March 1997, pp. 3-10.

145. Santosus, Megan and Surmacz, Jon, The ABC's of Knowledge Management, http://www.cio.com/research/knowledge/edit/kmabcs.html

146. Satija, Mohinder Partap, The plight of librarians: avenues for more jobs, Lucknow Librarian, 15(3), Sept 83, pp. 93-97.

147. Schatz, B. R., Building the Interspace: The Illinois Digital Library Project, Communications of the ACM, 38(4), 1995, pp. 62-63.

148. Schwartz, C, Web search engines, Journal of the American Society for Information Science, 49 (11) Sep 1998, pp. 973-82.

149. Scott Mace et. al., Weaving a better Web, Byte, March 1998, pp. 58-68.

150. Seamans, Nan and McMilan, Gail, Digital library definition for DL12, 1998, June 16, http://scholar.lib.vt.edu/DLI2/defineDL.html

151. Seetharama S, Collection Development/Management in an Information Technology-Based Environment: Current Initiatives and Issues, DESIDOC Bulletin of Information Technology, 17(1), January 1997, pp. 11-20.

152. Sen N B (ed.), Indian Book Trade and Library Directory 1950-51, Delhi, New Book Society of India.

153. Sharma, R. N., "Development of library and information science periodicals in Asia, with emphasis on South Asia: problems and solutions", 65th IFLA Council and General Conference, Bangkok, Thailand, August 20 - August 28, 1999, http://www.ifla.org/IV/ifla65/papers/006-118e.htm

154. Silberschatz, Abraham, Korth, Henry F., Sudarshan, S, Database System Concepts, New York, McGraw Hill, 3rd edition, 1997, xxii, 821 p.

155. Simpson, Alan, Understanding dBASE III+, New Delhi: BPB, 1st ed., 1986.

156. Smith, John, Summary of Public Libraries Survey, 1991, http://www.ukoln.ac.uk/services/ukoln/smith-1999-01.

157. Spink, Amanda and Cool, Colleen, Education for Digital Libraries, D-Lib Magazine, May 1999, 5(5), http://www.dlib.org/dlib/may99/05spink.html

158. Srinivasan, Padmini, "Digital Library Projects in the United States", DESIDOC Bulletin of Information Technology, 17(6), November1997, pp. 15-21.

159. Tedd, L. A., Yeates, R, A personalised current awareness service for library and information services staff: an overview of the NewsAgent for Libraries project, Program, 32(4), Oct 1998, pp. 373-390.

160. Thibadeau, Robert and Benoit, Evan, Antique Books, D-Lib Magazine, September 1997, http://www.dlib.org/

dlib/september97/thibadeau/09thibadeau. html

161. Tate, Marsha and Alexander, Jan, Teaching Critical Evaluation Skills for World Wide Web Resources, Computers in Libraries, 16(10), November/ December 1996, pp. 50-54.

162. Tenopir, Carol, and Barry, Jeff, The Data Dealers, Library Journal, May 15, 1997, pp. 33-34.

163. Tenopir, Carol, King, Donald W., Designing Electronic Journals With 30 Years of Lessons from Print, The Journal of Electronic Publishing, 4(2), December 1998, http://www.press.umich.edu/jep/04-02/king.html

164. Traditional Knowledge Digital Library, Information Today & Tomorrow, 20 (3), September 2001, pp. 16-17, http://itt.nissat.tripod.com/itt0103/tkdl.htm

165. Tucker, Bill, E-Learning and the Nonprofit Sector: White Paper discussion of the potential of e-learning to improve nonprofit management training, June 2000, http://www.smarterorg.com

166. Tuli, J. K., Evaluated nuclear structure data file, Nuclear Structure and Methods in Physics Research, A 369, 1996, pp. 506-510.

167. Ubois, J., Hassett, C, Cast system, Internet World, 7 (10) Oct 96, pp. 94-8, 100.

168. Ullman, Jeffrey D., Principles of Database Systems, 2nd edition, New Delhi: Galgotia, 1996, vii, 484 p.

169. Ulrich's International Periodicals Directory, 37th ed., NJ: R.R. Bowker, 1999, p.vii.

170. UNESCO Public Library Manifesto, http://www.ifla.org/documents/ libraries/policies/ unesco.htm

171. USbancorp – Piper Jaffray, Helping Investors Climb the e-Learning Curve (report by Robert W. Peterson, Mark A. Marostica, and Lisa M. Callahan), Nov. 1999.

172. Waller, Consuella Askew and Hipps, Kaylyn, Using LibQUAL+TM and Developing a Culture of Assessment

in Libraries, http://www.arl.org/newsltr/221/libqarl.html

173. Waller, Consuella Askew, et al., LibQUAL+ Policies and Procedures Manual, Association of Research Libraries, Washington, D.C., 2003, http://www.libqual.org/documents/admin/procedures3.8.pdf

174. Weisser, Christian R. and Walker, Janice R., Electronic Theses and Dissertations: Digitizing Scholarship for Its Own Sake, The Journal of Electronic Publishing, 3(2), December, 1997, http://www.press.umich.edu/jep/03-02/etd.html

175. Wilson, T.D. (2002) The nonsense of 'knowledge management, Information Research, 8(1), http://InformationR.net/ir/8-1/paper144.html

176. Wolf, Connie and Holland, Douglas, Digitizing and Preserving Plant Images: Linking Plant Images and Databases for Public Access, First Monday, 5(6), June 2000, http://firstmonday.org/issues/issue5_6/wolf/

177. World Information Report 1997/98, Paris: UNESCO, 1997.

178. Yovits M C, et al., Information Flow and Analysis: Theory, Simulation, and Experiments. 1, Basic Theoretical and Conceptual Development, Journal of the American Society of Information Science, May 1981, p. 187.

179. Zhao, D, The Personal Digital Library, ELINOR: Electronic Library Project. London: Bowker-Saur for British Library, 1998, pp. 97-103.

180. Zeithaml, Valarie A. et al., Delivering Quality Service: Balancing Customer Perceptions and Expectations, New York: Free Press, 1990.

WEBSITES

1. http://216.87.26.241/en/org/ raja%20 ram.htm
2. http://www.aiai.ed.ac.uk/~alm/kamlnks.html
3. http://www.ala.org/Template.cfm?Section=Collection_Development&template=/ContentManagement/

ContentDisplay.cfm&ContentID=26942

4. http://americanlibrary.in.library.net
5. http://bioweb.pasteur.fr
6. http://www.bl.uk/
7. http://www.britishcouncil.org/india/
8. http://www.cic.nic.in/mainblocks1.htm
9. http://www.digitalpreservation.gov/index.php?nav=1
10. http://dublincore.org/documents/dcmes-qualifiers/
11. http://www.dli.ernet.in/
12. http://www.esevaonline.com/
13. http://www.emeraldinsight.com/consortia/
14. http://www.fpbai.org
15. http://www.gutenberg.net/
16. http://www.headline.ac.uk/public/diss/jp-PIE-HybLib-model/
17. http://www.himachal.nic.in/lokmitra.htm
18. http://www.hindu.com/2004/04/05/stories/2004040504780600.htm
19. http://www.hotmail.com
20. http://web1.hry.nic.in/naidisha/aboutus.asp
21. http://www-4.ibm.com/software/developer/library/personalization/
22. http://www.keralaitmission.org/content/egovernance/
23. http://www.lib.nus.edu.sg/
24. http://libraries.mit.edu/ordering/ilb.html
25. http://library.caltech.edu/services/interlib.htm
26. http://www.licensingmodels.com/academic.htm
27. http://www.licensingmodels.com/consortia.htm
28. http://international.loc.gov/intldl/intldlhome.html
29. http://www.loc.gov/
30. http://www.mahitishakti.net/

31. http://macfadden.mit.edu:9500/networked/policy.html
32. http://mbcr.bcm.tmc.edu/databases.html
33. http://memory.loc.gov/
34. http://mobilelibrary.cdacnoida.com/
35. http://my.lib.ncsu.edu
36. http://nerdatabank.nic.in
37. http://www.nlindia.org/
38. http://www.onlineoriginals.com/
39. http://www.personalization.org/personalization.html
40. http://rajasthan.gov.in/it/eg/Janmitra.shtm
41. http://www.revdept-01.kar.nic.in/Bhoomi/web-page/Karnatakas%20Bhoomi%20Project.htm
42. http://web.simmons.edu/~schwartz/462-defs.html
43. http://www.smart-text.com/topical.html
44. http://sunsite.berkeley.edu/ARL/definition.html
45. http://www.tenet.res.in/sari/
46. http://www.thehindubusinessline.com/bline/2002/08/10/stories/2002081002500200.htm
47. http://www.usnews.com/usnews/edu/elearning/rankings/lib_reg_prof.htm
48. http://www.usnews.com/usnews/edu/elearning/rankings/lib_reg.htm
49. http://www1.worldbank.org/publicsector/egov/diskcs.htm#
50. http://www.worldwidelearn.com/library-science.htm

Index